Thinking in Sound

The Cognitive Psychology of Human Audition

Edited by

STEPHEN McADAMS

Laboratoire de Psychologie Expérimentale (CNRS),
Université René Descartes
and IRCAM, Paris

and

EMMANUEL BIGAND

Laboratoire d'Etudes des Acquisitions
et du Développement (CNRS),
Université de Bourgogne, Dijon

Clarendon Press · Oxford
1993

Oxford University Press, Walton Street, Oxford OX2 6DP

Oxford New York Toronto
Delhi Bombay Calcutta Madras Karachi
Kuala Lumpur Singapore Hong Kong Tokyo
Nairobi Dar es Salaam Cape Town
Melbourne Auckland Madrid
and associated companies in
Berlin Ibadan

Oxford is a trade mark of Oxford University Press

Published in the United States
by Oxford University Press Inc., New York

© The contributors listed on p. xiii, 1993

A catalogue record for this book is available from the British Library

Library of Congress Cataloging in Publication Data
(data available)
ISBN 0 19 852258 4 (hbk)
ISBN 0 19 852257 6 (pbk)

Typeset by
Graphicraft Typesetters Ltd, Hong Kong
Printed in Great Britain on acid-free paper by
St Edmundsbury Press, Bury St Edmunds

For Marie-Claire Botte

Preface

To our knowledge, no volume exists, either in English or French, which covers in a didactic fashion the whole range of subjects in the domain of auditory cognition. In order to rectify this deficit, a Tutorial Workshop was organized by the Hearing Group of the French Acoustical Society. Specialists in various domains of auditory perception and cognition were invited to participate and to write chapters on their area of expertise. This book is the result.

Auditory perception reveals a paradox similar to that encountered in all realms of perception: nothing seems more simple than to perceive the sound environment around us, and yet it is a phenomenon that appears to rebel against scientific analysis. What difficulty exists, for example, in recognizing one's name in a sentence pronounced by another person, in differentiating the noise of a car from that of an aeroplane, in perceiving the captivating rock rhythms of Bill Haley, in recognizing the voice of one's own child or the steps of a familiar person? All that seems to be needed is simply to 'open one's ears'.

Imagine for just an instant, however, the array of information and the set of procedures with which it would be necessary to endow a computer so that it could distinguish a violin from a flute in polyphonic music, extract an alarm signal from the sonorous background within which it is embedded, grasp the connection between a theme and a musical variation, analyse by simply listening to the noise of a car a problem with the engine, detect an inhabitual sound in the beating of a patient's heart, and so on. In spite of the high level of technological sophistication available today, it is quite likely that problems such as these could be resolved only after many years of research in artificial intelligence and signal processing, since the amount of necessary information is so great and the ways in which it must be combined are so complex.

This difficulty in analysing the process of listening underscores the great richness of information present in the world of sound around us. The main objective of this book is to evaluate the current state of what we know about cognitive aspects of human audition. The book is primarily oriented toward students in the cognitive sciences and scientists specializing in fields other than auditory psychology. Most of the material presented presumes at least an elementary knowledge of acoustic terminology and of the concepts and methods of experimental psychology.

REFERENCE

Coren, S. and Ward, L. M. (1989). *Sensation and perception*, (3rd edn). Harcourt, Brace, Jovanovich, San Diego.

Paris   S. M.
June 1992   E. B.

Acknowledgements

The Tutorial Workshop that resulted in the collective writing of this book was the fourth in a series organized by the Hearing Group of the French Acoustical Society (SFA). The first three Workshops covered cochlear physiology (Aran *et al.* 1988), psychoacoustics and auditory perception (Botte *et al.* 1989), and the central auditory nervous system (Roman 1992). The organization of the workshop and the preparation of the book were made possible by generous financial or infrastructural support from the Hearing Group of the SFA; the programme, entitled 'Sciences de la Cognition' of the French Ministries of Research and Technology and of National Education; the Direction de Recherches, Etudes et Techniques of the French Ministry of Defence, and the Institut de Recherche et Coordination Acoustique/Musique (IRCAM).

The Tutorial Workshop series was conceived and vigorously animated for several years by Marie-Claire Botte (then President of the Hearing Group, and Vice President of the SFA). Primarily due to the unflagging efforts of Dr Botte, auditory research in France has seen a particularly remarkable change in status over the past decade. It is thus with a profound gratitude, deep respect, and a great deal of affection that we dedicate this book to her.

The chapters to this book were submitted to *ad hoc* peer review, each being reviewed by from two to four referees in addition to the reviews made by the volume editors. Each co-editor ensured the review process for the other. We would like first of all to thank the authors for cooperating with us in this rather arduous task. Secondly we would like to thank the reviewers who include Alain Lieury, Brian Moore, Bruno Repp, Charles Watson, Christopher Darwin, Earl Schubert, Eric Clarke, Francis Eustache, Jay Dowling, Jean-François Camus, Jose Morais, Josiane Bertoncini, Karen Yankelovich, Ken Robinson, Rachel Clifton, Robert Zatorre, Stanislas Dehaene, and Stephen Handel. Three reviewers chose not to have their names listed. We would also like to thank Cécile Marin for preparing the subject and name indexes and Carolyn Drake and the authors for their helpful comments on the glossary.

This book is being published in both English and French. The French edition will appear in early 1993 as *Les aspects cognitifs de l'audition humaine*, published by Presses Universitaires de France.

REFERENCES

Aran, J.-M., Dancer, A., Dolmazon, J.-M., Pujol, R., and Tran Ba Huy, P. (1988). *Physiologie de la cochlée*. INSERM/EMI, Paris.

Botte, M.-C., Canévet, G., Demany, L., and Sorin, C. (1989). *Psychoacoustique et perception auditive*. INSERM/EMI/SFA, Paris.

Roman, R. (ed.) (1992). *Le système auditif central: anatomie et physiologie*. INSERM/EMI, Paris.

Contents

Contributors

Emmanuel Bigand Laboratoire d'Etudes des Acquisitions et du Développement (CNRS), Université de Bourgogne, 6 bd Gabriel, F-21000 Dijon, France

Albert S. Bregman Psychology Department, McGill University, 1205 Dr Penfield Ave., Montréal, Québec H3A 1B1, Canada

Robert G. Crowder Department of Psychology, Yale University, Box 11A Yale Station, New Haven, Connecticut 06520, USA

Mari Riess Jones Department of Psychology, The Ohio State University, 142 Townsend Hall, 1885 Neil Ave., Columbus, Ohio 43210, USA

Stephen McAdams Laboratoire de Psychologie Expérimentale (CNRS), Université René Descartes, 28 rue Serpente, F-75006 Paris; and IRCAM, 31 rue Saint-Merri, F-75004 Paris, France

Isabelle Peretz Département de Psychologie, Université de Montréal, CP 6128, Succ. A, Montréal, Québec H3C 3J7, Canada

Laurel J. Trainor Department of Psychology, McMaster University, 1280 Main St. W., Hamilton, Ontario L8S 4K1, Canada

Sandra E. Trehub Centre for Research in Human Development, University of Toronto, Erindale Campus, Mississauga, Ontario L5L 1C6, Canada

Richard M. Warren Department of Psychology, University of Wisconsin–Milwaukee, Box 413 Milwaukee, Wisconsin 53201, USA

William Yee Department of Psychology, The Ohio State University, 142 Townsend Hall, 1885 Neil Ave., Columbus, Ohio 43210, USA

1

Introduction to auditory cognition

Stephen McAdams and Emmanuel Bigand

1.0 WHAT IS COGNITIVE IN AUDITION?

Etymologically speaking, the term 'cognition' refers to the notion of knowledge. It has been used in a more specific sense to designate the conditions that allow humans to develop knowledge of the world. It almost goes without saying that no knowledge can be acquired in the absence of perceiving: in other words, no theory of knowledge is complete without a theory of its acquisition, and thus of perception. To emphasize the cognitive aspects of audition is thus primarily to remind us that auditory information participates in a fundamental way in the development of knowledge.

Of course the processes that are part and parcel of the perception of acoustic information can seem quite different from those that intervene in more abstract intellectual activities (thinking, logic, reasoning, decision making, imagination, etc.). Two remarks need to be made on this point, however. First of all, the originality of the cognitive project is the desire to present an integrated picture of the ensemble of intellectual processes, in making evident the continuity that exists between more elementary aspects of these activities (sensory information processing) and more abstract aspects (symbolic information processing). The cognitive project therefore goes beyond the traditional division into independent intellectual functions: perception, memory, learning, language, intellection, etc. To emphasize the cognitive character of human audition is also to manifest the will to situate the processes of auditory perception within this continuity.

The second remark more directly concerns the mental processes implied in auditory perception. The emphasis placed on the term 'cognitive' in this volume highlights the fact that beyond the elementary phases of processing, higher-level processes that bring into play mental representations, decision making, inference, and interpretations by the perceptual

Thinking in sound: the cognitive psychology of human audition, ed. S. McAdams and E. Bigand. Oxford University Press, 1993, pp. 1–9.

system are necessary to elaborate a coherent representation of the sound world.

The postulate of a cognitive approach to perception is that the sensory information must be interpreted in order to give rise to a coherent perception. Interpretation is necessary since the information contained in the stimuli that reach the sensory organs is not always sufficient to form a coherent image of the surrounding sound environment. In these cases, the perceptual system must represent and then compare auditory information that is not directly present at the sensory level. One of the main reasons for this is that sound events are events that succeed one another in time: perception of their structure requires the elaboration of a mental representation in order to be able, subsequently, to establish relations among events that are separated from one another by several minutes or even hours. Music offers a typical example here: how can we perceive the unity of a sound structure that develops over a very long time-span (one and a half hours in the case of Beethoven's ninth Symphony) without elaborating representations of the substructures (thematic ones, for example) that are developed in the work?

When the sensory data that are immediately available are found to be insufficient, the perceptual system analyses the situation by taking into consideration knowledge that it has acquired of the surrounding sound world. Information from the environment does not, with the exception of newborns, stimulate a completely naïve organism. Acquired knowledge interacts with the current sensory data to interpret the auditory stimulation. Imagine for an instant that we are being guided through an Amazonian rain forest: we would hear exactly the same noise as the native of the region that accompanies us but we would be incapable, because of our lack of knowledge of the environment, to extract from the sound background events corresponding to the cries of iguanas and Macaques, the songs of Wistiti monkeys, or the rustling of the leaves of tropical trees, nor would we be able to assign meanings to entire sound structure that might in the long run be important for survival. In the same way, the Golden Ears of the French Navy have been trained in sonar detection to listen to what most of us would hear as a noisy underwater sound field and to perceptually segregate and identify a multitude of underwater sources such as clicking shrimp, whales, porpoises, schools of fish, and ocean-going vessels. They even succeed in classifying such vessels as commercial or military, as surface or submarine, as diesel or nuclear, as Russian, American, or French. In particularly dramatic cases, an inability to perceptually segregate sound sources and recognize their nature could lead a listener to fail to deduce from these signals the presence of imminent danger: the appearance of a jaguar, or a clandestine submarine, for example.

In the case of sound structures like music, whose organization is highly determined by cultural rules, a simple observation of the information recorded at the level of the sensory organs does not suffice to explain the difference in our perception of a Mozart quartet or one by Beethoven. In many other situations, the information available at the level of the sense organs may be too ambiguous to give rise to a unique perception of the current situation. Imagine, for instance, that we are in an old country house at night: are the noises we perceive the result of the steps of an unwanted intruder seeking to enter the house, or of the creeking of old woodwork strained by the wind? The identification of the sources of sound can be different according to the kinds of information to which we pay most attention: regularities in the noise or the timbral qualities of the materials being set into vibration. Faced with ambiguous stimuli of this kind, the perceptual system normally makes a subconscious decision in order to organize the sound figure. The knowledge possessed by the listener certainly plays an important role at this level: in the preceding example, a child, an adult, or the owner of the house would arrive at different interpretations of the same situation since they do not have the same auditory knowledge base.

Auditory illusions also emphasize the interpretive work performed by the perceptual system: nevertheless, in this case, the inference realized on the basis of the available information is incorrect and results in the perception of an unreal sound object. Composers have known for centuries how to exploit these perceptual characteristics in order to create seductive sound figures. Bach's sonatas and partitas for violin are a remarkable example of auditory illusion: the listener perceives quite clearly the presence of two violins playing in different pitch registers although there is actually only one violinist rapidly alternating between registers. Or, by appropriately orchestrating several instruments playing the same melody in parallel at different pitches, Ravel, in his *Bolero*, succeeds in tricking the ear into hearing not the original set of familiar instruments, but a single, new 'virtual' sound source with a marvellous, previously un-heard timbral quality.

1.1   THE CURRENT STATE OF AUDITORY COGNITION RESEARCH

Our perception of the sound world thus greatly surpasses the quality of the sensory information available at each instant: it results from mental processing. The study of cognitive aspects of information processing by the different sensory modalities is currently making great progress in the cognitive sciences. Interest in higher-level processing is marked in the realm of vision by the publication of a large number of articles and books. The works of Marr (1982), Pinker (1984), and Humphreys and

Bruce (1989) present important syntheses of theoretical principles and basic experimental data from vision research. In the realm of audition, the study of cognitive processes has been dealt with in publications that are primarily limited to the understanding of spoken language. The range of subjects habitually covered in general psychology texts includes

- the perception of stimulus qualities or attributes and patterns (all senses);

- perceptual organization processes (usually confined to vision);

- perceptual categorization and perceptual constancy (confined to vision and speech);

- recognition and identification of objects, events, and patterns (confined to vision and speech);

- memory processes (vision and speech with occasional reference to audition);

- attentional processes (primarily visual although dichotic listening is often well represented);

- development, learning, and skill acquisition (rarely touching upon audition);

- grammars of large-scale temporal structures (exclusively linguistic, almost never referring to music);

- problem solving and reasoning (never related to auditory problem solving as might be involved in musical composition, for example).

Comparable volumes for non-verbal audition (e.g. Moore 1982; Warren 1982; Botte *et al.* 1989) are limited to data on peripheral physiology and to psychoacoustic aspects of hearing; studies of cognitive processes are discussed only to a limited extent. The more recent publications of Sloboda (1985), Dowling and Harwood (1986), Handel (1989), Dooling and Hulse (1989), and Bregman (1990), however, mark an extremely important turning point in addressing issues in audition that go beyond the simple laboratory stimuli and listening situations that have been the primary domain of exploration in psychoacoustics for over a century now.

It is particularly important to note that the realm where much truly auditory (non-verbal) cognitive research has taken place is music psychology. In the past 20 to 30 years this area has seen a substantial expansion in the problems posed and the methodologies developed for exploring the musical mind. Most human listeners possess and deploy a high level of perceptual and cognitive sophistication for understanding, appreciating, and participating in musical activity. The primary interest of this area for the cognitive sciences is that musical systems are ubiquitous in the cultures of the world, they have attained a degree of structural (i.e. grammatical) complexity which rivals that of language, and they can be learned without explicit training at a very early age—as is also the case with language. The importance of music psychology for auditory cognition in general is evidenced by the strong place it occupies in most of the chapters of this volume.

One of the areas that has not received much attention, with the exception of some studies in young children, is the understanding of the role of auditory cognitive processes and their integration with those of other sensory and more general cognitive systems in everyday activity, e.g. using acoustic cues for navigating safely through a city environment, for manipulating and monitoring the function of sophisticated machinery, or for evaluating the identity and significance of events that are not within one's current field of vision. Research programmes addressing some of these issues are sure to demonstrate a more important role for audition in everyday activity than has been granted to this perceptual system to date.

1.2 ORGANIZATION OF THE BOOK

There are many ways to subdivide a field of research. The division adopted in this book comprises the following (overlapping) domains of auditory research: perceptual organization (Bregman, Ch. 2), global pattern perception (Warren, Ch. 3), attentional processes (Jones and Yee, Ch. 4), memory processes (Crowder, Ch. 5), recognition (McAdams, Ch. 6), neuropsychology (Peretz, Ch. 7), music perception (Bigand, Ch. 8), and developmental psychology (Trehub and Trainor, Ch. 9).

The main types of auditory processing dealt with in this book, and their interactions, are summarized schematically in Fig. 1.1. Sound vibrations enter the inner ear where they are analysed and transduced into nerve impulses that are sent by way of the auditory nerve to the brain. (The process of *transduction* of vibrations into neural impulses is only briefly discussed in Chapter 6 by McAdams.)

Auditory grouping processes effect the fusion and segregation of concurrent sound elements into auditory events, as well as the temporal integration and segregation of successive sound events into auditory streams. These processes are daily brought into play in many different ways. For example, sitting in front of the television you may suddenly hear the beep of a car horn in the street outside. Without the slightest hesitation this newly arrived noise will be heard as separate from and superimposed upon that of the television and not as forming a single sound object with whatever happens to be sounding on the television at the

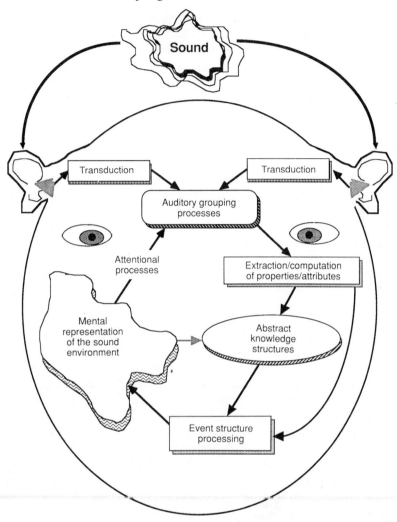

Fig. 1.1   The main types of auditory processing and their interactions.

moment. Such auditory grouping processes are the main focus of Bregman's chapter (Ch. 2), but are also discussed in the chapters by Warren (Ch. 3), Jones and Yee (Ch. 4), Bigand (Ch. 8), and Trehub and Trainor (Ch. 9).

According to the theory of auditory scene analysis, auditory grouping generally precedes the *extraction or computation of perceptual properties or attributes*. That is, attributes are the derived perceptual properties of the elements that have been grouped together. In Rimsky-Korsakov's *The flight of the bumble-bee,* for example, the notes follow in extremely rapid succession in such a way as to form a single sound stream, but come too fast to be heard separately. What imposes itself on a listener's perception is the overall form of the melodic line, anchored in time by the contour peaks and valleys as well as the accentuation of particular notes by the player. The global perception of sequential sound patterns and their temporal organization are discussed in the chapters by Warren (Ch. 3) and Jones and Yee (Ch. 4).

Once the perceptual qualities are represented in the auditory system, they can be interpreted with respect to evoked *abstract knowledge structures.* The result is the recognition and identification of, as well as the assignment of meaning or significance to, events and sequences of events with respect to the local stimulus context and the previous experience of the listener. If you are cooking in the kitchen and suddenly hear a loud kerfuffle in the dining room, auditory analysis of the noises heard allows you to identify a plate breaking on the floor, forks and knives tumbling around, the muffled sound of a dish crashing, and a cat's surprised meow. From this analysis you succeed in attaching meaning to the whole scene, the cat was perhaps playing with the corner of the table cloth and pulled everything with it off the table on to the floor. The psychological and neuropsychological processes underlying such auditory recognition of sound sources, sound events, and sound sequences are reviewed in the chapters by Crowder, McAdams, and Peretz (Chs 5, 6, and 7 respectively). A more general review of specifically auditory aspects implicated in memory processes is developed by Crowder. In adults, the perception of musical relations is in part conditioned by abstract knowledge structures that have been acquired in listening to the music of a given culture. The form of these knowledge structures for Western tonal/metric music is delineated in Chapter 8 by Bigand. In addition, the existence of precocious abilities that underlthat their development in children is reviewed by Trehub and Trainor (Ch. 9), while the impairment of access to such structures in brain-damaged patients is discussed by Peretz (Ch. 7).

The perceived relations among sound events can evoke a whole interpretive framework that affects the perception of subsequent events. This framework strongly influences the establishment of larger-scale structural relations (of a hierarchical or associative nature). The processes that are responsible for this level of perception and comprehension are labelled *event structure processing* in Fig 1.1. Seated in a concert hall you await the arrival of the conductor: the musicians are warming up and producing a great sound mass. Listening attentively, you do not hear any relation between what each one is playing. You deduce therefore that each player is individually rehearsing different parts of the score. Then the concert starts. This time the events seem to follow one another with ease and you clearly perceive that the music progresses and develops through time. The exposition of the themes finishes and you then hear chords that are quite different from those in the preceding section. These changes in key announce the section in which the themes are developed. The understanding of this progression supposes that each of the new sound events can be connected to the preceding events. In cases where the incoming sound material is completely unknown to the listener, or does not correspond to known systems of structural relations (as would be found in the music of a given culture, for example), more primitive structuring procedures, such as segmentation into groups of events, may still operate directly on the relations among perceived surface attributes.

The end result of event structure processing is the gradual elaboration of a *mental representation of the structure of the sound environment* currently being experienced by the listener. Studying the elaboration of a mental representation is important for cognitive psychology, since it is quite crucial for any sensory system whose input is entirely transitory, i.e. there are no persisting objects in audition, and information about acoustic events must be accumulated through time, attended to dynamically, and processed with respect to previous experience while new information is being received. You may be following the various paths of musical development in a symphony, but you have established a mental representation of what happened at the beginning, which allows you to realize that at this moment the music is progressively moving towards the recapitulation of the principal theme, and you understand that the movement is about to come to a close. Chapter 8 by Bigand reviews the processes implicated in event structure processing and the building up of a mental representation of the structure of the sound environment. These processes are shown to influence the degree to which listeners are capable of establishing larger scale relations and thus to appreciate musical form and the development of musical ideas.

One of the important implications of event structure perception is that these structures serve as a framework having implications for the structure of acoustic information that has not yet arrived. By way of the interpretive framework evoked from abstract knowledge structures, anticipations and expectations may be set up that orient the listener's attention to forthcoming events of a particular kind or at particular times. These *attentional processes* may also be simply affected by perceived regularities in the stimulus structure. It is possible that attending itself may influence the activity of lower-level organizational processes (and even the process of sensory transduction). This area of attending to auditory events and its implication for perception and action are developed in Chapter 4 by Jones and Yee.

REFERENCES

Botte, M.-C., Canévet, G., Demany, L., and Sorin, C. (1989). *Psychoacoustique et perception auditive*. INSERM / EMI / SFA, Paris.

Bregman, A. S. (1990). *Auditory scene analysis: The perceptual organization of sound*. MIT, Cambridge, MA.

Dooling, R. J. and Hulse, S. H. (ed.) (1989). *The comparative psychology of audition: perceiving complex sounds*. Erlbaum, Hillsdale, NJ.

Dowling, W. J. and Harwood, D. L. (1986). *Music cognition*. Academic, Orlando, FL.

Handel, S. (1989). *Listening: an introduction to the perception of auditory events*. MIT, Cambridge, MA.

Humphreys, G. W. and Bruce, V. (1989). *Visual cognition: computational, experimental, and neuropsychological perspectives*. Erlbaum, Hillsdale, NJ.

Marr, D. (1982). *Vision: a computational investigation into the human representation and processing of visual information*. Freeman, San Francisco.

Moore, B. C. J. (1982). *Introduction to the psychology of hearing*, 3rd edn. Academic, London.

Pinker, S. (ed.) (1984). *Visual cognition*. MIT, Cambridge, MA. [reprinted from *Cognition*, Vol. 18].

Sloboda, J. A. (1985). *The musical mind: the cognitive psychology of music*. Clarendon, Oxford.

Warren, R. M. (1982). *Auditory perception: a new synthesis*. Pergamon, New York.

2

Auditory scene analysis: hearing in complex environments

Albert S. Bregman

2.0 INTRODUCTION

I would like to introduce an approach to auditory perception that is concerned with quite different questions from those asked by traditional psychophysics. The latter is occupied with such questions as these: What is the minimum amount of energy that can be sensed by the auditory system? How far apart do the frequencies of two pure tones have to be in order to be distinguished when they are played either sequentially or at the same time? How does the experienced loudness of a tone grow as its physical intensity is increased? How do differences between the acoustic patterns registered at each ear tell us where the source of sound is?

The development of artificial intelligence in recent years has made us aware that even if the above questions were answered with certainty, we would still understand very little about how the auditory system worked. A useful exercise that can help us to see the problems is first to imagine the auditory system as being possessed by a robot, and then to ask what its hearing capacities (as presently conceived) would do for it.

Let us imagine that we equipped our robot with a pair of sensing devices as ears and embodied, in these devices, all the properties that had been found to be true of human audition. The robot would still have great difficulty using the information that it received. Its most difficult problem would be in dealing with mixtures of sounds. Its record of any incoming signal would represent the sum of all sound-producing sources that had been simultaneously active at the time of the recording. Suppose that our robot had a definition in its memory of the sound of a voice saying a particular word. It still might not be able to recognize the word because the presence of other sounds had created a situation in which no segment of the recording matched the definition closely enough. Even worse, it might mistakenly hear some accidental product of the mixture of two voices as a word.

Thinking in sound: the cognitive psychology of human audition, ed. S. McAdams and E. Bigand. Oxford University Press, 1993, pp. 10–36.

Here is another example of the difficulty that it might have. Psychophysicists tell us that the intensities of the sounds at the two ears can be used as a clue for the spatial position of a sound source. But how does the robot know, when it is comparing the intensities at its two 'ears', that it is comparing the energy derived from only one sound source? If there are two, each in a different place, the simple strategy of comparing intensities at the two ears will no longer work. It must do a separate comparison of the intensities derived from each source. How is it to know how much energy came from each source to each ear?

To recognize the component sounds that have been added together to form the mixture that reaches our ears, the auditory system must somehow create individual descriptions that are based on only those components of the sound that have arisen from the same environmental event. The process by which it does this has been called 'auditory scene analysis' (Bregman 1990).

The term 'scene analysis' was first used by researchers in computer vision to refer to how a computer might solve the following problem. In a photograph of a scene of normal complexity, the visible parts of a single object are often discontinuous because the camera's view of the object has been interrupted by the presence of another object that lies between it and the camera (e.g. Guzman 1969). Scene analysis is the name given to the strategy by which the computer attempts to put together all the visible properties—edges, surface textures, colours, distances, and so on—that belong to the same object. Only then can the correct global shape and properties of that object be determined. By analogy, *auditory* scene analysis is the process whereby all the auditory evidence that comes, over time, from a single environmental source is put together as a perceptual unit. This chapter will describe the methods that the auditory system employs and some of the research that has discovered them.

2.1   SCENE ANALYSIS IN AUDITION

When you describe the problem of mixtures to most people, they are inclined to say that they solve it simply 'by paying attention to one of the sounds at a time'. In saying this, they imply that the parts of the same sound are somehow a coherent bundle that can be selected by the process of attention. However, we must remember that the only thing received by the ear is a pattern formed by pressure changes over time, and if we look at a graph of the waveform of a mixture of sounds, there is nothing obvious in it that labels the sound as a mixture or tells you how to take it apart.

We know that the first stage in the analysis of sounds by the human auditory system takes place in the cochlea. There the sound is decomposed

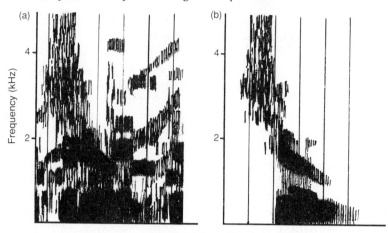

Time (1 division = 10 ms)

Fig. 2.1   Spectrogram of (a) a mixture of sounds and (b) one of the components of the mixture, the word 'shoe'.

into separate neural patterns that approximately represent the different frequencies in the signal (see Moore and Patterson (1986), for discussions on the limits of the ear's ability to separate very closely spaced frequencies). Decomposition into component frequencies is a technique also used by scientists in trying to understand hearing. The results are displayed in a spectrogram, a picture that shows time on the *x* axis and frequency on the *y* axis. The darkness at any point on the picture shows the intensity of the sound at a particular time and frequency. We can appreciate the limitations in the usefulness of the ear's frequency-based decomposition of the signal by considering the information shown in a spectrogram.

The one shown in Fig. 2.1(a) shows a mixture of sounds. The reader might think that the problem of finding the individual sources from mixtures might be solved immediately by using such a picture. This could indeed be done if the sources were steady, pure tones that were well separated in frequency. Then each horizontal streak on the picture would represent a separate environmental sound, persisting for some period of time. Figure 2.1(a), however, represents a more natural case in which each environmental sound has many frequency components and these are not constant over time. (It represents a mixture of a man saying 'shoe', another singing to himself, and an unrelated piece played by instruments in the background). A listener can easily hear the word 'shoe' in the recording from which this spectrogram was made. Figure 2.1(b) shows the word spoken in isolation. This is what must be extracted from the mixture. We can do it visually to some extent after seeing the isolated pattern, but listeners can do it even without being told which word is embedded in the mixture. The problem they face can be shown with reference to the spectrogram. We can see that in the mixture, the streaks that represent the components of the word are interlaced with and cross over those representing the components of the other sounds. Even a single streak can represent the sum of two or more components of the same or almost-the-same frequency that have been derived from different sounds. So separating the frequencies in the nervous system and laying them out over time, as illustrated in Fig. 2.1(a) does not, in itself, provide coherent bundles that can be selected by attention. The separate sound sources that listeners describe are not given in any simple way in the spectral decomposition of the signal. The problem of finding them is the job of auditory scene analysis.

It appears to me that there are three processes occurring in the human listener that serve to decompose auditory mixtures. One is the activation of learned schemas in a purely automatic way. It is a common observation that occasionally, people imagine they hear their names spoken in a noisy environment, for example a city street corner. Apparently, a chance co-occurrence of sounds can activate the mental schema that represents the sound of one's name. This hypersensitivity and automatic activation presumably occurs because people so frequently hear their names spoken that its schema is in a highly potentiated state. Whenever the incoming sound matches the schema's acoustic definition in even an approximate way, it becomes active. This method of analysis might penetrate some mixtures as long as the sound pattern recognized by the schema was not totally distorted.

A second process that can decompose mixtures is the use of schemas in a voluntary way. An example occurs when we are intent on trying to hear whether our name is being called out by a person announcing the next appointment in a busy office. The experience of 'trying' is an indication that voluntary attention is involved. Notice, however, that the schema for our name is also involved, though its operation is not automatic in this case. In general, whenever we are listening for a specific sound or class of sounds, some criterion for recognizing the targets must be employed. I call this criterion a schema because it is a mental representation of a particular set of characteristics.

Both of these methods, automatic and voluntary recognition, require that schemas (knowledge of the structure of particular sounds or sound classes that are important to us) have *already been formed* by prior listening. If these schema-based methods were the only ones for decomposing mixtures, it would be hard for us to form schemas for important sounds in the first place unless we frequently encountered these sounds in isolation. It would be valuable, therefore, for us to have general methods for partitioning an incoming mixture of sound into separate acoustic sources that could be used prior to any specific knowledge of the important sounds of our environment.

It appears that we do have such methods. I have referred to them collectively by the term 'primitive auditory scene analysis' (Bregman 1990, p. 38). By calling them primitive, I mean that instead of depending on knowledge of specific types of sound, such as voices, musical instruments, or machines, they depend on general acoustic properties that can be used for decomposing all types of mixture.

2.1.1 Using general acoustic regularities

There are certain relations between the acoustic properties of a sound that can be useful in solving the scene analysis problem even if the listener is not familiar with the signal. These relations are the result of general properties of sound-producing events and are not specific to voices, music, animal sounds, or any other individual class of sounds.

An example of a general property is the fact that many sounds of our environment are harmonic. That is, their frequency components are all multiples (approximately) of a fundamental frequency. This arises from the fact that when force is applied to certain types of bodies, they go into oscillatory motion. Their sub-parts also go into oscillation. Sub-parts forming halves, thirds, quarters (and so on) of the whole body go into oscillations whose frequencies are respectively twice, three times, four times (and so on) the frequency of the oscillations of the whole body. Examples of such bodies are the ones that produce animal vocalizations (including the human vocal cords), the strings in musical instruments, and parts of many machines.

The auditory system can employ a strategy that exploits this regularity. For example, what should it conclude about a signal, when it discovers from an analysis of its frequency components over a short span of time, that all the pure-tone components are multiples of a common fundamental? Are there many sounds present or only one? What are the odds in favour of a hypothesis that there are a number of sounds present, each with a different set of harmonics, all of which happen, by chance, to be multiples of a common fundamental? This would be a highly improbable accident. A better bet is that it is hearing only one acoustic event that is generating harmonics. Here is another example: What should the auditory system bet if it detects two subsets of components, the members of each of them being multiples of a different fundamental? Obviously, the best bet in this case is that the signal is a mixture of two harmonic sounds. The use of harmonicity is a case, then, where a general regularity of the world can be used to decide on the number of sounds being heard.

We find, however, that no single regularity can be trusted all the way. After all, it is not impossible that the harmonics of two sounds might briefly enter into an apparently regular relation with one another. But we would find, in all likelihood, that they were coming from different places in space or that they started and stopped at different times. Since the frequency components from a single acoustic event tend to come from the same place and to start and stop at roughly the same time, differences in these properties would protect us against accepting accidentally harmonic components as parts of a single sound. We therefore need to exploit many regularities at the same time if we are to come to the right answer.

Shepard (1981) has argued that because animals have evolved in a world that contains regularities, it is likely that their perceptual systems have evolved modes of operation that take advantage of them. That is, as animals evolved, the properties of their perceptual systems became tuned to the regularities of the physical world. The resulting match is referred to as 'psychophysical complementarity.' If Shepard is right, a good strategy for finding the laws of auditory organization would be to try to discover relations among the components of the incoming sound that are frequently present when parts of the sound have been created by different environmental events. Then we can do experiments to find out whether the human auditory system exploits these relations to decompose mixtures.

2.2   EFFECTS OF AUDITORY SCENE ANALYSIS ON PERCEPTION

The organization of sensory evidence which is carried out by auditory scene analysis, affects many aspects of auditory perception that we do not usually believe to be related to perceptual organization. Organization is often viewed as a grouping of raw auditory properties *after* they have been created by perception. However, even such apparently raw properties as loudness can be affected by organization.

Here is an example described by Warren (1982) as 'homophonic continuity' (see also Warren *et al.* 1972; Warren 1984). Suppose we are presented with a steady sound which first holds a fixed intensity for a few seconds, then suddenly becomes more intense, holds this new intensity briefly, and then returns to the original level and continues for some time. If the period of greater intensity is short, we hear it not as a change in the original signal, but as a second sound, identical in properties to the original one, joining it, and then disappearing. The first signal is heard as continuing, unchanged in loudness, behind the added one. The intensity, when it is at the higher level, is interpreted not as coming from a single loud sound, but as a mixture of two softer sounds. In other words, the intensity information is shared out between two perceived events. On the other hand, in experimenting with this stimulus, I have noticed that if the rise and fall in intensity are not sudden, then the two-sound interpretation does not occur (Bregman 1991). Instead, the original sound is heard as changing in loudness, and the full intensity at the high level is used to derive the perceived loudness of a single sound. To summarize, organizational processes will decide whether we hear one loud sound or two softer ones.

We can create a variation of this example to show how perceptual organization can affect even a sound's perceived spatial position (Bregman 1991). Let us present the signal I have just described, but this time to our right ear only. At the same time, we present to the left ear a sound that is identical to our original signal in all respects, except that it always remains at the lower intensity. During the initial phase, when both the left and right ear are receiving the same lower-intensity signal, we hear a single, steady sound in the middle. Then when the right-ear signal suddenly rises in intensity, stays briefly at this level, and then returns, we perceive the original sound continuing in the middle, accompanied briefly by a sound at our extreme right. With this procedure two sounds are heard, each with its own position.

Suppose, instead, we raise and lower the intensity at the right ear less suddenly. In this case, we hear the sound move over to the right and then back to the centre, our spatial perception following the changing balance of intensities at the two ears. We perceive only a single sound with a single location.

Regardless of whether the change is sudden or gradual, it leads to the same intensity balance between the two ears during the middle phase (when the sound is more intense at one ear). If perceived location were unaffected by the history of the event, we would hear the same thing in the two cases. But we do not. This tells us that when we perceive a location, it is not the location of 'sound' in the abstract, but of a particular sound. Depending on how many sounds are created by perceptual organization, the set of perceived locations will be different. The simple rules for spatial perception that classical psychophysics has discovered by testing listeners in simple, quiet environments cannot be applied without modification in acoustically complex ones.

Auditory scene analysis can also affect whether we hear one tone with a rich timbre or a number of tones with purer timbres (Bregman and Pinker 1978). It can affect the perceived identity of a speech sound by segregating acoustic components that might otherwise be part of it, and allocating them to another perceived event (Darwin 1984; Ciocca and Bregman 1989). It can determine whether two melodies, presented as a mixture, are heard individually or whether a new emergent melody, formed of all the notes, is heard instead (Dowling 1973). It can determine whether the instruments of an ensemble are heard with their individual properties or blend to form a global timbre (Bregman 1990, Ch. 5). In short, it affects every auditory experience in natural environments.

Although I have surveyed much of the research on auditory scene analysis at length in a separate volume (Bregman 1990), I will try here to convey a basic understanding of the approach. The presentation will be organized around the different environmental regularities exploited by the auditory system.

Regularity 1.   *Unrelated sounds seldom start or stop at exactly the same time.*

Acoustic components derived from independent environmental events tend not to start and stop at the same time. Instead, one is likely to be active already at the moment that another begins. The auditory system exploits this general truth when it uses what I have called the 'old-plus-new' strategy: when a spectrum suddenly becomes more complex but, as far as the nervous system can tell, it still contains the same frequency components as before, it is interpreted as a continuation of an old signal with a new one joining it. The old sound continues to be heard for a short time along with the new one. If the spectrum becomes simple again, so that it contains only the components of the old sound, this strengthens the perception of the old one as having been present all the time. The perceived qualities of the added sound are derived from the components of the complex spectrum that are left over after the components of the earlier simpler spectrum are subtracted out.

The various phenomena of perceived continuity (see Warren 1984) are derived from this strategy. In the best known example, a long pure tone is alternated with a short, louder noise burst that stimulates neural channels that include the one stimulated by the tone. A listener will hear the tone as continuing through the noise—it seems to be present all the time. Rather than hearing the tone turn suddenly into a noise burst, the auditory system determines that the neural activity occurring during the noise burst is consistent with the continuation of the tone. This allows it to generate a percept of the tone continuing behind the noise. Probably the rejection of the alternative interpretation, a tone turning into a noise, is due to the auditory system's exploitation of another environmental regularity that we will discuss later: when properties are derived from a single continuing sound, they tend not to change suddenly.

In the preceding example of continuity it is hard to determine whether the part of the neural activity that was interpreted as the continuing tone was allowed to contribute to the perception of the noise. A broad band of noise sounds very much the same whether or not the narrow band of frequencies allotted to the tone has been subtracted from it. A better stimulus for seeing how the total information from the noise is shared out is a signal in which a band of noise, say 0 to 1 kHz ('kHz' means 'thousands of cycles per second'), alternates with a wider band (say 0 to 2 kHz), with the narrower band of noise longer in duration than the wider one. The stimulus is generated so that the components shared by the two sounds (i.e. those in the 0–1 kHz range) are equal in intensity in the two sounds. In this demonstration, a listener will hear the narrow-band noise as continuing through the wide-band noise (Warren 1982, Ch. 2). In addition, it is the listener's impression that the short intermittent sound lacks the components that have been used by the auditory system to create the percept of the continuing narrow-band noise. The contribution of the 0–1 kHz components has been removed and the 'added' noise is experienced as having the same quality as a 1–2 kHz noise. The spectrum of the wider-band 0–2 kHz noise has been divided up, providing separate components for the continuing and the added sounds.

An example of the old-plus-new strategy in the field of speech perception is found in an experiment by Darwin (1984). Each vowel in a language can be distinguished from all the others by the positions of a number of formants (intensity peaks) in its spectrum. Each formant consists of an augmented intensity of a number of harmonics. Darwin lengthened one of the harmonics in the lowest formant of a vowel so that it started before the vowel and continued throughout its duration. In this stimulus pattern, the tone is the 'old' sound and the vowel is the 'new' one. The effect was to cause the vowel to sound more like a different one. This occurred because when the harmonic was heard alone, it was assigned an identity as a separate sound. Then when it was joined by the rest of the vowel, the total neural stimulation activated by the vowel was partitioned. A part was interpreted as the continuing (old) tone. Only the remainder, with this part removed, was interpreted as the vowel. The remaining sensory evidence pointed to a peak in the spectrum at a different place from that shown by the whole body of evidence, and, in doing so, changed the identity of the perceived vowel.

Regularity 2.   *Gradualness of change.*

    (a) *A single sound tends to change its properties smoothly and slowly.*

    (b) *A sequence of sounds from the same source tends to change its properties slowly.*

The environmental regularity concerning the sequential resemblance of sounds from the same source tends to take two forms. One of them relates to a *single sound-producing event* that extends over time. Examples (at different scales of time) are a single violin note, a single syllable being spoken, the roar of a lion, or the continuous noise of a motor. The sound coming from such an event tends to change continuously rather than abruptly in its properties as the event unfolds.

A second form of this sequential regularity is concerned with a *succession of sounds* from the same source. Many examples can be cited: a succession of footsteps, a series of chirps in a bird's or a frog's call, a series of pecks of a woodpecker, and so on. Sounds derived in succession from the same acoustic source tend to resemble one another, with only gradual changes in properties between members of the series.

Sometimes it is not the event that is occurring repeatedly, but our auditory access to it. In a mixture of sounds, each of which is waxing and waning in intensity, the auditory system may obtain a succession of exposures to the properties of one of the sounds relatively unmixed with properties of the others. The spectral samples caught in these successive 'glimpses' of the sound are likely to resemble one another.

An important fact about sequential resemblance is that sounds do, in fact, change. However, since the changes tend to be gradual, samples from the same acoustic event that are taken closer together in time tend to resemble each other more closely.

These facts about sequential change in the sounds of the world are encapsulated in two rules that seem to be followed by the auditory system. The first rule that is based on these regularities is the 'sudden-change rule'. The auditory system will treat a sudden change of properties as the onset of a new event. Examples of this were given earlier in this chapter. We had the example of homophonic continuity as well as the example in which one ear received an abrupt rise in intensity while the other ear's sound remained steady. In both cases, the suddenness of the change triggered the interpretation of an added sound. This set the stage for the old-plus-new strategy to decompose the spectrum into the components belonging to the old sound and those of the added one.

The use of this strategy requires a definition of suddenness. However, there is no clear boundary between gradual and sudden changes. This is illustrated in a recent unpublished study by Jean Kim and myself. We played a rapid sequence of four one-second tones to subjects and asked them to judge their order of onset. They were highly overlapped in time— for example each successive tone could begin as little as 0.15 s after the previous one. The suddenness of the rise in intensity of each tone, as it was turned on, helped the listener to decompose it from the mixture. When the onsets took 0.04 s, the tones sounded distinct and the listener could judge their order fairly well, but when it took 0.64 s, the tones were all blended together in an impenetrable mush of sound and it was almost impossible to judge their order. However, the change from sudden to gradual was not 'all or nothing' in nature. An intermediate onset time, 0.16 s, gave an intermediate result. The suddenness of spectral change works like every other clue for scene analysis. The stronger it is, the more it affects the grouping.

The range of durations (0.04 to 0.64 s) that I have described as embodying a wide range of suddenness may be a valid range only for changes in intensity. The values that count as sudden and gradual for changes in other features of sound, such as spatial location, timbre, or pitch, have not yet been pinned down quantitatively.

Sometimes the auditory system will not be able to find a close enough match in the spectra before and after the sudden change to support the old-plus-new interpretation. Therefore, instead of interpreting the change as a second sound being added to the mixture, or as a change in the qualities of a single continuing sound, it may conclude that a second sound has replaced the first. An experiment by Darwin and Bethell-Fox (1977) found an example of this in speech perception. First it is important to understand that the fundamental frequency and the frequencies of the formants can be varied independently of one another. The fundamental is the frequency of which all the components of the spectrum are multiples (harmonics). The formants are those parts of the spectrum in which the harmonics have been strengthened in intensity. The researchers synthesized a sample of continuous speech consisting of smooth formant transitions (gradual changes in the positions of spectral peaks) back and forth between two vowels. The vowels were represented by frequencies of the formants that were held steady for 0.06 s. In the middle of each transition, they suddenly changed the speaker's fundamental frequency, so that one vowel was always on a lower frequency, 101 Hz, and the other on a higher one, 178 Hz ('Hz' means 'cycles per second'). This caused a segregation of two apparently different talkers, one speaking in a lower pitch and the other in a higher. Furthermore, even though there was a continuous change in the formant frequencies, the parts of the transition before and after the abrupt change in pitch tended to be perceptually isolated from one another. Each voice seemed to be silent during the period in which the other was talking. Furthermore, the syllables that were constructed in perception tended *not* to be based on formant patterns that bridged the change in the fundamental. It was as if the auditory system did not want to make a mistake by creating syllables out of relations between the sounds from two different talkers.

A second rule that exploits the probable sequential resemblance of sounds from the same source is the 'grouping by similarity' rule. We do not yet know all the ways in which sounds can be similar. However, similarities in the frequencies of pure tones, in spatial location, and in the spectral content and fundamental frequency of complex tones has been shown to affect grouping (Bregman 1990, Ch. 2). We are also unsure about the measurement of similarity. For the frequencies of pure tones, the difference that affects grouping appears to be the difference between the logarithms of their frequencies, but for other dimensions, no one has yet tried to discover appropriate quantitative measures of the degree of similarity. It has been directed, instead, towards demonstrating that such similarities actually have an effect on grouping, using common sense assessments of similarity.

In some sense, we have already discussed similarity. We might argue that discontinuity, mentioned earlier, is merely the absence of sequential similarity. However, in mentioning the similarity rule separately, I am thinking of cases in which the sounds occur in discrete samples or episodes, such as a succession of footsteps or a succession of glimpses of one sound in a mixture whenever the others drop in intensity. These successive samples of sound are modelled in the laboratory by successions of tones, bursts of noise, tonal glides, and so on.

The effect of the rule is to take sounds that have similar properties, to link them together perceptually into groups, and to segregate these groups from one another. Each linked group is considered by the auditory system to have come from a distinct environmental source. As a result, pattern-recognition processes tend to treat the grouped sounds as the 'package' of evidence within which to look for familiar patterns.

The phenomenon of auditory streaming exemplifies the working of this rule (Bregman and Campbell 1971; van Noorden 1975, 1982). Suppose we start with two sets of tones, one of high tones and the other of low ones, in which there is a considerable frequency separation between the high and low sets, but where the frequency differences between the tones within each set are small. Suppose we then interleave the high (H) and low (L) tones together (e.g. HLHLHL . . .) to make a long sequence, and play it to listeners. Recall that I said that in the world at large, the closer in time two samples from the same acoustic source are, the more similar their properties are likely to be. The 'grouping by proximity' strategy takes this regularity into account. As long as the succession of tones is slow (i.e. the samples are far apart in time), the auditory system is willing to accept the entire set of tones as coming from a single source. However, when the sequence is speeded up, two perceptual 'packages', or auditory streams, are formed—the listener hears the sequence as if two distinct sources of sound were active at roughly the same time. Patterns formed by the high and low tones taken in combination tend to disappear in favour of patterns formed by the high tones alone and the low ones alone. For example, two melodies will be heard, one involving the high notes and the other the low ones. Also if the original mixed sequence is irregular, different temporal patterns will be heard in the high and low ranges. For example, the following sequence of high and low tones

...H H L H L L H L H H H L L H L...

will break into the streams

...H H – H – – H – H H – – H – ... and
...– – L – L L – L – – L L – L...

In these letter-diagrams, the dashes represent silences that appear in each stream as a result of the absence of the tones that have been placed into the other stream by the perceptual grouping. So, temporal patterns, including rhythms (in repetitive sequences), can be created or altered by the segregation into auditory streams.

The grouping is sensitive to the degree of difference between the frequencies of the high and low tones, the segregation becoming stronger as the separation in frequency becomes greater. This frequency difference can trade off against the speed of the sequence. A sequence in which the frequency difference is smaller must be sped up more before it will be segregated (van Noorden 1975).

The sensitivity of segregation to the speed of the sequence can be viewed as a sensitivity to the rate of change between high and low tones. When changes occur more rapidly, the sequence is less likely to be treated as issuing from the same environmental source. This property of the perceptual process is justified by the environmental regularity that, in a series of sounds from the *same* acoustic source, the properties tend to change only slowly.

An important fact about the segregation of the tones of two classes (at least when the classes are defined by frequency range) is that it is cumulative. Even at a high speed, the first few high and low tones are usually integrated into a single stream. As the auditory system continues to hear two populations of tones, segregation occurs. It appears that the segregative tendency builds up for at least four seconds. Just as the tendency to segregate takes some time to build up, it also takes at least four seconds to dissipate. Even if the sequence stops for a couple of seconds, some segregative tendency will remain, and if the sequence starts again, it will be segregated more quickly the second time (Bregman 1978). This auditory principle seems to correspond to the environmental fact that the best predictor of a sound occurring is the fact of having just heard it a moment earlier. Apparently the auditory system keeps an 'open slot' available for the return of the sound.

It appears that even simple perceptual judgments are affected by the segregation of components in different frequency ranges. The exact temporal separation between two tones, one higher in frequency than the other, becomes more difficult to judge as the frequency separation is increased (see Bregman 1990, pp. 159–63 for an account of this research).

2.3   MULTIPLE BASES FOR SEGREGATION

The frequencies of the tones are not the only differences that affect their sequential organization. Tones can also be grouped according to similarities in their spatial positions (described by Bregman 1990, pp. 73–83). In addition, if the sounds are complex, other factors can play a role. In tones formed of many harmonics, as voices and musical tones are, the grouping can depend on similarities in their fundamental frequencies and also in their timbres, if we define timbre by the relative strengths of harmonics in their spectra (Singh 1987; Bregman *et al.* 1990a). Tones (sounds whose waveforms repeat cyclically) will often segregate from noises (Dannenbring and Bregman 1976). Tones that glide from one frequency to another will connect together sequentially better when they have the same slopes and are in the same frequency range (Steiger and Bregman 1981).

These various types of difference compete and cooperate with one another in determining grouping. If different factors promote contradictory groupings of the sounds, the winner will be the grouping with the most factors favouring it or the grouping that is favoured by the factors that the auditory system prefers to use (Bregman 1990, pp. 165–71, 218, 335).

This brings up the point that not all acoustic differences are equally important in determining grouping. Hartmann and Johnson (1991) asked listeners to recognize pairs of melodies whose notes had been interleaved to form a new sequence of tones. In each sequence, the notes of the two melodies were made to differ from one another on a single acoustic characteristic. The most effective ways to help people to segregate the two melodies were to send them to different ears, to shift the notes of one melody up by an octave, or to introduce a timbre difference between them (pure sine-wave tones versus rich complex tones). Virtually no improvement of segregation was obtained when the difference involved the attack and decay times of the notes of the two sets or when the rhythm of the overall sequence was altered by shifting one set of notes so that they did not fall exactly half way between the notes of the other, or when noise was added to the notes of one melody.

When we observe, in an experiment, that segregation is more strongly affected by some acoustic factors than others, we still do not know whether the observed differences arose because of their effects on the primitive scene-analysing mechanism or because of the activity of more sophisticated mechanisms that use learning or attention. Evidence that there is more than one mechanism comes from the different effects that speed has, depending on the intentions of the subject. Van Noorden (1975) played his listeners a sequence in which tones in two different frequency regions alternated, and asked them about the perceptual segregation of the tones into high and low streams. He varied the frequency separation between the high and low tones and the speed of the sequence. The results he obtained depended on what he asked the listeners to do. When they were asked to hold the high and low tones *together* in a single stream as much as possible, he found a trade-off between frequency separation and speed. As the speed became higher, the tones had to be closer together in frequency before they could be integrated. However, there was no such trade-off when they were asked to try to *segregate* the high tones from the low ones as much as possible. As long as there was a minimum frequency separation of a few semitones, the sequence could be segregated equally well at any speed. To me this difference indicates that there is more than one mechanism of segregation. When listeners are trying to *integrate* the sequence, the segregation is involuntary, acting in *opposition* to their intentions. This sort of segregation is probably due to primitive scene analysis mechanisms. On the other hand, the segregation that occurs when listeners are trying to segregate the sounds, i.e. when the segregation is *consistent* with their intentions, is the product of a selection process carried out by attention (Bregman 1990, Ch. 4). The existence of two mechanisms explains another related finding. When we vary an acoustic difference among some sounds in a sequence, two aspects of the results are not always consistent with one another. For example, differences between notes on timbre may *assist* the listeners strongly when they are trying to segregate the sequence on that basis. However, those same timbre differences may *not* strongly oppose the grouping when listeners are trying to segregate the sequence on the basis of another factor, pitch differences (Bregman *et al.* 1990a). If only one process of segregation existed, you would expect that when it supported your intentions, it should give symmetrically opposite effects to those obtained when it opposed your intentions.

If more than one mechanism can be involved, experiments that study the role of acoustic differences in segregation must attempt to ensure that the variation among the results of different experimental conditions is due to only one of these mechanisms. We have tried in our own research at McGill University to engage the primitive mechanism by always giving subjects tasks that require them to hold the sequence together. When they cannot do so, the negative influence is attributed to a primitive mechanism.

Consider the Hartmann and Johnson experiment mentioned earlier (p. 23). The listeners were required to pull out a sub-sequence of sounds (a melody) whose tones were marked by a common property. Therefore, they could have set their attentional mechanisms to select tones with that property. The difficulty they had in using some of these properties could have come because either the primitive mechanism or the attentional mechanism made little use of them. It is likely, since all differences were discriminable, that the results were influenced primarily by primitive grouping. However, a purer test of primitive grouping would be to control the listeners' attentional strategies by asking them to try to use the same acoustic difference (e.g. attack time) on *every* test, but to oppose their intentions by introducing other differences that could be employed by primitive scene analysis to form groupings that opposed the intended ones. The effectiveness of this opposition would reveal the effectiveness with which primitive grouping used that property.

The readiness of the auditory system to group similar sounds when they occur in a sequence is the basis for a slightly different version of the 'old-plus-new' strategy from the one I described earlier. In the examples I gave before, one of the components of a mixture started ahead of the mixture as a whole and continued, without a break, into it. The clear glimpse that the auditory system obtained of the earlier-starting sound allowed it to be factored out of the mixture. A similar, but weaker, effect occurs when two sounds are used—a simpler one, and a more complex one that contains the simpler one as part of it, but there is a break between them. They are rapidly alternated, with brief silences between them, in a repeating cycle. Under favourable circumstances, the listener will experience the pure tone twice on each cycle, once when it is presented in isolation and once when the complex tone occurs. This means that the isolated pure tone has captured the corresponding frequency out of the complex tone into a pure-tone stream. As a result, the listener will hear the pure tone twice per cycle (the second occurrence is the component captured out of the complex tone). The remainder of the complex tone will form a second sound that seems to occur only once per cycle.

This extraction of an earlier-heard sound out of a complex one was described earlier as the old-plus-new strategy. The only difference in the present case is that there is a silence separating the isolated tone from its counterpart in the later mixture of components that comprises the complex tone. However, because the isolated tone (the captor) and its 'target' inside the complex tone are not continuous, this stimulus pattern allows us to manipulate the frequency proximity between them. If the captor and target are pure tones, then increasing the frequency difference between them reduces the capturing. With sufficient separation, the second occurrence of a pure tone on each cycle can no longer be heard (Bregman and Pinker 1978).

This influence of frequency proximity in the capturing of a tone from a complex spectrum is a direct counterpart to its influence in the sequential streaming of tones that occur in different frequency ranges. The two cases can be described in the same terms: an earlier tone (or stream of similar tones) tries to link itself to a newly arriving tone (*or a part of it*) in proportion to the proximity of the new component to those already in the stream. In both cases, there is a sequential grouping by proximity.

2.4   DIFFERENCES IN SPATIAL LOCATION

Regularity 2 (gradualness of change) applies to spatial location as well as to the other factors already mentioned. Sounds that are created by the same event typically come from the same position in space, or from a location that is changing slowly. Correspondingly, there is a scene-analysis principle that groups sounds that come from the same spatial location. Bregman (1990) describes cases in which this grouping occurs when the sounds appear sequentially (pp. 75–83), or when they are presented at the same time (pp. 293–312). An example of the latter can be created by sending the upper- and lower-frequency components of a speech sound to separate ears. In certain conditions, a separate sound will be heard on each side of the head (e.g. Cutting 1976). This segregation of speech components, while audible, often does not prevent their use together to form a speech sound. This freedom of speech perception from compulsion by primitive scene analysis resembles what happens in the case of seg-regation by harmonic relations. I discuss the latter further on, together with the reasons why it may occur (see also Bregman 1990, Ch. 7).

While the use of spatial location is central to many attempts by en-gineers to programme computers to segregate the sound of a person speaking from other co-occurring sounds, humans do not seem to depend so heavily on this cue. They do use spatial location, but when it competes against a sequential grouping based on frequency differences, it typically loses (e.g. Smith *et al.* 1982).

When two steady sounds are played at the same time in different spatial locations, the listener's ability to derive a separate estimate for the location is not very precise (Divenyi and Oliver 1989). Yet I believe that there *is* a role for spatial differences in auditory scene analysis. I would guess that, in general, they play a facilitating role, strongly enhancing segregation based on other factors such as asynchrony, or differences in frequency or timbre. They would probably greatly facilitate the follow-ing of sounds into mixtures when the earlier sound and the added ones were at different locations.

Why should the human not give absolute priority to the spatial cue? I can imagine both a reason based on the environmental information available to scene analysis and one based on the physiology of audition. First, consider the environmental argument. The gradualness of change of the location of an event in our environment should be just as strong a regularity as gradualness of change of frequency. While this may well be true, the physics of sound makes the evidence about location less reliable. We use differences in the sound received at our two ears or the way it is filtered by our outer ears to derive the direction from which it was coming. However, sounds can bounce around corners in the envir-onment, or reflect off walls near one of our ears, or an obstructing object

can move close to one of our ears, attenuating the sound. These phenomena cause the information about location to become incorrect. Such
events cannot, however, change the fundamental frequency of a sound
or its internal harmonic relations or add a frequency that was not there
before; therefore we should not be surprised that fundamental frequency,
harmonic relations, and frequency composition are used more strongly
than spatial location. Another possible reason for the conservative use of
the location cue may be found in the physiology of hearing. To segregate
sounds based on their locations, the auditory system must calculate which
frequency components have come from the same spatial location; that is,
it must assign a separate location estimate to each one. This may be
difficult to do when the components are densely packed in the spectrum.

Regularity 3.   *When a body vibrates with a repetitive period, its vibrations give rise to an acoustic pattern in which the
frequency components are multiples of a common
fundamental.*

I described this regularity earlier and outlined the corresponding
strategy that could be employed to group the partials (frequency
components) in a spectrum. Let me now describe a few observations and
experiments which show that people do indeed use such a strategy. The
most obvious observation is that people can hear the individual pitches
of two complex tones played at the same time, even if they start and stop
together. We have reason to believe that in a complex tone, many of its
partials contribute to its pitch (see Moore 1989, Ch. 5). But, to derive each
pitch correctly, the auditory system must be including only the partials
of one of the tones and excluding the partials of the other one. In the
present example, this could only be done by using the harmonic relations
between the partials of the same tone. This example shows only that the
auditory system can use harmonic relations for deriving two pitches at
the same time. It does not prove that harmonic relations can be used to
segregate groups of partials for any other purpose. This proof, however,
has come from laboratory studies.

Darwin and Gardner (1986) showed that a segregation based on harmonic relations could effect the perception of a vowel. They based their
procedure on a finding by Moore *et al.* (1986); so let me diverge a little
to describe this finding. These researchers started with a complex tone in
which all partials were harmonically related to the same fundamental.
Such a tone is perceived as a unified whole, with only a single pitch.
They found that when a low harmonic was mistuned from its harmonic
value by a sufficient amount, it was heard as a separate tone with a pitch
different from that of the complex tone. Accordingly, Darwin and Gardner

synthesized a vowel with a harmonic spectrum and then mistuned one of its harmonics. The perceived identity of the vowel was changed when the harmonic was mistuned by eight per cent. Apparently this occurred because the mistuned partial was removed from the package of evidence defining the vowel, and the remaining evidence pointed to a different vowel. So the segregation based on harmonicity can affect not just the pitch but other qualities of the sound.

None the less, there seems to be a discrepancy between two effects of harmonic relations—effects on the perception of how many sounds are present, and effects on the identification of speech. The discrepancy has been noticed in cases in which there is only a single speech sound in the spectrum. The spectrum is divided into two non-overlapping regions and a different fundamental frequency is used to derive the harmonics of each region. While listeners will segregate the two regions as far as the perception of pitch is concerned (they hear two), they will still integrate the regions to derive the identity of the speech sound (Cutting 1976; Darwin 1981). We encountered this discrepancy earlier in our discussion of the segregation of parts of a speech sound by their spatial locations.

The finding about fundamental frequencies seems to imply that speech perception does not make any use of differences on this factor to segregate mixtures of sounds. Yet this is not true. When *two* complete speech sounds are mixed, with their spectra *overlapping*, their identities are perceived much more clearly when the harmonics of the two are related to two different fundamental frequencies (Brokx and Noteboom 1982; Scheffers 1983). Spatial differences also make it easier to segregate two concurrent voices (Schubert and Schultz 1962). I believe that it is possible to resolve these contradictions by arguing that the grouping created by primitive scene analysis does not lead to separate percepts in a single step (Bregman 1990, Ch. 7). It merely lays constraints of a non-binding nature on a subsequent description-building process. The latter process is also governed by our schemas of speech sounds and other familiar sounds. The interaction of the two sorts of constraint leads to the final percept.

Regularity 4.   *Many changes that take place in an acoustic event will affect all the components of the resulting sound in the same way and at the same time.*

An example of this regularity can be found in the sound of a man dragging a load by fits and starts along an irregular gravel road. The sound made by the dragging has many frequency components in it, yet the intensities of all these components rise and fall together in synchrony as the load moves irregularly along. A correlated pattern of intensity change occurs across the spectrum. However, the frequency components arriving from other co-occurring events, such as a car passing or a person talking at the same time, have their own independent patterns of change.

The perceptual rule based on this regularity favours the grouping of components of the spectrum that have the same pattern of intensity variation. Its effects can be observed in the laboratory in a phenomenon called 'comodulation masking release' or CMR (Hall *et al.* 1984; see also review by Moore 1990). In one version of it, a target sound, such as a pure tone, is played together with a noise whose component frequencies fall in a narrow range (a 'narrow band') and are close to those of the masker. If loud enough, this noise (called the 'on-target band') tends to mask or drown out the target noise because noises that have frequencies close to those in a target are effective in masking it. The amplitude of the masker, but not of the target, fluctuates over time. The experiment proceeds as follows. First the on-target masker is made just intense enough that the target cannot be heard. Next, a second narrow band of noise is added to the signal. Its frequencies are too far from that of the target to mask it. This second band is called the 'flanking band'. Surprisingly, if the amplitude fluctuations of the flanking band are synchronized with those of the on-target band, the perception of the previously masked target signal is restored. Apparently the scene-analysis system can group neural activity across frequency ranges when it shows the same pattern of change. The information summed across the ranges concerning the fluctuations allows the two bands to be treated as a single source that is separate from the target tone, which does not have the same fluctuations. This example shows that not only does the auditory system have the power to group components that share the same pattern of fluctuation but that it can segregate them from others that do not share it.

It is not yet clear as to what exact process permits the segregation to take place in the CMR phenomenon. Clearly, in a natural environment, the combined information from two frequency bands would specify the fluctuations in a source event more exactly than either could do alone, since it is likely that the individual bands would contain a contribution from other events that had different fluctuation patterns. In the CMR case, the fluctuation in the on-target band is being altered through its mixture with the target tone, which is not fluctuating.

But how is the improved information about the fluctuation pattern employed to better detect the target? Is the fluctuation pattern subtracted from all spectral bands that show any sign of it? How would the system know how much to subtract? After all, the fluctuating event in the environment would probably not generate equally strong acoustic energy in all frequency bands. It is not clear how the auditory system solves these problems.

Another example of the grouping of components by their fluctuation patterns is found in listening to the human voice. The pulses of air through the vocal folds of the speaker give rise to a pattern of harmonics. These are spaced apart in frequency, as harmonics always are, by an amount equal to the fundamental frequency. (For example, the harmonics of a 100 Hz fundamental are 100, 200, 300, and so on, all separated by 100 Hz.) When they reach a listener's inner ear, a number of consecutive harmonics can affect the same region on the basilar membrane (see Glossary for explanation). Due to the geometry of the inner ear, this happens increasingly as the frequencies of the harmonics become higher. At higher frequencies, components having a given frequency difference affect places that are closer together on the basilar membrane. When this happens, that region tends to register beats at a rate that is equal to the frequency separation of the harmonics. Because the harmonics are all equally spaced in frequency, this beat rate is the same at different places on the basilar membrane, corresponding to different frequency bands in the incoming signal. This correlated beating in different frequency regions of the auditory system tells it that these regions have been stimulated by the same voice. This can be used as a reason for grouping the evidence from these neural channels. The amplitude fluctuations that are being discussed here are much faster in the case of the voice, even the male voice (mostly between 80 and 200 fluctuations per second), than in the CMR phenomenon (commonly around 10–25 Hz). However, laboratory studies have shown that amplitude modulation around 100 Hz can be used as a basis for fusing the perception of two spectral regions (Bregman *et al.* 1990*b*) and differences of as little as 5 Hz can measurably reduce the fusion (Bregman *et al.* 1985).

2.5   SYNCHRONIZED FREQUENCY CHANGES

When a sound-generating object changes its properties so that its fundamental frequency gets higher or lower, all the partials (pure-tone components) of the sound also change synchronously and in parallel (on logarithmic frequency coordinates). An example of this regularity can be found in the human voice. A voiced sound—a vowel, for example—contains many harmonics. When we raise the pitch of our voice by tightening our vocal folds, the frequencies of all the harmonics rise by a proportionate amount at the same time. The same thing holds true when we move the slide of a trombone.

Suppose that, in a particular listening situation, the auditory system encountered a spectrum in which two subsets of partials had the following properties: (i) the partials within each subset changed their frequencies in parallel, and (ii) the two subsets had independent patterns of frequency change. How should this evidence be used? Obviously it indicates the presence of two independent sounds, each formed of a set of partials.

The auditory system should fuse each subset, i.e. it should use only the partials within a subset to derive a description of a sound. The net effect would be the segregation of two sounds in a mixture.

It has been proposed that the auditory system does exploit this form of regularity. McAdams (1984) found that when a number of pure-tone components, played at the same time, were caused to move through small changes in frequency, the listeners heard fewer sources of sound when their frequencies changed in parallel (on a logarithmic frequency scale) than when they changed in a non-parallel way. This argues that the parallel components were fused. However, in another experiment by McAdams (1989), the auditory system did not seem to be able to use the independent movement of three subsets of components in order to segregate them. The author synthesized three vowels on different fundamental frequencies and mixed them. In all cases he jittered the fundamental frequency of the vowels over time, causing all the harmonics of any individual vowel to change in parallel. In some cases, the pattern of change was the same for all vowels, and in others, each vowel had a different pattern. One would think that in the former case the vowels would be segregated by the independence of their changes and in the latter case they would be fused and be hard to hear individually. However, no difference in the perceived prominence of the individual vowels was found in the two conditions. This called into question the idea that the auditory system uses parallel changes to group components and independent changes to segregate them. Another negative finding was reported by Gardner and Darwin (1986). They gave one of the harmonics in a synthesized vowel a different pattern of frequency change from the others and found that it did not reduce the contribution of that harmonic to the identity of the vowel.

There would be a problem of interpretation even if we found that the parallel movement of partials promoted their fusion and that non-parallel movement promoted their segregation. Consider a sound that is harmonic (i.e. all its partials are multiples of its fundamental). Suppose all the partials are to be changed in frequency. When all of them are changed in parallel (on a logarithmic frequency scale), they remain multiples of a common fundamental whose frequency is changing. Therefore if the auditory system groups a subset of partials whenever they change in parallel, it may not be reacting to the parallel movement but to the continued presence of harmonic relations. Any experiment on the independent effect of parallel movement over and above the harmonicity factor has to be done with partials that are not harmonically related. To my knowledge, only one experiment of this type has shown a facilitation of the recognition of two separate sounds in a mixture. It was done by Chalikia and myself in an unpublished study. Vowels were synthesized using inharmonic spectra. Two were played at the same time and the listener was asked to identify them. In some conditions they were more accurate when the partials of the two vowels glided in different paths than when they glided in parallel. However, the facilitating effect of independent motion was not large. Perhaps the auditory system's apparent neglect of this factor is due to the fact that frequency changes can be hard to detect in an environment in which there are reflections and reverberation. Hence they do not provide a robust clue to the structure of mixtures.

2.6   PHYSIOLOGICAL LIMITATIONS

In describing the use of these properties to group the components of the signal—properties such as the frequencies of components, the fit of all components into a harmonic series, their spatial origins, and so on—I have spoken as if there were no limits to the precision with which such properties and relations could be assessed by the auditory system. In actuality, this is not true. For example, assigning a separate estimate of spatial location may be difficult to achieve physiologically when the frequency components are closely packed or overlapped in the spectrum. Accordingly, the estimates would be unreliable. This is a good reason for using many clues to find the contributions of the individual acoustic sources to the incoming sound. Different ones may be reliably assessed under different acoustic circumstances. If they are allowed to compete and collaborate, the final decision should be more robust.

2.7   CONCLUSIONS

The principles of auditory scene analysis described in the foregoing paragraphs seem to resemble the principles of grouping described by the Gestalt psychologists. For example, these theorists described perceptual grouping in vision that was controlled by similarity in colour or proximity in space. Correspondingly, auditory grouping is promoted by similarity in timbre or in pitch, or by proximity in space. They also mentioned 'good continuation'. An example in vision is that when a contour is smooth, its parts are likely to be grouped and treated as the edge of a single object, whereas when a contour changes in a discontinuous way, its parts are less likely to be grouped. A corresponding example in audition is that if changes in the pitch of a voice are too sudden, as in the synthetic speech of Darwin and Bethell-Fox (1977) that I described earlier, the parts are not assigned to the same voice. There are some principles of grouping that seem to apply to only one sense or the other. For example bilateral symmetry in vision tends to group contours, but it would be stretching an analogy to apply this to audition. Conversely, harmonic relations unite auditory components, but there is no analogy in vision. However, it is reasonable to conclude that the principles of grouping that were discovered and named by the Gestalt psychologists exist in order to perform the role of scene analysis. They serve, on the whole, to group sensory evidence that has been derived from the same (or closely related) environmental objects and events. Whatever correspondences exist between the principles that affect vision and audition do so because similar problems in the grouping of evidence are found in the two sense modalities. I have discussed the issue at length elsewhere (Bregman 1990).

The rules that group sounds by their sequential similarities may not always correctly bind together those that have come from the same environmental source, but they are likely to do so. When there are many rules, each with a good chance of grouping the right parts, a correct solution is likely to emerge if they are all permitted to 'vote' for the groupings that they favour, and the grouping with the highest number of votes is selected. A correct solution is probable as long as the system is operating in the rich natural environment in which it evolved. When it is placed in a soundproof room and presented with sounds in which many of the natural properties of the sound are missing, it is likely to produce strange illusions, such as the phenomena of auditory streaming and homophonic continuity that were discussed earlier, or the musical illusions described by Deutsch (e.g. 1975). These percepts represent the best the system can do when its strategies are evoked by unnatural data. Fortunately, these illusions display the nature of the rules to the experimental psychologist.

When I call the processes 'strategies' and describe them as solving problems, voting, and so on, I do not mean to imply that the components of the system know that they are doing these things. The metaphorical language that I have selected emphasizes the *contribution* that the various processes play in the adaptation of humans to their environments. Rather than linking the processes downward to a causal, physiological account of how they work, it links them upward, describing their functional role in the larger process of perceiving. Obviously both sorts of explanation, physiological and functional, are necessary for a full understanding.

I believe that there are a large number of strategies for grouping and interpreting the sensory data. The necessity for a large number comes from the fact that each one is subject to error. The one that tries to group sounds by their spatial origins may not be effective in reverberant environments. The one that groups partials only when they are harmonically related will fail when the event gives rise to inharmonic partials or to noisy sound that has no definite partials. The ones that look for sequential resemblances will sometimes be fooled by acoustic events that give rise to discontinuities in the sound. Because the clues are redundant, all being the result of the same real-world events, the use of a number of relations will usually act as a protection against a failure of some of them. In the worst cases, listeners may simply not be able to penetrate the mixture of sounds. It is a testament to the power of the scene-analysis process that such total failures are quite rare.

REFERENCES

Bregman, A. S. (1978). Auditory streaming is cumulative. *Journal of Experimental Psychology: Human Perception and Performance*, **4**, 380–7.

Bregman, A. S. (1990). *Auditory scene analysis: the perceptual organization of sound*. MIT, Cambridge, MA.

Bregman, A. S. (1991). Using quick glimpses to decompose mixtures. In *Music, language, speech, and brain* (ed. J. Sundberg, L. Nord, and R. Carlson), pp. 284–93. MacMillan, London.

Bregman, A. S. and Campbell, J. (1971). Primary auditory stream segregation and perception of order in rapid sequences of tones. *Journal of Experimental Psychology*, **89**, 244–9.

Bregman, A. S. and Pinker, S. (1978). Auditory streaming and the building of timbre. *Canadian Journal of Psychology*, **32**, 19–31.

Bregman, A. S., Abramson, J., Doehring, P., and Darwin, C. J. (1985). Spectral integration based on common amplitude modulation. *Perception and Psychophysics*, **37**, 483–93.

Bregman, A. S., Liao, C., and Levitan, R. (1990a). Auditory grouping based on fundamental frequency and formant peak frequency. *Canadian Journal of Psychology*, **44**, 400–13.

Bregman, A. S., Levitan, R., and Liao, C. (1990b). Fusion of auditory components: effects of the frequency of amplitude modulation. *Perception and Psychophysics*, **47**, 68–73.

Brokx, J. P. L. and Noteboom, S. G. (1982). Intonation and the perceptual separation of simultaneous voices. *Journal of Phonetics*, **10**, 23–36.

Ciocca, V. and Bregman, A. S. (1989). Effects of auditory streaming on duplex perception. *Perception and Psychophysics*, **46**, 39–48.

Cutting, J. E. (1976). Auditory and linguistic processes in speech perception: Inferences from six fusions in dichotic listening. *Psychological Review*, **83**, 114–40.

Dannenbring, G. L. and Bregman, A. S. (1976). Stream segregation and the illusion of overlap. *Journal of Experimental Psychology: Human Perception and Performance*, **2**, 544–55.

Darwin, C. J. (1981). Perceptual grouping of speech components differing in fundamental frequency and onset-time. *Quarterly Journal of Experimental Psychology*, **33A**, 185–207.

Darwin, C. J. (1984). Perceiving vowels in the presence of another sound: constraints on formant perception. *Journal of the Acoustical Society of America*, **76**, 1636–47.

Darwin, C. J. and Bethell-Fox, C. E. (1977). Pitch continuity and speech source attribution. *Journal of Experimental Psychology: Human Perception and Performance*, **3**, 665–72.

Darwin, C. J. and Gardner, R. B. (1986). Mistuning a harmonic of a vowel: grouping and phase effects on vowel quality. *Journal of the Acoustical Society of America*, **79**, 838–45.

Deutsch, D. (1975). Musical illusions. *Scientific American*, **233**, 92–104.

Divenyi, P. L. and Oliver, S. K. (1989). Resolution of steady-state sounds in simulated auditory space. *Journal of the Acoustical Society of America*, **85**, 2042–52.

Dowling, W. J. (1973). The perception of interleaved melodies. *Cognitive Psychology*, **5**, 322–7.

Gardner, R. B. and Darwin, C. J. (1986). Grouping of vowel harmonics by frequency modulation: absence of effects on phonemic categorisation. *Perception and Psychophysics*, **40**, 183–7.

Guzman, A. (1969). Decomposition of a visual scene into three-dimensional bodies. In *Automatic interpretation and classification of images* (ed. A. Grasselli), pp. 243–276. Academic, New York.

Hall, J. W., Haggard, M. P., and Fernandes, M. A. (1984). Detection in noise by spectro-temporal pattern analysis. *Journal of the Acoustical Society of America*, **76**, 50–6.

Hartmann, W. M. and Johnson, D. (1991). Stream segregation and peripheral channeling. *Music Perception*, **9**, 155–84.

McAdams, S. (1984). *Spectral fusion, spectral parsing, and the formation of auditory images*. Ph.D. thesis, Stanford University. Stanford, CA.

McAdams, S. (1989). Segregation of concurrent sounds. I: Effects of frequency modulation coherence. *Journal of the Acoustical Society of America*, **86**, 2148–59.

Moore, B. C. J. (1989). *An introduction to the psychology of hearing* (3rd edn). Academic, London.

Moore, B. C. J. (1990). Co-modulation masking release: Spectro-temporal pattern analysis in hearing. *British Journal of Audiology*, **24**, 131–7.

Moore, B. C. J. and Patterson, R. D. (ed.) (1986) *Auditory frequency selectivity*, NATO-ASI Series. Plenum, New York.

Moore, B. C. J., Glasberg, B. R., and Peters, R. W. (1986). Thresholds for hearing mistuned partials as separate tones in harmonic complexes. *Journal of the Acoustical Society of America*, **80**, 479–83.

Scheffers, M. T. M. (1983). *Sifting vowels: auditory pitch analysis and sound segregation*. Ph.D. thesis, Groningen University. Groningen, The Netherlands.

Schubert, E. D. and Schultz, M. C. (1962). Some aspects of binaural signal selection. *Journal of the Acoustical Society of America*, **34**, 844–9.

Shepard, R. N. (1981). Psychophysical complementarity. In *Perceptual organization* (ed. M. Kubovy and J.R. Pomerantz), pp. 279–341. Erlbaum, Hillsdale, NJ.

Singh, P. (1987). Perceptual organization of complex-tone sequences: a tradeoff between pitch and timbre? *Journal of the Acoustical Society of America*, **82**, 886–99.

Smith, J., Hausfeld, S., Power, R. P., and Gorta, A. (1982). Ambiguous musical figures and auditory streaming. *Perception and Psychophysics*, **32**, 454–64.

Steiger, H. and Bregman A. S. (1981). Capturing frequency components of glided tones: frequency separation, orientation and alignment. *Perception and Psychophysics*, **30**, 425–35.

van Noorden, L. P. A. S. (1975). *Temporal coherence in the perception of tone sequences*. Ph.D. thesis, Eindhoven University of Technology. Eindhoven, The Netherlands.

van Noorden, L. P. A. S. (1982). Two channel pitch perception. In *Music, mind and brain: the neuropsychology of music* (ed. M. Clynes), pp. 251–70. Plenum, New York.

Warren, R. M. (1982). *Auditory perception: a new synthesis*. Pergamon, New York.

Warren, R. M. (1984). Perceptual restoration of obliterated sounds. *Psychological Bulletin*, **96**, 371–83.

Warren, R. M., Obusek, C. J., and Ackroff, J. M. (1972). Auditory induction: perceptual synthesis of absent sounds. *Science*, **176**, 1149–51.

3

Perception of acoustic sequences: global integration versus temporal resolution

Richard M. Warren

3.0 INTRODUCTION

Perception of acoustic sequences has long been a topic of major interest in psychoacoustics, due no doubt to the fact that speech and music consist of a succession of particular sounds occurring in specific orders. While the number of sounds employed in speech and the number employed in music are limited, their arrangements into extended sequential patterns are limitless. It seems quite reasonable to assume that comprehension of speech and appreciation of music could not be accomplished without the ability to identify component sounds and their order at some level of analysis. Thus, Hirsh (1959) related his measurements of thresholds for identification of order for pairs of items (consisting of sounds such as hisses, tones, and clicks) to the requirements for temporal resolution in speech perception. To illustrate these requirements, he cited the need for listeners to identify the order of /s/ and /t/ in order to discriminate between the words 'mist' and 'mitts'. More recently, Miller and Dexter (1988) stated: 'A major goal of research on speech perception is to explain how a listener derives the phonetic structure of an utterance during the course of language processing'. Similar statements have been made for music, with Winckel (1967) stating that when notes in music were played too rapidly, a perceptual metathesis (or permutation) of the order of the notes occurs, so that melody recognition becomes impossible.

However, there is a mounting body of evidence indicating that the comprehension of speech and the appreciation of music does not require their resolution into an ordered sequence of components, but rather involves global or holistic organization. It appears that this ability to perceive complex acoustic patterns globally occurs not only with verbal and musical sequences, but with sequences of arbitrarily selected brief

Thinking in sound: the cognitive psychology of human audition, ed. S. McAdams and E. Bigand. Oxford University Press, 1993, pp. 37–68.

sounds as well, and is a skill we share with other species. As will be discussed, mechanisms based upon the global integration of items in sequences of brief sounds can provide explanations for a number of otherwise puzzling perceptual phenomena.

3.1   BASIC CONCEPTS

3.1.1   Identification of order

The recent literature on the ability to identify the order of sounds can be considered to start with the study of Hirsh (1959). His procedure involved a pair of qualitatively different sounds with asynchronous onsets, and the listener was required to identify which of the two possible orders was heard. The threshold was considered to be the separation required for 75 per cent correct responses. Hirsh reported that the threshold for identification of order, regardless of the items employed, was about 20 ms.

Hirsh and Sherrick (1961) expanded the study of temporal order identification to pairs of sounds delivered to opposite ears, and again the threshold was found to be about 20 ms. They also used pairs of stimuli in other modalities (vision and touch), and in addition had one stimulus delivered via one modality and the other via a second. In all cases, roughly 20 ms was found to be the threshold for identifying order, and it was concluded that this value represents a fundamental limit for order identification.

Other laboratories used pairs of non-speech sounds (Kinney 1961; Fay 1966), and found values close to those reported by Hirsh. These thresholds were well within the values required for identifying the order of phonemes in speech and notes in music. Efron (1963) reported that phonemes in conversational speech were about 80 to 100 ms/phoneme. (Of course, phonemes vary considerably in duration, so that some are briefer and some longer in duration.) Oral reading is faster than conversation (about 70 ms/phoneme), and Joos (1948) stated that comprehension of speech declined if the average phoneme duration fell below 50 ms. Foulke and Sticht (1969) summarized evidence obtained using devices which accelerate or 'compress' speech, and stated that some degree of intelligibility was possible down to 30 ms/phoneme. Thus, the ability to resolve 20 ms items reported by Hirsh seemed quite adequate for the handling of the identification of phonemic order. The rate of occurrence of notes in melodies is much slower than phonemes in speech. Fraisse (1963) reported that the fastest rate normally used for melodic themes was about 150 ms/note, so that the 20 ms limit of resolution could handle the resolution of notes in melodic themes with ease.

However, an experiment by Broadbent and Ladefoged (1959) indicated that the identification of temporal order in the study by Hirsh (1959) was inferred and not perceived directly. They reported that untrained listeners were unable, initially, to discriminate the order of pairs of sounds when the onsets were separated by 150 ms, but with practice, thresholds dropped to 30 ms. The conclusion they reached was that discriminations of practiced listeners were made on the basis of the 'quality' of the pattern, not a difference of the kind usually considered as 'perceived order'. When the task presented to subjects involved discriminating between different orders of two sounds, then accurate performance was observed when durations were as brief as 2 ms (Patterson and Green 1970; Green 1971; Wier and Green 1975). In each of these studies, the thresholds for discriminating between permuted orders was considered as a measure of 'temporal acuity'. However, it should be emphasized that temporal acuity as so defined does not require the ability to identify the order of the component sounds. The importance of distinguishing between the ability to discriminate between orders and the ability to identify orders was emphasized by Efron (1973) in his study of 'micropatterns' consisting of two stimulus elements which were described as having temporal asynchronies well below the threshold for performing temporal order judgments.

Efron found that the two orders of the elements could be discriminated with ease not only when these elements consisted of sounds, but also when they were lights of different colours and vibrations of different frequencies delivered to the fingertips. Unlike Green and his associates, Efron made a sharp distinction between *discriminating* between permuted orders and *identifying* order, stating

It should be stressed that the [subjects] had no knowledge of the temporal order of the elements or that their perceptual experience of each micropattern was correlated with the temporal order of its elements. When they were ultimately informed of the correlation (at the *end* of the series of experiments), the [subjects] could then *infer* the temporal order of the stimulus elements. However, during the course of the experiments, this information was not available to them and their inference could not have been made.

The studies described thus far have employed pairs of sounds to investigate the temporal limits for identification of order and discrimination between orders. However, the sequences forming speech and music consist of many more than two items. Two-item sequences follow special rules, one reason being that the initial and terminal items can be identified with a special ease (Warren 1972).

However, there is a way to study temporal order with extended sequences consisting of a limited number of sounds. The method involves 'recycling' sequences of three or more items by iterating the pattern over and over, without pauses separating successive statements of the acoustic pattern. Identification of initial and terminal sounds in such sequences does not help to establish their order relative to other items. When three sounds are used (A, B, and C), there are two possible arrangements (ABCABCA . . .) and (ACBACBA . . .). Four sounds can be arranged to produce six possible patterns (there are factorial $n-1$ possible arrangements for n items when recycled). The first observations made with recycled sequences indicated that there was a surprising inability to identify the order of components.

When four unrelated sounds (tone, hiss, buzz, and the speech sound 'ee') are presented at matched levels of 80 dB, listeners cannot identify the order of the sounds at item durations of 200 ms. Even when all four components could be heard clearly and individuals could listen to the recycled sequence as long as they wished, groups of 30 college students could not identify the order at levels above chance (Warren 1968; Warren et al. 1969). Listeners reported that the order seemed frustratingly elusive, and were generally quite surprised that items could be heard clearly and yet could not be ordered. A subsequent study found that the threshold was between 450 and 670 ms/item when separate groups of 30 listeners responded by calling out the order. When other groups were instructed to arrange cards bearing the names of the sounds in appropriate order, thresholds dropped to between 200 and 300 ms/item (Warren and Obusek 1972). The card ordering permitted listeners to handle the problem in parts: they could start with whichever sound they chose and then determine which sound preceded or followed it, continuing the process until the entire sequence was described. With three-item sequences, the task involved only a single judgment of order: listeners could choose any one of the three sounds and determine which of the sounds came next. The problem was then completely solved since the third sound of the recycled sequence was located between the other two. By using a card-ordering response, the threshold for order identification with three unrelated sounds was found to be between 100 and 200 ms/item (Warren and Ackroff 1976).

A number of laboratories have used recycled four-item sequences for studying the lower limits for identification of order of tones and of vowels. Threshold for pure (sinusoidal) tones was reported to be 125 ms/item (Thomas and Fitzgibbons 1971). Threshold for steady-state vowels was 125 ms, with values dropping to 100 ms when brief silent intervals separated successive vowels (Thomas et al. 1970, 1971). It had been reported earlier (Warren and Warren 1970) that silent intervals cause recycled vowel sequences to seem more speech-like by eliminating the abrupt transition from one vowel to the next (which would be impossible for a speaker to produce). Cole and Scott (1973) and Dorman et al. (1975) reported that linking successive items with normal articulatory transitions facilitated identification of order within recycled phonetic sequences.

Why is the threshold for identifying order of items in extended recycled multi-item sequences so high? A possible explanation is that recycling disrupts our ability to perceive order, perhaps by causing repetitions of the same item to form a separate auditory stream of the sort described and elaborated by Bregman and his colleagues (Bregman 1990; see also Ch. 2, this volume). Such streaming would prevent the recognition of cross-stream temporal relations. However, this possibility is weakened by the observation that recycled sequences having different arrangements of the same components can be discriminated even when the item durations are well below the threshold for identifying order. (This ability to recognize and discriminate between different orders of tones, vowels or unrelated sounds having items as brief as 5 or 10 ms will be discussed subsequently.) There is another possibility which was suggested by Teranishi (1977). He measured the thresholds for order identification with recycled sequences consisting either of unrelated sounds or Japanese vowels, and independently arrived at the same explanation suggested by Warren (1974a) that the time required for naming individual items determines the threshold for order identification within extended sequences. When a listener tries to identify the order of items within a sequence, he or she attaches a verbal label to each item. If the naming is not completed by the time the item is terminated, then less time is available for naming the following item of the sequence before its termination, and even less time is available for the next item. Soon the listener is trying to attach a name to one sound while hearing another, and the entire process halts in confusion. There is evidence going back to Helmholtz (1954) that the time required for verbal labelling is about 200 ms/item. Helmholtz was listening to pairs of pure tones mistuned from unison and trying to determine the time required to count a fixed number of beats (the number of beats per second is a measure of the frequency difference). Counting the beats involved attaching a verbal label (in this case, a number) to a sound as it occurred, and Helmholtz found that his limit was about 5 or 6 beats/second. Garner (1951), apparently unaware of this earlier work, published an article which reported the same limit for the counting of identical events (in this case, tone bursts) presented in long sequences.

If we accept the hypothesis that the time required for attaching a verbal label to a sound determines the threshold for order identification in recycling sequences, why is the threshold lower for verbal sequences then for sequences of other sounds? Teranishi (1977) and Warren (1974a) both reasoned that vocal productions are unique in having a name which is the same as the sound. Thus, an echoing response suffices for naming the item, eliminating the time required for the verbal encoding of other sounds, and resulting in the lowest threshold for order identification. Yet phonemes in speech occur at an average rate which is still faster, and it seems that we can perceive these phonemes in their proper order. However, evidence will be presented subsequently indicating that this common-sense observation may be false, and that phonetic identification and ordering is not accomplished directly but is inferred following a prior recognition of holistic patterns corresponding to syllables or words.

3.1.2   Holistic pattern recognition

It is generally accepted that at durations above the threshold for identifying components and their orders, some sequences also form recognizable holistic patterns. The melodic organization of a succession of notes is an example of such holistic pattern recognition. However, the rules for melodic organization are quite complex, and show considerable cultural dependence (see Dowling and Harwood 1986).

Garner and his associates have used extended binary sequences having item durations permitting direct identification of order as relatively simple stimuli for studying the holistic organization of acoustic patterns (Garner and Gottwald 1967, 1968; Royer and Garner 1970; Royer and Robin 1986). These sequences consisted of two easily discriminated sounds (for example, tone A and tone B) arranged in a sequence (such as the nine-item arrangement AABABBABB) which was repeated without pause. 'Unary' sequences were also employed in which one item of a binary sequence was removed and replaced with silence (for a review, see Garner 1974, pp. 49–72). Listeners tended to perceive such patterns as particular groupings with definite starting positions. The rules governing organization and starting positions were quite complex, and Garner concluded that classical rules of Gestalt psychology could not be applied directly. Jones (1976) examined various types of complex sequence at durations above the threshold for order identification, and formulated rules of hierarchical organization based upon attentional factors linked to multidimensional analyses (see also Jones and Yee, Ch. 4 this volume). Experiments by Martin (1972) emphasized the rhythmic structure of complex sequences as organizational bases for pattern recognition (again with item durations permitting direct identification of components and their orders).

The ability of listeners to organize acoustic patterns in a global fashion when component items are above the durational threshold for the direct identification of order seems to have led some investigators to conclude that temporal resolution into an ordered series of elements is a prerequisite for the holistic recognition of patterns and the discrimination between permuted orders of components. As mentioned previously, Winckel (1967) stated that melody recognition becomes impossible when the presentation of items is too rapid for identification of order due to a 'metathesis' causing different arrangements of notes to become perceptually indistinguishable. More recently Jones (1978, p. 282) stated that perception of speech and music required that 'somehow people preserve order amongst successive sounds' at the durations represented by these 'rapid-fire sequences' (see also Boltz *et al.* 1985). Miller and Eimas (1982, p. 111) considered that, 'A critical component of language comprehension . . . is the initial analysis of the waveform which yields a sequence of ordered phonetic segments'. Finally, Miller and Dexter (1988), in the first sentence of their paper, stated that, 'A major goal of research on speech perception is to explain how a listener derives the phonetic structure of an utterance during the course of language processing'.

Relatively few laboratories have studied the identification and discrimination of multi-item sequences at item durations below the threshold for direct identification of order. Watson and his associates have utilized tasks involving the discrimination of changes in single components within complex sequences (see Watson (1987) for a review). In their typical experiments, they used 'word-length' sequences consisting of ten different 40 ms sinusoidal tones presented as unrecycled single statements. The item duration was chosen to correspond to the duration of brief phonemes in rapid speech, and the frequencies of the tones were chosen to cover 'the major portion' of the speech spectrum (Watson 1987). One of the principal goals of these studies was to determine the extent of training required under various experimental conditions to discriminate changes in dimensions such as frequency, intensity, and duration of single target tones within the sequence. The task was quite difficult and could require many hours (or even months) of training to reach asymptotic performance when the task involved recognition of changes in single components under 'high stimulus uncertainty' conditions, such as those in which listeners did not know which pattern to expect nor where within the pattern the target tone might occur. Under these conditions, changes in a tone (which were readily noticed when presented in isolation) were subject to what was called informational masking, and went unnoticed when the tone served as a target and was embedded within a sequence of other tones. Under conditions of 'minimal uncertainty' in which listeners were familiarized with a particular pattern and the temporal position of the target tone within the pattern, the ability to detect changes in the target could approximate that obtained with single isolated tones. It was suggested by Watson and Kelly (1981) that with such minimal uncertainty, listeners first organize the sequences of tones globally, using 'whole-pattern features' such as pitch-contour and rhythm to identify a given pattern, and then use these cues to process the stored details of an individual component.

The experiments in Watson's laboratory were concerned chiefly with the detection of changes in single components. Bashford and Warren

(1988) reasoned that 'whole-pattern features' of the ten-tone sequences could also be used to detect changes in the order of the 40 ms components. When the order of two of the adjacent tones was interchanged to create different arrangements, it was found that listeners allowed to switch between a pair of word-length sequences could accurately discriminate between same and different orders within a few tens of seconds. Bashford and Warren next substituted different 'frozen' noise segments (40 ms segments excised from noise) for each of the ten tones in word-length sequences, and found that when two of the frozen noise segments were interchanged in their positions, listeners could again discriminate accurately between same and different stimulus pairs. Hence, it would appear that the discrimination of sequences through recognition of 'whole-pattern features' does not require that the items of the sequence consist of discrete sounds such as tones.

As discussed earlier, Broadbent and Ladefoged (1959) and Efron (1973) had concluded that identification of order within a sequence consisting of two brief sounds can be accomplished through a whole-pattern or global recognition of the pattern followed by a learned recitation of the order corresponding to that pattern. Such a procedure could not be used with ten-item word-length sequences, since there would be ten factorial (over three million) different arrangements (one-tenth this number if the sequence is recycled). However, it is feasible to examine the process of learning to identify the order of components within sequences of moderate complexity. Warren (1974a) used sequences consisting of pairs of sounds as well as sequences consisting of three items presented in recycled and non-recycled formats. Feedback concerning the accuracy of responses was given, and the time course of learning the correct order of items determined for durations down to 5 ms/item. Neisser and Hirst (1974) and Nickerson and Freeman (1974) also provided feedback to their subjects and determined the accuracy of performance as a function of training.

However, feedback is not required for listeners to learn the correct identification of components and their orders (Warren 1974a). When listeners were presented with different arrangements of the component sounds at various item durations, they could name the order of sounds directly for the longer item durations (100 ms or more), and they could then name the order of components for briefer items through a recognition of qualitative similarities in the global pattern. It was found that by a series of successive generalizations to briefer items, a lower limit or 'threshold' for order identification of 10 ms could be reached for three-item recycled sequences without once ever providing information or feedback concerning the actual order of items.

Thus, there is ample evidence that with sufficient practice and training, listeners can identify order of sequences consisting of up to four sounds down to item durations of 10 ms or less. However, identifying

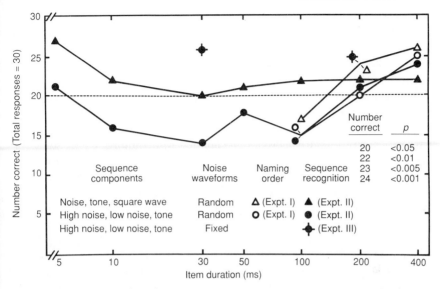

Fig. 3.1 Accuracy of naming the order of components and accuracy of sequence recognition (reporting whether two sequences with the same components had identical or permuted orders) for three-item recycled sequences. On-line generation of random noise bursts was used in experiment I (naming) and experiment II (recognition). 'Frozen' or fixed waveform noise bursts were used for recognition in experiment III. The broken horizontal line corresponds to the limit of performance that is significantly better than chance. (From Fig. 1, Warren and Ackroff (1976) p. 389. © Psychonomic Society, Inc., 1976. Reprinted with permission.)

order on this basis does not furnish information concerning the mechanisms normally employed for sequence recognition since it involves the rote application of an ordered sequence of names to a pattern which is recognized first as a global entity. In order to compare directly listeners' ability to recognize patterns with their ability to identify the order of components directly without the possibility of such rote learning, Warren and Ackroff (1976) used recycled sequences of three sounds (A, B, and C) which were presented either in the order (ABCABCA . . .) or (ACBACBA . . .).

There are two ways to eliminate the possibility that experience with naming order at longer item durations could influence judgements at shorter durations: listeners could be presented with sequences in order of increasing item durations, or separate groups of listeners could be used for each item duration. Warren and Ackroff chose the latter procedure.

Separate groups of 30 university students were used for each of the 22 conditions shown in Fig. 3.1 (a total of 660 subjects). The three-item recycled sequences either consisted of a 2000 Hz sinusoidal tone, a high-frequency noise band ($\frac{1}{3}$-octave band centred on 5000 Hz), and a low-frequency noise band (500–1000 Hz), or a broad-band noise, a 2000 Hz sinusoidal tone, and a 1000 Hz square wave. In experiment 1 (naming of order), each listener in a group heard a single sequence at a single item duration and could listen to the recycled sequence as long as desired. Half the listeners in a group heard one of the two possible arrangements, the other half of the listeners heard the other arrangement. Listeners performed significantly better than chance in arranging cards with the names of the sounds in the order of their occurrence for item durations of 200 and 400 ms, but could not identify the order at levels above chance at 100 ms/item for both types of sequence (noise, tone, square wave, and high noise, low noise, tone). In experiment 2 (distinguishing between permuted arrangements), the same sequences of sounds were used as in the order identification experiment, but in addition to the durations of 100 to 400 ms used in experiment 1, durations ranging down to 5 ms (as shown in Fig. 3.1) were also employed. Listeners were presented with a pair of recycled sequences having either identical or permuted orders, and they were required to tell whether the sequences were the same or different. They could listen as long as they wished, and switch between sequences at will. Fifteen subjects in each group were given 'same' pairs and 15 were given 'different' pairs. Figure 3.1 shows that at 200 and 400 ms item durations, performance was above chance, and the accuracy of the same/different judgements was similar to the accuracy obtained in the naming of order with the same sequences in experiment 1. However, at item durations of 100 ms or less, performance was significantly better than chance at all item durations for the stimuli consisting of two periodic sounds and broad-band noise, but it was no better than chance for sequences consisting of the tone, high-frequency noise band, and low-frequency noise band (except for the 5 ms item duration). At 5 ms, the entire three-item sequence repeated each 15 ms, corresponding to a repetition frequency of 67 Hz (lying in the range that gives rise to a perception of pitch), and it appeared that differences in timbre of the two arrangements could furnish a clue to whether the sequences were identical or different. However, there is still the curious finding that orders could not be distinguished for the sequences containing the tone and two noise bands at durations from 10 ms to 100 ms. This observation suggested that the individual bursts of the same noise band, even though they came from the same generator and passed through the same filter, might have been treated as different sounds. Sequences containing the tone and the two noise bands consisted of a single periodic sound (the sinusoidal tone) surrounded by randomly determined waveforms that were uncorrelated and changed with each presentation. However, the sequences containing both a sinusoidal tone and a square wave have two periodic sounds, each having a fixed repeated waveform. Decisions concerning identity or difference could be based upon the relative positions of these periodic sounds even if the broad-band noise in the sequence did not enter into judgements. This line of reasoning raised the interesting possibility that recognition of the sequences consisting of brief items involved memory based upon the waveform of the pattern rather than the memory of separate components and their orders. This possibility was put to the test in experiment 3 by using 'frozen' noise bursts—that is, recorded segments with fixed waveforms that had been excised from an ongoing noise. It can be seen in Fig. 3.1 that when the frozen high-frequency noise band and frozen low-frequency noise band were used along with the tone, accuracy of same/different judgements improved dramatically. However, when the two frozen noise bands and the tone all had durations of 200 ms, the orders of the high noise, low noise, and tone could be named for the sequences whether or not the noise bands were frozen or were constantly changing, and performance was no better for the frozen noises.

3.1.3 Distinguishing between the two types of sequence perception

The observations described in the previous section suggest that there are two basically different types of sequence perception. The type of greater importance in everyday life has been called 'holistic pattern recognition' by Warren and Ackroff (1976). It involves the global recognition of overall patterns without the need for decomposition into component elements. Such familiar recognizable patterns have been considered as 'temporal compounds' (Warren 1974a) in analogy with chemical compounds. The auditory compounds of psychoacoustics and the molecular compounds of chemistry both consist of elements that are combined to form structures with emergent non-colligative or global properties (that is, characteristics which do not represent the sum of properties of the constituent elements). Isomeric compounds consisting of different arrangements of the same elements have recognizably different characteristics. While it may not be possible for an observer to analyse compounds into constituent elements directly, once the components and their arrangements within a compound have been learned, then a two-stage process is possible. First, the compound is recognized, then a remembered analytical description may be given in terms of component elements and their internal arrangement. Auditory temporal compounds are encountered not only in laboratory experiments, but also when we attend to speech, and it may be that the decomposition into an ordered sequence of phonemes reflects learned descriptive terms.

The second type of sequence perception has been called 'direct identification of components and their orders' by Warren and Ackroff

(1976). Sequences of long-duration items do not form temporal compounds, but, through use of linguistic skills, listeners can name the successive items in proper order as they occur. However, such identification of order is not needed for perception of speech or perception of music. Evidence concerning the characteristics of holistic pattern recognition when used in the perception of speech and music will be presented subsequently.

When item durations within a sequence are changed, listeners employing direct identification of order have no difficulty in distinguishing between the same and permuted arrangements since the orders of the names of components are easily compared despite the durational changes. However, experiments have shown that this is not the case for holistic pattern recognition. It appears that holistic pattern recognition requires that durations of the components of a sequence fall within a restricted range corresponding to a 'temporal template' in order for listeners to perceive whether or not the arrangement of items is the same or different.

An experiment by Warren (1974b) was designed to measure the durational limits of a temporal template by determining the effect of durational mismatch upon accuracy of same/different judgements with recycled sequences. Sequence A and sequence B consisted of the same four items arranged in different orders: sequence A always had the order tone, noise, speech sound 'ee', buzz, with each item lasting 200 ms; sequence B had item durations ranging from 127 to 600 ms as shown in Fig. 3.2 and had either the identical order as sequence A ('same' order pairs) or had the position of the noise and the buzz interchanged ('different' order pairs). Separate groups of 30 university students were used for each of the durations (a total of 240 subjects). Each listener received both a same-order pair and a different-order pair, and they were required to decide whether the order of components in the two sequences was the same or different. Earlier experiments with recycled sequences of the same sounds had found that order could not be identified at the 200 ms item duration used for sequence A when heard alone (Warren and Warren 1970), and that the threshold for identifying order of these items was between about 250 and 560 ms, depending upon response procedure (Warren and Obusek 1972). Figure 3.2 shows that the accuracy of same/different judgements was not improved when item durations in sequence B were increased to values which would permit the direct identification of order, providing further evidence that order identification could not be accomplished for sequence A. Figure 3.2 gives the shape of the temporal template: accuracy of same/different judgements was highest when sequence B had durations of 200 and 215 ms, and fell off more rapidly at shorter than at longer item durations.

Sorkin (1987) reported results consistent with the concept of temporal

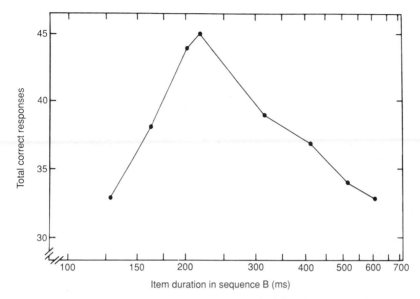

Fig. 3.2   Global pattern recognition with temporal mismatch. Scores for correct same-or-different judgements are shown for pairs of recycled sequences consisting of the same four sounds arranged in either identical or permuted orders. Sequence A of the pair always had component sounds lasting 200 ms, and the duration of items in sequence B is given by the abscissa. The maximum score for correct response is 60. Each data point is based on the responses of separate groups of 30 subjects. (From Fig. 1, Warren (1974*b*) p. 498. © Psychonomic Society, Inc., 1974. Reprinted with permission.)

template matching in sequence recognition. He had listeners attempt to judge if two sequences of tone bursts separated by intertone gaps had the same or different pattern of frequencies. The temporal envelopes of the sequences were varied by changing the inter-burst intervals and durations of the tones. Two conditions were employed. In the uncorrelated condition, temporal envelopes varied within and across trials; in the correlated condition, while the temporal envelopes varied across trials, the pairs of sequences used for judgements of identity or difference within trials always had the same temporal envelope. In keeping with observations for same/different judgements described above for sequences with matched and unmatched tone durations (see Fig 3.2), it was found that the use of correlated temporal patterns within trials greatly enhanced the ability of listeners to determine whether or not the same frequency patterns were presented. The quantitative data obtained by Sorkin was used by him to extend a mathematical model for auditory discrimination originally proposed by Durlach and Braida (1969).

3.2   APPLICATION OF BASIC CONCEPTS

3.2.1   Tone sequences and melodies

Tone sequences are interesting for several reasons. Music, of course, involves a special subclass of tone sequences of considerable interest. But, in addition, tone sequences are valuable research tools for investigating perception of multi-item sequences, since it is possible to control the extent of frequency differences in a continuous manner from near identity (with overlapping loci of stimulation on the basilar membrane), to large differences (involving different loci and different populations of receptors).

Warren and Byrnes (1975) compared holistic pattern recognition with direct identification of components and their orders for four-item recycled tone sequences using listeners (college students) without special training or prior experience with such sequences. Among the variables employed were frequency separation of tones (steps ranging from 0.3 to 9 semitones), frequency range (either within the pitch range of orchestral instruments or extending above the 4500 Hz limit of this range), tone durations (200 ms and 50 ms), as well as the effect of brief silent intervals. The results are summarized in Fig. 3.3. Each data point in the figure represents results from a separate group of subjects so that each of the listeners performed only one task with one set of stimuli. In experiments 1, 2, and 3, item durations were 200 ms. It can be seen that matching (accomplished by choosing which of six different arrangements of the four-item sequences was identical with an unknown sequence) was always superior to the naming of order (accomplished by ordering cards—labelled highest, next highest, next lowest, lowest—in the order of occurrence). Some other results with interesting implications are shown in Fig. 3.3. Accuracy of matching did not decrease with increasing frequency separation as might be anticipated on the basis of experiments with auditory stream segregation of tones (Bregman, Ch. 2 this volume; Bregman and Campbell 1971). However, Barsz (1988) suggested that this lack of evidence of streaming might result from differences in procedure from those normally used to demonstrate this phenomenon with tones.

Figure 3.3 shows that the naming of order was relatively difficult when tones were separated by 0.3 semitones (less than the one semitone corresponding to the smallest pitch interval used in most Western music), yet matching was accurate and comparable to that obtained with larger frequency separations. Matching was always more accurate than naming, even though each had a chance proportion of correct guesses of one in six. Brief silence between tones did not enhance performance in identification of order, although it has been reported that introduction of equivalent silent gaps facilitated order identification with vowel sequences

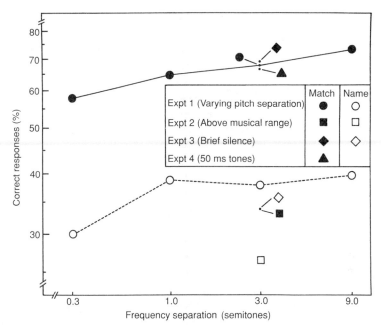

Fig 3.3 Accuracy of matching and of naming permuted orders of recycled sequences consisting of four sinusoidal tones. (From Fig. 1, Warren and Byrnes (1975), p. 276. © Psychonomic Society, Inc., 1975. Reprinted with permission.)

(Thomas *et al.* 1971; Warren and Warren 1970). Strangely, accuracy in matching dropped dramatically for sequences with three semitone separations when the frequencies were raised from those within the musical range (68 per cent correct) to those above the musical range (34 per cent correct). Another unexpected finding not shown in Fig. 3.3 was that while the accuracy of matching monotonically increasing or decreasing pitches ('glissandi') was higher than the accuracy with non-monotonic pitch changes within the musical range (stimulus frequencies from 1000 Hz to 2378 Hz), performance in matching glissandi was no better than with other arrangements of the same tones above the musical range (stimulus frequencies from 4500 Hz to 7569 Hz). (For a discussion of the upper limit of musical pitch, see Semal and Demany (1990).) A duration of 200 ms/ tone is within the range of durations of notes in melodies while 50 ms/ tone is well below this range, yet Fig. 3.3 shows that accuracy in matching was equivalent at both item durations. This equivalency suggests that the lower durational limits employed for notes in melodies of about 150 ms/note (Fraisse 1963) does not result from an inability to recognize different global properties associated with different arrangements at briefer durations, as has been suggested by some theorists (e.g. Winckel 1967). As we shall see, subsequent experiments support this suggestion.

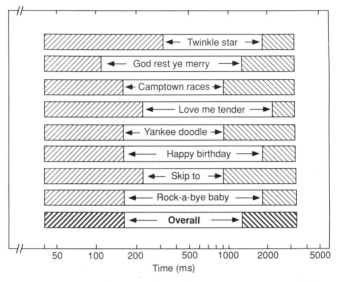

Fig. 3.4 Note durations required for melody recognition. The range of durations investigated ranged from 40 ms to 3.6 s. The arrows indicate the median limits for recognition of the eight melodies by 30 subjects without formal musical training. For durations below the recognition limit, it was possible to hear distinctive patterns for each of the sequences of notes, but the corresponding melodies could not be identified. For durations above the recognition limit, the notes were heard as individual pitches lacking melodic organization. (From Fig. 1, Warren *et al.* (1991), p. 281. © the Regents of the University of California, 1991. Reprinted with permission.)

Sequences of tones forming melodies are perceived as more than a series of pitches, and seem to have an emergent property characteristic of the particular pattern—in other words, they form distinctive auditory gestalten or temporal compounds. If melodies can be considered as temporal compounds, then we would expect to find a 'temporal template' for melody recognition that has both upper and lower durational limits (see Fig. 3.2 and associated discussion). An experiment by Warren *et al.* (1991) was undertaken to determine whether such a temporal template based upon note durations does exist and, if so, the limiting durational values of the template. Eight familiar melodies, each consisting of a seven- to nine-note phrase, were presented to undergraduate students without formal musical training (i.e. they could not name or transcribe notes of melodies). The importance of this restriction will be discussed later.

The melodies employed and the durational limits of their temporal templates are shown in Fig. 3.4. Presentation of the repeated sequences of notes always started with a note in the middle of the melodic phrase. Subjects could listen for as long as they wished before attempting to identify the melody. For determining the upper boundary of the recognition template, note durations started well above the range normally employed for melodies (5.6 s/note), and decreased systematically in duration until either recognition was achieved, or the notes were 320 ms in duration. The importance of starting the repeated melodic phrase in the middle for long-duration notes was determined in earlier preliminary experiments—if presentation started at the beginning of the phrase, identification was often possible after the first two or three notes, with listeners extrapolating from this limited information and identifying the rest of the melody even if it was not played. By starting the melody in the middle of the phrase and recycling without pause, such extrapolation was minimized. However, when listeners who were musically literate (i.e. could read and transcribe music) were presented with the same stimuli consisting of long-duration notes, most of them could recognize the melodies regardless of starting position, apparently through notational coding of the musical intervals. To return to the formal experiment, it can be seen in Fig. 3.4 that the grand median for the upper limit for note durations permitting melody recognition was 1280 ms.

In determining the lower limit for melody recognition, the recycled sequences were first presented at durations much too brief to permit recognition (40 ms/note), and durations were increased systematically until either recognition was accomplished or note durations reached 320 ms/note. It can be seen in Fig. 3.4 that the grand median for the lower limit of melody recognition was 160 ms/note. The range of the melody recognition template determined in this study is not too different from the values of roughly 150 to 900 ms/note cited by Fraisse (1963) as the range of durations normally used for melodies.

It was observed that while melodies could not be identified at rapid rates, the pattern of notes seemed to be distinctive for each of the tunes. It did not appear that there was a temporal smear or metathesis of notes as described by Winckel (1967) for rapid playing, but rather that a recognizable non-melodic pattern was created. The recognizability of sequences of brief items is in keeping with the report cited earlier that the six possible patterns formed by a recycled sequence of four 50 ms sinusoidal tones were each discriminable from the others (see Fig. 3.3). It has also been reported by Bashford and Warren (1988) that listeners presented with recycled sequences of ten 40 ms tones could accurately discriminate minimal changes in temporal order produced by interchanging the position of two contiguous tones. Finally, Warren *et al.* (1991) undertook an experiment involving a wide range of item durations to determine whether any upper and/or lower limit of item durations could be found for discriminating between different orders of tones. The recycled sequences of three sinusoidal tones employed in this study were well within the musical pitch range (988, 1661, and 2791 Hz), and their

Table 3.1 Pitch-based tone pattern judgements. Accuracy of same/different judgements for recycled sequences of three tones differing in pitch (sinusoidal tones of 988, 1661, and 2791 Hz) arranged in identical or permuted orders.

Duration of items (ms)	Percentage correct (out of 108)	Z score[a]
10	77	5.58*
30	89	8.08*
100	86	7.51*
300	95	9.43*
1000	95	9.43*
3000	95	9.43*
5000	96	9.62*

[a] Z score by binomial expansion (see Bruning and Kintz 1968).
* Significant at $p < 0.0001$.

item durations ranged from 10 ms through 5 s as shown in Table 3.1. Listeners (36 undergraduate students selected without regard for musical training) heard pairs of sequences presented in order of increasing item durations, and were required to tell if the sequences were the same or different. It can be seen in Table 3.1 that they could readily recognize sequences as same or different on the basis of their temporal arrangement at all of the durations employed, including those above and below the item durations representing the limits for melody recognition (see Fig. 3.4). These results with brief item durations support the observations described earlier for melodic sequences which suggested that rapid playing produced recognizable temporal compounds, even though melodic organization could not take place.

Warren *et al.* (1991) carried out a final experiment in which each tone of a recycled three-item sequence had the same pitch but a different timbre or tone quality. The tones were a sinusoidal tone of 1000 Hz, a 1000 Hz filtered unipolar pulse train, and a 1000 Hz filtered square wave. The experimental procedure was identical to that employed with the three-item sequences with different pitches described above and in Table 3.1. It might be thought that the three tones with different timbres would not form temporal compounds since they would normally be associated with different sound sources, and hence would form three separate streams each consisting of iterations of the same item (see Bregman 1990, pp. 92–126). However, as shown in Table 3.2, same/different judgements could be accomplished readily by untrained listeners, and their performance was similar to that observed with tones differing in pitch (shown in Table 3.1). At item durations below the threshold for direct identification of order (100 ms and less) it appeared that an ensemble quality or timbre served as the basis for judgements. At item durations above the threshold for direct identification of order (300 ms and greater), listeners could apply identifying verbal labels to each of the three tones in the

Table 3.2   Timbre-based tone pattern judgements. Accuracy of same/different judgements for recycled sequences of three tones differing in timbre, but having the same fundamental frequency and pitch value (1000 Hz sinusoidal tone, filtered unipolar pulse train, and filtered square wave), which were arranged in identical or permuted orders.

Duration of items (ms)	Percentage correct (out of 108)	Z score[a]
10	86	7.51*
30	86	7.51*
100	93	8.85*
300	92	8.66*
1000	95	9.43*
3000	91	8.47*
5000	95	9.43*

[a] See Table 3.1.
* Significant at $p < 0.0001$.

order of occurrence, and to make same/different judgements on this basis.

Perhaps we should not be too surprised at the lack of streaming and the ability to distinguish between permuted arrangements of tones with different timbres at brief item durations. Vowels of the same pitch can be considered as tones which are readily distinguished by their timbre or quality. By moving the articulatory structures in our vocal tract such as our tongue, jaw, and velum, we are able to shape the spectrum of the periodic buzz produced by our vocal chords and produce the resonant spectral bands known as formants which give vowels their individual identities. As we shall see, sequences of brief vowels readily form temporal compounds, even when each is a steady-state sound lacking the formant glides or transitions linking successive sounds in normal speech.

3.2.2   Phonetic sequences and their perceptual organization

Recycled sequences of vowels have been used by a number of investigators as a means of studying the mechanisms employed for perceptual organization of phonemes in speech. The earlier experiments with vowel sequences were concerned with the lower durational limits for the direct identification of components and their orders (Warren 1968; Thomas *et al.* 1970; Warren and Warren 1970; Thomas *et al.* 1971; Cole and Scott 1973; Dorman *et al.* 1975; Cullinan *et al.* 1977). None of these reports described the perception of vowel sequences below the limit for order identification. However, the perception of sequences of brief vowels has some interesting characteristics which appear to provide information concerning the nature of organizational processes employed for speech.

Warren *et al.* (1990) employed recycled sequences of three vowels (the

Table 3.3   Accuracy of same/different judgements for recycled sequences of three vowels arranged in identical or permuted orders.

Duration of items (ms)	Percentage correct (out of 108)	Z score[a]
10	78	5.82*
12[†]	91	8.52*
30	83	6.86*
100	91	8.52*
300	94	9.15*
1000	95	9.35*
3000	98	9.98*
5000	99	10.18*

[a] See Table 3.1.
* Significant at $p < 0.0001$.
[†] Items with locked waveform switching.

vowels present in 'hud', 'had', and 'heed') using a procedure similar to that described earlier for three-item tone sequences. Listeners (undergraduate students) were required to tell whether pairs of recycled sequences of the three vowels (which either had the vowels in identical or in permuted orders) were the same or different. The vowels were prepared from single 10 ms glottal pulses and were repeated to provide steady-state vowels. The durations employed varied from 10 ms to 5 s as shown in Table 3.3. At the briefest item duration (10 ms) listeners heard only a single glottal pulse of each vowel in turn. The switching was not locked to a particular portion of the waveform of each glottal pulse, and hence a slow drifting of the ensemble waveform occurred, which listeners perceived as a slow change in the quality of the recycled sequence. In order to eliminate this drifting, a pair of same/different sequences was synthesized with 'locked' waveforms (12 ms item durations). A brief silent interval separated the single glottal pulses of each vowel, and by switching during the silent interval, an unchanging repetition of the ensemble waveforms was maintained for each arrangement. Table 3.3 shows that the untrained listeners could distinguish between same and different orders with accuracy at all item durations from 10 ms through to 5 s. Preservation of the exact waveforms with continued repetition (12 ms items) resulted in a significant increase in the accuracy of judgements over that obtained with the slowly changing ensemble waveforms of the 10 ms vowels.

Informal questioning of listeners after completion of the formal experiment indicated that their observations concerning the strategies employed for discriminating between different orders of vowels agreed with the observation of the laboratory personnel. There appear to be three discrete durational ranges with clearly different procedures employed for each. At durations above 100 ms, as would be expected from previous experiments with recycled vowel sequences, listeners easily named the vowels in their appropriate orders and used the order of items to distinguish between the two arrangements. At durations below 30 ms, the vowel sequences did not seem to consist of speech sounds, but formed temporal compounds with different ensemble timbres for the different orders of vowels (for example, a listener described one order as 'dull' and the other as 'crisp'). However, the most interesting range extended from 30 through to 100 ms. Within this range, listeners heard syllables and words as their temporal compounds, with different words perceived for the different arrangements of vowels (for example, a listener heard one order as 'kettle' and the other as 'puddle').

These informal observations led to the second experiment reported by Warren *et al.* (1990). Ten steady-state, 40 ms vowels were synthesized (vowels in 'heed', 'hid', 'head', 'had', 'hod', 'hawd', 'hood', 'hud', 'hoot', and 'herd' as pronounced in American English) each vowel being derived from a single glottal pulse. A total of 48 recycled sequences were constructed by sampling the ten vowels randomly without replacement. The duration of the sequences (400 ms) corresponded to that of words in normal conversation. Thirty-two college students were presented with twelve sets of four such word-length sequences (two practice sets and ten formal sets), and they wrote down what the voice seemed to be saying for each sequence in each set. Following this initial presentation, they were then presented with the sequence sets again in a different random order, and were required to match the individual sequences with the appropriate verbal descriptions transcribed earlier. The task proved to be quite easy. These untrained listeners were able to match their verbal organizations correctly for each of the four sequences in a set in 94 per cent of the formal trials ($p < 0.05$ for getting all four correct by chance in a single trial). It appears that the sequences of brief vowels underwent an obligatory transformation into verbal temporal compounds. While each of the 40 ms vowels was readily identifiable when presented alone, when presented in a sequence they lost their separate identity and became transformed into monosyllabic or polysyllabic forms which could be either lexical or non-lexical (i.e. representing a word or not, respectively).

The characteristics of the verbal forms reported for vowel sequences may provide clues concerning the global processing of phonetic sequences. The unit for this organization of these phonetic patterns appears to be the syllable, with the illusory consonants and vowels invariably following the rules of English phonemic clustering within syllables. There is another curious feature of the global organization of the vowel sequences— listeners usually reported hearing two simultaneous verbal forms. For example, a listener in the experiment described above reported hearing a ten-vowel sequence as both 'Frankie' and 'go animal' spoken simultaneously by voices differing in timbre. Subsequent observations with bandpass vowel sequences by Chalikia and Warren (1990) indicated that different spectral regions were involved in the simultaneous voices. Despite the fact that all spectral regions are integrated to form a unified percept with single steady-state vowels, when presented with other vowels the normal perceptual integrity of individual vowels is lost, and both spectral splitting and phonetic transformations occur. It should be noted that it is impossible for listeners who are aware of the nature of the stimulus to decompose the global temporal compound formed by a vowel sequence and recover the actual phonetic components, even if they have training in phonetic analysis and transcription.

How can repeating sequences of steady-state vowels be misperceived as syllables and words? It has been suggested that these illusory perceptual organizations result from the operation of a 'criterion shift rule'. I will first describe this rule, and then will discuss how it applies to the illusory verbal organization of vowel sequences.

The rule is a simple one with broad applicability. It states that the criteria used to evaluate stimuli or events are displaced in the direction of simultaneous or recently experienced values (Warren 1985). Various consequences attributable to this rule have been reported earlier, and aspects of this effect have been rediscovered several times over the past century. Among the many names given to this general phenomenon are: central tendency effect, diabetic effect, attunement, persistence effect, law of contrast, adaptation with negative after-effect, and adaptation level changes. Effects consistent with this rule have been reported in psycholinguistics. Following repetition of a syllable, perceptual boundaries of subsequently heard speech sounds are shifted temporarily towards a closer correspondence to values represented by the repeated stimulus (for a discussion of the criterion shift rule as applied to these 'category boundary shifts', see Warren and Meyers 1987). Warren and Meyers have pointed out that the effects of repetition are even greater when observed while a stimulus is still being repeated.

It appears that during exposure to a repeated vowel sequence, a linguistic template employed for syllabic or lexical recognition can change sufficiently for the sequence to be accepted as an exemplar of a particular utterance. This match can be facilitated not only by a criterion shift, but also by a spectral split. Rather than matching the entire acoustic pattern to the template, matching can be based upon a limited spectral region. The remaining spectral components of the stimulus are either perceived as an extraneous non-linguistic noise, or matched to a second linguistic template, as reported by Chalikia and Warren (1990). Riener and Warren (1990) have observed that continued listening to repeated vowel sequences can lead to perceptual reorganization related to the verbal transformations heard with repeated syllabic stimuli (for a discussion of verbal transformations, see Warren 1982, pp. 181–5).

We have seen that the actual acoustic–phonetic components of vowel sequences cannot be identified, even with durations of individual vowels as long as 100 ms. Yet each of these vowels is a pristine steady-state exemplar which can be identified with ease when presented in isolation. The illusory phonemes corresponding to the illusory words heard with vowel sequences are apparently derived from an obligatory, prior syllabic organization, since as discussed earlier, they invariably follow the clustering rules of English. Is this dependence of phonetic analysis upon syllabic organization restricted to sequences of vowels, or does it represent a more general principle concerning a global organization of speech sounds?

There are several lines of evidence in the literature indicating that speech is organized initially as syllables, rather than as a succession of phonemes which are subsequently linked to form verbal structures. Savin and Bever (1970) and Warren (1971) independently reported that listeners could identify a target nonsense syllable in a series of such syllables faster than they could identify a target phoneme within that syllable. Warren also used target syllables which were meaningful monosyllabic words within sentences. As would be anticipated, a sentence in which the preceding syntactic and semantic information enhanced the probability of the occurrence of the target word at its particular location had a shorter identification time than a target word in a sentence which lacked this high prior probability of occurrence. But, in addition, the identification times for constituent phonemes were also reduced to an extent corresponding to the reduction in the identification time required for the word with high prior probability. Subsequent studies involving bisyllabic words have produced results indicating that an initial organization takes place on a syllabic level. The time required to identify a word-fragment target was faster when it corresponded to the first syllable of a bisyllabic word than when it did not, when the testing involved words in Romance languages having clear syllabic boundaries. For example, in French, identification time for the target 'pa' was faster in the word 'pa'lace' than in the word 'pal'mier', while changing the target to 'pal' resulted in a shorter identification time for 'pal'mier' than for 'pa'lace'. However, results with English may not always conform to this rule for bisyllabic words, apparently due to an occasional ambiguity in syllabic boundaries, for example, 'ba'lance' versus 'bal'ance' (for a discussion of this literature see Segui *et al.* 1990).

Another relevant observation is the mislocalization of clicks in sentences, first reported by Ladefoged (1959) and Ladefoged and Broadbent (1960), and subsequently replicated by many laboratories. When a click was placed within a phoneme (care being taken to leave most of the phoneme intact), it was found that the location of the click seemed indeterminate, and when required to guess, listeners sometimes mislocalized by a word or two. The inability to localize a click has usually been attributed to attentional factors and their interaction with phrase boundaries and other features of higher level linguistic processing. But another possible explanation is that it is not only clicks that cannot be located within the phonetic sequences forming sentences, but the phonemes themselves cannot be localized directly and are only identified in their proper order after prior organization at the syllabic or lexical level. Strong evidence that phonemes are not identified directly in connected discourse is provided by phonemic restorations. It has been reported that when phonemes in sentences are completely deleted and replaced by a louder extraneous sound, listeners not only cannot localize the extraneous sound within the sentence (as in the experiments dealing with click mislocalization), but in addition they cannot distinguish between the illusory 'restored' phoneme and the speech sounds that are actually present (Warren 1970; Warren and Obusek 1971). Contextually appropriate phonemes are 'restored' even when the missing speech sound was deliberately mispronounced before deletion and replacement by a louder noise so that coarticulation information could not be used as an acoustic cue to the missing segment (Warren and Sherman 1974). Perhaps the inability to distinguish 'restored' phonemes from those actually present reflects the fact that auditory analysis does not reach down to the phonetic level when temporal compounds are formed during speech perception. This explanation is in keeping with the observation that when syllabic organization occurs with vowel sequences, listeners are unable to identify the phonemes actually present. Even though it may seem obvious that we perceive component speech sounds in the words and sentences of normal discourse, perhaps this is an illusion. Perhaps when we identify the phonetic components of speech we are describing by rote a learned analytical description of syllabic and lexical temporal compounds, much as listeners can be taught to name components in their proper order for sequences consisting of unrelated sounds each lasting only 10 ms (Warren 1974*a*).

There is evidence indicating that what may be called the 'phonetic illusion'—that is, the belief that we can detect individual phonemes in normal discourse—is a consequence of experience with our alphabetic writing system. There are several fundamentally different writing systems, and Gleitman and Rozin (1977) described three major types. The earliest type consists of pictures or symbols representing concepts, which are not necessarily related directly to words or sentences, and is represented by palaeolithic cave paintings. The next type employs symbols for words and for morphemes (that is, meaningful linguistic components within words), and this type has been used for several languages including Mayan, Egyptian, and Chinese. Alphabetic writing was apparently invented only once, originally appearing in the Middle East as a system employing only consonants, and then appearing shortly thereafter in Greece in its full representation of vowels and consonants some time during the first millennium BC. Alphabetic writing can be considered to be a temporally ordered symbolic representation of the limited number of articulatory gestures employed in a language. For someone familiar with this system, it is possible to use the alphabetic description to articulate words never heard before (or to recognize a written word which was heard but never seen in writing before). Of course, with writing systems for some languages (such as English), there are traps in spelling for the uninitiated, but it is still possible to make a good guess concerning the pronunciation of an unfamiliar written word.

Several studies have reported that children who are just starting to read find it difficult or impossible to segment words they hear (or speak) into individual speech sounds corresponding to letters in words (Calfee *et al.* 1972; Savin 1972; Gleitman and Rozin 1973; Gibson and Levin 1975). Syllabic units (temporal compounds?) are identified by children at this stage much more readily then phonetic components. Thus, Liberman *et al.* (1974) found that when children between four and six years of age played a 'game' requiring them to produce either one tap for each syllable or one tap for each speech sound, all children could tap out the number of units (which varied from one to three) more accurately when the units were syllables than when the units were phonemes. Before receiving instruction in reading, a group of four-year-olds could not tap to phonemes at all, but performance improved when some reading skills were acquired at age five, and performance was still better for the six-year-olds with additional training in reading. It might be considered that the ability to hear speech as a sequence of separate sounds reflected maturation rather than reading skills. However, a study by Morais *et al.* (1979) avoided this confound with maturation. They tested two groups of adults living in a poor rural region of Portugal. One group was illiterate, and the other group attended classes in reading as adults. Each group was asked to add the sounds 'sh', 'p', or 'm', to one group of utterances of a speaker, or to delete the sound from another group of utterances. The illiterates could not perform the task, while those with reading skills could perform both tasks quite easily.

Thus, it appears that phonetic segmentation, rather than being the basis for linguistic skills, is the consequence of these skills. Further, it appears that an ability to perceive acoustic patterns holistically is employed for the perception of speech, and that we share this mode of perceiving acoustic sequences with other animals.

3.3   CROSS-SPECIES COMPARISONS

There have been a few studies that have looked at the ability of mammals other than humans to distinguish between permuted orders of discrete sounds. It has been reported that these animals can discriminate between different arrangements of the same sounds, but only when the items had brief durations (or the pauses between successive items were not too long). When the time separating items was greater than a few seconds, the discrimination of order became impossible. Let us look more closely at these experiments, and then discuss their implications.

Dewson and Cowey (1969) trained monkeys to discriminate between the four possible two-item patterns that can be generated using a hiss and a tone (tone-tone, tone-hiss, hiss-tone, and hiss-hiss). The task could be accomplished when the individual sounds had durations of less than about 1.5 s. But when the items had durations of 3 s or more, the monkeys could not perform the task. It appeared that they were unable to remember the first item after the second item ended (they could not respond until after the entire sequence was finished). Since monkeys are generally considered to rely primarily on vision rather than hearing, their inability to accomplish the task at long item durations could be the result of a general difficulty in dealing with auditory tasks. However, an experiment with sequence perception in dolphins yielded similar results. Dolphins are generally considered to be highly intelligent and to rely primarily upon hearing rather than vision in their normal activities. They also are easily trained. Thompson (1976) used four sounds which can be designated as A, B, C, and D. They were used to construct sequences of two sounds which were delivered through hydrophones. The dolphin received a reward if it pressed one paddle after hearing the sequences AC or BD, or if it pressed a different paddle following the sequences AD or BC. The sounds had a fixed duration, and a silent interval of variable length was inserted between the first and second sound of the stimulus pair. In order for the dolphin to respond appropriately it was necessary to remember the identity of the first sound until the second sound occurred. Thompson reported that nearly perfect performance was observed when the interval used for separating sounds was less than 2 or 3 s. When the temporal separation was longer, performance fell to chance level. He concluded that the ability to hear the stimulus pair as an overall pattern had an upper limit of a few seconds, and that without the ability to perceive the entire pattern as a gestalt the task could not be accomplished. Cats were used in a study by Colavita *et al.* (1974) that tested their ability to discriminate between sequences consisting of intensity changes in tones (loud-soft-loud vs. soft-loud-soft), with each intensity level lasting 900 ms and with 100 ms separating successive levels. As a result of changes in performance and the ability to relearn the task following brain lesions, these investigators concluded that the original sequence discrimination accomplished by the cats was global, and not based upon discrimination of the actual order of individual items. This conclusion that cats process tone sequences holistically has subsequently received support from electrophysiological evidence.

A series of electrophysiological measurements involving responses of single neurones in the primary (AI) and secondary (AII) auditory cortex of waking cats has provided evidence for the global processing of tone sequences. Weinberger and McKenna (1988) and McKenna *et al.* (1989) used sequences of five iso-intensity tones which either increased or decreased in frequency in a monotonic fashion, or had a non-monotonic frequency pattern. They found that the vast majority of neurones in both auditory fields responded to the tone patterns in a global fashion, so that the responses to individual tone components were changed by the presence and the position of the other tones. Referring to the concept of 'holistic pattern recognition' put forward by Warren (1982), McKenna *et al.* (1989) stated: 'This "wholistic [sic] pattern recognition" may be related to the present results because neurons in AI and AII can encode permutations of tone sequences as discharge patterns which are not simply a concatenation of the responses to the individual tones.' (p. 151).

These tasks involving the ability to discriminate between permuted orders which were presented to monkeys, dolphins, and cats would be quite easy for humans, even if the temporal separation of items were greater than the temporal limits observed with animals. Of course, we can identify individual sounds with verbal labels and remember these labels and their orders for indefinite durations.

3.4 SUMMARY AND CONCLUSIONS

It appears that there are two fundamentally different mechanisms employed by listeners for the recognition of acoustic sequences and for distinguishing between different arrangements of their constituents. The mechanism of greater importance in everyday life (serving as an initial stage in the comprehension of speech as well as the recognition of melodic themes) involves the recognition of patterns formed by component sounds. These patterns, or 'temporal compounds', need not be resolved into an ordered sequence of elements. The other basic method, which has been the subject of many laboratory studies, involves the identification of component sounds in their proper order, and requires the application of linguistic skills in naming the successive items. The threshold for such direct identification of order in extended sequences has as its rate-limiting stage the time required for attaching verbal labels to component sounds. Studies with multi-item sequences reporting identification of order for components with durations less than 100 ms involve a two-stage process: the initial holistic pattern recognition of a familiar temporal compound followed by a previously learned description of component elements in the order of occurrence.

Application of the concept of temporal compound formation to speech perception suggests that the recognition of individual phonemes is not required for speech perception, and provides an explanation for several otherwise puzzling observations involving click mislocalization in sentences, phonemic identification time, phonemic restorations, and the perceptual organization of steady-state vowel sequences. While syllables appear to be the smallest organizational units, speech perception, of course, involves much more than the concatenation of a series of temporal compounds represented by syllables. The mechanisms available for the organization and comprehension of speech are variable and opportunistic, with the nature of perceptual processing observed in laboratory experiments depending upon both the nature of the stimulus (isolated syllables, words, sentences, or connected discourse) and the particular task presented to the subject. It is suggested that the 'global organizations' employed for speech perception can occur at various levels simultaneously on the bases of lexical, prosodic, syntactic, and thematic information. The LAME model (lateral access from multilevel engrams) considers that integration can occur simultaneously within and across different levels of linguistic organization, each level having its own global principles (Warren 1981). However, the simplest or lowest level of verbal organization appears to be the organization of the succession of speech sounds into syllabic groupings.

Experiments with sequences of sounds presented to mammals other than humans have indicated that they also group sounds holistically. It is suggested that our use of speech and our production and enjoyment of music are based upon an elaboration of global organizational skills possessed by our prelinguistic ancestors.

REFERENCES

Barsz, K. (1988). Auditory pattern perception: The effect of tonal frequency range on the perception of temporal order. *Perception and Psychophysics*, **43**, 293–303.

Bashford Jr, J. A. and Warren, R. M. (1988). Discrimination of recycled word-length sequences. *Journal of the Acoustical Society of America*, **84**, S141(A).

Boltz, M., Marshburn, E., Jones, M. R., and Johnson, W. W. (1985). Serial-pattern structure and temporal-order recognition. *Perception and Psychophysics*, **37**, 209–17.

Bregman, A. S. (1990). *Auditory scene analysis: The perceptual organization of sound*. MIT Press, Cambridge, MA.

Bregman, A. S. and Campbell, J. (1971). Primary auditory stream segregation and perception of order in rapid sequences of tones. *Journal of Experimental Psychology*, **89**, 244–9.

Broadbent, D. E. and Ladefoged, P. (1959). Auditory perception of temporal order. *Journal of the Acoustical Society of America*, **31**, 1539–40.

Bruning, J. L. and Kintz, B. L. (1968). *Computational handbook of statistics*. Scott, Foresman, Glenview, IL.

Calfee, R., Chapman, R., and Venezky, R. (1972). How a child needs to think to learn to read. In *Cognition in learning and memory* (ed. L. W. Gregg), pp. 139–82. Wiley, New York.

Chalikia, M. H., and Warren, R. M. (1990). Spectral factors in the organization of vowel sequences into words. *Journal of the Acoustical Society of America*, **88**, S54(A).

Colavita, F. B., Szeligo, F. V., and Zimmer, S. D. (1974). Temporal pattern discrimination in cats with insular-temporal lesions. *Brain Research*, **79**, 153–6.

Cole, R. A. and Scott, B. (1973). Perception of temporal order in speech: the role of vowel transitions. *Canadian Journal of Psychology*, **27**, 441–9.

Cullinan, W. L., Erdos, E., Schaefer, R., and Tekieli, M. E. (1977). Perception of temporal order of vowels and consonant–vowel syllables. *Journal of Speech and Hearing Research*, **20**, 742–51.

Dewson III, J. H. and Cowey, A. (1969). Discrimination of auditory sequences by monkeys. *Nature*, **222**, 695–7.

Dorman, M. F., Cutting, J. E., and Raphael, L. J. (1975). Perception of temporal order in vowel sequences with and without formant transitions. *Journal of Experimental Psychology: Human Perception and Performance*, **104**, 121–9.

Dowling, W. J. and Harwood, D. L. (1986). *Music cognition*. Academic, Orlando, FL.

Durlach, N. I. and Braida, L. D. (1969). Intensity perception. I: Preliminary theory of intensity resolution. *Journal of the Acoustical Society of America*, **46**, 372–83.

Efron, R. (1963). Temporal perception, aphasia, and *déjà vu*. *Brain*, **86**, 403–24.

Efron, R. (1973). Conservation of temporal information by perceptual systems. *Perception and Psychophysics*, **14**, 518–30.

Fay, W. H. (1966). *Temporal sequence in the perception of speech*. Mouton, The Hague.

Foulke, E. and Sticht, T. G. (1969). Review of research on the intelligibility and comprehension of accelerated speech. *Psychological Bulletin*, **72**, 50–62.

Fraisse, P. (1963). *The psychology of time* (trans. J. Leith from French, 1st edn, 1957). Harper and Row, New York.

Garner, W. R. (1951). The accuracy of counting repeated short tones. *Journal of Experimental Psychology*, **41**, 310–16.

Garner, W. R. (1974). *The processing of information and structure*. Erlbaum, Potomac, MD.

Garner, W. R. and Gottwald, R. L. (1967). Some perceptual factors in the learning of sequential patterns of binary events. *Journal of Verbal Learning and Verbal Behavior*, **6**, 582–9.

Garner, W. R. and Gottwald, R. L. (1968). The perception and learning of temporal patterns. *Quarterly Journal of Experimental Psychology*, **20**, 97–109.

Gibson, E. J. and Levin, H. (1975). *The psychology of reading*. MIT Press, Cambridge, MA.

Gleitman, L. R. and Rozin, P. (1973). Teaching reading by use of a syllabary. *Reading Research Quarterly*, **8**, 447–83.

Gleitman, L. R. and Rozin, P. (1977). The structure and acquisition of reading. I: Relations between orthographies and the structure of language. In *Toward a psychology of reading* (ed. A. S. Reber and D. L. Scarborough), pp. 1–53. Erlbaum, Hillsdale, NJ.

Green, D.M. (1971). Temporal auditory acuity. *Psychological Review*, **78**, 540–51.

Helmholtz, H.L.F. (1954). *On the sensations of tone as a physiological basis for the theory of music* (trans. A. J. Ellis from German, 4th edn, 1877). Dover, New York (reprinted from English 2nd edn, 1885).

Hirsh, I. J. (1959). Auditory perception of temporal order. *Journal of the Acoustical Society of America*, **31**, 759–67.

Hirsh, I. J. and Sherrick, C. E. (1961). Perceived order in different sense modalities. *Journal of Experimental Psychology* , **62**, 423–32.

Jones, M. R. (1976). Time, our lost dimension: toward a new theory of perception, attention and memory. *Psychological Review*, **83**, 323–55.

Jones, M. R. (1978). Auditory patterns: studies in the perception of structure. In *Handbook of perception, Vol. 8: perceptual coding* (ed. E. C. Carterette and M. P. Friedman), pp. 255–88. Academic, New York.

Joos, M. (1948). Acoustic phonetics. *Supplement to Language*, **24**, 1–136 (Language Monograph No. 23).

Kinney, J. A. S. (1961). Discrimination of auditory and visual patterns. *American Journal of Psychology*, **74**, 529–41.

Ladefoged, P. (1959). The perception of speech. In *Mechanisation of thought processes*, National Physical Laboratory Symposium, No. 10, Vol. 1, pp. 399–417. Her Majesty's Stationery Office, London.

Ladefoged, P. and Broadbent, D. E. (1960). Perception of sequence in auditory events. *Quarterly Journal of Experimental Psychology*, **12**, 162–70.

Liberman, I. Y., Shankweiler, D., Fischer, F. W., and Carter, B. (1974). Reading and the awareness of linguistic segments. *Journal of Experimental Child Psychology*, **18**, 201–12.

Martin, J. G. (1972). Rhythmic (hierarchical) vs. serial structure in speech and other behavior. *Psychological Review*, **79**, 487–509.

McKenna, T. M., Weinberger, N. M., and Diamond, D. M. (1989). Responses of single auditory cortical neurons to tone sequences. *Brain Research*, **481**, 142–53.

Miller, J. L. and Dexter, E. R. (1988). Effects of speaking rate and lexical status on phonetic perception. *Journal of Experimental Psychology: Human Perception and Performance*, **14**, 369–78.

Miller, J. L. and Eimas, P. D. (1982). Feature detectors and speech perception: a critical evaluation. In *Recognition of pattern and form* (ed. D. G. Albrecht), pp. 111–45. Springer, New York.

Morais, J., Cary, L., Alegria, J., and Bertelson, P. (1979). Does awareness of speech as a sequence of phonemes arise spontaneously? *Cognition*, **7**, 323–31.

Neisser, U. and Hirst, W. (1974). Effect of practice on the identification of auditory sequences. *Perception and Psychophysics*, **15**, 391–8.

Nickerson, R. S. and Freeman, B. (1974). Discrimination of the order of the components of repeated tone sequences: effects of frequency separation and extensive practice. *Perception and Psychophysics*, **16**, 471–7.

Patterson, J. and Green, D. M. (1970). Discrimination of transient signals having identical energy spectra. *Journal of the Acoustical Society of America*, **48**, 894–905.

Riener, K. R. and Warren, R. M. (1990). Verbal organization of vowel sequences: effects of repetition rate and stimulus complexity. *Journal of the Acoustical Society of America*, **88**, S55(A).

Royer, F. L. and Garner, W. R. (1970). Perceptual organization of nine-element auditory temporal patterns. *Perception and Psychophysics*, **7**, 115–20.

Royer, F. L. and Robin, D. A. (1986). On the perceived unitization of repetitive auditory patterns. *Perception and Psychophysics*, **39**, 9–18.

Savin, H. B. (1972). What the child knows about speech when he starts to learn to read. In *Language by ear and by eye* (ed. J. F. Kavanagh and I. G. Mattingly), pp. 319–29. MIT Press, Cambridge, MA.

Savin, H. B. and Bever, T. G. (1970). The nonperceptual reality of the phoneme. *Journal of Verbal Learning and Verbal Behavior*, **9**, 295–302.

Segui, J., Dupoux, E., and Mehler, J. (1990). The role of the syllable in speech segmentation, phoneme identification, and lexical access. In *Cognitive models of speech processing: psycholinguistic and computational perspectives* (ed. G. T. M. Altmann), pp. 263–80. MIT Press, Cambridge, MA.

Semal, C. and Demany, L. (1990). The upper limit of 'musical' pitch. *Music Perception*, **8**, 165–76.

Sorkin, R. D. (1987). Temporal factors in the discrimination of tonal sequences. *Journal of the Acoustical Society of America*, **82**, 1218–26.

Teranishi, R. (1977). Critical rate for identification and information capacity in hearing system. *Journal of the Acoustical Society of Japan*, **33**, 136–43.

Thomas, I. B. and Fitzgibbons, P. J. (1971). Temporal order and perceptual classes. *Journal of the Acoustical Society of America*, **50**, 86–7(A).

Thomas, I. B., Hill, P. B., Carroll, F. S., and Garcia, B. (1970). Temporal order in the perception of vowels. *Journal of the Acoustical Society of America*, **48**, 1010–13.

Thomas, I. B., Cetti, R. P., and Chase, P. W. (1971). Effect of silent intervals on the perception of temporal order for vowels. *Journal of the Acoustical Society of America*, **49**, 84(A).

Thompson, R. K. R. (1976). *Performance of the bottlenose dolphin* (Tursiops truncatus) *on delayed auditory sequences and delayed auditory successive discriminations*. Ph.D. thesis, University of Hawaii.

Warren, R. M. (1968). Relation of verbal transformations to other perceptual phenomena. In Institution of Electrical Engineers, London. Conference Publication No. 42, Supplement No. 1, pp. 1–8.

Warren, R. M. (1970). Perceptual restoration of missing speech sounds. *Science*, **167**, 392–3.

Warren, R. M. (1971). Identification times for phonemic components of graded complexity and for spelling of speech. *Perception and Psychophysics*, **9**, 345–9.

Warren, R. M. (1972). Perception of temporal order: special rules for initial and terminal sounds of sequences. *Journal of the Acoustical Society of America*, **52**, S167(A).

Warren, R. M. (1974*a*). Auditory temporal discrimination by trained listeners. *Cognitive Psychology*, **6**, 237–56.

Warren, R. M. (1974*b*). Auditory pattern discrimination by untrained listeners. *Perception and Psychophysics*, **15**, 495–500.

Warren, R. M. (1981). Mode of representation in production and perception,

Chairman's comments. In *The cognitive representation of speech* (ed. T. Myers, J. Laver, and J. Anderson), pp. 34–7. North-Holland, Amsterdam.

Warren, R. M. (1982). *Auditory perception: a new synthesis*. Pergamon, Elmsford, NY.

Warren, R. M. (1985). Criterion shift rule and perceptual homeostasis. *Psychological Review*, **92**, 574–84.

Warren, R. M. and Ackroff, J. M. (1976). Two types of auditory sequence perception. *Perception and Psychophysics*, **20**, 387–94.

Warren, R. M. and Byrnes, D. L. (1975). Temporal discrimination of recycled tonal sequences: pattern matching and naming of order by untrained listeners. *Perception and Psychophysics*, **18**, 273–80.

Warren, R. M. and Meyers, M. D. (1987). Effects of listening to repeated syllables: category boundary shifts versus verbal transformations. *Journal of Phonetics*, **15**, 169–81.

Warren, R. M. and Obusek, C. J. (1971). Speech perception and phonemic restorations. *Perception and Psychophysics*, **9**, 358–62.

Warren, R. M. and Obusek, C. J. (1972). Identification of temporal order within auditory sequences. *Perception and Psychophysics*, **12**, 86–90.

Warren, R. M. and Sherman, G. L. (1974). Phonemic restorations based on subsequent context. *Perception and Psychophysics*, **16**, 150–6.

Warren, R. M. and Warren, R. P. (1970). Auditory illusions and confusions. *Scientific American*, **223** (December), 30–6.

Warren, R. M., Obusek, C. J., Farmer, R. M., and Warren, R. P. (1969). Auditory sequence: confusion of patterns other than speech or music. *Science*, **164**, 586–7.

Warren, R. M., Bashford Jr, J. A., and Gardner, D. A. (1990). Tweaking the lexicon: organization of vowel sequences into words. *Perception and Psychophysics*, **47**, 423–32.

Warren, R. M., Gardner, D. A., Brubaker, B. S., and Bashford Jr, J. A. (1991). Melodic and nonmelodic sequences of tones: effects of duration on perception. *Music Perception*, **8**, 277–90.

Watson, C. S. (1987). Uncertainty, informational masking, and the capacity of immediate auditory memory. In *Auditory processing of complex sounds* (ed. W. A. Yost and C. S. Watson), pp. 267–77. Erlbaum, Hillsdale, NJ.

Watson, C. S. and Kelley, W. J. (1981). The role of stimulus uncertainty in the discrimination of auditory patterns. In *Auditory and visual pattern recognition* (ed. D. J. Getty and J. H. Howard), pp. 37–59. Erlbaum, Hillsdale, NJ.

Weinberger, N. M. and McKenna, T. M. (1988). Sensitivity of single neurons in auditory cortex to contour: toward a theory of neurophysiology of music perception. *Music Perception*, **5**, 355–90.

Wier, C. C. and Green, D. M. (1975). Temporal acuity as a function of frequency difference. *Journal of the Acoustical Society of America*, **57**, 1512–15.

Winckel, F. (1967). *Music, sound and sensation: a modern exposition*. Dover, New York.

4

Attending to auditory events: the role of temporal organization

Mari Riess Jones and *William Yee*

4.0 INTRODUCTION

Attending is an activity we take for granted. If you don't 'pay attention' to something you cannot expect to perceive, understand, or remember it. Conversely, it is difficult to 'attend to two things at once'. Even psychologists who rarely agree about anything else concur that these are two important aspects of attending, referred to respectively as *selective attending* and *divided attending* (Fig. 4.1). Selective attending requires focusing upon one of several possible stimuli; it can be seen as a limiting case of divided attending where one must 'spread attending' over several concurrent stimuli.

The most famous example of selective attending involves the so-called cocktail party conversation phenomenon where one listens exclusively to one of several speakers (Cherry 1953). It captures a general feature of attending, namely that we often effortlessly 'tune out' distracting sound patterns which arise from various sources (e.g. speakers, instruments, vibrating objects, etc.), and follow the output from just one source. Dividing attention among several different conversations seems more effortful and difficult. Much early research on selective and divided attending confirms these intuitions using tasks that bring different elements of attending into the laboratory.

4.0.1 What is attention?

While attention is something that can be selectively focused or divided, it remains unclear just what attention *is*. Indeed, Johnston and Dark (1986) have observed a 'widespread reluctance to define attention' (p. 43). Some authors, such as Shiffrin (1988), have ventured a general definition:

Attention has been used to refer to all those aspects of human cognition a subject can control . . . , and to all aspects of cognition having to do with limited resources or capacity and methods of dealing with constraints. (p. 739.)

Thinking in sound: the cognitive psychology of human audition, ed. S. McAdams and E. Bigand. Oxford University Press, 1993, pp. 69–112.

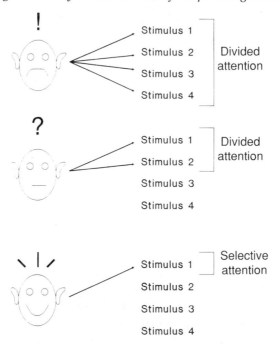

Fig. 4.1   Selective attention as a limiting case of divided attention.

This suggests that attention involves ubiquitous constraints of a specific sort. Others define attention differently. Johnston and Dark emphasize the 'differential processing of simultaneous sources of information' (1986, p. 44) in selective attention, where an information source is either internal (e.g. memories) or external (e.g. environmental objects). Using still other terms, William James (1950) assures us that attention involves the mind's tendency to focus and concentrate. Finally, it seems that not only is there a general reluctance to define attention, but those intrepid psychologists who do offer definitions cannot precisely agree. Their definitions engage different processes and terms (e.g. limited resources, processing, mind).

This state of affairs exists because attention itself is an inferred construct. Any meaningful definition of it quickly becomes 'theory bound', virtually compelling a commitment to 'what' attention is. Ultimately, definitions of attention become theories of attention.

4.0.2   Tasks

Tasks used to study attention are as varied as its definition, and they too shift with theoretical orientation (Kahneman and Treisman 1984).

Early experimentation centred upon limits of attention associated with processing simultaneous information sources. Subjects attended to one or both of two concurrent messages. These two tasks engage selective and divided attending, respectively. Thus, in a dichotic listening task, different auditory messages (prose, digit strings, or letter strings) were presented simultaneously to each ear via headphones. The subject might monitor certain information by overtly responding to all items (shadowing), or to a single embedded item (target detection), or by immediately recalling strings of items (memory probe). When messages were extended for significant time periods, sustained attending was involved.

Over the past decade, new theories have brought other attention tasks. Nowadays, many prominent theories envision attention as spatially oriented, leading to widespread concern with visual search tasks. Sets of visual items called display sets (e.g. letters, digits, etc.) are successively or simultaneously presented in various spatial arrays and viewers must locate a predesignated target amidst distractor items. Other contemporary approaches envision attention as responsive to various temporal and spectral properties of events, leading to interest in auditory patterns. Tasks may require overt monitoring of sequential events or selective responding to predesignated acoustic targets within various temporal arrays.

This chapter considers theory and research on attending to auditory events. It is divided into two main sections. The first section presents a selective overview of theoretical approaches to attention, with special emphasis on those relevant to auditory events. The second section considers current issues in attending to auditory events, including auditory sequences, musical patterns, and speech events.

4.1   CURRENT APPROACHES TO ATTENDING

Contemporary theories offer different conceptions of attention. All aim to explain why people seem constrained in their abilities to respond to the myriad environmental energies bombarding them. Some offer explanations based on a general view of attention while others rest on more delimited definitions (e.g. visual or auditory events). The first part of this section presents a highly selective introduction to certain general theories of attention; the second part considers in detail recent theories that have special applicability to auditory events.

4.1.1   General theories of attention

Many approaches to attention build upon an information processing metaphor. An individual is viewed as a communication system through which information flows. Attention is conventionally conceived either in terms of a bottleneck which occurs at certain *stages* in the flow, or in terms of certain processing limits. This section briefly outlines information-processing models that espouse a stage analysis and others which do not.

Stage models

All stage models assume that incoming stimulus energy is treated to a succession of different operations reflecting increasingly more abstract encoding, namely from shallow (i.e. physically based) codes, to deep (i.e. semantically based) ones. Most distinguish an initial parallel stage, in which all information is assumed to be processed simultaneously, from a second serial stage, in which a subset of information is processed successively. Selective attention is associated with a bottleneck in information flow caused by onset of the serial processing stage.

Filter theories of attending, originated by Broadbent (1958), assumed that the bottleneck arose from a filter which blocked parallel information flow on certain information *channels*. Thus, limits associated with attention were cast in terms of filters that permit more extensive (serial) processing of information in a selected channel (see reviews by Eysenck 1982; Parasuraman and Davies 1984; Hirst 1986).

The *dichotic* listening task was popular with these theories. When people selectively shadowed words or tones presented to one ear (an information channel), they presumably filtered out inputs at the other ear (an unattended channel), either wholly (Broadbent 1958) or partially (Treisman 1969). To divide attention, one had to switch quickly between channels. The 'channel' construct was not well specified; most often it referred to a physical distinction among stimuli (e.g. frequency versus time dimensions or high versus low frequencies). In this sense, it neatly explained the cocktail party phenomenon where, for example, one might attend selectively to a female speaker in the context of lower pitched male voices.

Filter models raised numerous persisting issues, the most prominent of which involved the location of the bottleneck (for reviews see Lambert 1985; Hirst 1986). Some argued for early attentional selectivity, based on physical features (e.g. Broadbent 1958), while others argued for late selectivity (e.g. Deutsch and Deutsch 1963). Early location of the bottleneck implies that people should have no comprehension of semantically meaningful events on a rejected, i.e. unattended, physical channel. While there is some support for this prediction (e.g. Treisman 1969), there is also evidence that people respond to meaningful words (e.g. their names) presented within unattended messages (Moray 1959; Lewis 1970). Further attention is not allocated in an all-or-none fashion with task expectancies affecting 'how much' is remembered from an unattended message (Shinar and Jones 1973). Finally, the issue is more complex than stage models imply; it appears that pinpointing a particular stage where some attentional bottleneck occurs is impossible (Lambert 1985; Hirst 1986; Allport 1989).

Resource theories of attending derive largely from Kahneman (1973) and Norman and Bobrow (1975). Kahneman builds upon Neisser's (1967) stage analysis, distinguishing an initial preattentive stage from a subsequent attentive stage. In the preattentive stage, coherent object percepts are effortlessly formed via Gestalt principles. This reflects a greater concern with relations that determine object perception than is evident in channel theory. In contrast, however, constraints that realize attention belong in the second, resource allocation, stage. Attentive resources (effort) have fixed limits. But because they are preferentially allocated to object percepts, attention can enhance perception.

Other stage models also build upon the distinction between parallel and serial processing. Some refine the idea of resources, assuming multiple task-specific resources (e.g. Wickens 1984), while others see presentation rate as limiting attentional resources (e.g. Massaro 1972).

Of special interest are those which extend Kahneman's position on object-based attending (e.g. Duncan 1979; Treisman and Gelade 1980; Treisman 1982; Duncan and Humphreys 1989). For example, Treisman and Gelade assume that object features (colour, shape) are processed directly and independently (in parallel), regardless of spatial location, in an initial stage. In a second focal attending stage, serial processing integrates (i.e. 'glues together') spatially and temporally coincident features to create object percepts (e.g. green is combined with the shape 'O' by attention when a green circle appears). Again attention and perception are intimately linked: object percepts are literally constructed by attention.

Other contemporary theories

The metaphor of information flow takes on a different character in other theories which, nevertheless, endorse the preattentive and attentive distinction. Preattentive processes are automatic, effortless, unconscious, and operate in parallel, while attentive ones are serially controlled, effortful, and conscious (e.g. Posner and Snyder 1975; Schneider and Shiffrin 1977; Shiffrin and Schneider 1977). However, Shiffrin (1988) maintains that automatic and controlled processes do not mandate a stage theory; they operate concurrently and interact.

The metaphor of an attentional spotlight is evident in still other approaches which are concerned with *visual attention* and the role of spatial location in search tasks (Posner 1980; Posner *et al.* 1980; Broadbent 1982). Attention is voluntarily moved, with either constant (Shulman *et al.* 1979; Tsal 1983) or variable velocity (Remington and Pierce 1984), over static spatial arrays to illuminate and heighten processing of certain visual events within the attention 'beam'. Others eschew this metaphor, relying simply on spatial gradients of attention (e.g. LaBerge and Brown 1989).

Finally, scheme theories derive from Bartlett's theory of reconstructive memory and link attentional control to learning and memory (Bartlett 1932; Neisser 1976). Schemes are simplified, but structured, hypotheses about the environment which Neisser maintains explain differential performance in attention tasks. In challenging stage models, he claims that attention is not *caused* by some special mechanism (e.g. fixed resources, spotlights, filters), but rather is the *effect* of hypothesis testing (cf. Johnston and Dark 1986):

Organisms are active: they do some things and leave others undone. To pick one apple from a tree you need not filter out all the others; you just don't pick them. (Neisser 1976, p. 85.)

Schemes embody learned skills that are sensitive to the relational structure of objects. Thus, attentional control is linked to both memory and selective perception of objects, and its influence on coherent performance will vary depending upon task and function (see also Allport 1989). Support for this view is found in divided attention tasks (e.g. Spelke *et al.* 1976; Hirst *et al.* 1980) and in perceptual learning of complex auditory patterns (Neisser and Hirst 1974; Leek and Watson 1984, 1988).

Summary

Originally stage models emphasized physically defined channels and early selectivity of incoming information via filters. Later stage models distinguished between preattentive and attentive stages in which the second (attentive) stage could involve resources or controlled attending of various sorts. In a second category of models, automatic and controlled (attentional) processes are viewed not in terms of stages but as concomitant processes. Others relate performance in attentional tasks to acquired schemes. A thread running through several contemporary theories connects attending to object perception.

4.1.2   Contemporary approaches to attending to auditory events

Analysis of our auditory environment invites still different perspectives on attention which continue the trend toward a relational, object-based, approach. However, in contrast to models concerned with attention to static spatial arrays (e.g. spotlight models), theories about attending to auditory events address dynamically changing arrays of acoustic information. For instance, a melody is such an array; elementary sounds are experienced not as strings of unrelated events but as integrated dynamic wholes based on connections in pitch and loudness in time. The term 'event' is used here to refer interchangeably to elementary sounds or to whole patterns; an auditory event is any relationally intact acoustic pattern. Event relationships contribute to the perception of acoustic arrays as perceptual objects.

This section describes three different relational approaches to attending. The first is a stage theory; the others are not.

Auditory scene analysis

Bregman (1990 and Ch. 2 this volume) adapts stage theory to explain the way in which listeners segregate (both simultaneously and sequentially) the mixture of acoustic energies that reaches our ears from various environmental sources. Following Kahneman (1973), he assumes that scene analysis involves a preattentive stage, which is characterized by primitive partitioning processes effortlessly driven by innate Gestalt laws. Perceptual objects associated with preattentive groupings feed into a second, attentive stage, which is characterized by the operation of acquired schemes that effortfully and selectively guide attention. Attentional constraints derive partly from Gestalt groupings, but also from the use of acquired schemes themselves which permit selective attending only among items that can be discriminated from one another (Bregman 1990, pp. 406–7).

Consider the fast and slow sequences of alternating low (L) and high (H) frequency tones shown in Fig. 4.2. These are *isochronous* sequences in that the time period, T, between successive tone onsets is fixed. Typically, people are asked to report what they hear via serially recalling successive tones or rating the pattern's coherence. With fast patterns, as frequency distance between the two tones increases, listeners tend to report less overall coherence. In fact, they often report hearing two overlapping *auditory streams*, one based on relations among high tones (H . . H . . H . .), the other based on low tone relations (. . L . . L . .). Bregman assumes that at fast rates (i.e. small T) preattentive processes automatically yield stream segregation: tones within each stream group via Gestalt proximity rules applied to frequency and time. With slow patterns, a melodic trill pattern relating both frequencies (HLH . . .) is reported, especially when H and L tones are close in frequency. This results from controlled attentive processes following learned, domain-specific schemes that operate on preattentive groups (e.g. 'trills' derive from musical training). Effort also constrains listeners' use of schemes; it is

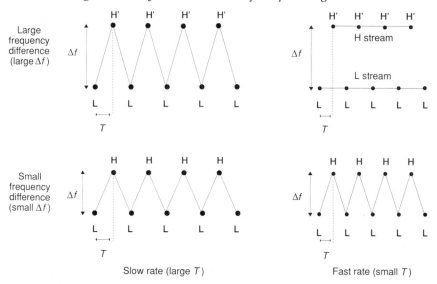

Fig. 4.2   The perception of trills and streams as a function of frequency differ-ences, Δf (small, large) and rate, T (fast, slow), of alternating high (H or H') and low (L) tone sequences. Perceptual relations corresponding to percepts of trills and streams are shown as solid lines connecting tones. Note that stream percepts form only with fast rates (small T) and large frequency differences.

related to discriminability limits among similar frequencies (e.g. only H tones) within the trill (Bregman and Campbell 1971; Bregman 1990).

Streaming is a fascinating phenomenon that has been greatly illumin-ated by Bregman's extensive research. It challenges channel theories of attention because streams are formed on the basis of *joint* frequency and time relationships (see Fig. 4.2), not simply on the basis of a single, chan-nel-based, physical dimension (e.g. frequency or time). In this respect, Idson and Massaro (1976) pushed channel theory to its limits, concluding that it fails to accommodate numerous streaming effects determined by relationships among tones in complex pitch sequences and endorsing Bregman's approach.

Van Noorden's approach

Van Noorden's approach (1975) focused on streaming. Based on an im-pressive series of studies, he proposed that listeners attend to frequency motions, which he defined as frequency change relative to pattern rate. He examined attentional set and time discrimination with auditory event sequences that varied in rate and frequency structure.

Attentional set was manipulated via instructions. He told some subjects

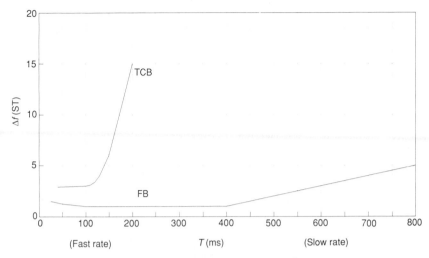

Fig. 4.3 An illustration of van Noorden's temporal coherence (TCB) and fission boundaries (FB) as a function of frequency (Δf in semitones, ST) and time (T) separation between adjacent tones in alternation (e.g. HLH . . .) tone sequences. (From Fig. 2.9, van Noorden (1975) p. 15. © L.P.A.S. van Noorden, 1975. Adapted with permission.)

to follow the trill rhythm of alternating high and low tones (e.g. as in Fig. 4.2) and to 'hold on to this rhythm for as long as possible'. Others, he told to 'focus attention selectively on the string of low tones . . .'. These two sets encourage, respectively, divided attending among two different frequencies, and selective attending to only low tones. However, note that in this context the divided attention set clearly implies more than simply 'spreading' attention over high and low tones. It emphasizes *the role of relational properties* in integrating the two frequencies to form a trill percept. To distinguish this condition from the more conventional divided attention task, we use the term *integrative attending*.

Sequences themselves varied in rate, T, and frequency distance, Δf, between H and L tones. Figure 4.3 indicates points where different listeners (integrative versus selective attending) failed to perform their respective tasks as these two pattern relationships changed. Listeners in the integrative attending condition had trouble hearing a coherent trill as both rate and frequency distance increased. The upper line indicates points where their trill percepts 'broke', yielding stream percepts; this is called the temporal coherence boundary (TCB). By contrast, listeners in the selective attending condition, told to monitor low tones, could perform this task until the two frequencies were very similar, yielding a fission boundary (FB).

Van Noorden's thresholds have been variously interpreted. Van

Noorden himself relates the temporal coherence boundary threshold to the idea that frequency and time coalesce perceptually to form a single higher-order relation, frequency motion based on $\Delta f/T$; the temporal coherence boundary is seen as a limiting frequency motion. Thus, constraints on attending derive from both attentional set and implied frequency motion (rate, frequency change). These ideas differ from those of channel theories where independent capacity limits obtain for the separate dimension of frequency and time. They also differ from Bregman's theory which attributes limits on integrative attending to separate frequency and time proximities. Further, Bregman (1990) connects the flatter fission boundary threshold to limits on schema-driven selective attending, which is inherently different from preattentive (integrative) processes, in that schema limits depend on a listener's frequency discriminabilities (i.e. fission boundary) and are independent of time (T). However, a moment's reflection suggests that attending to a series of low tones may not be inherently different from attending to the low–high series; it is simply based on a slower tone rate (i.e. L to L takes a time of $2T$, while L to H takes T).

Van Noorden's hypothesis joins a small set of attentional theories which address time perception (e.g. Underwood and Swain 1973; Thomas and Weaver 1975; Jones 1976; Massaro and Idson 1978; Jones and Boltz 1989). Because frequency and time are psychologically interlocked, this approach implies that frequency changes affect time judgements. Van Noorden asked listeners to detect small time changes in the base time period, T, of alternating sequences in which rate and frequency distance varied. Using an integrative attentional set, listeners adjusted timing (ΔT) of the lower tone until a just noticeable time difference (jnd) in T appeared (see Fig. 4.4(a)). He discovered that when people could integrate high with low tones to yield a trill percept, they were quite good at the timing adjustment.

Conventionally, time discrimination is indexed by a temporal Weber fraction, $\Delta T/T$, namely the ratio of a temporal jnd to the base period. Small Weber fractions (e.g. 0.05) imply good time discrimination. Figure 4.4(b) shows Weber fractions van Noorden observed with different values of T and Δf. Notice that

1. The Weber fraction changes with pattern rate, T, and this means that time discrimination does not conform to Weber's law. Weber's law (see horizontal broken line, Fig. 4.4(b)) states that $\Delta T/T$ should be constant as T changes.

2. Deviations from Weber's law are related to the 'velocity' ($\Delta f/T$ ratio) of a frequency motion, with good discrimination limited to relatively low $\Delta f/T$ values.

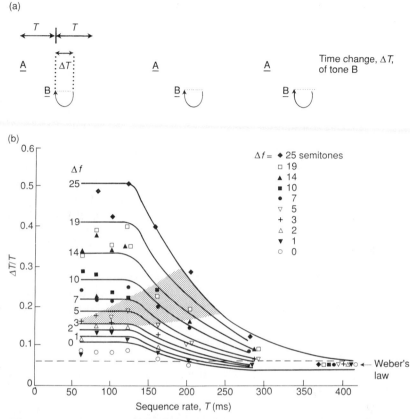

Fig. 4.4 (a) The onset timing of low tones in an alternating tone sequence is adjusted until a time difference, ΔT (a temporal jnd) is perceived. (b) Weber fractions, $\Delta T/T$, observed by van Noorden as a function of rate (T) and frequency distance (Δf in semitones, ST) in time discriminations of (a). The broken line represents a hypothetical Weber's law function for $\Delta T/T = 0.06$. (From Fig. 6.4, van Noorden (1975) p. 50. © L.P.A.S. van Noorden, 1975. Adapted with permission.)

Others, using different tasks, also find that time discrimination defies Weber's law in part because it is influenced by unexpected and/or large changes in frequency (Penner 1976; Divenyi and Danner 1977; Allan 1979; Hirsh *et al.* 1990). One reading of such findings maintains listeners who hear an integrated object percept (e.g. a trill below the temporal coherence boundary) use the time period of that pattern (i.e. T) as a psychological referent when discriminating ΔT. Listeners who cannot integrate frequencies (i.e. hear streams above the temporal coherence boundary) also rely on the time period of the perceived object for their referent but in this case, it is $2T$, the period within an attended-to stream. Thus, a given change (ΔT) must be larger to be noticed.

A dynamic attending approach

Jones offers a third relational approach (Jones 1976, 1981, 1990b; Jones and Boltz 1989). While also object-based, it emphasizes that time relations are part of perceived object structure. The primary attentional vehicle involves internal rhythms whose synchronous operations permit graded, not all-or-none, allocations of attentional energy to parts of the environment, thus subtly tethering a listener to his or her surroundings. Attentional periodicities tend to form simply nested sets where each component frequency has a potential to synchronize, with variable energy (amplitude), with a corresponding environmental time period. Specifically attentional rhythms synchronize with auditory events as a function of two broad categories of temporal relationships within the events themselves: motion-like relations and rhythmic relations.

This is not a stage theory. Motion-like and rhythmic relations appear concurrently within any auditory event and are responded to as such. Constraints associated with attending arise from relational limits on attentional synchrony; these limits differ for motion-like and rhythmic attending activities. Following Johnston and Dark (1986), who distinguish between *cause* and *effect* attention theories, this approach is an effect theory because attentional limits are by-products of other psychological processes.

Motion-like relations involve dimensional changes (e.g. frequency, intensity, etc.) gauged relative to concomitant time changes. Thus, frequency or intensity changes are gauged relative to their time spans leading to a continuous motion-like experience. Frequency motion trajectories, summarized by rates of frequency change, can direct attending along paths of implied motion to certain expected frequencies and times. Using a visual example, attending tends to follow coherent space–time paths such as those traced by the trajectory of a tossed ball rather than incoherent, i.e. irregular paths. Similarly, smooth ups and downs of fundamental frequency in speech or music reflect these motion-like properties (Jones 1976; Jones et al. 1978; Jones and MacCallum 1987; Kronman and Sundberg 1987).

Constraints on motion-like attending take the form of 'frequency velocity' thresholds in integration tasks, an idea akin to van Noorden's temporal coherence boundary threshold, although it was developed independently. Patterns with large frequency velocities (i.e. large $\Delta f / T$ ratios) hamper full attentional synchronicity and so constrain integrative attending. Such constraints are depicted in Fig. 4.5, which relies upon

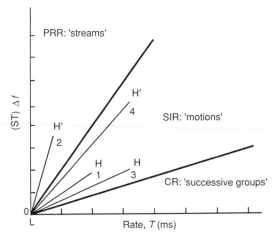

Fig. 4.5 An illustration of 'frequency velocity' thresholds for four alternating (*L, H* and *L, H'*) tone sequences. Sequences which manifest a frequency / time ($\Delta f / T$) ratio that occurs within the serial integration region (SIR) are perceived in an integrated an ordered manner, leading to a 'trill' percept. When 'frequency velocity' becomes extreme, the sequence can segregate into separate auditory streams (PRR). The four alternating tone patterns are defined by the following table:

Tone	Δf	T	$\Delta f / T$
1. L–H	Small	Medium	SIR
2. L–H'	Large	Medium	PRR
3. L–H	Small	Large	SIR
4. L–H'	Large	Large	SIR

a frequency–time coordinate system to show frequency / time ($\Delta f / T$) trajectories associated with four different two-tone sequences (e.g. LHL . . .). Two limiting rates of change outline a central 'serial integration region' (SIR). The serial integration region corresponds to patterns that produce smooth coherent motion-like percepts based on synchronous attending. Upper and lower serial integration region thresholds (bold lines in Fig. 4.5) reflect limits on synchronous attending created respectively by relatively high and low frequency velocities. Regions outside these serial integration region limits suggest different ways of 'breaking' attentional synchrony and hence preventing smooth extrapolations of implied motions. Thus, one trajectory (2) of Fig. 4.5 is so fast that it exceeds the upper threshold and falls in the parallel representation region (PRR); it evokes asynchronous attending plus a potential for perceptual time distortions and stream formation. The chunking region (CR), which obtains with lower frequency velocities, leads to percepts of temporally discrete groups (chunks) of repeated tones (e.g. frequency proximities). Such limits realize relational constraints on attending.

Evidence for motion-like properties comes from tasks where people must relate all tones of a sequence (i.e. integrate) and/or extrapolate their implied relations. In addition to van Noorden's data, other research suggests the importance of rates of change: listeners group together frequency glides having the same slope especially if they share the same central frequency (Steiger and Bregman 1981), and they interpolate or extrapolate frequency patterns along implied motion paths (Howard *et al.* 1984; Ciocca and Bregman 1987; Freyd *et al.* 1990). Not all experiments support a simple trajectory hypothesis (e.g. Steiger and Bregman 1981; Tougas and Bregman 1990). However, some suggest the nature of trajectory limits, which derive from very fast frequency motions (e.g. van Noorden 1975; Jones and MacCallum 1987), or very slow frequency motions (i.e. based on frequency proximities, as shown by Steiger and Bregman 1981; Tougas and Bregman 1990).

Research on time perception is relevant. Because time is conceived as an integral part of the structure of an attended-to pattern, the perceptual 'break-up' of a pattern implied by the threshold of the parallel representation region suggests that temporal judgements should suffer. A number of studies confirm this for discrimination of time intervals, as discussed earlier, and for temporal order judgments (Warren *et al.* 1969; Bregman and Campbell 1971; Jones *et al.* 1978; Warren 1982, and Ch. 3, this volume).

Rhythmical relations refer to other relative time properties of events. The rhythm of a patterned event arises from relations among its various time spans, as these are *marked* by changes in frequency, intensity, timbre, and duration. An event's rhythm and motion-like structure emerge together as shown in Fig. 4.6. Pitch, loudness, and/or duration changes denote breaks in auditory motion and simultaneously mark rhythmic groups. Accordingly, psychological responses to these properties also transpire concurrently. As we have seen, time percepts are affected by motion changes and phenomenal time expansions can produce groupings: listeners perceive accented rhythmic groups or segments within seemingly continuous auditory sequences (e.g. speech, music). These accents signal attending over higher-order time periods (i.e. periods of groups as AAA . . .) by breaking lower-level attentional synchrony. In short, in unfolding events, lower-order motion properties periodically evoke various higher-order attentional periodicities, thereby facilitating a concurrent 'locking in' of nested attentional rhythms.

The facility with which higher-order attending rhythms 'lock in' to a sequence depends upon relationships among its nested time levels. Simple nesting relationships arise when breaks in lower-order trajectories

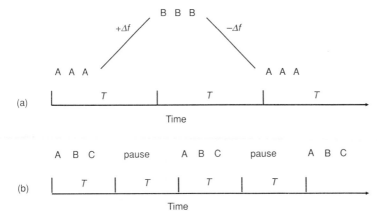

Fig. 4.6 Let A, B, C represent different tones. Changes in frequency (a), loudness, duration (b), etc., produce changes in motion like ($\Delta f/T$) relations. These changes mark tonal subgroups (e.g. AAA) within the sequence.

occur with periodic regularity. In Fig. 4.7 regular and irregular temporal groupings are shown to result from temporal lengthening at, respectively, even and uneven time intervals within the sound series. However, only the former has regularity at higher-order time levels, and hence accents regularity (full lines). Time patterns with such simple nestings of time levels are *hierarchical*. Let T_n denote a time span at level n. A simple time hierarchy emerges when nested time levels yield a constant and integer (harmonic) ratio (T_n/T_{n-1}) of a higher time period (T_n) to a lower one (T_{n-1}). In Fig. 4.7 the hierarchical ratio has a constant value of 3.0 in the regular pattern, but no constant value in the irregular one.

Attentional constraints associated with rhythmic relationships involve time hierarchies. Jones assumes that people abstract hierarchical time ratios, and these function as rhythmic generators which support dynamic attending schemes. These constraints stem directly from Jones' assumption that rhythms naturally organize along lines of harmonic ratios (Jones 1976, 1990*b*; Hahn and Jones 1981; Jones and Boltz 1989). Hierarchical time structure can help or hurt performance depending on the task. Tasks that require attending to all parts of a pattern (integrative attending) will yield best performance (synchronous attending) when these parts are related according to a simple (harmonic) time hierarchy (Jones and Boltz 1989). Conversely, tasks that require focusing upon certain subparts of a pattern (selective attending) will yield best performance when *only* to-be-attended subparts are linked within a common (harmonic) time hierarchy (e.g. via accentuation) and to-be-ignored subparts are distinctly excluded from this relational scheme. In general, dynamic schemes based on simpler time hierarchies are more quickly learned and more likely to

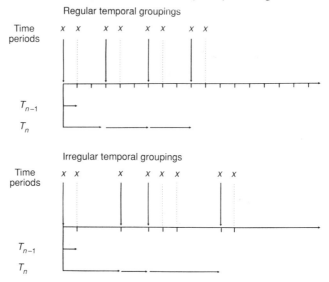

Fig. 4.7   Regular rhythmic groupings of time periods and accents (solid lines) lead to higher-order isochrony; irregular ones do not. Here n denotes level and T_n denotes the time period at level n.

support timed anticipations, i.e. *temporal targeting of attention*, to pattern subparts. Schemes based on more complex timing patterns, as in speech and music, involve non-harmonic ratios and are acquired with experience (Jones 1990*b*).

Summary

Three relationally oriented approaches to attention and perception of auditory events place different emphases on a stage analysis. Bregman's theory distinguishes a preattentive from an attentive stage, maintaining that selective attention is controlled by schemes and is specific to the second stage. Van Noorden and Jones are do not offer stage theories. Van Noorden focuses on frequency motions; Jones focuses on listeners' interactive and synchronous attentional responses to both motion-like and rhythmic properties of events. Relational constraints which define attention differ for these theories.

4.2   CURRENT ISSUES IN ATTENDING TO
AUDITORY EVENTS

Issues surrounding attending to auditory events that emerge from current theories fall into two categories—those concerned with relatively fast events and lower-order motion properties, and those concerned with relatively slow events and determinants of sustained attending. Topics associated with fast and/or brief auditory patterns include streaming, harmonic/spectral grouping, and determinants of perceived temporal order. These matters are considered in the chapters by Bregman and Warren (Chs 2 and 3 respectively, this volume). The present chapter is confined to issues within the second category, namely those involving sustained attending to extended auditory patterns.

Several contemporary theories address issues of sustained attending. They assume that listeners rely upon some abstract structure to control attending to longer and/or slower auditory events (Neisser 1976; Jones and Boltz 1989; Bregman 1990). These abstractions have been termed schemes. Although the term 'scheme' is routinely criticized for its vagueness, in lieu of a better term it is used here to mean abstractions based on either long term (e.g. music or speech), or immediate (e.g. shadowing a novel acoustic event) experience. Bregman maintains that attentional schemes arise from long term experience and are domain specific (speech, music). Jones maintains that all abstracted schemes function as covert dynamic action patterns based partly on timing invariances that derive from either immediate or long term experience. Finally, Neisser's analysis is most general, maintaining that schemes evidence refined attending skills.

The remainder of this chapter considers elements of the scheme notion as these apply to attending to novel auditory events and to music and speech patterns. It considers first 'what' schematic relations listeners might abstract from various auditory sequences. Both immediate memory (reproduction tasks) and integrative attending tasks are used to assess this. Secondly, it considers 'how' scheme information selectively directs attending.

Various attending tasks are relevant. Integrative attending tasks encourage, via instructions and/or response requirements, covert or overt responses to *all* elements of an extended sound pattern. If, as some suggest, attentional constraints are manifest in 'behavioral coherence and univocal perceptual–motor control . . .' (Allport 1989, p. 631), then accuracy and variability of sequential responding can provide a wealth of information about prominent structural determinants of attentional control. The rationale is that differences in performance as a function of manipulations of auditory event structure will reveal elements of coherent schemes which guide attention. One drawback in this reasoning is that variations in overt performance may reflect simple motor constraints, not properties of attentional schemes. Thus, caution is in order.

Selective attending is also manipulated by instructions regarding 'what' target(s) to listen for. These tasks often require single responses to *subparts* of auditory events (e.g. single-item targets). Of interest is the relationship of the whole pattern to the subpart to be detected. The speed and/or accuracy of responding to the predesignated target element(s) provides information about the way listeners guide attending to selected parts of an auditory event.

4.2.1   Attending to auditory events

This section considers sustained attending to auditory events that are not explicitly speech or music patterns. It is divided into two parts which deal respectively with integrative and selective attending.

Integrative attending

In a celebrated paper on the 'problem of serial order', Lashley (1951) maintained that mistakes (order confusions, anticipation errors) people make in generating certain kinds of auditory patterns (e.g. speech, music) reveal their reliance upon general schemes, in particular rhythmic schemes. Nowadays, elementary aspects of such schemes are studied using patterned sequences of unfamiliar sounds in tasks which probe listeners' memory for salient pattern properties or assess synchronous shadowing. It turns out that when required to shadow (tap) these sequences, people can synchronize responses to and continue isochronous or simple time patterns quite well (e.g. Michon 1967; Wing and Kristofferson 1973*a,b*). However, with more complex (i.e. anisochronous) timing patterns, performance declines in interesting ways that reveal something about the schemes people use, at least in synchronous shadowing tasks (judgement tasks are less sensitive; cf. French-St.George and Bregman 1989). Two general proposals for these schemes involve 'clocks' and 'time hierarchies', respectively.

The clock model developed out of Povel's attempts to test hypotheses of Fraisse (1963, 1982, 1984). Fraisse suggested that in anisochronous sequences two different kinds of contrastive and lower-order time intervals (short, long) function psychologically to define temporal groupings. Further, listeners are biased to perceive and reproduce sequences so that long intervals between groups are twice the size of short ones within groups. Povel (1981) asked listeners to covertly or overtly shadow (tap) sequences of 150 ms beeps separated by long and short intervals bearing simple (2:1, 3:1, 4:1) and complex (3:2, 5:2, 4:3) time ratios. They then continued the pattern after the sequence ceased (immediate reproduction). Listeners' timed responses were most accurate for sequences with the 2:1 time ratio that Fraisse specified. More interesting, Povel also found that people can accurately reproduce rhythms involving other simple ratios (3:1, 4:1) when groups based on these were embedded within certain higher-order structures.

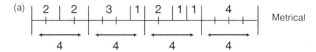

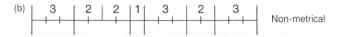

Fig. 4.8 Povel's metrical and non-metrical patterns. The metrical pattern requires the existence of an invariant higher-order time period. The non-metrical pattern does not.

Povel later formulated a beat-based clock model to explain his findings. He tested it in tasks that involved shadowing and immediate memory. The rationale was that during shadowing listeners develop a clock code (scheme) based on a division of the whole sequence into equal higher-order time-spans called *beat periods* plus subdivisions of these spans. This scheme is revealed when a listener immediately reproduces the pattern because certain temporal properties of the sequence will be distorted via filtering through a fixed, higher-order time-span, i.e. the clock beat period. However, distortions should be fewer for *metrical* than for *non-metrical* sequences because the former afford ready divisions into equal time spans whereas the latter do not (see Fig. 4.8). That is, a metrical pattern might have successive time spans of 2–2–3–1–2–1–1–4 (where 1 refers to a time unit), hence yielding a higher-order time span of four time units which would align better with some clock scheme (Essens and Povel 1985; Povel and Essens 1985).

Essens and Povel (1985) tested the clock model by requiring listeners to shadow (tap), then reproduce metrical and non-metrical sequences created from successive 50 ms bursts of square-wave sounds (830 Hz) having pairs of time intervals with time ratios of either 2:1 or 3:1. Figure 4.9 presents one measure of reproduction errors (mean deviations from the norm of long intervals) as a function of metrical (M) and non-metrical (NM) structure. Notice that metrical structure facilitates performance with temporal groupings based on 3:1 time ratios as the clock model predicts.

What schemes, if any, apply to non-metrical sequences? According to Povel, many do not induce clocks. People rely instead on figural or numerical codes. For example, a numerical–verbal code '2–1–2' might represent the number of tones, respectively, in three temporally segregated groups. But exact time separations among elements are absent; in fact only two ordinal time categories are implied (i.e. 'shorter' and 'longer'). Such schemes would explain why shadowing and timed

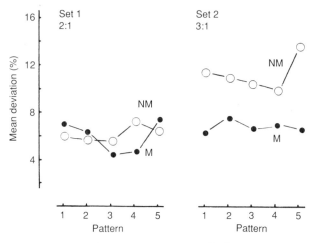

Fig. 4.9   Mean percentage of tapping responses which deviated from presented time intervals within each of five metrical (*M*) and five non-metrical (NM) sequences in conditions where 'between' and 'within group' time periods had ratios of either 2:1 (set 1) or 3:1 (set 2). (From Fig. 4, Essens and Povel (1985) p. 6. © Psychonomic Society, Inc, 1985. Reprinted with permission.)

reproductions are poorer with non-metrical sequences. However, it is not clear that they have sufficient generality to apply to time patterns in speech and music where it is argued that non-metrical structures abound. Further, they do not explain the fact that infants, who cannot verbalize number codes, are sensitive to more than simply ordinal time relations in non-metrical sequences (Demany *et al.* 1977).

Clock models are quite popular. As immediate memory structures, their parsimony makes them prime candidates for attentional schemes. However, they also suffer difficulties. Essens (1986) tested the prediction of simple clock models that higher level time structure consists of a single recurrent beat period. Listeners shadowed and then immediately reproduced various metrical sequences by tapping. The sequences were composed of 50 ms bursts of a 830 Hz square wave. He varied the context in which certain subdivisions of the fixed beat period occurred. This is shown in Fig. 4.10. Note that the two example sequences are identical with the exception of hierarchical ratios (T_n/T_{n-1}) in the first 800 ms beat period. In sequence (a), a non-hierarchical sequence occurs when the first beat period embeds two smaller time periods each having a hierarchical ratio to the beat period of 2.0 (= 800/400). In sequence (b), a hierarchical subdivision occurs where the first beat period is subdivided into three 267 ms periods yielding an an embedding ratio of 3.0. The latter yields a hierarchical pattern because the third (test) period of both sequences

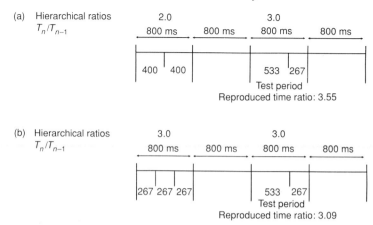

Fig. 4.10 An illustration of non-hierarchical (a) and hierarchical (b) subdivisions. In hierarchical time sequences, all subdivisions of level $n(T_n)$ are based on the same hierarchical time ratio: T_n/T_{n-1} (=3.00). In non-hierarchical sequences this is not the case. Essens (1986) finds that produced time ratios from tapping to the test period are poorer for non-hierarchical sequences. (From Essens (1986). © Psychonomic Society, Inc., 1986. Adapted with permission.)

involves a ratio of 3.0 (i.e. 533 and 267 ms). Timing accuracy was greater for the hierarchical sequence, (b), which possessed a constant embedding ratio. Thus, the nature of specific constraints on embeddings between the clock interval and lower time spans are more important than simple clock schemes imply.

Essen's work fleshes out certain hierarchical properties suggested earlier by Povel (1981). It shows that memory is better when clock subdivisions conform to constant time ratios. Hierarchical time ratios apply to hierarchical levels (T_n, T_{n-1}) and not merely to time-spans within and between groups proposed by Fraisse (see Jones 1990a). More generally, this work suggests that people are more likely to recreate accurately timings of patterns in which multiple time levels are simply (harmonically) related (see Fig. 4.11).

If memory schemes for time patterns tend to rest on hierarchical time ratios, then these ratios may also systematically influence synchronous perceptual–motor shadowing in integrative attention tasks. This was tested by Deutsch (1983), who manipulated ratio complexity in a dichotic listening task. Listeners heard two concurrent isochronous sequences of brief (50 ms) tones, each of different sine-wave frequencies (880, 1100 Hz), presented respectively to left and right ears. Each hand was to shadow (via synchronous tapping) sounds reaching the ipsilateral ear. A constant time ratio related the time periods of the two sequences—it was

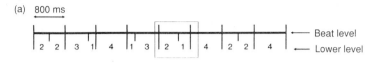

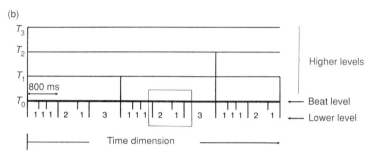

Fig. 4.11 An illustration of a simple clock model (a) and a simple hierarchical model (b). The clock model permits various subdivisions of a single beat level. The time-hierarchy model permits both multiples and subdivisions of a beat level ($n = 0$), but assumes that levels are related by a constant hierarchical ratio, T_n / T_{n-1}.

either an integer (1, 2, 3 . . .) or a fraction ($\frac{3}{2}$, $\frac{5}{2}$, $\frac{4}{3}$ . . .) (see Fig. 4.12 for an example). Synchronous performance, measured in terms of response time variability, was directly related to ratio complexity: larger integers and more complex fractions yielded correspondingly poorer shadowing. Also using two handed tapping, Jagacinski *et al.* (1988) varied the frequency separation of two isochronous sequences, related by a 3:2 ratio (see Fig. 4.12): they found that response synchronicity declines with larger separations. This and related work that controls for motor responding suggests that coherent schemes involve attentional/perceptual constraints as well as motor ones. Further, these schemes seem to be relationally sensitive in that they work best when notes are related by small pitch differences and simpler time ratios (Klapp *et al.* 1985). Finally, given that listeners must respond to both of two co-occurring sequences, these tasks conform to the standard divided attention format. Accordingly, such findings reinforce observations of both Van Noorden (1975) and Hirst (1986) that people can effectively 'divide' their attention among different sequences when these are integrated into a single scheme.

Summary Both clocks and time hierarchies offer structural bases for schemes that guide integrative attending. However, time hierarchies fare better than clock models. Formally, time hierarchies were shown to differ from clocks in two major ways, summarized in Fig. 4.11.

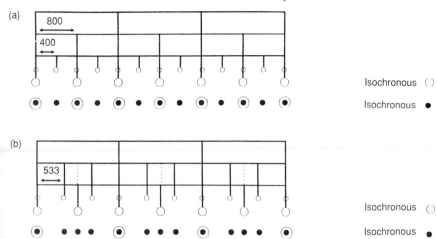

Fig. 4.12 Two concurrent isochronous sequences of different (O versus o) frequencies form simple (a) or complex (b) temporal sequences depending on the value of their hierarchical time ratios (2:1 or 3:2 = 1.5) from their respective periods. The hierarchical ratio, T_n / T_{n-1}, is 800/400 = 2.0 for (a), and 800/533 = 1.5 for (b).

1. Clock models emphasize subdividing a fixed beat period but do not imply that invariant time ratios facilitate subdividing whereas simple hierarchical time models do.

2. Clock models do not posit time levels higher than the beat period level, whereas hierarchical time models do.

In addition to formal differences between clocks and time hierarchies, experiments based on immediate memory and divided attention tasks suggest that

(1) listeners integrate sequences along lines implied by simple time hierarchies and that

(2) sequences that incorporate smaller pitch distances and/or harmonic time ratios yield better synchronous attending.

Scheme theories of sustained attending must therefore accommodate these findings.

Selective attending

Selective attending requires a person to listen for one or several targets embedded within a longer, more complex, auditory event. Targets may involve merely the presence or absence of some sound element in the case of a detection task, or they may involve a change in some aspect of a comparison sequence relative to a standard sequence in a discrimination task. The rationale is that if focused attention occurs, it will enhance detection or discrimination. Most research on this topic concerns 'how' such focusing occurs within extended auditory events, if indeed it does.

A touchstone for assessing performance in detection and discrimination of events (subparts) within larger auditory contexts is performance with these same events presented in isolation. The probe–signal method, introduced by Greenberg and Larkin (1968), is often used to study frequency detection of isolated tones that occur with some uncertainty. People first learn to detect which of two stipulated time intervals contains a tone of some fixed (expected) frequency; next, *probe* tones of different (unexpected) frequencies are sometimes introduced. Detection of unexpected probe frequencies is a function of their frequency distance from the expected frequency (Greenberg and Larkin 1968; Scharf *et al.* 1987). This extends to cases where listeners learn to expect two different frequencies (Macmillan and Schwartz 1975; Johnson and Hafter 1980) although greater signal uncertainty decreases performance levels (e.g. Green 1961). Underlying this procedure is the assumption that probability of occurrence determines an attentional set, or expectancy, for a given frequency. Observed selectivity is then interpreted to derive from the operation of a narrow frequency-specific attention band (e.g. a critical bandwidth roughly corresponding to the response region of an auditory filter), centred on an expected frequency. Thus, both predictability (or, conversely uncertainty) and frequency contribute to attentional focusing (cf. Johnson and Hafter 1980).

Expectancy is often manipulated by varying the probability of item occurrence (e.g. of a tone's frequency). However, a *conceptual* equation of expectancy with simple probability overlooks many factors, including the fact that, in practice, such probabilities are always conditional upon some context and that they tacitly apply to certain temporal regions. Some effects of a patterned context on frequency detection are shown in a study by Howard *et al.* (1984). Using a forced-choice task, they presented listeners with two similar sequences: one with 12 tones where the 11th tone frequency functioned as a probe tone, and another in which the probe location was filled with a temporal gap. Listeners heard the sequences in random order against noise backgrounds and had to indicate which pattern contained the temporal gap. Detection of a specific probe frequency (and hence of the time gap) was influenced by pattern context (ascending versus descending frequencies) and also by the overall probability that a particular frequency occurred in the probe location regardless of its fit into the surrounding pattern context. To the extent that a probe tone frequency 'fit' into an ascending or descending frequency pattern, and/or was likely to occur in a given context, detection of it was better. These findings suggest that pattern structure and conditional probabilities influence pitch (or frequency) expectancies about tones which occur at certain temporal locations.

Watson and his colleagues extensively explored probabilistic influences on frequency discrimination arising from both experimental context and pattern structure (e.g. Watson and Kelly 1981). Listeners were better at discriminating frequency changes of pure tones in isolation than when they were embedded in sequences and presented in experimental contexts that introduced uncertainty by including many different sequences (e.g. Green 1961; Leek and Watson 1984). Consistent with a general scheme interpretation, they showed that perceptual learning improves frequency discrimination and can even overcome uncertainty effects (Spiegel and Watson 1981; Watson *et al.* 1981; Watson 1987; Kidd and Watson 1989).

Relatively little research addresses uncertainties associated with temporal structure in selective attending. Yet, the concept of expectancy implies some reliance on time relations since listeners must focus their attentional energies not only at certain frequencies but also at certain future times. Kidd *et al.* (1984) confirmed that temporal pattern context influences discrimination of certain pitches. They used a standard-and-comparison task in which listeners indicated whether or not a ten-tone comparison sequence was identical to its standard when it contained a small pitch change in one tone half the time. Performance was best when both standard and comparison were isochronous; it declined when one or both were anisochronous and when there was an increase in uncertainties associated with the number and types of rhythms listeners heard in a session (see also Jones *et al.* 1981). Specific temporal patterns also affect attention; standard rhythm patterns can direct listeners' attention towards or away from the temporal location of a target tone in the comparison, leading respectively, to good or poor discrimination of changes in target tone pitch (Jones *et al.* 1982). These findings suggest that both temporal uncertainty and rhythmic structure influence attentional targeting in selective attending tasks.

Finally, listeners' ability to distinguish timing changes also varies with pitch and time context. This was evident in the research of Van Noorden and others mentioned earlier. Discrimination of time intervals within a sequence may be better or worse than among two isolated time intervals (e.g. as in Abel 1972). A study by Halpern and Darwin (1982) shows that in isochronous rhythms time discrimination is fairly good. Listeners judged whether the fourth in a series of three equally spaced clicks was 'early' or 'late' (actual ΔT varied from 10 per cent early to 10 per cent late). The data, shown in Fig. 4.13, reveal small Weber fractions and rough conformance to Weber's law over base time periods from 400 ms

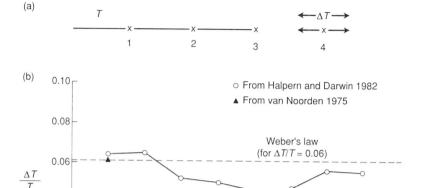

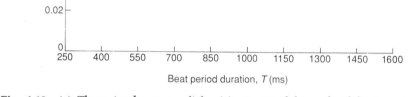

Beat period duration, *T* (ms)

Fig. 4.13 (a) Three isochronous clicks (x) separated by a fixed beat period of length *T* are followed by a fourth click with variable onset times. (b) Weber fractions (Δ*T*/*T*) based on temporal jnds for the fourth click are shown as a function of *T* (also see van Noorden's data in Fig. 4.4).

to 1450 ms (see also Monahan and Hirsh 1990).[1] With less metrical sequences, poorer time discrimination is reported even with significant training (Kidd and Watson 1990).

Summary Findings drawn from detection and discrimination of selected targets suggest some elements that determine how listeners focus selectively within a sequence.

1. Within a specified context, detection of a given tone frequency and of similar frequencies improves as the probability of that frequency increases.

2. Discrimination of frequency changes in a target embedded within larger patterns improves as uncertainties about pattern frequencies decrease.

3. Detection of embedded target frequencies is influenced by pattern structure in the form of frequency configurations.

1. Direct comparisons of thresholds across different studies must be undertaken with caution, because not only do rhythmic context and the range of *T* vary, but so also do intensities, types of tones, and threshold criteria.

4. Discrimination of embedded target frequencies is affected by temporal pattern structure in the form of temporal uncertainties and rhythmic configurations.

5. Discrimination of target durations is affected by pattern structure, in the form of both pitch and metric/rhythmic relationships.

6. Perceptual learning usually improves performance. Such findings suggest that the direction of attending according to schemes is sensitive to context-specific, probabilistic, and structural information.

4.2.2 Attending to musical events

Musical events differ from non-musical ones in many ways, including their artful construction, which combines explicit use of special frequencies and tonal relationships based on changes along a logarithmic frequency continuum (e.g. as in musical scales) with various temporal constraints associated with tempi, meters, and rhythmic patterns. Few disagree that listeners rely on some relationships when they attend to novel music and that both general perceptual learning and specific musical training increase their sensitivity to other relationships. However, a complete understanding of musical schemes requires a theory of learning and is beyond the scope of this chapter (but see Jones 1990b). Instead, research considered here relies upon music composed via a familiar idiom to examine a few fairly general aspects of musical schemes and their function in integrative and selective attending tasks. Some of these properties are familiar ones in that they relate to frequency and time structures; distinctions between metrical and non-metrical rhythms as well as between clocks and time hierarchies again become relevant.

Integrative attending to music

Western music seems to invite us to tap our foot and follow a beat, suggesting an apparent metricality. Indeed, to Western listeners, one general aspect of any tune which seems to 'hold it together' involves its metrical time structure. It is surprising, therefore, that on closer scrutiny even musical time patterns defy straightforward descriptions in terms of metric schemes, whether based on clocks or time hierarchies.

On paper, namely a musical score, there is plenty of evidence for metricality in music. Consider the most obvious example of this: musical meter. In fact, duple and triple metres are easily described in terms of hierarchical time ratios of two and three, respectively (Lerdahl and Jackendoff 1983; Jones 1987; Jones and Boltz 1989). Further, composers reinforce a multi-level time hierarchy implied by a stipulated meter by additionally marking higher metric time levels with more important melodic and harmonic elements (structural accents) in a score (Palmer and Krumhansl 1990). Thus, musical scores imply metrical time hierarchies. A problem comes when a performer translates the score into an acoustic pattern. Here the precise outlines of a metric time hierarchy usually become blurred as a performer modifies various time-spans and shifts accent locations (e.g. Shaffer 1981, 1982; Gabrielsson 1985, 1986; Palmer 1992). If we continue to define a metrical stimulus event as one in which there is a precisely recurrent higher-order time-span (Povel and Essens 1985) or in which simple and invariant hierarchical time ratios obtain (Jones 1976; Jones and Boltz 1989), then truly metrical sound patterns may only exist in synthesized performances, not in human ones!

This presents a puzzle. It is undeniable that musical events seem metrical to listeners in spite of the fact that their manifest structure does not conform to strict definitions of this term. What then governs listeners' sense of metricality? Although technically, observed deviations from metricality imply that musical events are, in a sense, non-metrical patterns, it seems implausible that listeners' perceptions are based on non-metrical schemes suggested by Povel's numeric codes. This puzzle is the challenge that motivates much contemporary research (see Gabrielsson 1986 for a review). One clue to a solution comes from performance studies which explicitly manipulate the attentional set of performers (pianists) by asking them to interpret the same score in different ways when they produce it (Palmer 1992). By carefully analysing all of the produced frequencies and their timings, it is possible to determine that the produced timings, while not strictly metrical, nevertheless contain small meaningful deviations from the stipulated (scored) time hierarchies. This suggests that performers, at some level, continue to rely on time hierarchies. While this topic is hotly debated, one interpretation of such findings is that performers intentionally control their responses to create musical sound patterns which systematically violate listeners' expectations about hierarchical time relations, and thereby communicate one interpretation of the score (Gabrielsson 1986; Jones 1990a; Palmer 1992).

Nevertheless, the fact that musical events do not measurably conform to precise time hierarchies, as defined here, continues to pose an interesting theoretical problem for simple adaptations of attentional schemes based on either clocks or time hierarchies. If, strictly speaking, musical sound patterns are non-metrical, then how can they induce an attentional scheme which involves a clock or a time hierarchy, assuming that a sense of experienced metricality depends on such things? One solution appeals to learning and domain-specific schemes. This assumes that experienced listeners have abstracted certain metrical properties that permit them to generate an implied time hierarchy in certain contexts. Consider a study by Palmer and Krumhansl (1990). They presented listeners with nine isochronous context beats all of the same frequency and intensity in which no higher-order time-spans were explicitly marked (Fig. 4.14(a)).

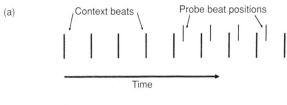

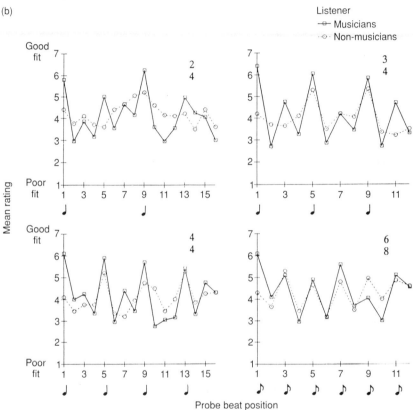

Fig. 4.14 (a) Example of temporal sequences used by Palmer and Krumhansl (1990) as stimulus materials for goodness-of-fit ratings and (b) mean goodness-of-fit ratings for musicians (solid line) and non-musicians (broken line) as a function of attentional set for metre and probe location (1 = poor fit; 7 = good fit to imagined metric context). (From Figs 2A, 3, Palmer and Krumhansl (1990) pp. 733, 734. © American Psychological Association, Inc., 1990. Adapted with permission.)

Somewhere amidst the last five beats a higher pitched probe beat could occur. Attentional set was manipulated by instructing listeners to 'hear' context beats according to one of four different metrical schemes (e.g. in groups of two, three, four, or six beats), and to rate how well probes fit into each scheme. Ratings differed as a function of both attentional set and experience (musicians, non-musicians) as shown in Fig. 4.14(b). When listeners were set to hear duple metre (two or four beats), a probe occurring near the onset of these imagined metric groups received high ratings while a probe near onsets of groups of three or six beats (triple metre) did not. The reverse was true for listeners set to hear triple metre (groups of three or six beats). These findings indicate that ready integration of a given probe depends its location and imagined metric scheme (i.e. attentional set). Differences as a function of set were more pronounced for musicians, supporting the role of experience. Thus so long as no directly conflicting evidence exists in a sound pattern, it appears that listeners can generate metric schemes that determine perceived groupings and that trained listeners are more effective in doing this. These findings also imply that such attentional schemes are based on time hierarchies.

Complementing these findings is direct evidence that musically experienced listeners can even generate missing parts of time hierarchies. Jones and Boltz (1989) presented listeners with several measures of incomplete folk tunes. In some tunes, musical accents outlined simple binary time hierarchies (i.e. time ratios of two), while in others these accents outlined violated time hierarchies. Listeners had to complete the final time-span of each tune by pressing a button at the correct ending time. They performed this very accurately with hierarchical tunes. However, they were also sensitive to systematic violations of time hierarchies, producing lawful over- and under-estimations of time-spans with these tunes. Jones and Boltz proposed (1989) that experienced listeners base expectancies on time hierarchies, but that systematic violations of these hierarchies, conferred by non-metrical aspects of a pattern, also play a role.

Many other aspects of musical structure (e.g. tonality, pitch contour, melodic and rhythmic structure, etc.) undoubtedly determine both scheme acquisition and application (e.g. Lerdahl and Jackendoff 1983; Sloboda 1985; Dowling and Harwood 1986; Krumhansl 1990). However, this area of research is relatively new, and these aspects remain to be explored. As such, it offers opportunities to study the way attending and attentional schemes change as listeners become more familiar with various musical events.

Summary Musical patterns are putatively among nature's most metrical events. Yet as sound patterns, their metricality is often blurred by a performer. Nevertheless, listeners can generate and apply metrical relationships to relate groups of tones, and can temporally complete folk tunes based on simple time hierarchies while responding lawfully to those with systematic violations of simple time hierarchies. Finally, however, the formal role of metricality (clocks, time hierarchies) in musical schemes is a much debated one.

Selective attending to music

Selective attending to music is intuitively comprehensible. We seem to be able to attend to different aspects of musical structure (e.g. phrasings versus timbre), or follow one of several melodic lines within a larger music tapestry, or even await with anticipation a single tone or turn of phrase. All are characteristic of selective attending.

Boltz (1991) manipulated attentional set by instructing people to listen for targets within one or another of two temporally distinct levels within a single, unfamiliar melody. Some listeners had to selectively attend only to the tune's higher-order tonal phrase structure while others monitored only its lower-order changes in pitch contour. Using judged duration as a dependent measure, Boltz found that the two groups differed significantly in their duration estimates of the same melody. Others, using tune identification as a dependent measure, studied selective attending to one of two familiar, temporally interleaved, melodies. Here it is possible that acquired schemes, based on knowledge of one or both tunes, facilitated performance (e.g. Dowling 1990). However, Dowling (1973) showed that tune frequencies also matter. He alternated tones from two folk tunes so that together they formed a more complicated and rapid sequence. When the frequency ranges of the two tunes overlapped, listeners could not name the target melody. However, as their frequency ranges were separated, selective tracking of a target melody became effortless and theme identifications improved. These findings are consistent with Bregman's hypothesis that acquired schemes selectively guide attending but are limited by frequency discriminability.

However, use of schemes in selective attending may involve more than reliance on frequency differences between target and distractor tunes. According to Jones (1976, 1990b), attending must also be appropriately timed with respect to target tones. Metric regularity of target tones would permit application of simple schemes to guide attending to the right neighbourhood in time as well as in pitch (frequency). Dowling *et al.* (1987) pursued this by asking listeners to identify a familiar 'hidden target melody' (e.g. *Frère Jacques*) in interleaved contexts where target tones occurred either 'on' or 'off' an implied beat (see Fig. 4.15). As a dynamic interpretation of schemes suggests, listeners were better when notes of the target melody occurred at metrically expected times. This was true even when the frequency ranges of target and distractor melodies

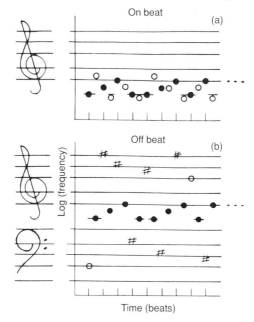

Fig. 4.15 An illustration of two different conditions: (a) target notes (filled symbols) on the beat, with distractor tones (open symbols) interleaved in the same pitch range as the target; and (b) target notes off the beat, with distractor tones (open symbols and # symbols) in separate pitch ranges. Implicit beats are indicated on the abscissa. (Targets were actually 16 beats long, with sustained notes in the familiar versions broken into separate notes on successive beats.) (From Fig. 2, Dowling *et al.* (1987) p. 646. © Psychonomic Society, Inc., 1987. Reprinted with permission.)

overlapped, indicating that 'well-timed' attending may overcome frequency discriminability limits which Bregman (1990) suggests constrain the use of schemes in selective attending.

Explicit manipulation of relative timing of two interleaved tone sequences also confirms the role of time ratios in sustained selective attending. When two isochronous sequences are interleaved to create polyrhythms based on complex time ratios among their respective time periods (e.g. 2:3, 3:4; see Fig. 4.12(b)), listeners rarely tap to *all* the tones when asked to tap the beat. Instead, they selectively follow only one line, and their choice is relationally determined by tempo, differences in tone frequency, and the time ratio involved (Handel 1989, pp. 404–6).

Thus far this research speaks to attending with interleaved melodies. Less is known about selective attending to single targets embedded within musical contexts. Some studies confirm results found with simpler tone sequences. That is, detection of small pitch changes of a target tone is better in isochronous than anisochronous rhythms (DeWitt and Samuel 1990). Even with musically complex rhythms, temporal expectancies stimulated by a preceding context facilitate detection of pitch changes in embedded targets (Dowling *et al.* 1987). Converging findings from a pattern comparison task suggest that detection of time changes is also affected by a preceding rhythmic context. Bharucha and Pryor (1986) presented listeners with 18 rhythmic monotone sequences, all implying a duple metre according to Povel's technique. Standard-comparison pairs were based on combinations of rhythmic sequences and their variants where the latter contained a randomly located, metrically disruptive, target pause. Listeners were better at detecting this pause when the rhythmic pattern, rather than the variant, served as the standard; this suggests that listeners relied heavily on the meter implied by the standard to detect the time change. Finally, Dowling *et al.* (1987) studied detection of both pitch and time changes within music-like patterns. He found that when distractor sounds are interleaved with a target tune, listeners seemed to narrow attention in pitch space to a smaller frequency range at an expected time to detect changes in anticipated targets. Their data support the hypothesis that listeners rely on dynamic aspects of musical pattern structure to aim attention in pitch space and time.

Summary Selective attending to musical events, whether it involves a sustained following of a whole theme or merely targeting attention to a single note, indicates that guiding attention selectively to subparts of complex music-like sequences is facilitated by

(1) attentional set (instructions);

(2) increasing the pitch distance between to-be-attended themes and to-be-ignored ones;

(3) metrically relating target subparts in time; and

(4) dynamic contexts that imply expected pitch and time neighbourhoods within which a target will occur.

4.2.3 Attending to speech

While it is a truism that speech is rhythmical, the nature of speech rhythmicity is much debated. One aspect of this debate involves the putative metricality of speech, as expressed by the *isochrony principle* (Classe 1939; Pike 1945; Lehiste 1977; Hayes 1984). In English, which is a stress-timed language, this principle implies (minimally) that timing of successive stresses within an unbroken utterance should conform to a simple clock model, namely evidence-invariant time periods between stresses.

This final section on speech patterns is brief and selective. It parallels earlier sections.

Integrative aspects of attending to speech

Speech, like music, is produced by humans for the purpose of communicating to other humans. Integrative attending involves monitoring, shadowing or producing all successive parts of an utterance. These activities clearly encompass much of what people do in conversations. But the dynamic interactions within a speaker–listener pair obviously partake heavily of sophisticated schemes that incorporate semantic, syntactic, phonemic knowledge, etc., of speech patterns. A detailed consideration of these schemes is beyond the scope of this chapter. Accordingly, this section focuses simply upon issues relating to schematic time structures.

A clock model, embodied in the isochrony principle, implies metricality. Consider the phrase 'Andrew must have been in this department' (adapted from Giegerich 1980). Assuming that underlined vowels are all salient time markers, then this utterance is metrical if these markers are temporally equidistant. Unfortunately, careful time measurements on such utterances shows this not to be the case. While there is a general alternation of weakly and strongly stressed syllables (i.e. *stress rhythm*), speech, like music, is not exactly metrical.

Yet listeners are clearly attuned to many aspects of speech timing. For example, they are sensitive to stress rhythms (e.g. Lieberman 1965). Gleason and Bharucha (1990) found that both production and perception of English sentences are disturbed when a repeating tone of alternating strong (loud) and weak (soft) stress is misaligned with their normal linguistic stress points. In addition, people are sensitive to the likelihood that strong syllables (i.e. containing a full vowel) tend to mark word onsets (Cutler and Norris 1988). They are also sensitive to characteristic durational patternings among syllables associated with different words (Smith *et al.* 1989).

There are curious parallels between timing in speech and in music. Discussions of speech rhythms often turn on the role of violations of the isochrony principle. For example, Lehiste (1977) has argued for a *perceptual isochrony* principle, claiming that because listeners *expect* regularity in utterances, violations of strict isochrony (e.g. via pauses, stress shifts, etc.) are meaningful. Both rhythmic expectations and their temporal violations do seem important. Just as musical performers shift musical accents for emphasis, speakers modify stressed locations and insert pauses in their utterances to convey intended meanings and disambiguate syntax; this information is reliably used by listeners (e.g. Lehiste 1973; Lehiste *et al.* 1976; Scott 1982). Violations of rhythmic expectations even systematically change how listeners hear consonant sounds (e.g. Kidd 1989).

Finally, as Cutler and Isard (1980) showed, even certain disruptions of isochrony appear, in the end, to reinforce some version of an isochrony principle: when speakers increase interstress durations that straddle a syntactic boundary (relative to fixed time periods between stresses within syntactic boundaries), these increases are lawful violations of isochrony that simply 'skip a beat'.

However, even with modifications to incorporate expectancy violations, it is unlikely that a simple clock can accommodate the complexity of multiple timing deviations and stress patterns in speech. On the other hand, if speech utterances are in fact non-metrical, does this mean that people develop speech schemes based on Povel's figural–numeric codes? This too seems unlikely. A number of mysteries remain. However it is described, speech, timing is finely woven; it is part of complex schemes that experienced speakers have acquired. Finally, it seems that to achieve the necessary flexibility, speed, and economy in attending, time structures which support attending to speech must be more complex than clock schemes but they cannot be too complicated.

It is possible that speech patterns seem more 'non-metrical' than they are simply because researchers have not divined all the ways sophisticated speakers and listeners differentially *mark* higher and lower levels of time structure (e.g. Jones and Boltz 1989). While there is evidence for multiple time levels based on studies of pause placements in speech, where longer pauses mark correspondingly higher time periods (e.g. Cooper *et al.* 1978; Grosjean *et al.* 1979), pause segmentations cannot explain how listeners hear distinct word segments from continuous speech where markings are more subtle. In fact, as in performed music where strong stresses marking measure onsets can be missing, so in produced speech, strongly stressed syllables which tend to signal word onsets are sometimes absent. Here expectancies based on domain specific knowledge may be at play. Cutler (1990) suggests that sophisticated listeners 'know' that stressed syllables are more likely to signal word boundaries and therefore segment a continuous speech pattern accordingly, leading to occasional misperceptions.

Summary Evidence for isochrony and strict metricality of speech is not in abundance. Nevertheless, listeners are sensitive to

(1) speech timing patterns;

(2) meaningful violations of stress / accent regularities; and

(3) probabilistic aspects of stress functions.

These data do not rule out the possibility that domain-specific knowledge of speakers and listeners includes complex, and subtly marked, time hierarchies. As with music this issue remains a source of continued debate.

Selective attending to speech

Most studies concerned with attention to speech involve selective attending. Here, initially stimulated by the isochrony principle, there exists a narrow tradition of investigating the influence of speech rhythmicities on attention. It originated with a hypothesis by Martin (1972) concerning attentional targeting to major lexical or emphatic stress points in English, and interest in this topic continues to the present.

Martin proposed that listeners automatically target their attention in time to anticipate more stressed elements of speakers' utterances. This idea makes adaptive sense since nouns and verbs, which carry more information, often bear greater stress than other words. While this hypothesis is consistent with either clock or time-hierarchy descriptions in that it focuses upon the role of certain regular higher-order (interstress) time-periods, Martin favoured a time hierarchy model, maintaining that stronger stresses mark correspondingly higher time levels.

A common paradigm used to address the targeting hypothesis involves phoneme monitoring: a listener monitors an utterance both for its meaning and for the occurrence of a specified target phoneme (to which the response is made). Often the utterance context, including rhythm, is of experimental interest. Performance is measured in terms of speed and accuracy of a target detection response. The attentional targeting hypothesis implies that listeners should be faster and/or more accurate in detecting target phonemes in stressed than in unstressed syllables. While some research supports this prediction (Shields *et al.* 1974; Meltzer *et al.* 1976), a tricky aspect of evaluating the idea surrounds the fact that stressed syllables are not only higher in pitch and louder than unstressed ones, but are also longer. Thus, performance may be better when the stressed targets are marked by increased duration merely because they allow more processing time.

Recent research controls for differences between stressed and unstressed syllables by holding constant the acoustic properties of targets in different contexts. Stressed neutral words are spliced into various test utterances. In these cases, small but significant influences of rhythmic context and implied stress are evident (Cutler 1976; Pitt and Samuel 1990). Cutler, for example, varied emphatic (contrastive) stress via intonational contour changes of utterances such as 'She managed to remove the dirt from the rug, but not the berry stains' (where the word 'dirt' is stressed) and, 'She managed to remove the dirt from the rug, but not from their clothes' (where 'dirt' has low stress), but held constant acoustic properties of 'dirt'. Listeners nonetheless responded significantly more quickly to /d/ when it occurred in high stress contexts.

Summary The approximate regularity of various kinds of stresses in unbroken speech utterances provides a basis for research on temporal targeting of attention to embedded phonemic targets. This research shows small but consistent effects on target detection as a function of manipulations of speech rhythms.

4.3 CONCLUSIONS

Contemporary approaches that address attending to extended auditory events implicate the role of both immediate and prior experience in shaping schemes that control attending. In simpler auditory events which involve unfamiliar sounds and patterns, listeners reveal tendencies to direct attending over successive tones that are of roughly similar frequencies and which trace out relatively simple (harmonic) nested time levels (i.e. time hierarchies). Similar properties influence selective attending to these sorts of sequences, although here perceptual learning of probabilistic contingencies also shapes performance. However, within a corpus of familiar auditory patterns (music, speech), sophisticated listeners may use more complex time patterns, although there remains evidence for some influence of frequency similarities/proximities and temporal constraints. In general, whenever simpler and/or more familiar time patterns connect distinctive subparts (e.g. accents) of a music or speech pattern, selective attending to and perception of these subparts improves.

Finally, a theme within this chapter involves the role of time structure in attending. While often neglected, current theory and research with auditory events suggest that temporal structure and dynamic pattern properties are receiving increasing interest. Thus, many problems posed in this chapter may eventually find solutions—such solutions may, in turn, have general ramifications for understanding attention.

ACKNOWLEDGEMENTS

The authors are indebted Carolyn Drake, Susan Holleran, James Klein, Caroline Palmer, Mark Pitt, Ken Robinson, and two anonymous reviewers who read and commented on earlier versions of this chapter.

REFERENCES

Abel, S. M. (1972). Discrimination of temporal gaps. *Journal of the Acoustical Society of America*, **52**, 519–24.

Allan, L. G. (1979). The perception of time. *Perception and Psychophysics*, **26**, 340–54.

Allport, A. (1989). Visual attention. In *Foundations of cognitive science* (ed. M. I. Posner) pp. 631–82. MIT Press, Cambridge, MA.

Bartlett, F. C. (1932). *Remembering: an experimental and social study*. Cambridge University Press.

Bharucha, J. J. and Pryor, J. H. (1986). Disrupting the isochrony underlying rhythm: an asymmetry in discrimination. *Perception and Psychophysics*, **40**, 137–41.

Boltz, M. (1991). Time estimation and attentional perspective. *Perception and Psychophysics*, **49**, 422–33.

Bregman, A. S. (1990). *Auditory scene analysis: the perceptual organization of sound*. MIT, Cambridge, MA.

Bregman, A. S. and Campbell, J. (1971). Primary auditory stream segregation and perception of order in rapid sequences of tones. *Journal of Experimental Psychology*, **89**, 244–9.

Broadbent, D. E. (1958). *Perception and communication*. Pergamon, London.

Broadbent, D. E. (1982). Task combination and selective intake of information. *Acta Psychologica*, **50**, 253–90.

Cherry, E. C. (1953). Some experiments on the recognition of speech, with one and two ears. *Journal of the Acoustical Society of America*, **25**, 975–9.

Ciocca, V. and Bregman, A. S. (1987). Perceived continuity of gliding and steady–state tones through interrupting noise. *Perception and Psychophysics*, **42**, 476–84.

Classe, A. (1939). *The rhythm of English prose*. Blackwell, Oxford.

Cooper, W. E., Paccia, J. M., and Lapointe, S. G. (1978). Hierarchical coding in speech timing. *Cognitive Psychology*, **10**, 154–77.

Cutler, A. (1976). Phoneme-monitoring reaction time as a function of preceding intonation contour. *Perception and Psychophysics*, **20**, 55–60.

Cutler, A. (1990). Exploiting prosodic probabilities in speech segmentation. In *Cognitive models of speech processing: psycholinguistic and computational perspectives* (ed. G. T. M. Altmann), pp. 105–21. MIT, Cambridge, MA.

Cutler, A. and Isard, S. D. (1980). The production of prosody. In *Language production: Vol. 1. Speech and talk* (ed. B. Butterworth), pp. 245–269. Academic, New York.

Cutler, A. and Norris, D. G. (1988). The role of strong syllables in segmentation for lexical access. *Journal of Experimental Psychology: Human Perception and Performance*, **14**, 113–21.

Demany, L., McKenzie, B., and Vurpillot, E. (1977). Rhythm perception in early infancy. *Nature*, **266**, 718–19.

Deutsch, D. (1983). The generation of two isochronous sequences in parallel. *Perception and Psychophysics*, **34**, 331–7.

Deutsch, J. A. and Deutsch, D. (1963). Attention: some theoretical considerations. *Psychological Review*, **87**, 272–300.

Dewitt, L. A. and Samuel, A. G. (1990). The role of knowledge-based expectations in music perception: evidence from musical restoration. *Journal of Experimental Psychology: General*, **119**, 123–44.

Divenyi, P. and Danner, W. F. (1977). Discrimination of time intervals masked by brief acoustic pulses of various intensities and spectra. *Perception and Psychophysics*, **21**, 125–42.

Dowling, W. J. (1973). The perception of interleaved melodies. *Cognitive Psychology*, **5**, 322–37.

Dowling, W. J. (1990). Expectancy and attention in melody perception. *Psychomusicology*, **9**, 148–60.

Dowling, W. J. and Harwood, D. L. (1986). *Music cognition*. Academic, Orlando, FL.

Dowling, W. J., Lung, K. M., and Herrbold S. (1987). Aiming attention in pitch and time in the perception of interleaved melodies. *Perception and Psychophysics*, **41**, 642–56.

Duncan, J. (1979). Divided attention: the whole is more than the sum of its parts. *Journal of Experimental Psychology: Human Perception and Performance*, **5**, 216–28.

Duncan, J. and Humphreys, G. W. (1989). Visual search and stimulus similarity. *Psychological Review*, **96**, 433–58.

Essens, P. J. (1986). Hierarchical organization of temporal patterns. *Perception and Psychophysics*, **40**, 69–73.

Essens, P. J. and Povel, J. D. (1985). Metrical and nonmetrical representations of temporal patterns. *Perception and Psychophysics*, **37**, 1–7.

Eysenck, M. W. (1982). *Attention and arousal, cognition and performance*. Springer, New York.

Fraisse, P. (1963). *The psychology of time*. Harper and Row, New York.

Fraisse, P. (1982). Rhythm and tempo. In *The psychology of music* (ed. D. Deutsch), pp. 149–80. Academic, New York.

Fraisse, P. (1984). Perception and estimation of time. *Annual Review of Psychology*, **35**, 1–36.

French-St. George, M. and Bregman, A. S. (1989). Role of predictability of sequence in auditory stream segregation. *Perception and Psychophysics*, **46**, 384–6.

Freyd, J. J., Kelly, M. H., and DeKay, M. L. (1990). Representational momentum in memory for pitch. *Journal of Experimental Psychology: Learning, Memory and Cognition*, **62**, 423–32.

Gabrielsson, A. (1985). Interplay between analysis and synthesis in studies of music performance and music experience. *Music Perception*, **3**, 59–86.

Gabrielsson, A. (1986). Rhythm in music. In *Rhythm in psychological, linguistic and musical processes* (ed. J. R. Evans and M. Clynes), pp. 131–67. Charles C. Thomas, Springfield, Ill.

Giegerich, H. J. (1980). On stress-timing in English phonology. *Lingua*, **51**, 187–221.

Gleason, T. and Bharucha, J. J. (1990). Speech accompanied by a tone with aligned or misaligned stress. Unpublished paper presented at the Meeting of the Psychonomic Society, New Orleans, November 1990.

Green, D. M. (1961). Detection of auditory sinusoids of uncertain frequency. *Journal of the Acoustical Society of America*, **67**, 1304–11.

Greenberg, G. Z. and Larkin, W. D. (1968). Frequency-response characteristic of auditory observers detecting signals of a single frequency in noise: The probe–signal method. *Journal of the Acoustical Society of America*, **44**, 1513–23.

Grosjean, F., Grosjean, L., and Lane, H. (1979). The patterns of silence: performance structures in sentence production. *Cognitive Psychology*, **11**, 58–81.

Hahn, J. and Jones, M. R. (1981). Invariants in auditory frequency relations. *Scandavian Journal of Psychology*, **22**, 129–44.

Halpern, A. R. and Darwin, C. J. (1982). Duration discrimination in a series of rhythmic events. *Perception and Psychophysics*, **31**, 86–9.

Handel, S. (1989). *Listening: an introduction to the perception of auditory events*. MIT Press, Cambridge, MA.

Hayes, B. (1984). The phonology of rhythm in English. *Linguistic Inquiry*, **15**, 33–74.

Hirsh, I. J., Monahan, C. B., Grant, K. W., and Singh, P. G. (1990). Studies in auditory timing: 1. Simple patterns. *Perception and Psychophysics*, **47**, 215–26.

Hirst, W. (1986). The psychology of attention. In *Mind and brain: dialogues in cognitive neuroscience* (ed. J. E. LeDoux and W. Hirst), pp. 105–41. Cambridge University Press.

Hirst, W., Spelke, E., Reaves, C., Caharack, G., and Neisser, U. (1980). Dividing attention without alternation or automaticity. *Journal of Experimental Psychology: General*, **109**, 98–117.

Howard Jr, J. H. O'Toole, A. J., Parasuraman, R., and Bennett, K. B. (1984). Pattern-directed attention in uncertain frequency detection. *Perception and Psychophysics*, **35**, 256–64.

Idson, W. L. and Massaro, D. W. (1976). Cross-octave masking of single tones and musical sequences: the effects of structure on auditory recognition. *Perception and Psychophysics*, **19**, 155–75.

Jagacinski, R., Marshburn, E., Klapp, S. T., and Jones, M. R. (1988). Tests of parallel versus integrated structure in polyrhythmic tapping. *Journal of Motor Behavior*, **20**, 416–42.

James, W. (1950). *The principles of psychology*. Dover, New York. (First published in 1890 by Henry Holt, New York.)

Johnson, D. M. and Hafter, E. R. (1980). Uncertain-frequency detection: cuing and condition of observation. *Perception and Psychophysics*, **28**, 143–9.

Johnston, W. A. and Dark, V. J. (1986). Selective attention. *Annual Review of Psychology*, **37**, 43–75.

Jones, M. R. (1976). Time, our lost dimension: toward a new theory of perception, attention, and memory. *Psychological Review*, **83**, 323–55.

Jones, M. R. (1981). Only time can tell: on the topology of mental space and time. *Critical Inquiry*, **7**, 557–76.

Jones, M. R. (1987). Dynamic pattern structure in music: recent theory and research. *Perception and Psychophysics*, **41**, 621–34.

Jones, M. R. (1990a). Musical events and models of musical time. In *Cognitive models of time* (ed. R. Block) pp. 207–40. Erlbaum, Hillsdale, NJ.

Jones, M. R. (1990b). Learning and the development of expectancies; an interactionist approach. *Psychomusicology*, **9**, 193–228.

Jones, M. R. and Boltz, M. (1989). Dynamic attending and responses to time. *Psychological Review*, **96**, 459–91.

Jones, M. R. and MacCallum, R. (1987). An application of principal directions in scaling to auditory pattern perception. *Multidimensional scaling: they and application* (ed. F. Young and R. Hamer), pp. 259–78. Erlbaum, Hillsdale, NJ.

Jones, M. R. Maser, D. J., and Kidd, G. (1978). Rate and structure in memory for auditory patterns. *Memory and Cognition*, **6**, 246–58.

Jones, M. R., Kidd, G., and Wetzel, R. (1981). Evidence for rhythmic attention. *Journal of Experimental Psychology: Human Perception and Performance*, **7**, 1059–73.

Jones, M. R., Boltz, M., and Kidd, G. (1982). Controlled attending as a function of melodic and temporal context. *Perception and Psychophysics*, **32**, 211–18.

Kahneman, D. (1973). *Attention and effort*. Prentice-Hall, Englewood Cliffs, NJ.

Kahneman, D. and Treisman, A. M. (1984). Changing views of attention and automaticity. In *Varieties of attention* (ed. R. Parasuraman and D. R. Davies), pp. 29–61. Academic, Orlando, FL.

Kidd, G. (1989). Articulatory-rate context in phoneme identification. *Journal of Experimental Psychology: Human Perception and Performance*, **15**, 736–48.

Kidd, G. R. and Watson, C. S. (1989). Detection of relative frequency changes in tonal patterns. *Journal of the Acoustical Society of America*, **86**, S121(A).

Kidd, G. R. and Watson, C. S. (1990). Detection of relative-duration changes in tonal patterns. *Journal of the Acoustical Society of America*, **88**, S147(A).

Kidd, G., Boltz, M., and Jones, M. R. (1984). Some effects of rhythmic context on melody recognition. *American Journal of Psychology*, **97**, 153–73.

Klapp, S. T., Hill, M., Tyler, J., Martin, Z., Jagacinski, R., and Jones, M. R. (1985). On marching to two different drummers: perceptual aspects of the difficulties. *Journal of Experimental Psychology: Human Perception and Performance*, **11**, 814–27.

Kronman, U. and Sundberg, J. (1987). Is the musical ritard an allusion to physical motion? In *Action and perception in rhythm and music* (ed. A. Gabrielsson), pp. 57–68. Royal Swedish Academy of Music, Stockholm.

Krumhansl, C. L. (1990). *Cognitive foundations of musical pitch*. Oxford University Press, New York.

LaBerge, D. and Brown, V. (1989). Theory of attentional operators in shape identification. *Psychological Review*, **96**, 101–24.

Lambert, A. J. (1985). Selectivity and stages of processing—an enduring controversy in attentional theory: a review. *Current Psychological Research and Review*, Fall, 239–56.

Lashley, K. S. (1951). The problem of serial order in behavior. In *Cerebral mechanisms in behavior* (ed. L. A. Jeffress), pp. 112–46. Wiley, New York.

Leek, M. R. and Watson, C. S. (1984). Learning to detect auditory components. *Journal of the Acoustical Society of America*, **76**, 1037–44.

Leek, M. R. and Watson, C. S. (1988). Auditory perceptual learning of tonal patterns. *Perception and Psychophysics*, **43**, 389–94.

Lehiste, I. (1973). Rhythmic units and syntactic units in production and perception. *Journal of the Acoustical Society of America*, **54**, 1228–34.

Lehiste, I. (1977). Isochrony reconsidered. *Journal of Phonetics*, **5**, 253–63.

Lehiste, I., Olive, J. P., and Streeter, L. (1976). Role of duration in disambiguating syntactically ambiguous sentences. *Journal of the Acoustical Society of America*, **60**, 1199–202.

Lerdahl, F. and Jackendoff, R. (1983). *A generative theory of tonal music*. MIT Press, Cambridge, MA.

Lewis, J. (1970). Semantic processing of unattended messages using dichotic listening. *Journal of Experimental Psychology,* **85**, 225–8.

Lieberman, P. (1965). On the acoustic basis of the perception of intonation by linguists. *Word,* **21**, 40–54.

Macmillan, N. A. and Schwartz, M. (1975). A probe–signal investigation of uncertain frequency detection. *Journal of the Acoustical Society of America,* **58**, 1051–8.

Martin, J. (1972). Rhythmic (hierarchical) versus serial structure in speech and other behavior. *Psychological Review,* **79**, 487–509.

Masaro, D. W. (1972). Preperceptual images, processing time, and perceptual units in auditory perception. *Psychological Review,* **79**, 124–45.

Massaro, D. W. and Idson, W. L. (1978). The temporal course of perceived auditory duration. *Perception and Psychophysics,* **20**, 331–52.

Meltzer, R. H., Martin, J. G., Mills, C. B., Inhoff, D. L., and Zohar, D. (1976). Reaction time to temporally-displaced phoneme targets in continuous speech. *Journal of Experimental Psychology: Human Perception and Performance,* **2**, 277–90.

Michon, J. A. (1967). *Timing in temporal tracking.* Van Gorcum, Assen, The Netherlands.

Monahan, C. B. and Hirsh, I. J. (1990). Studies in auditory timing: 2. Rhythm patterns. *Perception and Psychophysics,* **47**, 227–42.

Moray, N. (1959). Attention in dichotic listening: affective cues and the influence of instructions. *Quarterly Journal of Experimental Psychology,* **11**, 56–60.

Neisser, U. (1967). *Cognitive psychology.* Appleton-Century-Crofts, New York.

Neisser, U. (1976). *Cognition and reality.* Freeman, San Francisco.

Neisser, U. and Hirst, W. (1974). Effect of practice on the identification of auditory sequences. *Perception and Psychophysics,* **15**, 391–8.

Norman, D. A. and Bobrow, D. B. (1975). On data limited and resource-limited processes. *Cognitive Psychology,* **7**, 44–64.

Palmer, C. (1992). The role of interpretive preferences in music performance. In *Cognitive bases of muscial communication* (ed. M. R. Jones and S. Holleran), pp. 249–62. American Psychological Association, Washington, D.C.

Palmer, C. and Krumhansl, C. L. (1990). Mental representations for musical meter. *Journal of Experimental Psychology: Human Perception and Performance,* **16**, 728–41.

Parasuraman, R. and Davies, D. R. (eds) (1984). *Varieties of attention.* Academic, Orlando, FL.

Penner, M. (1976). The effect of marker variability on the discrimination of temporal intervals. *Perception and Psychophysics,* **19**, 466–9.

Pike, K. L. (1945). *The intonation of American English.* University of Michigan Press, Ann Arbor, MI.

Pitt, M. A. and Samuel, A. G. (1990). The use of rhythm in attending to speech. *Journal of Experimental Psychology: Human Perception and Performance,* **16**, 564–73.

Posner, M. I. (1980). Orienting of attention. *Quarterly Journal of Experimental Psychology,* **32**, 3–25.

Posner, M. I. and Snyder, C. R. R. (1975). Attention and cognitive control. In *Information processing and cognition: the Loyola symposium* (ed. R. L. Solso), pp. 55–85. Erlbaum, Hillsdale, NJ.

Posner, M. I., Snyder, C. R. R., and Davidson, B. J. (1980) Attention and the detection of signals. *Journal of Experimental Psychology: General,* **109**, 160–74.

Povel, D. J. (1981). Internal representations of simple temporal patterns. *Journal of Experimental Psychology: Human Perception and Performance*, **7**, 3–18.

Povel, D. J. and Essens, P. J. (1985). Perception of temporal patterns. *Music Perception*, **2**, 411–40.

Remington, R. and Pierce, L. (1984). Moving attention: evidence for time-invariant shifts of visual selective attention. *Perception and Psychophysics*, **35**, 393–9.

Scharf, B. S., Quigley, S., Akoi, C., Peachey, N., and Reeves, A. (1987). Focussed auditory attention and frequency selectivity. *Perception and Psychophysics*, **42**, 215–23.

Schneider, W. and Shiffrin, R. M. (1977). Controlled and automatic human information processing: I. Detection, search, and attention. *Psychological Review*, **84**, 1–66.

Scott, D. R. (1982). Duration as a cue to the perception of a phrase boundary. *Journal of the Acoustical Society of America*, **71**, 996–1007.

Shaffer, L. H. (1981). Performances of Chopin, Bach, and Bartók: studies in motor programming. *Cognitive Psychology*, **13**, 326–76.

Shaffer, L. H. (1982). Rhythm and timing in skill. *Psychological Review*, **89**, 109–22.

Shields, J., McHugh, A., and Martin, J. (1974). Reaction time to phoneme targets as a function of rhythmic cues in continuous speech. *Journal of Experimental Psychology*, **102**, 250–5.

Shiffrin, R. M. (1988). Attention. In *Stevens' handbook of experimental psychology. Vol. 2: learning and cognition.* (ed. R. C. Atkinson, R. J. Herrenstein, G. Lindzey, and R. D. Luce), pp. 739–811. Wiley, New York.

Shiffrin, R. M. and Schneider. W. (1977). Controlled and automatic human information processing: II. Perceptual learning, automatic attending, and a general theory. *Psychological Review*, **84**, 127–90.

Shinar, D. and Jones, M. R. (1973). Effects of set-inducing instructions on recall from dichotic inputs. *Journal of Experimental Psychology*, **98**, 239–44.

Shulman, G. L., Remington, R. W., and McLean, J. P. (1979). Moving attention through visual space. *Journal of Experimental Psychology*, **93**, 73–82.

Sloboda, J. (1985). *The musical mind: the cognitive psychology of music.* Clarendon, Oxford.

Smith, M. R., Cutler, A., Butterfield, S., and Nimmo-Smith, I. (1989). The perception of rhythm and word boundaries in noise-masked speech. *Journal of Speech and Hearing Research*, **32**, 912–20.

Spiegel, M. F. and Watson, C. S. (1981). Factors in the discrimination of tonal patterns. III. Frequency discrimination with components of well-learned patterns. *Journal of the Acoustical Society of America*, **69**, 223–30.

Spelke, E., Hirst, W. and Neisser, U. (1976). Skills of divided attention. *Cognition*, **4**, 215–30.

Steiger, H. and Bregman, A. S. (1981). Capturing frequency components of glided tones: Frequency separation, orientation and alignment. *Perception and Psychophysics*, **30**, 425–35.

Thomas, E. and Weaver, W. (1975). Cognitive processing and time perception. *Perception and Psychophysics*, **17**, 363–7.

Tougas, Y. and Bregman, A. S. (1990). Auditory streaming and the continuity illusion. *Perception and Psychophysics*, **47**, 121–6.

Treisman, A. M. (1969). Strategies and models of selective attention. *Psychological Review*, **76**, 282–99.

Treisman, A. M. (1982). Perceptual grouping and attention in visual search for features and for objects. *Journal of Experimental Psychology: Human Perception and Performance*, **8**, 194–214.

Treisman, A. M. and Gelade, G. (1980). A feature-integration theory of attention. *Cognitive Psychology*, **12**, 97–136.

Tsal, Y. (1983). Movements of attention across the visual field. *Journal of Experimental Psychology: Human Perception and Performance*, **9**, 523–30.

Underwood, G. and Swain, R. (1973). Selectivity of attention and the perception of duration. *Perception*, **2**, 101–5.

van Noorden, L. P. A. S. (1975). Temporal coherence in the perception of tone sequences. Ph. D. thesis, Eindhoven University of Technology, The Netherlands.

Warren, R. M. (1982). *Auditory perception: a new synthesis*. Pergamon, New York.

Warren, R. M., Obusek, C. J., Farmer, R. M., and Warren, R. P. (1969). Auditory sequence: confusion of patterns other than speech or music. *Science*, **164**, 586–7.

Watson, C. S. (1987). Uncertainty, informational masking and the capacity of immediate memory. In *Auditory processing of complex sounds* (ed. W. A. Yost and C. S. Watson), pp. 267–77. Erlbaum, Hillsdale, NJ.

Watson, C. S. and Kelly, W. J. (1981). The role of stimulus uncertainty in the discrimination of auditory patterns. In *Auditory and visual pattern recognition* (eds D. J. Getty and J. H. Howard, Jr), pp. 37–59. Erlbaum, Hillsdale, NJ.

Watson, C. S., Lehman, J. R., and Kelly, W. J. (1981). Relation between sensation level and frequency discrimination under conditions of information masking. *Journal of the Acoustical Society of America*, **69**, S64(A).

Wickens, C. D. (1984). Processing resources in attention. In *Varieties of attention* (eds R. Parasuraman and D. R. Davies), pp. 63–102. Academic, Orlando, FL.

Wing, A. M. and Kristofferson, A. B. (1973a). The timing of inter-response intervals. *Perception and Psychophysics*, **13**, 455–60.

Wing, A. M. and Kristofferson, A. B. (1973b). Response delays and the timing of discrete motor responses. *Perception and Psychophysics*, **14**, 5–12.

5

Auditory memory

Robert G. Crowder

5.0 INTRODUCTION

With this review, I have two purposes: firstly, to suggest some orienting attitudes towards memory storage in general, and secondly, to survey a few of the most active research programs that are specifically about auditory memory. In past reviews of this sort (Crowder 1975, 1978), I have been at pains to include many individual experiments that used novel or clever methodologies for studying auditory memory, even if they had not led to replication and programmatic extensions. I have not become cynical about those experiments. This time, however, I am widening the definition of auditory memory beyond what used to be called 'sensory memory' and I am describing several forms of memory that are specific to the auditory system. This I take to be the important criterion—that the memory under study be authentically auditory—not quibbling over what 'sensory' means or whether the auditory sensory store matches established wisdom about visual sensory storage. The reason for celebrating a diversity of experimental techniques for studying auditory memory, rather than despairing of the inconsistent results in the field, is related to the guiding *procedural* attitude about memory that I now endorse more clearly than in the past, as will be discussed in Section 5.0.2.

5.0.1 Memory and knowledge

When a person recognizes a clap of thunder as such, the tune of the national anthem, or when he or she understands the statement 'You have a double chin,' auditory memory is being used, without any question. The learning of naturalistic sounds, familiar tunes, and the learning of the forms of the mother tongue, respectively, surely cannot have been innate, and thus they must be information retrieved from memory. At

Thinking in sound: the cognitive psychology of human audition, ed. S. McAdams and E. Bigand. Oxford University Press, 1993, pp. 113–45.

several points in this review, I shall recognize the existence and importance of this *auditory knowledge*. However, our main attention will go to cases in which a specific auditory experience was retained in memory for a measurable time delay, and then retrieved afterwards. This is the auditory version of what Tulving (1983) has called *episodic memory*.

The review will be organized partly historically and partly on the basis of complexity of the information being retained. We first consider manifestations of auditory memory in which a strong verbal component underlies the task, immediate memory span. The interest here (Section 5.1) is in whether the information arrives over the visual or auditory sense modality. The remainder of the survey (Sections 5.2 and following) concerns situations in which verbal coding is unlikely to support performance. The coverage roughly follows a principle of increasing complexity, from memory of the pitch of pure tones to memory for the rich timbres of voice quality.

This survey will not dwell on auditory memory as a largely *theoretical* entity. Numerous formal models have found it indispensable to posit a form of memory for the purely auditory properties of stimuli, from the speech-perception models of Fujisaki and Kawashima (1969, 1970) and McClelland and Elman (1986) to the psychoacoustic model of intensity perception by Braida and Durlach (1988; see also McAdams, Ch. 6 this volume). Although experiments have been undertaken to illuminate specific properties of such storage agencies (Pisoni 1973), concentration, here, will give priority to empirical research programmes rather than to formal models. Before commencing our survey, however, we pause to reflect on the nature of memory storage itself.

5.0.2   The storage and procedural attitudes about memory

Two perspectives guide work on memory in general, and auditory memory in particular. The *storage* position is that retention of experiences (episodic memory) informs us about the existence of dedicated memory stores—receptacles, as it were. Roediger (1980) has demonstrated that our previous attitudes about memory in cognition largely commit us implicitly to this *library metaphor* of memory storage. By this view, evidence for auditory memory defines the existence of a memory store for that modality. The task for scientists, then, would be to enumerate the different stores that can be proven, experimentally, and to describe their properties.

Early evidence from the visual modality (Sperling 1960) suggested such a sensory store in vision (iconic memory) and, from the auditory modality, a corresponding echoic store (Crowder and Morton 1969). Subsequent evidence showed that different experimental techniques for *measuring* the presumed iconic and echoic stores yielded storage properties for each of a puzzling variability (Coltheart 1980; Cowan 1984). In the visual case, the contrast was between Sperling's (1960) original experimental preparation and the 'fusion technique' introduced by Haber and Standing (1970). (The former procedure was to measure information extracted from a brief glimpse of an array of letters or digits. The latter procedure was for subjects to superimpose a remembered, meaningless pattern upon a current, also meaningless, one, when the combined pattern would be meaningful and identifiable.) In the auditory case a corresponding distinction was made between the suffix-modality work of Crowder and Morton (1969) and Massaro's (1970) recognition-masking techniques (see Sections 5.1 and 5.2, respectively).

The response by partisans of the storage position to this inconsistency of the properties of a visual sensory store and of an auditory sensory store was to postulate multiple sensory memory stores. In Coltheart's (1980) usage, iconic memory was distinguished from visible persistence. In Cowan's (1984) corresponding survey of the auditory domain, 'short' and 'long' auditory stores were distinguished.

I begin this survey by introducing the proceduralist assumption that memory is not a mental faculty or capacity, as such. There are not places or even units in the nervous system that are devoted to memory. Rather, memory is depicted as *the persistence that is a by-product of some original mental activity*, which activity, in turn, comprised the learning episode.[1] This proceduralist position (Kolers and Roediger 1984; Crowder 1989) denies that information is retained in memory stores similar in any way to receptacles. Instead, this proposal is that retention is a natural consequence of the information processing that was originally engaged by the experience in question (see also Crowder and Morton (1969) and Craik and Lockhart (1972) for early versions of this attitude). *Where* that original experience was played out, in brain activity, is where the memory for it will correspondingly reside afterwards. If two different auditory experiences, for example, recruit two different kinds of information processing, by virtue of stimulus or task properties, then they may well show two different kinds of retention, afterwards, not because they are served by different auditory memory stores but because different, perhaps anatomically distinct, portions of the nervous system were active in processing the original information (Farah 1988).

Hebb (1949) clearly embraced this proceduralist assumption when he supposed that synaptic changes underlying learning and memory occur in those units engaged by an original perception. In his specific example,

---

1. In the same way, the bombardments of neutrino particles observed several years ago, from Supernova 1987A, were not records laid down by that event, unimaginably remote both in time and space. They were not, in any sense, 'astronomical memory traces'. They were the (cataclysmic) event itself, viewed from a great distance in time and space (Crowder 1989).

these would have been units in the visual and motor projection areas involved in perceiving a triangle, and the associative cortical units aroused during that processing. Among those workers committed to investigating memory as a brain function, much the same attitude is now taken for granted, perhaps as too obvious for words. Squire (1987) says the following, in reference to vertebrate habituation, an established learning/memory experimental task:[2]

Findings from the invertebrate cases support this analysis of habituation in vertebrates. Behavior change arises from modifications in already existing circuitry, specifically in the same circuitry specialized to perform the behavior that is modified. This simple type of learning apparently requires no additional brain regions, no additional circuitry, and no additional neurons and synapses, beyond those already required to perform the reflex ... (p. 88).

The pure proceduralist position is that this summary extends broadly across species and tasks, as a characterization of learning and memory in general. It follows from proceduralism that there should be variable sorts of memory to the extent that the nervous system realizes variable sorts of perception, thinking, and information processing.

Accordingly, auditory processing results in auditory memory. At a minimum, auditory memory will tend to be located in auditory processing centres of the brain, surely including the temporal cortex, and visual memories will tend to be located in visual processing areas, including the occipital visual projection areas. Auditory brain activity of different kinds will furthermore tend to engage different loci in the auditory central nervous system, and accordingly, different memory loci. This proceduralist attitude contrasts with efforts in the past twenty-five years to discover more and more memory 'stores' such as echoic, iconic, short term, and long term.

However, allegiance to proceduralism is not required for readers of this review. Grouped under the headings that follow are active research programmes that define our knowledge about types of auditory memory, whatever attitude we may find congenial for the nature of memory. These foci of research, to some, define different stores with differing properties. In the style of theory based on information-flow diagrams, these stores would be drawn as a multiplicity of separate 'boxes.' The reader is free to interpret the evidence described in these terms, if that perspective is preferable to him or her than the proceduralist perspective.

What follow are several kinds of auditory activity that show appreciable memory retention following experiences, and in which the medium of verbal coding of information can be discounted.

---

2. It should be said that Squire's (1987) overall position, nevertheless, would hold that more complex forms of learning are not as 'procedural' as vertebrate habituation.

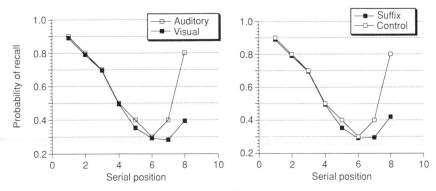

Fig. 5.1 Schematic serial position curves showing the modality effect in the left panel and the suffix effect in the right panel. In both cases probability of recall is plotted against serial position.

5.1 AUDITORY RETENTION IN SHORT-TERM VERBAL MEMORY

Manifestations of genuine auditory memory are particularly unambiguous when non-auditory forms of coding, such as verbal coding, are virtually ruled out by the stimuli or by the task. Notwithstanding, one of the first sources of evidence came from tasks using auditory presentation of *familiar verbal material*. Crowder and Morton (1969) proposed that auditory sensory (that is, precategorical) memory lay behind the *modality effect*, a consistent advantage of auditory over visual presentation in serial, immediate recall situations in which the subject was to report the items in the order received immediately following presentation. They suggested that following a spoken stream of characters, or words, people had access not only to the interpretations they had made of these items (categorical memory) but also to the most recent item or items, as actual sounds (precategorical acoustic storage).

The argument for auditory coding in this situation must not be that verbal codes are ruled out—that would be preposterous for familiar characters in the subjects' native language. Instead, we can assert that verbal coding has been effectively *equalized* across auditory and visual presentations of exactly the same material. The advantage of the auditory modality over the visual modality in serial recall for verbal lists is shown in the left-hand side of Fig. 5.1, in schematic form.

Following auditory input, presentation of an extra item, called a stimulus suffix, although posing no additional load on memory, was shown to erase most or all of the auditory advantage. This *suffix effect* explains why, in modality comparisons, auditory presentation results in superior performance, but only for the last few positions in the list. Each item in the series acted as a sort of suffix with regard to the previous item. Only the last item, in a control condition, was free of this interference. The suffix effect is shown schematically on the right-hand side of Fig. 5.1. The figure makes obvious that presentation of a redundant suffix after the list has the effect of removing, more or less, the advantage that came from having the list presented auditorially in the first place.

Ensuing experiments (reviewed by Crowder (1976)) showed that the meaning of this suffix item had no effect on the tendency of the suffix to reduce performance at the end of auditory lists (see Fig. 5.1). However, differences between the list to be remembered and the redundant suffix had a large effect if they were changes in physical properties such as spatial location or voice quality (e.g. male versus female). This sensitivity to physical attributes, along with an insensitivity to conceptual attributes, is what would be expected of a precategorical memory store (Morton *et al.* 1971). By a proceduralist attitude, we would say that it is just what would be expected of the residue from precategorical information processing, because processing of only precategorical features should be unaffected by meaning but sensitive to acoustic features.

Another consequential finding for precategorical acoustic storage was that lists of spoken syllables differing only in their initial stop consonants (bah, dah, gah) showed no auditory superiority over visual presentation, and no suffix effect in the case of the former. However, similar lists of syllables varying in vowel sounds (gah, goo, gee) showed both, just as did lists of spoken symbols or words (Crowder 1971; Darwin and Baddeley 1974).

The modality–suffix experiments on immediate memory (Fig. 5.1) were rather generally attributed to precategorical acoustic storage until experiments by Spoehr and Corin (1978) and by Campbell and Dodd (1980) showed that the original hypothesis had been too simple. These authors showed that silent lip-reading and related procedures produced results in immediate memory that were almost indistinguishable from auditory presentation, and were readily differentiated from orthographic visual presentation. One response has been to make revisions in the precategorical acoustic storage model, but leaving its essential features unchanged (Crowder and Greene 1987). Another option has been to seek a different interpretation of the suffix–modality results altogether. So far, however, it is warranted to say that no single, satisfactory candidate has emerged.

For example, Shand and Klima (1981) proposed that recency is produced in the serial recall task when the stimulus series involves a *primary linguistic code* (for most normal subjects language comes to them first, as children, over the auditory channel). This accounts for why deaf users of American sign language showed recency in serial recall (Shand and Klima 1981), but it does not accommodate the finding mentioned above that recency is a consequence of remembering vowel sounds but not the sounds of stop consonants (Crowder 1971). Both are, after all, in the same auditory presentation mode. Nor has the primary linguistic code hypothesis survived experiments designed specifically to test it (Manning *et al.* 1989).

A second alternative idea was advanced by Campbell and Dodd (1980), to the effect that recency is a property of stimuli with *changing-state* information. (Auditory stimuli inherently unfold over time but static visual stimuli do not.) This hypothesis is not entirely without support from experiments attempting to incorporate changing-state presentation formats for visual stimuli (Kallman and Cameron 1989; Glenberg 1990). However, the sizes of the recency effects found in those two experiments were tiny compared with the usual auditory recency effect (Fig. 5.1). Furthermore, other experiments that used different ways of making visual information dynamic (changing state) were completely unsuccessful in affecting recency (Crowder 1986).

Still a third idea proposed as an alternative to precategorical acoustic storage is directed mainly at the modality effect and not the suffix effect: Glenberg (1987; Glenberg and Swanson 1986; Glenberg and Fernandez 1988) suggested that recency results from well-defined temporal coding, that is, that good recall of the last items on a list is later supported by good information about the relative (or absolute) times that these items occurred. This assumes that time of occurrence can be used as a retrieval cue. For example, if people use the retrieval strategy of seeking the 'last item' first, then a precisely defined encoding of time of occurrence, for that item, will help. A further suggestion was that this coding of time is inherently better in the auditory modality than in the visual modality. Crowder and Greene (1987) and Schab and Crowder (1989) have performed direct comparisons of the accuracy of temporal coding for visual and auditory events, however, and have reported no differences.

Thus, the original data of Fig. 5.1 are stable and may be said to represent *some* form of auditory memory. With the verbal contribution to coding equalized across modalities, the auditory modality shows a consistent advantage in memory over the visual modality. This seems to be particularly true for linguistic stimuli (Crowder and Surprenant 1992). Beyond that, the task of theoretical explanation remains somewhat open. The postulation of a dedicated auditory store—precategorical acoustic storage—for materials arriving through sound is notoriously too simple a formulation (Spoehr and Corin 1978; Campbell and Dodd 1980). However, alternatives have not shown promise of clearing up the disarray in the literature. One hypothesis that captures elements of both the changing-state hypothesis and the data on lip-reading is that the auditory memory summarized by precategorical acoustic storage is a property of the mental system responsible for language perception and analysis (Morton *et al.* 1981; Surprenant *et al.* 1993).

5.2   AUDITORY BACKWARD RECOGNITION MASKING

At about the same time the modality–suffix work was accumulating, experiments on the masking of pure tones were also being used as an inferential basis for auditory (sensory) memory. Note that these pure-tone stimuli make a strong claim to engage purely auditory processing, and not verbal processing, as will be remarked below. In this section, the target behaviour is *identification* of single tones, whereas in Section 5.3, pairs of single tones are compared with respect to a same/different criterion.

Massaro (1970) delivered subjects one of two possible pure tones, 20 ms long and pitched at either 770 or 870 Hz. The main task was to identify which of these two—the high or the low one—had been presented. After this target, and at delays of 0 to 500 ms, a masking tone (820 Hz) was presented. In general, presentation of the masking tone reduced subjects' abilities to identify correctly, or recognize, which of the two tones had come before, especially if the masker came within about 250 ms of the target. This result is shown in Fig. 5.2. The three curves correspond to the three different subjects tested in this way.

The logic of this experiment (see also Massaro 1972) is that if the original target tone had been fully processed before the masker arrived, there would have been no decrement in its identification caused by a backward masker. If the target were still being processed when the masker arrived, however, there must have been a sensory trace of it still available somewhere in the auditory system, i.e. in auditory memory. This is because presentation of the target tone was complete before the masker occurred.

Comparable experiments with speech have given much the same result (Massaro 1974). Moore and Massaro (1973) showed that the tone properties of loudness and spatiality (where the sound occurred) are also subject to backward masking in this paradigm, with time constants that are largely consistent with those shown in Fig. 5.2. Kallman and Massaro (1983) have summarized much of the work on backward masking in this paradigm and have suggested its relation to the modality–suffix experiments described above.

From a detailed review of results and models of auditory integration and auditory persistence, Cowan (1984, 1987) distinguished two types of auditory sensory memory, which he called, respectively, short and long. The short auditory store was to have a useful life of about 250 ms and is represented in Massaro's experiments on recognition masking and related techniques. Cowan argued that the same short auditory store participated in experiments on subjective auditory duration (Efron 1970) and other examples of auditory integration. The long auditory store was

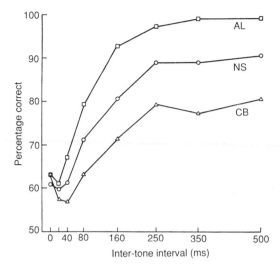

Fig. 5.2 Proportion of correct identifications of a test tone (as high or low in pitch) as a function of the interval between it and a subsequent masking tone. The three functions represent performance of three subjects. (From Fig. 1, Massaro (1970) p. 559. © American Psychological Association, Inc. Adapted with permission.)

to last as long as 2–10 s, or roughly an order of magnitude greater, and underlies the suffix and modality comparisons (Fig. 5.1).

These two stores may alternatively be viewed, from a proceduralist point of view, as the residues of distinct kinds of information processing. By the storage view, it was always troubling that these two techniques for showing auditory sensory memory gave storage times so discrepant from each other. However, by the proceduralist view, experiments on verbal short-term memory and on recognition of single tones would depend on somewhat different brain activities and so *of course* they would show different retention characteristics.

Precisely the same state of affairs was produced in visual sensory memory. Years after Sperling's (1960) classic demonstration experiments, another technique, called the fusion method (Haber and Standing 1970; Di Lollo *et al.* 1988) gradually began to produce discrepant results. Because they used different stimuli and tasks, one might have expected these two methods to converge on a common form of iconic storage. However, Coltheart (1980) distinguished them as two modes of retention—visible persistence and iconic memory—with dissociated properties. One can choose to view these as two different dedicated memory stores, or as the persistence properties of two kinds of different visual information processing.

Massaro's experiments on recognition masking have *prima facie* plausibility as evidence for true auditory memory, because the stimuli are non-verbal to start with. The strategy of verbal recoding of the individual tones is quite unlikely, except perhaps for possessors of absolute pitch (who appear to have rapid access to a verbal code). However, we should not dismiss the possibility of a verbal strategy lightly: with only two target tones, of quite different pitches, the verbal designations 'high' and 'low' could be used for a two-tone sequence. Also, the two-tone sequence formed by the target and the masker could be encoded as 'rising' or 'falling.'

These possibilities of verbal coding cannot be dismissed in principle, but they are rendered unlikely by several facts. First, versions of the task arranged to test for *detection masking*, where identification of the target is not at stake—only whether or not some stimulus occurred—show a generally similar dependence of performance on masker delay, as do experiments on *loudness masking*, where the subject must identify the loudness level of a tone (see Moore and Massaro 1973). Second, to the extent that verbal recoding was important to the task, an interfering tone should have had only a minimal effect, and an interpolated word should have been very damaging to performance. We do not have this result, but in its absence we can assume that the tone is vastly more interfering than a word would be.

5.3   SAME/DIFFERENT PITCH COMPARISONS IN PAIRS OF TONES

The comparison between tones and words as masks for targets that are tones is available in research by Deutsch (1970, 1975) on memory for single tones. In her experiments, as in Massaro's, the task was based on a pair of target tones separated by several seconds. The two tones were either identical in pitch or separated by a half tone, and the task assignment was to say 'same' or 'different' in those situations, respectively. Each tone was 0.2 s in duration. The first tone, the standard, was followed by the comparison tone after 5 s. In the experiment by Deutsch (1970) four conditions were defined by what occurred during this five-second interval. A comparable experiment without any distracting activity during the pause ('no distractor') produced essentially perfect performance. Performance in this condition, and the four comparison conditions, is shown in Table 5.1. In the second condition ('ignore tones'), six interfering tones were played during the delay between the two target tones. These were randomly chosen from the same octave as the target tones but none was allowed to come within 1.5 semitones of these targets.

Table 5.1 Listeners' average performance (percentage correct) in the Deutsch (1970) experiment

Condition	Pitch comparison task	Digit recall task
No distractors	100.0	—
Ignore tones	67.7	—
Ignore digits	97.6	—
Recall digits	94.4	74.7
Only digits	—	72.6

Subjects were told to ignore these interfering tones, but as we see in the table, performance was reduced from 100 per cent correct to 67.7 per cent correct just by virtue of their presentation. In the third condition of Table 5.1 ('ignore digits'), a list of six spoken digits was presented at the same times the six interfering tones had been in the previous condition. They obviously had negligible effect on the target task. In the fourth condition ('recall digits'), the presentation sequence was exactly the same except that subjects were responsible for recalling the six digits after each trial. Performance on the same/different task with tones was not reliably lower, indicating that even if people had to attend to the interfering digits those digits did not threaten the tone-comparison task. We can be assured that they did indeed attend to the digits because recall of them was as good as 74.7 per cent. The last condition ('only digits'), in which no tones were ever presented, not even the target tones, yielded essentially the same performance, establishing that the tones and spoken digits did not mutually interfere.

Semal and Demany (1991) have extended this work by dissociating the properties of pitch, in single tones, from their timbres (timbre is roughly 'tone colour' or instrumental colour; see McAdams, Ch. 6 this volume). Spoken digits differ from the comparison tones, in Deutsch's experiments, by both dimensions (pitch and timbre) after all. In a series of experiments based on the Deutsch method, Semal and Demany found consistently that pitch was the important factor. Like Deutsch and Feroe (1974) they found that interference tones did the most damage if they were from the same pitch region as the two tones being compared. This was true whether or not the interfering tones shared timbre (basically, the overtones present above the fundamental frequency). We may surmise, then, that timbre differences between tones and voices were not responsible for their lack of interaction.

To perform a delayed same–different task absolutely requires that the first stimulus be preserved in some form—remembered—until the second stimulus arrives. Deutsch's experiment as a whole assures us that verbal coding was not the medium of such memory, otherwise verbal digits would have challenged the tone-comparison task. The case for an authentically auditory memory is greatly enhanced by the selective interference shown in the tone-distractor task. The comparison of these conditions emphasizes what has been a broad strategy in memory research for a long time: one can judge what type of coding has been involved in a memory task by determining what events will interfere with that memory. Deutsch chose to emphasize that this was a variety of short-term memory, but no evidence suggests that remembering a single tone over a longer period of time, if it could be done by people without absolute pitch, would engage different storage mechanisms.

Thus, the results of Deutsch (1970) presented in Table 5.1, as well as those of Semal and Demany (1991), bespeak a tidy modularity in memory, wherein the different formats of storage (pitch, timbre, verbal) are not corrupted by interference from the inappropriate code. Following the proceduralist attitude described at the beginning of this chapter, we might prefer to consider this modularity as a modularity of *processing* in which memory storage is the outgrowth, or by-product, of that processing. Proceduralism of memory and modularity of processing, together, make sense of the patterns of agnosia discussed by Peretz (Ch. 7, this volume). She argues with force that the linguistic and non-linguistic aspects of auditory perception are not lost together in neuropsychology patients (usually stroke victims). More tentatively, she proposes that among the latter, musical and other auditory processing (environmental sounds, for example) might be capable of dissociation. (See her comments on the musical lexicon, Section 7.3.3). If the same neural equipment is used for the perceptual recognition of these auditory events as for the episodic storage of them in recognition experiments, then patterns of dissociation should, indeed must, match experimental dissociations such as those shown in Table 5.1.

A recent report by Pechmann and Mohr (1992) qualifies our conclusions about strict modularity in a way that introduces a new dimension into the problem of memory for tones. They showed that the Deutsch result of Table 5.1 is reliably characteristic of trained musicians. However, a musically naïve group of otherwise comparable subjects showed some 'cross-talk.' That is, for the latter group, verbal and visual interference activities caused interference in memory for single tones, as well as tone interference. Experimentally, this shows that individual subject factors figure prominently into even such musically meaningless tasks as pure-tone pitch comparison.

The added dimension for auditory memory is the *knowledge base* against which such pitches occur. Just as single letters and single words, in a memory laboratory, are learned against a knowledge base provided by the natural language, remembered auditory knowledge of the tonal system influences how tonal events are remembered.[3] As Bigand (Ch. 8, this volume) has argued, this knowledge base may well be implicit, a sort of tacit knowledge, but generally a lifetime of experience with tonal music (whatever the idiom) lies behind it. Just as we cannot apprehend linguistic units, the letters and words of our native language, other than against a background of tacit linguistic knowledge, the tacit guidance provided by schemas for even musically naïve listeners is profound. Hebb (1949) claimed that such an organized knowledge base is an inescapable property of all learning by mature organisms, but not immature organisms.

Having recognized the pervasiveness of some knowledge base against which tonal experience is laid, for adult humans, we should not be complacent in assuming that it is all *learned* knowledge. Trehub and Trainor (Ch. 9, this volume) have provided bounds on this learning assumption by discussing the capabilities of newborn infants, and even such species as starlings, to process musical stimuli. But the nature/nurture issue really has to do with where this background knowledge originally came from. Neither answer to that question would deter us from believing that new tonal experiences are necessarily registered against the background.

The recent reviews of Krumhansl (1990, 1991) may be consulted for the kinds of auditory knowledge listeners show in the perception of individual pitches. Some of Krumhansl's own early work (Krumhansl 1979) provides a convenient transition from the current discussion of memory for individual pitches to the next section, which treats memory for melodic sequences. Krumhansl (1979, experiments 2 and 3) performed same–different pitch judgements similar to those introduced by Deutsch (1970). In all Krumhansl's experimental conditions, interference tones separated the two tones being judged as same or different. These interference tones were sometimes members of the same tonal scale as the target and comparison tones: for example, if the target and comparison tones were F and G, both F, or both G, the eight interference tones in this tonal condition were C, A, E, F, D, G, B, and C. In another condition, which she called 'atonal', the interference tones were foreign to the tonality of the target and comparison tones: in this second case, with F and G the target-comparison set, the interfering tones would be C#, A, E, F, D#, G, A, C#.[4] Her finding was that more interference occurred if the interfering set was consistent with the tonality of the tones being judged than otherwise. (That is, poor performance was obtained if both the tones being judged and the interference tones were from the same diatonic set, C, D, E, F . . . .) Conversely, if the two tones being compared were outside that

---

3. In considering the influence of this background knowledge, we shall increasingly refer to musical cognition in this survey.
4. Note that F and G occur in both interference sets.

same tonal context (as for example G# would be) then the pattern reversed, with the atonal interference causing poorer performance than the tonal interference. Thus, we must conclude that even when there is no obvious melody, individual tones are not heard independently of a tonal context. Subjects' implicit knowledge of the conventional tonal relationships in Western music supplies this framework, or schema, (see Bigand, Ch. 8 this volume). In ordinary music, such a tonal context is almost inevitable, so we should move from the examination of memory for individual tones to collections of tones in a melodic context, with the understanding that a harmonic, or tonal, context is carried by melody whether or not it is 'accompanied.'

5.4   MEMORY FOR MELODY

The experiments of Deutsch (1970), shown in Table 5.1, employed the same/different task with respect to single pitches. The same/different methodology is one of several that have been applied to more complex auditory stimuli, melodies, where the critical information is contained in the sequence of pitch intervals rather than the absolute pitches themselves. These explicit same/different tasks will be described later (Section 5.4.4), after we discuss memory for familiar tunes.

5.4.1   Melodies in auditory knowledge

We have already stipulated that *auditory knowledge* and *auditory memory* can be differentiated according to whether the information is specific to the time–space context in which it occurred (as is the case in episodic memory). Although our main attention is to episodic memory, matching the emphasis in the literature, retrieval of auditory knowledge of melodies has been examined in at least three experimental contexts and these should properly be included in our survey. These techniques are usually described as 'melody perception' experiments but they might just as well be considered retrieval experiments (of remembered knowledge).

Interleaved melodies

Dowling (1973) presented pairs of interleaved melodies to subjects. He found that if the pitch ranges of the two were non-overlapping, they could easily be distinguished and identified. Interleaving a familiar melody with an unfamiliar one impaired recognition of the former, however, most especially when the two were played in the same pitch range, i.e. the same range of keys on a keyboard (see Bregman, Ch. 2 and Jones and Yee, Ch. 4 this volume, for discussions of sequential auditory

Fig. 5.3 The notes of 'Frère Jacques' and 'Twinkle, twinkle little star' interleaved, but in different pitch ranges. (From Fig. 5.1A, Dowling and Harwood (1986) p. 125. © Academic Press. Adapted with permission.)

Fig. 5.4 An octave-scrambled version of 'Mary had a little lamb'. (From Fig. 5.3A, Dowling and Harwood (1986) p. 129. © Academic Press. Adapted with permission.)

organization). These two situations are portrayed in Fig. 5.3: the two melodies are in different pitch ranges.

Providing the title of a familiar tune can overcome the interference from an interleaved distractor, even when both are in the same pitch range. This last finding (Dowling 1973) shows that auditory knowledge can be accessed through verbal cues, at least sometimes, which would agree with most people's intuitions. These and other subsequent results using this paradigm are reviewed, with examples, by Dowling and Harwood (1986, Ch. 5).

Octave-scrambled melodies

Octave-scrambled melodies are defined by an exact sequence of the familiar pitch *chromas* for a melody (sequence of the chromatic set C, C#, D, D#, and so on) but with unpredictable jumps of one or several octave steps between successive tones. An octave-scrambled version of 'Mary had a little lamb' is shown in Fig. 5.4.

Deutsch (1972) showed that melody recognition (retrieval of the name of a familiar tune) is very difficult under these conditions. Providing correct labels for the tunes has similar effects on octave-scrambled melodies as on interleaved melodies (see also Dowling and Harwood 1986). Dowling and Hollombe (1977) and Idson and Massaro (1978) showed experimentally that one factor of these distorted melodies, as compared with the originals, is that their *contours* are seriously changed.

Contour is a property psychologists have used to abstract the patterns in melodies—namely their patterns of up–down pitch changes between adjacent notes, disregarding their distances (Teplov (1966) called this the *courbe mélodique*). The contour for 'Mary had a little lamb'—in its original, unscrambled version—begins down–down–up–up. . . . Notice that the pattern of ups and downs in Fig. 5.4 begins down–up–down–up. . . . Dowling and Hollombe (1977) and Idson and Massaro (1978) demonstrated that if octave-scrambled melodies are prepared, *preserving* the original sequence of ups and downs, they are easier to recognize than when the contour is violated. We shall discuss melody contour again in Section 5.4.4 on recognition of unfamiliar melodies.[5]

Recycled melodies

A third technique of studying memory, as represented by retrieval of auditory knowledge, has been examined by Warren *et al.* (1991; see also Warren, Ch. 3 this volume). It is possibly the simplest of all: these authors presented cycling repetitions of familiar tunes played at different tempi or speeds. The tunes were started somewhere in the middle of the sequence and recycled without pause (otherwise the task was too easy). Recognition was possible at a range of rates that covered approximately one order of magnitude, from about 200 ms per tone to about 2000 ms per tone, with best performance at a rate of about three per second (320 ms per tone on the average). These temporal parameters were compared with those obtained for non-melodic auditory sequences (see Warren, Ch. 3 this volume). This technique makes a good case for getting to the heart of melody perception in that it does not depend on distorting the pitches of original melodies, on distorting the relative timing relations among those pitches, or on adding extraneous pitches

5.4.2   Comment on priming

Studies on the perception/identification of familiar melodies examine the problem of auditory knowledge. Likewise, the study of perceptual recognition thresholds for familiar words, in vision, studies our visual knowledge of the language. Perhaps the dominant discovery in memory psychology during the 1980s was that the threshold for word perception is reduced if that same word had been recently processed. This episodic priming defines the flourishing contemporary field of *implicit memory* (Jacoby and Dallas 1981; Jacoby 1983; Roediger 1990). The priming

5. Some workers believe that contour is a property abstracted and processed by individual subjects as well as by psychologists.

methodology is a ripe candidate for study in melody recognition, perhaps using one of three methods that have been discussed in this section. Announcing the titles of familiar tunes to be presented, in the octave-scrambled and interleaved-melodies paradigms, facilitates their perception, as we have said, presumably through priming by means of auditory imagery (Halpern 1988).

Next, we consider studies where the target information is melodic and explicit memory is at stake (direct tests). Finally, we shall consider implicit measures of memory for melody.

5.4.3 Episodic memory for new melodies: recall

Our first impulse, in wondering whether a person remembers something, is simply to ask him or her what it was. Indeed, much of the vast literature on memory for verbal experiences is based on just that technique. In these experiments on free recall we are essentially never concerned that a person reproduce the tone of voice or typographic form in which the target words originally were presented. It is understood, by all concerned, that an abstraction from that original experience is called for.

In a study by Balch (1984) subjects were asked to abstract all but directional (contour) information from presented melodies. He found evidence from modality-specific-interference comparisons that both visual (experiments 1 and 2) and auditory (experiment 3) coding could underlie the immediate retention of such information.

Also committed to the notion of contour, Davies and his associates asked listeners to draw graphic representations of musical contours (maintaining interval sizes) for well-known melodies (Davies and Jennings 1977) or for randomly produced (unfamiliar) melodies (Davies and Yelland 1977). They concluded that melody recognition, in both cases, is related to the production of an internal representation that differs from a memorized, ordered sequence of measured pitch skips.

As Sloboda and Parker (1985) explained, the problem of finding a consensual form of abstraction is vastly more problematic in music recall than in verbal recall.[6] Constraints on some forms of recall by reproduction (singing or keyboard media, for example) are all too obvious. Nor do all our subjects have fluency with musical notation. Even if they did know the rudiments of notation, subjects would be powerfully swayed by conventional cognitive structures about the style of music they know. Worse, in many ways, the experimenter would also have to interpret recall efforts from within those same constraints. As it were, both subjects

---

6. Provided one wants to go beyond the schematic drawing of contours.

and experimenters would approach the task through the same 'cognitive filters.' Sloboda and Parker surmise that, for reasons such as these, recall has not been a popular methodology in memory-for-melody research.

Undaunted by these challenges, and believing that recognition tests constrain our knowledge of melodic memory too severely, Sloboda and Parker (1985) collected a data base on eight subjects' recall for unfamiliar melodies. Each of several Russian folk-songs was played six times in a row on the piano. Subjects were asked to recall, after each presentation, by singing 'la-la-la . . .' or some other meaningless verbalization. The recorded recall efforts were then analysed by several musical features, including metrical, rhythmic, harmonic, and structural. These same analyses had been performed on the stimulus tunes, and the agreement between the analyses of stimuli and the analyses of recall efforts were compared, to indicate recall accuracy.[7]

Perhaps the most unexpected, and therefore the most interesting, results of Sloboda and Parker (1985) were the following two. First, recall in this situation was subject to such powerful proactive inhibition (earlier melodies' intruding into recall of later melodies) that all except the very first melody tested had to be discarded. Secondly, for five of the six different response criteria, the four musically trained subjects did not perform better than the four musically naïve subjects. Only on the retention of harmonic relations did the subjects' training seem to make a difference. Thus, a recall technique can, after all, be used with musical stimuli. Beyond that existence proof, the Sloboda and Parker (1985) study seems to have stimulated little or no subsequent research activity, even by those authors themselves.

5.4.4   Episodic memory for new melodies: recognition

We turn now to explicit melody recognition, in the episodic sense. But the logic of recognition testing raises a formidable problem, immediately: with Deutsch's (1970) same/different recognition tests of a single pitch, no uncertainty attaches to which test events should be called 'same' and which 'different.' With melodies, this issue is not so clear. Figure 5.5 shows five variants on the tune 'Pop goes the weasel' in which the four versions (b) through (d) bear various degrees of similarity to the original version (a). For example, version (b) transposes (a) into a new key signature, but the exact pitch intervals between adjacent notes are the same. Version (c) changes not only the key signature but also the mode of the original (from major to minor). The same pitch intervals are *not* maintained in (c), as compared with (a) or (b). Version (d) preserves the contour of (a), but not its tonality, while version (e) destroys all of these features,

---

7. Explicitly recognizing the cognitive filters mentioned above.

Fig. 5.5 The first part of the song 'Pop goes the weasel'. (a) Original version, (b) transposed to another key, (c) same contour with some different intervals, but tonal, (d) same contour but atonal, and (e) changed contour. (From Fig. 5.4, Dowling and Harwood (1986) p. 130. © Academic Press. Adapted with permission.)

and even the contour (up–down sequence of skips) of the original.[8] With respect to (a), which of these should be called 'same' and which 'different?' The convention has been to regard B as the same melody and the others, (c)–(e), as different melodies. Such a seemingly arbitrary division of the similarity dimension (calling (a)–(a) and (a)–(b) 'same' and (a)–(c), (a)–(d), and (a)–(e), etc. 'different') is defensible in the context of Western music practices, where a change only in starting pitch for a melody—leaving all subsequent pitch intervals the same—is not regarded as a change at all.[9]

A series of experiments by Dowling and his colleagues has used such materials as those of Fig. 5.5 to identify factors important in the recognition of melodies. The premise of these recognition experiments is that *confusions* between an original melody and a transformed one (version a versus versions b, c, or d) indicate that the maintained features are characteristic of the memory record of the original melody.

First of all, we return to familiar melodies for a moment. Bartlett and Dowling (1980) showed that people easily recognize 'wrong-note' deviations in the specific intervals of a well-known tune (see also Attneave and Olson (1971), who showed that subjects had excellent memory for

8. Notice that all four variants are completely faithful to the rhythm of the original.
9. Although most mature, Western listeners agree with musicologists that transpositions are the 'same melody'.

the pitch intervals of a familiar radio chime). However, with unfamiliar melodies, heard for the first time, the picture changes—immediately after hearing such a melody, subjects are poor at distinguishing an exact transposition of it (Fig. 5.5(b)) from a test item that has the same contour as the original but slightly different interval skips (Fig. 5.5(c)), usually involving a minor-to-major change (cf. Dowling and Fujitani 1971; Dowling 1978; Bartlett and Dowling 1980). It is as though subjects were relying on a representation of the melody's contour, for a melody they just heard, with less emphasis on the exact pitch intervals.

With a delay following presentation of a novel melody, however, the balance changes so that exact intervals play a larger role (Dowling and Bartlett 1981). Performance does not actually improve over increasing retention intervals, but the balance of dependence on contour information and dependence on interval information seems to change, with contour dominating at short intervals and the two playing a more equal role at longer intervals. This active area of research has seen criticisms of Dowling's inferences about the factors concerned in melody recognition (Croonen and Kop 1989), but other recent evidence with somewhat different testing protocols supports the argument for a shift in the preponderance of different types of false-alarm errors over increasing, short retention intervals[10] (Edworthy 1985; DeWitt and Crowder 1986; Dowling 1991).

We may accept these conclusions as features of auditory memory for melodies, but they depend on our axiomatic belief in the process of abstraction in hearing and remembering music. The fact is that an exact transposition of a melody (Fig. 5.5(b)) is *different* from an original (Fig. 5.5(a)), by one criterion—the pitch on which it starts. With respect to meter and rhythm, all melodies in the set (Figs 5.5(a) to (e)) are unquestionably the *same*. To any individual subject, the complexities of the experimental definitions of 'same' and 'different' are challenging (see footnote 9 on p. 131). For group comparisons, such as musicians versus non-musicians, the understanding of those experimental instructions is unlikely to be equalized. To young children, the definitions of 'same' and 'different' are likely to be downright baffling. So group comparisons involving children (Bartlett and Dowling 1980) might well be tapping differences in memory for melodies, across age, but they might just as well be tapping differences across age in ability to understand the instructions.

These issues do not arise in implicit memory techniques (Jacoby and Dallas 1981; Jacoby 1983; Roediger 1990) because the subject is not deliberately declaring anything about the contents of his or her memory. We turn now to experiments on implicit memory, for the remainder of this section and in Section 5.5 below.

---

10. From this most authors infer a shift in the storage format of the remembered information.

5.4.5 Implicit memory for unfamiliar melodies

In a series of experiments on memory for song (Serafine *et al.* 1984, 1986; Crowder *et al.* 1990) melodies were taken from a heterogeneous group of unfamiliar folk-song fragments. We were interested in the relation between memory for the two streams—verbal and musical—that define a song. As has been noted above, the melodic constituent involves mostly genuine auditory memory because the verbal–linguistic code is not ordinarily available for it.[11]

The procedure we employed was as follows. Subjects heard a serial presentation of a 'list' of about 24 short, unfamiliar folk-song excerpts, each about 6 s long and each only once. A recognition test followed immediately, in which subjects were asked to indicate, for a series of similar fragments, whether or not they had heard the melody previously, *and* whether they had heard the text previously. The test fragments included some with words from the presentation list, some with tunes from it, and some with new words and melodies. Our main concern was with two conditions we called MISMATCH conditions and OLD SONG conditions. In these two conditions, both the words and the melodies had occurred in the previous presentation list of song fragments. The distinction between them was whether they had occurred *together*, in the same fragment, as in the OLD SONG condition, or in different presentation fragments, as in the MISMATCH condition. An advantage of recognizing words or melodies with exactly the same companion (respectively melodies or words) as they had been presented with before—which is what we found in these experiments, repeatedly—indicates that the two constituents are stored together in memory. Thus, we had evidence that a song heard some minutes previously is represented in memory as 'those particular words' in conjunction with 'that particular melody.' This we called the *integration effect*.

The integration effect was reliably obtained with nonsense materials, verifying that the presence of the original text—even nonsense words— facilitates melody recognition in the OLD SONG condition over that obtained with the different, but equally familiar text, in the MISMATCH songs. Thus, even though words and text in songs seem intuitively to be readily separable codes, perhaps even processed in different hemispheres, the experiments suggest that they are at least partially integrated. Furthermore, we can surmise that ordinary meaning, as such, is not the agency for this integration effect.

Memory for either constituent on its own—melody or word—can be estimated by comparing performance in the OLD SONG or MISMATCH conditions with performance when either the words or melody was in fact

---

11. This is not to say that speech does not entail non-verbal (prosodic) levels of communication and processing.

new, that is, not on the presentation list. For example, memory for melody is established by comparing a new-melody/old-words condition with the MISTMATCH and OLD SONG conditions, where both constituents are old. In most of our experiments we were mainly concerned with memory for melodies, because recognition of the sentences in folk-song lyrics was always near ceiling. However, when memory for words could be measured at less than perfect performance (for example, when we used nonsense words) the integration effect was shown to be symmetrical: a text was best remembered in the presence of its original melody and a melody was best remembered in the presence of its original text (Serafine *et al.* 1986; Crowder *et al.* 1990).

As regards implicit auditory memory, when instructions call for recognizing the lyrics (words), but people show better word recognition in the OLD SONG condition than in the MISTMATCH condition, they *must* be remembering the original melody. Explicit recognition of melodies in these experiments, outside the context of the original words, was close to chance. Thus, under conditions where a list of unfamiliar song fragments were heard some half hour or so previously, explicit memory for melodies— when subjects are reflecting on the previous occurrence of a melody—is virtually absent. But the memory can be 'titrated out' by means of an implicit test, where a remembered melody can make it easier to recognize words that were originally paired with that melody than would have been possible otherwise.

The experiments reviewed above on explicit memory and common experience make it obvious that, of course, melodies are sometimes remembered explicitly, especially after repeated hearing. But in everyday life, relatively few of us spend much time doing this explicit retrieval. The more ecologically general kinds of melody memory may occur implicitly, when we cannot express the retention verbally but when it nevertheless affects our musical processing. The re-entry of a fugue theme, the occurrence of a leitmotif, or the development section of a remembered sonata-movement subject may all be examples of implicit music memory. The appreciation of these devices may not be restricted to musicologists.

5.5   MEMORY AND IMAGERY FOR MUSICAL TIMBRE

Timbre (see Section 5.3) is an auditory quality of great interest for two reasons. First, we cannot verbally describe the quality itself, adequately. Try, for example, to write a paragraph distinguishing the sounds of a tenor saxophone from those of a bassoon, without using non-musical descriptors (foggy, nasal, and so on). We can try to *communicate* these timbres with such adjectives, but we cannot *describe* them. Second, we cannot produce these timbres vocally, either. Among us, some gifted individuals can simulate some timbres—in an earlier generation the Mills brothers were known for this—but the point remains that for straight-forward acoustic differences we are gravely limited in simulating timbral differences with our vocal apparatus. It follows that memory for timbre is likely to be uncontaminated by internal motor recoding, unlike simple melodies (which we can produce internally or externally) or spoken language units (such as letters, which have tremendously overlearned names). Memory for this auditory quality, which is not likely to be recoded into some other format, is accordingly an excellent candidate for consideration as auditory memory.

Hebb (1968) believed that the same neural organizations (cell assemblies or phase sequences) were active both in imagery and the original experience. Such neural activity derived from the sensory surface in the case of the original perception and from top-down induction in the case of imagery. Hebb's favourite example was the 'phantom-limb phenomenon' where itching, for example, may be experienced from a part of the body that has actually been removed, surgically. We may suppose that the same neural centres were stimulated by the limb itself, before amputation, and of course by some other agency after the limb in question was amputated. But itching in the amputated toe, for example, would be represented neurally in the same higher neural centres standing, before and after surgery, for that itching.

What sets an image apart from any memory must be that it preserves the coding format of the original experience, untransformed by any process or recoding. Thus a visual image of an American flag must carry some one-for-one isomorphism with the object originally seen, not a verbal description of it or a meaningful association to it (Shepard 1978). Imagery is usually the term used when the memory was derived 'top-down', as from an instruction to 'picture an American flag.' The term image, or afterimage, is reserved for the case when this information—coded in the same way—results from actually seeing the target object. We shall see evidence for both in the projects on timbre, described below. Recently, I investigated imagery for musical timbre. As stated above, timbre can be defined as the characteristic qualities of a sound—beyond its pitch, loudness or duration—which identify it uniquely (as a bassoon or saxophone, in the earlier example) (Crowder 1989; McAdams, Ch. 6 this volume).

A primary aim of the study had been to demonstrate that auditory imagery is based on sensory (auditory) processing but not on motor (articulatory) processing. Some of the studies that had examined imagery for pitch (Segal and Fusella 1970; Farah and Smith 1983) can be explained by assuming that subjects produced internal correlates of a 'to-be-imagined' event by singing or humming it, rather than by a process of 'hearing the event in the mind's ear.' As a result, these studies do not unequivocally demonstrate the existence of genuinely auditory imagery, as opposed to some motor mediation. A similar argument applies to investigations of mental imagery for songs (Halpern 1988), which can be assigned either to a process of mental 'hearing' or, alternatively, to a process of 'singing to oneself.'

Since the normal human vocal tract cannot faithfully reproduce the timbres of most musical instruments, examining imagery for musical timbre provided a straightforward means of showing that this kind of auditory imagery (auditory memory) is sensory-based, rather than somehow motor-based. I used an experimental technique that had been employed to study visual imagery (Posner *et al.* 1969). Essentially, the technique was designed to assess whether imagery mirrors perception.

In the first experiment (Crowder 1989, experiment 1), subjects were asked to judge whether two consecutively presented tones, which could also vary in timbre, were of the same or of a different diatonic pitch. The results showed that correct same-pitch responses were significantly faster when the timbres of the two notes were also the same than when they were different, documenting that timbre information was stored with the memory trace of the first pitch, at least until arrival of the second pitch. This qualifies as a form of auditory memory because, of course, a 'same' or 'different' judgement cannot be made, without the retention of the first stimulus, until the arrival of the second. The implausibility of recoding the timbre cues, within the time allowed, makes any agency other than auditory memory remotely unlikely (see also Pitt and Crowder 1992).

An earlier report by Beal (1985) had demonstrated essentially the same effect as found in the first part of my imagery project. People recognized repetition of chords better if they were played in the same timbre than if in different timbres. This was especially true of non-musicians in Beal's study. In a study of explicit similarity comparison, Wolpert (1990) also showed that timbre is relatively more salient to untrained subjects, whereas melody and harmony are the more salient cues to trained musicians. From the Beal and Wolpert experiments, and from the first of my experiments (Crowder 1989, experiment 1) we may be confident, at the very least, that the residue from perceiving a musical tone carries information about the timbre in which it was played. Alternatively, a storage advocate would say that auditory memory-stores 'contain' information about timbre.

The same procedure was used in the second part of my study (Crowder 1989, experiment 2) as in the first (experiment 1) except that subjects were first played a pitch that was simple in timbre (a sine-wave tone) and then asked to *imagine* this sine-wave pitch as it *would sound* when played by a particular instrument (e.g. a flute, trumpet, or guitar). After subjects had indicated that an image had been formed, the second tone of the pair was presented for a same/different pitch judgement. Although reaction times were slower, overall, in this imagery experiment than in the two-tone comparison (experiment 1), the same pattern of results was found: 'same' pitch responses were faster when the imagined timbre (of the first tone) was the same as that presented (the second tone) than when it was different. I interpreted these findings as support for the existence of sensory-based auditory imagery. Subjects in this imagery experiment could well have ignored the instruction to form an auditory image and simply compared the pitch of the sine-wave tone to that of the instrumental tone which came next. The fact that same-pitch times were faster when the imagined timbre matched the presented timbre indicates, however, that subjects did not do this. A report by Pitt and Crowder (1992) confirms and extends these findings, especially as regards individual differences. Pitt and I found that some subjects seem virtually unable to respond on the basis of pitch, independently of timbre (see also Wolpert 1990).

The first study with this technique, where two instrumental tones were presented for pitch comparisons, demonstrates auditory retention of timbre for about one second.[12] The second study, comparing an imagined timbre with the second tone, demonstrates the generation of 'long-term' auditory images based on prior learning. The qualitative effect on pitch comparisons was the same, in both cases—facilitating same-pitch responses when timbres matched. This suggests the neural consequences of hearing an instrumental timbre and imagining that it were, to some extent, equivalent. This is just what Hebb (1968) meant, in discussing the nature of imagery.

Both are persisting mental representations, by definition. By reference to the storage metaphor of memory, or representation, the two kinds of traces, then, would have been 'stored in the same place'. How puzzling it would be to describe the properties of such a store, one 'top-down' and one 'bottom-up', one from an auditory event of a few seconds or less ago, and the other from long-term knowledge! An advocate of the storage metaphor would have to conclude that it is a coincidence that timbre affects pitch judgements in the same way in both cases.

The proceduralist, or processing, metaphor also maintains that the two forms of retention depend on a common resource, but this resource is the auditory neural machinery responsible for handling the cues to timbre, engaged either by a presented timbre or by an instruction to generate a mental image of one.

Here we can comment again on the difference between auditory knowledge and auditory memory. Recognition of the timbre of a bassoon,

---

12. Naturally, this is implicit memory, for subjects are not asked to reflect consciously on it.

as such, must necessarily indicate storage in memory for the timbre cues. In my experiments, however, the issue was whether the timbre of a presented tone matched a timbre presented or assigned several seconds before. This capacity indicates authentic auditory episodic memory and not generic auditory knowledge.

5.5½   MEMORY FOR SPEAKER'S VOICE

The preceding discussion of timbre brings to mind immediately the quality of speakers' voices in humans. There also, the fundamental frequency itself is not at stake, but rather resonant frequency characteristics, as resulting from an 'instrumental' filter (the vocal apparatus). I have (rather fancifully) labelled the section describing this source of evidence as $5.5\frac{1}{2}$ rather than 5.6 because the studies I know of, on memory for a speaker's voice, lead to the conclusions that this is true auditory memory, but it is a modest human ability, once it is separated from semantic connotations.

5.5½.1   Implicit memory for speaker's voice in word recognition

Craik and Kirsner (1974) presented subjects with a series of over 400 spoken words, each one eventually presented twice, and subjects had 4 s to indicate whether the word just heard, at any time, was the first or the second presentation of that word. Two voices, one male and the other female, were used to present the words. For a given word, the voices presenting it on the two occasions might be the same or different. The main finding was that correctly recognizing that a word had occurred before, when indeed it had, was facilitated if the presentation voices were the same on both occasions. This facilitation was measured as a difference of approximately 3 per cent in accuracy; in recognition latency, the facilitation was just over 20 ms. The same-voice advantage lasted over three minutes. This finding seemed at first to be unequivocal evidence for auditory memory. It parallels exactly the first part of the timbre demonstrations I have just described. On the face of it, recognition facilitation for same-voice items would indeed indicate that the voice itself had been incorporated into the memory traces.

However, subsequent research in the voice-recognition-facilitation paradigm challenged this conclusion in two ways. Geiselman and Glenny (1977) showed that instructions to imagine a verbal stimulus in either of two voices resulted in recognition facilitation if that same imagined voice presented the stimulus later for recognition judgement. This result is of course conceptually identical to the second of the two parts of my (Crowder 1989) pitch-recognition studies, where there was an advantage when the imagined timbre of a tone matched the presented timbre of the recognition probe.

But, secondly, Geiselman and Glenny (1977) found that recognition was facilitated if *two different* female, or two different male, voices spoke the item on both original presentation and recognition testing, as opposed to one male and one female token of that item. This result suggested to the authors that it was not so much a faithful record of the sound of the individual voice in memory as it was the connotation of a male or female pronouncing the word that affected the nature of the memory trace. Experiments by Geiselman and Bellezza (1977) supported this interpretation, essentially that the (connotative) meaning of an utterance was changed by the gender of the speaker presenting it. These authors reasoned that this connotation hypothesis predicts that a sentence neutral as to gender should be more influenced by the speaker's gender than one that is well defined. Accordingly, a sentence such as 'The puppy ate the food' might be more malleable, and lead to a larger facilitation effect, than a sentence such as 'The gentleman entered the house'. Geiselman and Bellezza (1977) showed this to be the case.

5.5½.2 Explicit recognition of unfamiliar voices

In experiments where pains are taken to measure memory for unfamiliar voices, performance seems modest at best. For example Legge *et al.* (1984) presented varying numbers of 'inspection' voices to over 400 subjects in groups. Later, they were given forced-choice recognition tests in which one voice had been a member of the original array and another not. The results showed that performance was nearly at chance unless prolonged exposures (60 s) to the voices had been given originally, only a short 'list' (5) of voices had been presented as targets, and faces given as context either in presentation or testing. When all these factors were optimal, recognition performance was only at about 70 per cent successful. By contrast, tests of visual face-recognition by the same subjects showed nearly perfect performance.

Note that as poor as voice recognition is, in this and other experiments (see also Hollien *et al.* 1982; Legge *et al.* 1984; Yarmey 1986; Papcun *et al.* 1989), it represents an *upper bound* estimate on episodic auditory memory for voice quality. To the extent that target voices carry idiosyncratic accents, speech impediments, or the like, subjects can use these non-vocal characteristics, rather than vocal timbre itself, for recognition. For example, Australians speak differently from Texans, given their common language, English. To the extent that subtle manners of speaking, less obvious than these two, were present in voice-recognition studies, they cannot be assigned completely to auditory memory.

Thus, the experiments reviewed in this section concern both implicit memory for voice quality and explicit voice recognition for unfamiliar voices. Neither is impressive. The former situation is compromised because, on close inspection, the studies can be explained by processes other than those involved in auditory memory. The latter situation is compromised because people seem to be rather poor at it.

In this context, we should remember that auditory knowledge for voice quality (identifying, as such, the voice of a famous personage) is surely quite impressive, but so far relatively unstudied.

5.6   CONCLUDING SUMMARY: DIMENSIONS OF AUDITORY MEMORY

In this survey, we have travelled across a variety of tasks and stimulus preparations. Several guiding dimensions organize this material: Sections 5.1 and 5.5$\frac{1}{2}$ concerned auditory aspects of natural human speech (auditory presentation and voice quality, respectively). Aside from language, the other major, complex mode of auditory cognition is music, and so it was natural that musical cognition was a major concern in Sections 5.4 and portions of 5.3 (respectively about melody and musical aspects of tone memory). Sections 5.2 and 5.3, and portions of Section 5.5, all covered cases in which single tones were the stimuli being processed (with respect to their identification, recognition, and timbral properties, respectively). Deliberate recognition was the prevailing task in Sections 5.3 and 5.4 and in portions of Sections 5.5 and 5.5$\frac{1}{2}$. The recognition criterion was of tones, melodies, tones again, and voice qualities, in these sections. Implicit memory, *not* requiring subjects' direct evaluation of what happened in the past, was particularly stressed in Sections 5.4 (the integration effect in memory for songs) and 5.5 (faster pitch judgements if the timbre of two tones were the same than if not).

What these situations have in common is their reliance on memory for past auditory experiences, under conditions making it unlikely that these experiences have been recoded into verbal form. The reader is welcome to postulate multiple 'stores' for these situations and distribute the corresponding boxes in some hypothetical information-processing flowchart. I have tried to stress how a proceduralist orientation deals with this variety as reflecting the variety of *kinds of auditory information processing*, with memory as a side effect of this processing in all cases.

REFERENCES

Attneave, F. and Olson, R. K. (1971). Pitch as medium: A new approach to psychophysical scaling. *American Journal of Psychology*, **84**, 147–66.

Balch, W. R. (1984). The effects of auditory and visual interference on the immediate recall of melody. *Memory and Cognition*, **12**, 581–9.

Bartlett, J. C. and Dowling, W. J. (1980). The recognition of transposed melodies: a key-distance effect. *Journal of Experimental Psychology: Human Perception and Performance*, **6**, 501–15.

Beal, A. L. (1985). The skill of recognizing musical structure. *Memory and Cognition*, **13**, 405–12.

Braida, L. D. and Durlach, N. L. (1988). Peripheral and central factors in intensity perception. In *Auditory function: neurobiological bases of hearing* (ed. G. M. Edelman, W. E. Gall, and W. M. Cowan), pp. 559–83. Wiley, New York.

Campbell, R. and Dodd, B. (1980). Hearing by eye. *Quarterly Journal of Experimental Psychology*, **32**, 85–99.

Coltheart, M. (1980). Iconic memory and visible persistence. *Perception and Psychophysics*, **27**, 183–228.

Cowan, N. (1984). On short and long auditory stores. *Psychological Bulletin*, **96**, 341–70.

Cowan, N. (1987). Auditory memory: procedures to examine two phases. In *Auditory processing of complex sounds* (ed. W. A. Yost and C. S. Watson), pp. 289–98. Erlbaum, Hillsdale, NJ.

Craik, F. I. M. and Kirsner, K. (1974). The effect of speaker's voice on word recognition. *Journal of Experimental Psychology*, **26**, 274–84.

Craik, F. I. M. and Lockhart, R. S. (1972). Levels of processing: a framework for memory research. *Journal of Verbal Learning and Verbal Behavior*, **11**, 671–84.

Croonen, W. L. M. and Kop, P. F. M. (1989). Tonality, tonal scheme, and contour in delayed recognition of tonal sequences. *Music Perception*, **7**, 49–68.

Crowder, R. G. (1971). The sound of vowels and consonants in immediate memory. *Journal of Verbal Learning and Verbal Behavior*, **10**, 587–97.

Crowder, R. G. (1975). Inferential problems in echoic memory. In *Attention and Performance V* (ed. P. M. A. Rabbit and S. Dornic), pp. 218–29. Academic, London.

Crowder, R. G. (1976). *Principles of learning and memory*. Erlbaum, Hillsdale, NJ.

Crowder, R. G. (1978). Sensory memory systems. In *Handbook of perception. Vol. VIII* (ed. E. C. Carterette and M. P. Friedman), pp. 343–73. Academic, New York.

Crowder, R. G. (1986). Auditory and temporal factors in the modality effect. *Journal of Experimental Psychology: Learning, Memory, and Cognition*, **12**, 268–78.

Crowder, R. G. (1989). Imagery for musical timbre. *Journal of Experimental Psychology: Human Perception and Performance*, **15**, 472–8.

Crowder, R. G. and Greene, R. L. (1987). On the remembrance of times past: the irregular list technique. *Journal of Experimental Psychology: General*, **116**, 265–78.

Crowder, R. G. and Morton, J. (1969). Precategorical acoustic storage (PAS). *Perception and Psychophysics*, **5**, 365–73.

Crowder, R. G. and Surprenant, A. M. (1992). On the linguistic module in auditory memory. In *Language and literacy* (ed. B. de Gelder and J. Morais). MIT, Cambridge, MA.

Crowder, R. G., Serafine, M. L., and Repp, B. (1990). Physical interaction and association by contiguity in memory for the words and melodies of songs. *Memory and Cognition*, **18**, 469–76.

Darwin, C. J. and Baddeley, A. D. (1974). Acoustic memory and the perception of speech. *Cognitive Psychology*, **6**, 41–60.

Davies, J. B. and Jennings, J. (1977). The reproduction of familiar melodies and the perception of tonal sequences. *Journal of the Acoustical Society of America*, **61**, 534–41.

Davies, J. B. and Yelland, A. (1977). Effects of training on the production of melodic contour in memory for tonal sequences. *Psychology of Music*, **5**, 3–9.

Deutsch, D. (1970). Tones and numbers: specificity of interference in short-term memory. *Science*, **168**, 1604–5.

Deutsch, D. (1972). Octave generalization and tune recognition. *Perception and Psychophysics*, **11**, 411–12.

Deutsch, D. (1975). The organization of short-term memory for a single acoustic attribute. In *Short-term memory* (ed. D. Deutsch and J. A. Deutsch), pp. 107–51. Academic, New York.

Deutsch, D. and Feroe, J. (1974). Disinhibition in pitch memory. *Perception and Psychophysics*, **17**, 302–4.

DeWitt, L. A. and Crowder, R. G. (1986). Recognition of novel melodies after brief delays. *Music Perception*, **3**, 259–74.

Di Lollo, V., Clark, C. D., and Hogben, J. H. (1988). Separating visible persistence from retinal afterimages. *Perception and Psychophysics*, **44**, 363–8.

Dowling, W. J. (1973). The perception of interleaved melodies. *Cognitive Psychology*, **5**, 322–37.

Dowling, W. J. (1978). Scale and contour: two components of a theory of memory for melodies. *Psychological Review*, **85**, 341–54.

Dowling, W. J. (1991). Tonal strength and melody recognition after long and short delays. *Perception and Psychophysics*, **50**, 305–13.

Dowling, W. J. and Bartlett, J. C. (1981). The importance of interval information in long-term memory for melodies. *Psychomusicology*, **1**, 30–49.

Dowling, W. J. and Fujitani, D. S. (1971). Contour, interval, and pitch recognition in memory for melodies. *Journal of the Acoustical Society of America*, **49**, 524–31.

Dowling, W. J. and Harwood, D. L. (1986). *Music cognition*. Academic, Orlando, FL.

Dowling, W. J. and Hollombe, A. W. (1977). The perception of melodies distorted by splitting into several octaves: Effects of increasing proximity and melodic contour. *Perception and Psychophysics*, **21**, 60–4.

Edworthy, J. (1985). Melodic contour and musical structure. In *Musical structure and cognition* (ed. I. Cross, P. Howell, and R. West), pp. 169–88. Academic, London.

Efron, R. (1970). The minimum duration of a perception. *Neuropsychologia*, **8**, 57–63.

Farah, M. J. (1988). Is visual imagery really visual? Overlooked evidence from neuropsychology. *Psychological Review*, **95**, 307–17.

Farah, M. J. and Smith, A. F. (1983). Perceptual interference and facilitation with auditory imagery. *Perception and Psychophysics*, **33**, 475–8.

Fujisaki, H. and Kawashima, T. (1969). On the modes and mechanisms of speech perception. *Annual Report of the Engineering Research Institute*, Vol. 28, pp. 67–73. Faculty of Engineering, University of Tokyo.

Fujisaki, H. and Kawashima, T. (1970). Some experiments on speech perception and a model for perceptual mechanism. *Annual Report of the Engineering Research Institute*, Vol. 29, pp. 207–14. Faculty of Engineering, University of Tokyo.

Geiselman, R. E. and Bellezza, F. S. (1977). Incidental retention of speaker's voice. *Memory and Cognition*, **7**, 201–4.

Geiselman, R. E. and Glenny, J. (1977). Effects of imagining speakers' voices on the retention of words presented visually. *Memory and Cognition*, **5**, 499–504.

Glenberg, A. L. (1990). Common processes underlying enhanced recency for auditory and changing-state stimuli. *Memory and Cognition*, **18**, 638–50.

Glenberg, A. M. (1987). Temporal context and memory. In *Memory and learning: the Ebbinghaus centennial conference* (ed. D. S. Gorfein and R. R. Hoffman), pp. 173–90. Erlbaum, Hillsdale, NJ.

Glenberg, A. M. and Fernandez, A. (1988). Evidence for auditory temporal distinctiveness: Modality effects in order and frequency judgments. *Journal of Experimental Psychology: Learning, Memory and Cognition*, **14**, 728–39.

Glenberg, A. M. and Swanson, N. C. (1986). A temporal distinctiveness theory of recency and modality effects. *Journal of Experimental Psychology: Learning, Memory and Cognition*, **12**, 3–24.

Haber, R. N. and Standing, L. (1970). Direct estimates of the apparent duration of a flash. *Canadian Journal of Psychology*, **24**, 216–29.

Halpern, A. R. (1988). Mental scanning in auditory imagery for songs. *Journal of Experimental Psychology: Learning, Memory and Cognition*, **14**, 434–43.

Hebb, D. O. (1949). *Organization of behavior*. Wiley, New York.

Hebb, D. O. (1968). Concerning imagery. *Psychological Review*, **75**, 466–77.

Hollien, H., Majewski, W., and Doherty, E. T. (1982). Perceptual identification of voices under normal, stress, and disguised speaking conditions. *Journal of Phonetics*, **10**, 139–48.

Idson, W. L. and Massaro, D. W. (1978). A bidimensional model of pitch in the recognition of melodies. *Perception and Psychophysics*, **24**, 554–65.

Jacoby, L. L. (1983). Remembering the data: analyzing interactive processes in reading. *Journal of Verbal Learning and Verbal Behavior*, **22**, 485–508.

Jacoby, L. L. and Dallas, M. (1981). On the relationship between autobiographical memory and perceptual learning. *Journal of Experimental Psychology: General*, **110**, 306–40.

Kallman, H. J. and Cameron, P. (1989). Enhanced recency effects with changing-state and primary-linguistic stimuli. *Memory and Cognition*, **17**, 318–28.

Kallman, H. J. and Massaro, D. W. (1983). Backward masking, the suffix effect, and preperceptual storage. *Journal of Experimental Psychology: Learning, Memory and Cognition*, **9**, 312–27.

Kolers, P. A. and Roediger, III, H. L. (1984). Procedures of mind. *Journal of Verbal Learning and Verbal Behavior*, **23**, 425–49.

Krumhansl, C. L. (1979). The psychological representation of musical pitch in a tonal context. *Cognitive Psychology*, **11**, 346–74.

Krumhansl, C. L. (1990). *Cognitive foundations of musical pitch*. Oxford University Press, New York.

Krumhansl, C. L. (1991). Music psychology: tonal structures in perception and memory. *Annual Review of Psychology*, **42**, 277–303.

Legge, G. E., Grosman, C., and Pieper, C. M. (1984). Learning unfamiliar voices. *Journal of Experimental Psychology: Learning, Memory and Cognition*, **10**, 298–303.

McClelland, J. L. and Elman, J. L. (1986). The TRACE model of speech perception. *Cognitive Psychology*, **18**, 1–86.

Manning, S. K., Silverstein, B., and Schreier, H. (1989). Recency and suffix effects in first, second, and unknown languages: a test of the Primary Linguistic hypothesis. *American Journal of Psychology*, **102**, 385–92.

Massaro, D. W. (1970). Perceptual processes and forgetting in memory tasks. *Psychological Review*, **77**, 557–67.

Massaro, D. W. (1972). Preperceptual images, processing time, and perceptual units in auditory perception. *Psychological Review*, **79**, 124–45.

Massaro, D. W. (1974). Perceptual units in speech perception. *Journal of Experimental Psychology*, **102**, 199–208.

Moore, J. J. and Massaro, D. W. (1973). Attention and processing capacity in auditory recognition. *Journal of Experimental Psychology*, **99**, 48–54.

Morton, J., Crowder, R. G., and Prussin, H. A. (1971). Experiments with the stimulus suffix effect. *Journal of Experimental Psychology: Monographs*, **91**, 169–90.

Morton, J., Marcus, S. M., and Ottley, P. (1981). The acoustic correlates of 'speechlike': a use of the suffix effect. *Journal of Experimental Psychology: General*, **110**, 568–93.

Papcun, G., Kreiman, J., and Davis, A. (1989). Long-term memory for unfamiliar voices. *Journal of the Acoustical Society of America*, **85**, 913–25.

Pechmann, T. and Mohr, G. (1992). Interference in memory for tonal pitch: Implications for a working memory model. *Memory and Cognition*, **20**, 314–20.

Pisoni, D. (1973). Auditory and phonetic memory codes in the discrimination of consonants and vowels. *Perception and Psychophysics*, **13**, 253–60.

Pitt, M. A. and Crowder, R. G. (1992). The role of spectral and dynamic cues in imagery for musical timbre. *Journal of Experimental Psychology: Human Perception and Performance*, **18**, 728–38.

Posner, M. I., Boies, S. J., Eichelman, W. H., and Taylor, R. L. (1969). Retention of visual and name codes of single letters. *Journal of Experimental Psychology: Monographs*, **79**, 1.

Roediger III, H. L. (1980). Memory metaphors in cognitive psychology. *Memory and Cognition*, **8**, 231–46.

Roediger III, H. L. (1990). Implicit memory: retention without remembering. *American Psychologist*, **45**, 1043–56.

Schab, F. R. and Crowder, R. G. (1989). Accuracy of temporal coding: auditory–visual comparisons. *Memory and Cognition*, **17**, 384–97.

Segal, S. J. and Fusella, V. (1970). Influence of imagined pictures and sounds on detection of visual and auditory signals. *Journal of Experimental Psychology*, **83**, 458–64.

Semal, C. and Demany, L. (1991). Dissociation of pitch from timbre in auditory short-term memory. *Journal of the Acoustical Society of America*, **89**, 2404–10.

Serafine, M. L., Crowder, R. G., and Repp, B. H. (1984). Integration of melody and text in memory for songs. *Cognition*, **16**, 285–303.

Serafine, M. L., Davidson, J., Crowder, R. G., and Repp, B. H. (1986). On the nature of melody–text integration in memory for songs. *Journal of Memory and Language*, **25**, 123–35.

Shand, M. A. and Klima, E. S. (1981). Nonauditory suffix effects in congenitally deaf signers of American sign language. *Journal of Experimental Psychology: Learning, Memory and Cognition*, **7**, 464–74.

Shepard, R. N. (1978). The mental image. *American Psychologist*, **33**, 125–37.

Sloboda, J. A. and Parker, D. H. H. (1985). Immediate recall of melodies. In *Musical structure and cognition* (ed. I. Cross, P. Howell, and R. West), pp. 143–67. Academic, London.

Sperling, G. (1960). The information available in brief visual presentations. *Psychological Monographs*, **74**, (Whole No. 498).

Spoehr, K. T. and Corin, W. J. (1978). The stimulus suffix effect as a memory coding phenomenon. *Memory and Cognition*, **6**, 583–9.

Squire, L. R. (1987). *Memory and brain*. Oxford University Press, New York.

Surprenant, A. M., Pitt, M. A., and Crowder, R. G. (1993). Auditory recency in immediate memory. *Quarterly Journal of Experimental Psychology*, (In press).

Teplov, B. M. (1966). *Psychologie des aptitudes musicales* (trans. from the Russian into French by J. Deprun). Presses Universitaires de France, Paris.

Tulving, E. (1983). *Elements of episodic memory*. Oxford University Press, New York.

Warren, R. M., Gardner, D. A., Brubaker, B. S., and Bashford Jr, J. A. (1991). Melodic and nonmelodic sequences of tones: effects of duration on perception. *Music Perception*, **8**, 277–90.

Wolpert, R. S. (1990). Recognition of melody, harmonic accompaniment, and instrumentation: musicians and nonmusicians. *Music Perception*, **8**, 95–106.

Yarmey, A. D. (1986). Verbal, visual, and voice identification of a rape suspect under different levels of illumination. *Journal of Applied Psychology*, **71**, 363–70.

6

Recognition of sound sources
and events

Stephen McAdams

6.0 INTRODUCTION

Imagine playing for listeners an acoustic demonstration of a pile of ceramic dinner plates sliding off a counter, tumbling through the air knocking against one another, and finally crashing on to a relatively hard surface upon which all but one of the plates break—the unbroken one is heard turning on the floor and then finally coming to rest.[1] Then we ask the listeners the following questions. What kinds of objects were heard? How many were there? What was happening to them? And finally, did they all stay in one piece throughout the whole event? Even in the absence of visual cues or a situational context that might predict this event, any listener from a culture that makes use of such objects in such surroundings would easily describe what has been heard, recognizing the nature of the global event, the individual objects that played a role in it, and the transformation of most of them from a whole to a shattered state.

Humans have a remarkable ability to understand rapidly and efficiently aspects of the current state of the world around them based on the behaviour of sound-producing objects, or sound sources, even when these sources are not within their field of vision. For instance we recognize things knocking together outside the window, footsteps approaching from behind, and objects that have been dropped unexpectedly. Though, of course, we use all of our sensory systems together, the above examples suggest that listening can contribute significantly to the perception of the environment in order to act appropriately with respect to it. This ability is due in part to the existence of processes of perceptual organization as discussed by Bregman (1990, Ch. 2 this volume). Once the acoustic information stimulating the ears has been analysed into mental descriptions of sound sources and their behaviour through time, their

Thinking in sound: the cognitive psychology of human audition, ed. S. McAdams and E. Bigand. Oxford University Press, 1993, pp. 146–98.
1. The demonstration cited may be found on track 5 of the compact disc *Sound Effects 7* (Dureco 1150582).

recognition may be considered to be one of the primary, subsequent tasks to be accomplished based on information supplied by the auditory system (Schubert 1975).

Recognition means that what is currently being heard corresponds in some way to something that has already been heard in the past, as when a voice on the telephone, or the footsteps of someone walking down the hall, or a piece of music on the radio, are each recognized. Recognition may be accompanied by a more or less strong sense of familiarity, by realizing the identity of the source (e.g. a car horn), and often by an understanding of what the source being heard signifies to the listener in his or her current situation, thereby leading to some appropriate action. For instance, you might be on the verge of walking carelessly across the street when a horn beeps. You immediately understand it as a very specific danger signal and quickly jump back off the road.

According to the *information processing* approach to psychology (cf. Anderson 1985; Lindsay and Norman 1977), the link between the perceptual qualities of the sound source, its abstract representation in memory, its identity, and the various meanings or associations it has with other objects in the listener's environment are hypothesized to result from a multi-stage process. This process progressively analyses and transforms the sensory information initially encoded in the auditory nerve. Recognition is accomplished by matching this processed sensory information with some representation stored in a lexicon of sound forms in long-term memory. The degree of match may determine whether the sound is recognized or not and may also determine the degree of familiarity that is experienced. The form(s) the sound event may assume and various semantic information associated with it through experience are also linked in memory (cf. Frauenfelder 1991). The activation of these associations follows from the activation of the particular entry in the lexicon. Which associations are activated and which subsequent actions are taken depend on the local context. For example, a listener's experience of the significance of a car horn would be different depending on whether he or she were crossing a street absent-mindedly, sitting in a cinema, or waiting at a stop light. So the recognized identity and significance of the sound event are the result of analysis, matching, and association processes.

Another approach is that of *ecological psychology* (see Gibson 1966, 1979 for the original writings on this approach, and Michaels and Carello 1981 for an excellent, accessible introduction). Ecological theory hypothesizes that the physical nature of the sounding object, the means by which it has been set into vibration, and the function it serves for the listener (as well as its name, presumably) are perceived directly, without any intermediate processing. That is, perception does not pass through an analysis of the elements composing the sound event and their reconstitution into a mental image that is compared with a representation in memory. The perceptual system itself is hypothesized to be tuned to those aspects of the environment that are of biological significance to the listener or that have acquired behavioural significance through experience. In a sense the claim that the recognition of the function of an object in the environment is perceived directly without processing would seem to evacuate the whole question of *how* (i.e. by what neurophysiological or mental process) organisms in possession of auditory systems that are stimulated by sound vibrations come to be aware of the identity of a sound source or how such sources acquire identity and significance for these listeners. The most appealing aspect of this approach, however, concerns the endeavour to develop descriptions of the structure of the physical world that make evident the properties that are perceived as being invariant, even though other properties may be changing. For example, you may still be able to recognize your grandmother's voice though she may have a cold, or be speaking over a noisy telephone line, or be speaking rapidly and in a higher pitch register because she is excited about something. Once such invariants have been isolated, the subsequent (psychological) task would then be to determine how listeners detect these properties. As such, ecological acoustics places more emphasis on the structure of acoustic events that are relevant to a perceiving (and exploring) organism than has been the case in the information processing tradition (at least in non-verbal hearing research). Being interested in the mechanisms by which recognition occurs, and given the relative paucity of research in ecological acoustics (aside from a growing body of research on speech perception), this chapter will primarily adopt the information processing approach in the discussion that follows, making reference to possible contributions by the ecological stance where these are appropriate.

The terms 'recognition' and 'identification' have been operationally distinguished in experimental psychology. Recognition is often measured as the proportion of times a subject correctly judges whether a stimulus item has been heard before, usually within the time frame allotted for one (or a series of) experimental session(s). A simple 'old item/new item' type of judgement may be accompanied by a rating of the degree of confidence in the judgement or by a rating of the degree of familiarity with the item. Identification experiments, on the other hand, require listeners to name or label the item, e.g. 'that's an oboe', or 'that's intensity number 5'. In a certain sense, identification can be considered a more narrowly focused kind of recognition that involves access to a (perhaps hierarchically organized) lexicon of names. For example, imagine that you hear a familiar bebop trumpet player on the radio, and you know that you have heard this person playing often while you were in college, but the name of the person escapes you. We would certainly say that recognition has occurred. We could even say that certain degrees of recognition have taken place, since you have recognized the sound source as a trumpet, the music as jazz, probably as being of a particular period of bebop style, and even more specifically as being played by a person you listened to in college. It is only the last level of the classification hierarchy that has not given rise to lexical activation, i.e. the name of the musician.

The purpose of the present chapter is to examine aspects of auditory representations and the nature of the processes operating on them that result in the recognition of sound sources and events. For the purpose of illustration, the discussion will be primarily confined to musical instruments and a few simple, 'natural' acoustic events. Relatively little work has been done on systematically investigating the various stages of the recognition process in audition. Therefore, I am obliged to examine a number of experiments that were directed at other experimental issues in an attempt to glean, indirectly, information that will help us piece together a picture of non-verbal auditory recognition. While the purpose of this chapter is to examine auditory recognition in general, most of the experiments that have dealt directly with the recognition of musical instruments and natural sound events have been confined to identification experiments.

The structure of the rest of this chapter is as follows. First I will consider in abstract terms the stages of processing that may be imagined to contribute to recognition as conceived within the information processing approach and extract from this consideration a number of important issues that should be analysed. Next I will examine experimental data from the literature on perception and identification of musical instrument tones and natural acoustic events. These experiments variously involved asking listeners to discriminate between sounds, to judge the degree of similarity among them, to classify them, or to identify them by name or by an arbitrarily chosen label. The data obtained from these experiments will be used to complete a more concrete, if tentative, picture of the stages of auditory processing previously discussed in abstract terms. Finally, I will discuss the properties of a number of models of recognition drawn from the domains of nonverbal audition, speech, and visual form recognition and analyse them in terms of what they might contribute to further clarification of the process of auditory recognition.

6.1 STAGES OF PROCESSING IN AUDITORY RECOGNITION

The recognition process may be conceived as involving several hypothetical stages of auditory information processing. This conception is shown schematically in Fig. 6.1. Different models of recognition hypothesize different stages of processing (some of the ones in Fig. 6.1 being

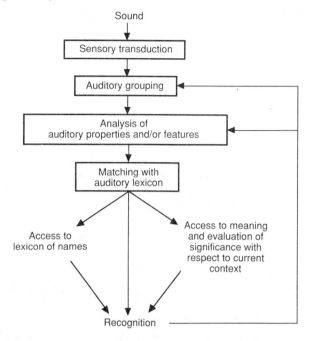

Fig. 6.1 Schematic diagram of the stages of processing involved in recognition and identification. The representation in flow-diagram form does not necessarily imply that the processing of each type is organized sequentially. Some models view things otherwise, as is discussed in the text. Further, some models regroup two or more 'types' of processing under one mechanism or bypass them altogether.

completely bypassed, for example). They also differ in the degrees to which the results of later stages feed back to influence the operation of earlier ones.

6.1.1   Peripheral auditory representation of the acoustic signal

The first stage is the 'raw' representation of the acoustic signal in the peripheral auditory nervous system (labelled *sensory transduction*) (cf. Aran *et al.* 1988; Pickles 1982; Roman 1992). This process involves the transmission of vibrational information to the cochlea in which the signal sets into motion different parts of the basilar membrane depending on its frequency content. Higher frequencies stimulate one part of the membrane and lower ones another part. The movement of the basilar membrane at each point is transduced into neural impulses that are sent through nerve fibres composing the auditory nerve to the brain. They then undergo a series of operations in the central auditory processing centres. Each nerve fibre encodes information about a relatively limited range of frequencies, so the acoustic frequency range is essentially mapped on to the basilar membrane and encoded in the array of aud- itory nerve fibres. This tonotopic mapping is to some extent preserved through all of the auditory processing centres up to cortex. At low in- tensity levels the band of frequencies encoded within a given fibre is very narrow. With increasing intensity, this band increases in extent. At very high intensities, the frequency selectivity of an individual fibre is rather broad. In spite of this change of frequency selectivity with intens- ity, the spectral (or frequency) aspects of a sound are thus represented in part by the degree of activity present in each nerve fibre. However, each fibre also encodes information about temporal characteristics of the in- coming waveform in its own frequency region by way of the detailed timing of neural impulses. As the part of the basilar membrane that is sensitive to a given frequency region moves, the pattern of activity in the population of nerve fibres connected to that part also fluctuates such that the nerve firings are to some degree time-locked to the stimulating wave- form. Taken together, these two general forms of encoding (average rate of activity and temporal fine-structure of the nerve firing pattern) ensure that the auditory system represents a large variety of acoustic properties. If we consider that the array of frequency-specific fibers represents a kind of spectral dimension and their average level of activity across dif- ferent populations of nerve fibres represents a kind of intensive dimen- sion, the ensemble of activity as it evolves through time can be thought of as a mean-rate neural spectrogram. The global pattern of spectral evolution encoded in the auditory nerve would be in part captured in this representation. Another possible visualization of the auditory rep- resentation would plot the evolution through time of the degree of synchrony among the neural impulse patterns of neighbouring fibres as a function of the frequency to which each group is most sensitive, result- ing in a kind of neural synchrony spectrogram. This representation would capture aspects of the temporal fine structure of the sound stimulus that are reliably encoded in the auditory nerve. Limitations in the spectral and temporal resolving power of the auditory transduction process in turn impose limits on the aspects of an acoustic waveform that are en- coded in the auditory nerve.

6.1.2   Auditory grouping processes

Bregman (Ch. 2, this volume) discusses principles according to which this array of time-varying activity is then believed to be processed in order to constitute separate auditory representations of the various sound sources present in the environment (labelled *auditory grouping* in Fig. 6.1). One principle that arises from work on auditory grouping is that the properties of a sound event cannot be analysed as such until its constituent components have been integrated as a group and segregated from those of other sound events. This principle represents the primitive (or 'bottom-up') processes that are primarily driven by an analysis of the incoming sensory information. One should not rule out, however, a possible contribution of schema-driven (or 'top-down') processes by way of which more familiar or well-known sound events (such as one's name) would be more easily separated from a noisy sound environment than less well-known events (represented by the feedback arrows in Fig. 6.1). Most experiments on perception of auditory qualities and on auditory recognition present isolated sounds to listeners. In such cases, this particular level of processing has little influence on the final result, though of course the situation is quite different in everyday listening.

6.1.3   Analysis of auditory properties and features

Once the sensory information has been grouped into representations of sound sources, a series of processes are engaged that, according to some theories of recognition, progressively analyse the perceptual features or properties that are relevant to listening activity at a given moment (labelled *analysis of auditory properties and/or features* in Fig. 6.1). This analysis process may extract information over both local (milliseconds to centiseconds) and global (centiseconds to a few seconds) time spans (subsequently referred to as micro- and macrotemporal properties).

The analysis of *microtemporal properties* would be concerned with simple sound events such as one plate sliding over, or striking, another plate, or like a single note of a musical instrument. These properties are determined by the nature of the resonant structure being set into vibration (resulting from the geometry and materials of the sound source), as well as by the means with which it is excited (sliding, striking, bowing, blowing, etc.). The resonance properties (such as those of a vibrating crystal glass or a violin string and body) generally give us information about the physical structure of the sound source itself and will later serve to allow us to identify it. This class of properties would be involved in the detection of what ecological psychologists call the *structural invariants* of a sound source, i.e. those aspects of the acoustic structure that are 'shared by objects that, at some level of description, can be considered the same' (Michaels and Carello 1981, p. 25). For example, a violin will often be identifiable as such whether it plays in the low or high register, whether it is plucked or bowed, whether it was made by Stradivarius or is a factory-made training instrument. It should be noted, however, that the exact cues concerning the properties that are present in the acoustic waveform are far from clearly delineated at this point, although some progress is being made as will be summarized in Section 6.3. Alternatively, a plucked string event (i.e. the way the string is excited) can be recognized whether it is a guitar, violin, harpsichord, or wash-tub bass. In the terminology of ecological psychology, this class of properties would involve a listener's detection of *transformational invariants*, i.e. those acoustic properties that specify what is happening to the sounding object. Each of these sets of properties remains constant in spite of variation in other properties. The role of psychological experimentation is to isolate the classes of invariants to which the listener is sensitive and to try to understand how the auditory system extracts and makes use of these invariants, at least in the case of the information processing framework.

The analysis of *macrotemporal properties* is concerned with the rhythmic and textural aspects of a whole environmental event that allow us to identify, for instance, a set of dinner plates sliding, tumbling, and crashing on the floor. The identification of a breaking event is interesting in that it involves a change in the resonant properties of the object in question, since its size and geometry are changed. It also involves a change in the number of sound sources. Here more than a single excitation of a plate is involved, since there is a whole series of frictional and impact events that have an identifiable macro-organization. These kinds of events are also identified on the basis of transformational invariants.

So structural invariants are those properties that specify the nature of the object or group of objects participating in an event, while transformational invariants are the patterns of change in the stimulus that specify the nature of the change occurring in or to the object. In Section 6.3 we will examine the nature of the micro- and macrotemporal properties that play a role in auditory recognition.

6.1.4 Matching auditory properties to memory representations

According to the diagram in Fig. 6.1, the initial auditory representation has, by this stage, been recoded as a group of abstract properties that characterize the invariants in the sound source or event (such as spectro-temporal structure of the onset of a musical tone, or the accelerating rhythmic pattern of a bouncing ball slowly coming to rest). This group of properties (which constitutes the input representation to the recognition process) is then matched to classes of similar sound sources and events in memory (labelled *matching with auditory lexicon* in Fig. 6.1). The stimulus is recognized as the class that gives the closest match to the auditory representation. Two kinds of matching process have been conceived and will be discussed in more detail in Section 6.4. Briefly, some researchers conceive of this matching as a *process of comparison* whereby the auditory feature representation is compared with stored memory representations and the most closely matching one is selected. Such a comparison process would be mediated by a kind of executive agency (homunculus) or mental algorithm that performs the comparison and then returns the result. In other conceptions, access to memory structures involves the *direct activation* of memory representations of sources and events that are sensitive to configurations of features in the perceptual representation. This latter mechanism has a certain elegance and computational economy in being able to avoid postulating an outside agent that must receive the analysed sensory data, search available memory while comparing the two, and then decide upon which bit of memory best corresponds to the sensory data. It also avoids having to postulate a memory 'storage' that is independent of the auditory processing elements (see Crowder, Ch. 5 this volume, for more on this proceduralist approach to memory). Recognition of the sound event is then determined by the memory representation that receives the highest degree of activation by the auditory representation and occurs when the memory representation achieves some threshold of activation. Memory representations of this sort are probably of a relatively abstract nature, i.e. you may never have heard this particular sound of breaking plates before but you recognized it as such anyway. For both the mediated and direct approaches, if no category is matched, or if too many categories are matched with about the same degree of fit, no recognition can occur.

6.1.5   Activation of the verbal lexicon and associated semantic structures

The selection or activation of an appropriate representation in memory may then be followed by the activation of items in the listener's lexicon of names, concepts, and meanings that are associated with that class of sound events. It would be at this point that identification would take place since the listener would then have access to the name of the sound source or event (e.g. a struck plate, a trotting horse). In the sound example described above, it would be the identification of ceramic objects and their behaviour: there were several of them, they were dinner plates, they slid and fell to the ground, knocking against one another on the way down, and broke on the hard surface, except for one that was heard turning at the end. Lexical activation gives access to associated knowledge about properties of the class as it relates to the perceiver and the local situation. These associations would allow the listener to plan appropriate action without having to verbalize what was heard. Children and animals can recognize sources and events (one might even say 'identify', in the sense of recognizing the identity of them), and act appropriately with respect to them without having mastered language skills. Once language is available, however, the recognition process also gives access to a verbal lexicon that allows the listener to name or describe the event verbally. At and beyond this stage, the processing is no longer purely auditory in nature.

6.1.6 Interactions between stages of processing

Information processing does not proceed uniquely from the bottom up, that is, from sensory transduction to recognition. For example, it seems likely that under certain conditions, knowledge of the form of a sound event can help with separating it from background noise. Everyone has had the experience of being in a noisy environment where it is difficult to understand what other people are saying, and yet to suddenly hear one's name emerge out of the din. Another anecdotal example experienced by many bilingual people is that the noise levels at which speech remains intelligible can be higher for one's mother tongue than for a second language; ingrained knowledge of one's mother tongue assists in recognizing words on the basis of partial information. These phenomena are examples of what Bregman (1990) calls schema-based processing in auditory organization, and they reflect influence from later stages of processing both on auditory grouping and on the analysis of auditory properties and features. One of the most clear-cut examples of top-down influence on phoneme recognition is the phonemic restoration illusion (Warren 1970). If a phoneme is cut out of a word and replaced with silence, interrupted speech is heard. If it is replaced with a burst of noise, listeners have the impression of having heard the missing phoneme 'behind' the noise. If one postulates a partial match of the available phonetic material plus the perceptual assumption that the missing material is truly there but has been masked, the restoration demonstrates a reconstructed analysis of perceptual elements that are completed on the basis of recognition. Other similar effects of this nature are well known in speech recognition (cf. Frauenfelder and Tyler 1987; Segui 1989).

6.2 IMPORTANT ISSUES IN AUDITORY RECOGNITION RESEARCH

Based on this speculative summary description of the recognition process, let us now isolate a few important issues that need to be considered. These concern the auditory input representations to the matching process, long-term memory representations of classes of sound sources and events, and the process by which the analysed auditory input is matched to these memory representations.

6.2.1 Auditory input representations

One of the most important problems concerns determining the nature of the auditory representation of sound stimuli at different stages of processing. At any given stage, the representation of sounds may be conceived as specific values or distributions along *continuous* dimensions in a multidimensional 'space' of auditory properties or they may be analysed into a configuration of *discrete* features or elements. Further, the representation may be transformed from continuous to discrete at some particular stage of processing. Some models of recognition postulate a transformation of continuous information into discrete features at a very early (preperceptual) stage. This featural representation would then be used to compare the current stimulus with the contents of long-term memory (Massaro 1987; McClelland and Elman 1986). In other models, the segmentation of the perceived source or event into parts or components occurs quite late in processing, i.e. the stimulus is categorized as a whole only at the point of recognition (Ashby and Perrin 1988; Braida 1991; Klatt 1989; Nosofsky 1986). It is equally important to determine the nature of the represented properties or features, i.e. the information in an acoustic signal that is necessary and sufficient for perception and recognition. And finally, we need to evaluate how these various descriptions capture the appropriate invariants in the acoustic structure so that it is correctly categorized.

6.2.2 Long-term memory representations

What is the functional form of representation of previous auditory experience in long-term memory? Some recognition models postulate abstract representations of categories in terms of rules (propositions), descriptions, or patterns (Massaro 1975, 1987; Klatt 1989; Marr 1982; McClelland and Elman 1986). These kinds of model often imply a separation between generic (abstract) and episodic (specific) memories. For other models, a more diffuse representation is hypothesized where categories are conceived as bounded regions in a continuous auditory-parameter space (Durlach and Braida 1969; Ashby and Perrin 1988; Miller 1982), or else categories are composed of a set of memory traces of individual episodes that are each specific instances of a given category (Hintzman 1986; Nosofsky 1986). These latter two may not be so different in form since the set of all points in a continuous space that are closer to a given exemplar than to other exemplars could also be considered to constitute a bounded region (cf. Braida 1991). The issue of the form of representation in memory is crucial since it could be argued to impose strong constraints on the sensory information that is useful in recognizing familiar sound events as well as new instances of a familiar class of sound events that have never been specifically encountered (e.g. a different oboe or words spoken by a person speaking with a foreign accent). Associated with this problem is the fact that sound sources remain recognizable despite enormous variability in the acoustic signals they produce, so it might be presumed that the forms of the memory representations used in recognition are isomorphic at some level of description with the stimulus invariants available to the auditory system.

6.2.3 Matching auditory to memory representations

What is the nature of the process by which newly formed auditory representations are matched to memory representations of previous experience? Is the matching of incoming sensory information with the contents of long-term memory performed by some specialized outside (executive) agent or by a process of direct activation by the contents of the information? What is the relation between the kinds of errors people make in recognition and identification tasks and the nature of the matching process? And how does the nature of this process give rise to the experience of differing degrees of familiarity and recognizability of sound events?

With these issues in mind let us now examine the available evidence concerning the perception and recognition of sound sources and events.

6.3   EXPERIMENTS ON PERCEPTION AND RECOGNITION OF SOUND SOURCES AND EVENTS

In this section, a number of experiments will be examined whose aim was to study perceptually relevant aspects of the auditory representation and identification of acoustic sources and events. The usefulness of the various potential cues for auditory recognition in general will then be considered.

Several kinds of sound sources and events have been studied in terms of the dimensions and features that contribute to their comparison and recognition. The ones that will be considered here include musical instruments (as an example of a class of sound *sources*) and complex acoustic *events* other than speech and musical sounds. Recognition of speech and speakers' voices will not be discussed since the emphasis of this book as a whole is on non-verbal audition, though some models of speech recognition will be included in Section 6.4. An introduction to the representation and identification of simple speech sounds and speakers' voices may be found in Handel (1989, Chs 8 and 9). Other areas of audition that have received much attention in both psychoacoustics and music psychology include pitch and rhythm perception and recognition.

It may be argued that both are as much meaningful 'events' (at least in music) as a musical instrument is a meaningful 'source'. These areas acquire additional interest by the fact that what listeners represent and compare mentally when listening to them are patterns of relations within a sequence (cf. Dowling and Harwood 1986; Sloboda 1985). Melodies and rhythms are thus extended auditory events of considerable complexity. However, aspects of their recognition are dealt with in other chapters in this volume (Warren, Ch. 3, Crowder, Ch. 5, Peretz, Ch. 7, and Trehub and Trainor, Ch. 9), so they will not be discussed here.

The process of non-verbal recognition in audition has not been systematically studied aside from a few studies on source or event identification. In order to evaluate the framework proposed in Section 6.2, therefore, we are obliged to consider research that has posed other experimental questions. As such, I will examine a number of different experimental tasks that are cogent to the present discussion and will then describe the results obtained with these tasks in listening to musical instrument tones and natural acoustic events.

6.3.1   Experimental tasks used to study source and event perception

Discrimination

Discrimination performance is measured for sounds that have been modified in some way to determine which modifications create significant perceptual effects. If no one was capable of hearing the difference between an original sound and a somewhat simplified version of that sound, we might conclude that the information that was removed from the sound was not represented in the auditory system, so there would be no sense in taking that level of detail into consideration in trying to explain auditory recognition. In one version of a discrimination task, listeners are presented with a pair of sounds that are identical or different in some way and are asked to decide whether they are the same or different. The experimenter varies the degree of difference between the two sounds in an attempt to understand the listener's sensitivity to the amount of change along a given stimulus dimension. Or the experimenter might make some kind of structural modification to a complex sound event in order to find out if the listener is sensitive to the modification when comparing it with the original sound. What this task is not good for is indicating a listener's perception of invariance in a class of stimuli, since the members of a class can each be discriminably different from one another, but would be treated as perceptually equivalent in some other kind of perceptual situation (such as listening to music or trying to understand what someone is saying or trying to detect a certain class of nuclear submarine on the basis of sonar signals). Some models do relate discrimination performance to identification performance in an explicit way, however, in the sense that sensitivity to change along a stimulus dimension can influence the way in which a listener categorizes the perceptual continuum (cf. Durlach and Braida 1969; Macmillan 1987; Rosen and Howell 1987).

Psychophysical rating scales

Unidimensional rating scales have been used in psychophysics since its inception by Fechner in the latter part of the 19th century (Fechner 1966). They have been particularly popular in attempting to describe the relation between physical quantities and perceptual values, such as the relation between sound intensity and loudness (cf. Thurstone 1927; Stevens 1956, 1957). In essence they may be considered to determine some psychological parameter that characterizes a given sensory continuum (Shepard 1981). Typically listeners are presented with a set of stimuli, one at a time, that vary along some analytic acoustic parameter (such as intensity) or along some more complex physical continuum (such as hardness of a percussion mallet). They are asked to rate each sound with respect to the continuum on some kind of numerical scale. The scale can be fixed (by comparison with a standard stimulus of predetermined value) or freely chosen by the subject. The experimenter then tries to establish the relation between the ratings (as a measure of perceived value) and some physical measure of the sound stimulus. If lawful relations of this kind can be established, the experimenter is in a position to make hypotheses about the auditory representation of the physical continuum being varied.

Similarity ratings

Similarity (or dissimilarity) ratings are used to discover the salient dimensions that underly the perceptual experience of a small set of sounds. A typical experiment involves presenting all possible pairs from a set of sound stimuli to a listener who is asked to rate how dissimilar they are on a given scale (say 1 to 8, where 1 means very similar and 8 means very dissimilar). In one variant of the analysis technique (called 'multidimensional scaling'; cf. Kruskal and Wish 1978; Schiffman *et al.* 1981), the ratings are then treated as psychological distances between the judged items and a computer program tries to map the distances on to a spatial configuration in a given number of dimensions. This mapping yields a geometrical structure that is interpreted as reflecting the perceptual qualities listeners used to compare the sounds, or, alternatively, as reflecting the structure of mental representations that allows them to make orderly comparisons. The interpretation of these structures is often focused on giving a psychoacoustic meaning to the spatial representation by relating the dimensions of the space to acoustical properties of the tones. What the structures may be considered to represent are the common *salient* dimensions to which listeners pay attention in the context of such an experiment. It is quite likely that the dimensions on which listeners do focus are determined by the set of sounds used in the experiment, i.e. their representations may be coded with respect to the stimulus context provided within an experimental session. In addition to giving us an idea of the auditory representations that listeners use in comparing sounds, these kinds of results can also contribute to an analysis of the processes underlying recognition when compared with identification tasks. A strong correlation has been demonstrated between similarity structures and the kinds of confusions people make among stimulus items in identification tasks (Shepard 1972; Grey 1977; Nosofsky 1986; Ashby and Perrin 1988), i.e. perceptual similarity and confusability are constrained by similar (or perhaps the same) limitations in the representation and comparison of auditory events. More recent techniques are beginning to refine this theoretical relation between similarity and identification within a signal detection framework (Braida 1991).

Matching

A matching task can be used to investigate recognition without requiring the listener to attach a verbal label to the sound source or event (Kendall 1986). A test stimulus is presented and then several comparison stimuli are presented, one of which is of the same class or category as the test stimulus. The listener is asked to say which of the comparison stimuli matches the test stimulus. The comparison stimuli may vary along perceptual dimensions that are irrelevant to the identity of the source or event being tested. This task would appear to be quite useful for answering questions about perceptual invariance within classes of stimuli as well as for investigating which aspects of the stimulus structure are used by listeners to effect an appropriate match. For example, the experimenter might perform various simplifying modifications on the test stimuli with respect to the (unmodified) comparison stimuli and estimate the degree to which such changes affect the listener's ability to make correct matches. As such, this task could give insight into the issues of both auditory and long-term memory representations and their comparison in the act of recognition.

Classification

A classification task consists of a listener being presented with a set of sound stimuli and being asked to sort them into classes on the basis of which ones go best together. A free classification task places no constraints on the number of classes, i.e. it is up to each listener to decide the appropriate number of classes and their contents. Some classification tasks may involve predefined (and named) classes within which the listener is to sort the sound events, this latter task being somewhat closer to an identification task. Based on the sorting results, the experimenter must then try to relate the class structure to properties of the stimuli, usually looking for structural similarities among stimuli that are classed together and differences among those that have been placed in separate classes. For the purposes of studying auditory recognition, these relations would indicate something about the properties that listeners use in organizing classes of sound sources and events in memory. While not a very refined technique, this experimental paradigm is easily performed by listeners and can help sketch out in rough detail the kinds of sound properties that are worth investigating more systematically.

Identification

In an identification experiment a set of sound stimuli is presented to listeners and they are asked to assign names or labels to them, one at a time. In free identification, listeners are required to draw upon whatever lexicon of names or descriptions they have acquired in their lives up to that point. More restricted identification tasks provide listeners with a list of labels for the items from which they are to choose (such as names of musical instruments, or arbitrary labels such as the numbers one to ten). Analysis of identification performance often proceeds by creating a confusion matrix in which the number of times a given item was called by a given name is recorded. This allows a detailed analysis of the confusions that listeners make among sound sources or events. Such confusions are informative about stimulus features that different items may share in their internal representations. In some studies, sound stimuli are modified in various ways and the degradation in their identification is measured as a function of the amount of modification. The main idea is that if an element in a sound is removed or is degraded too much, and that element is essential to the successful comparison of the sound with a representation in long-term memory, identification performance will deteriorate. A comparison between discrimination and identification experiments using similar stimuli is often fruitful for qualifying the utility of discrimination results for understanding recognition. The extent to which an event can be simplified without affecting identification performance is the extent to which the information is not used by the listener in the identification process, even if it is discriminable.

6.3.2 Musical instruments

A number of experiments have investigated the representation of auditory properties that distinguish the timbres of musical instrument sounds and allow listeners to identify them. In the discussion that follows the focus on timbre is not intended as a study of the perceptual quality for its own sake, but rather on its role as a perceptual vehicle for the identity of a particular class of sound sources. Musical instruments are good candidates for this kind of research since they have been thoroughly studied from the standpoints of both physical acoustics and experimental psychology (cf. Benade 1976; Leipp 1980; Barrière 1991). The search for the dimensions and features used in perception and recognition can be justified as a search for an economy of description of the stimulus and, ultimately, as an attempt to relate experimental data to models of perceptual processing. The focus in this section will be on the auditory cues listeners use to compare and identify acoustic and synthesized instrument tones. A discussion of the issues of memory representation and the matching process is deferred until Section 6.3.4.

Discrimination and identification studies

Experiments that have helped reveal the cues that are encoded in auditory representations of musical tones have studied the discrimination and identification of instrument tones that have been simplified in one way or another. One methodological issue in this kind of experiment concerns choosing the appropriate (i.e. auditory perceptual) conception of an 'element' or 'part'. While some of the studies described below have rather simplistic views of what constitutes an appropriate part of a sound event, to examine them will nevertheless be instructive.

The most simplistic of these approaches arbitrarily considers a musical sound event as composed of three parts: an attack (or onset) portion, a middle sustain (or relatively stable) portion, and a final decay (or offset) portion. Based on this conception of the sound event, manipulations involve removing or modifying various portions and determining whether any appreciable perceptual effects result. The modifications have been achieved either by cutting and splicing magnetic tape on to which sounds have been recorded (Saldanha and Corso 1964) or by editing them on a computer in digital form (Luce 1963; Kendall 1986), where the cuts and splices can be performed with much greater precision and run less risk of introducing discontinuities in the signal which would perturb listeners perceptions of them.

Saldanha and Corso (1964) investigated the identification of conventional musical instruments of the Western orchestra playing isolated tones both with and without vibrato. They sought to evaluate the relative importance, as cues in musical instrument identification, of onset and offset transients, spectral envelope of the sustain portion, and vibrato. Identification performance was surprisingly poor for some instruments even without modification, perhaps indicating that some of the information listeners normally use to identify instruments is accumulated across several tones. On the whole, however, Saldanha and Corso found that the attack and sustain portions were important for identification, i.e. performance decreased when these portions were removed, whereas cutting the decay portion had very little effect. The largest drop in performance occurred when the attack was cut out, leaving only the sustain portion. For tones with vibrato, on the other hand, the reduction was not as great with a cut attack as for tones with no vibrato. This result indicates that important information for instrument tone identification exists in the very first part of the sound event, but that in the absence of this information, additional information still exists in the sustain portion and is augmented slightly when a pattern of change that specifies the resonance structure of the source is present, as occurs with vibrato. McAdams and Rodet (1988) have shown that vibrato helps listeners extract information about the spectral envelope of synthesized vowel-like sounds. One might conclude that information in the tone that indicates how the instrument is set into vibration (i.e. the pattern of transients in the attack) contains the most important cues, followed by information concerning the global spectral structure that can be extracted during the sustain portion of a tone.

Another kind of simplification involves performing a fine-grained acoustic analysis of instrument tones and then resynthesizing them with modifications. Instruments from the string, woodwind, and brass families were employed. Grey and Moorer (1977) and Charbonneau (1981) presented listeners with different versions of each tone: the original recorded tones (Fig. 6.2(a)) and resynthesized versions of each one with various kinds of modifications. For each instrument, musician listeners were asked to discriminate among the versions and to rate how different they were. Charbonneau also used the rating scale to assess recognizability of the modified tones. These experiments showed that simplifying the pattern of variation of the amplitudes and frequencies of individual components in a complex sound (Fig. 6.2(b)) had an effect on discrimination for some instruments but not for others. Tones in which the attack transients were removed (Fig. 6.2(c)) were easily discriminated from the originals, confirming with greater precision the results from the cut-and-splice studies. Applying the same amplitude variation to all of the components (thus replacing the individual variations normally present; not shown in Fig. 6.2) grossly distorted the time-varying spectral envelope of the tone and was easily discriminated though it did not always adversely affect recognizability. Complete removal of frequency change during the tone (Fig. 6.2(d)) was also easily discriminated, although

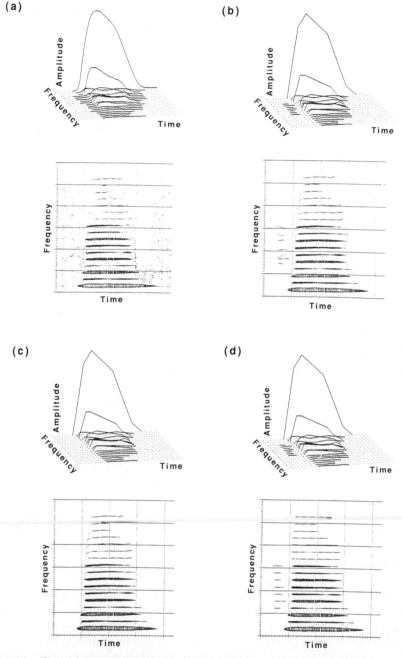

Fig. 6.2 Time–frequency perspective plots and spectrograms illustrating the modifications to a bass clarinet tone. The curves in the time–frequency plots represent the amplitude envelope for each frequency component. (a) The original tone. (b) Line-segment approximations of the amplitude and frequency variations. (c) Line-segment approximations with deletion of initial transients. (d) Line-segment approximations with flattening of the frequency variations. (From Figs 2, 3, 4, 5, Grey and Moorer (1977) pp. 457–8. © Acoustical Society of America, 1977. Reprinted with permission.)

applying a common frequency variation to all components (not shown) had only a weak effect on discriminability and none on recognizability. This latter result suggests that small modifications to the coherence of change among the frequencies of the components, while noticeable, do not much affect the identification of the instrument, which is more based on spectral structure and attack characteristics.

One difficulty in generalizing these results to everyday situations should be mentioned. All of the experiments described above employed isolated tones played at the same pitch, loudness, and duration. The temporal and spectral features of musical instrument tones change quite noticeably across pitch and loudness levels and so the features that contribute to identification of individual tones at one pitch and loudness may not be the same as those that contribute at another. In addition, the way an instrument's tones vary with pitch and loudness may be a strong cue in itself for recognition when listening to the instrument in a musical context. Two studies have investigated discrimination and recognition of modified instrument tones within musical contexts.

Grey (1978) used the kind of simplified tones shown in Fig. 6.2(b) for three instruments (bassoon, trumpet, and clarinet). He created notes at other pitches by transposing the instrument spectrum to higher or lower frequencies. He then asked listeners to discriminate the simplifications of a given instrument for either isolated tones or the same tones placed in musical patterns that differed in the number of simultaneous melodic lines, rhythmic variety, and temporal density. An effect of musical context would thus be measured as a difference in discrimination performance among the conditions. An increasingly complex musical context did not affect discrimination between original and modified versions of the bassoon, but hindered such discrimination for the clarinet and trumpet. An acoustic analysis of the bassoon tone showed that the simplification involved a change in the spectral envelope, which was not the case for the other instruments. Changes for the bassoon were described by listeners as differences in 'brightness' or 'high frequencies' which seem to be related to the spectral envelope, while those for the clarinet and trumpet were in 'attack' or 'articulation'. It seems that small spectral differences were slightly enhanced in single-voice contexts compared with isolated tones and multi-voiced contexts, though discrimination remained high. Articulation differences, on the other hand, were increasingly disregarded as the complexity and density of the context increased. These results suggest that in cases where demands on perceptual organization and the storing and processing of sequential patterns are increased, fine-grained temporal differences are not preserved as well as spectral differences. Since such differences are not used for discrimination in musical contexts, it seems unlikely that they would be available to the recognition process.

One possible confounding factor in Grey's (1978) study is the fact that the different pitches were created by transposing a single tone's spectrum and then concatenating and superimposing these tones to create the musical patterns. This removes any normal variation of spectral envelope with pitch as well as any articulation features that would be involved with passing from one note to another in a melody. Kendall (1986) controlled for these problems in an experiment in which the tone modifications were of the digital cut-and-splice variety. In his experiment, listeners heard two different melodies played in legato (connected) fashion. The first one was an edited version of the melody played by one of three instruments (clarinet, trumpet, or violin). The second melody was then played in unedited form by each of the three instruments in random order. Listeners had to decide which of the instruments playing the second melody matched the one playing the first melody. Several kinds of modifications were presented: normal tones, sustain portion only (cut attacks and decays), transients only (with either a silent gap in the sustain portion, or an artificially stabilized sustain portion). The results suggest that transients in isolated notes provide information for instrument recognition when alone or coupled with a natural sustain portion, but are of little value when coupled to a static sustain part. They are also of less value in continuous musical phrases where the information present in the sustain portion (most probably related to the spectral envelope) is more important. This conclusion confirms that of Grey (1978) with a recognition task and stimuli that include more realistic variations.

From these studies of the effects of musical context on discrimination and recognition we can conclude that the primacy of attack and legato transients found in all of the studies on isolated tones is greatly reduced in whole phrases (particularly slurred ones). The spectral envelope information present in the longer segments of the sustain portion is thus of greater importance in contexts where temporal demands on processing are increased.

A caveat on the interpretation of studies in which attack and decay transients are excised should be mentioned. The cutting out of an attack is quite simplistic in its conception of an instrument tone's morphology. It does not really remove an attack altogether; it replaces the original attack with another one. The new attack may be considered strong perceptual evidence *against* the instrument in question and so a reduction in identifiability is not surprising. This phenomenon may be related, to some extent, to that of phonemic restoration (Warren 1970). When a phoneme is removed and replaced by silence the word is less well identified than when the silence is replaced by a noise burst of appropriate spectral composition, i.e. the noise could have masked the phoneme were it actually present. Silence in this case is strong evidence against the phoneme, since abrupt stops and starts in the signal are encountered.

The masking noise burst is only weak evidence against the phoneme since the phoneme might, in fact, still be present. It is possible that different results might be obtained in the musical tone studies mentioned above, if similar procedures were used. Having a wrong attack (i.e. the cut attack) plus the right sustain may give lower identification performance than having a (potentially) masked attack plus the right sustain. In the latter case, the auditory recognition process, not being confronted with contradictory evidence, would be able to make better use of the sustain portion of the sound in making a partial match to the memory representation for the tone.

Multidimensional scaling studies

Several studies have performed multidimensional scaling analyses on dissimilarity ratings for musical instrument tones or synthesized tones with characteristics that resemble those of musical instruments (Plomp 1970, 1976; Wedin and Goude 1972; Wessel 1973; Miller and Carterette 1975; Grey 1977; Krumhansl 1989). In all of these studies, the perceptual axes have been related either qualitatively or quantitatively to acoustic properties of the tones as will be described below.

Grey (1977) recorded, digitized, and then analysed tones from 16 instruments played with equal pitch, loudness, and subjective duration. Listeners then rated the dissimilarities for all pairs of tones. Grey settled on a three-dimensional structure as capturing the greatest amount of the variation in the data structure while not having so many dimensions as to make the structure difficult to interpret. The final perceptual structure is shown in Fig. 6.3.

Grey qualitatively related the axes to acoustic properties in the following way. The first dimension represents the spectral energy distribution in the sound (or its spectral envelope) and is primarily a spectral dimension. This can be thought of as representing the degree of 'brightness' of the sound quality (Wessel 1979). Instruments with low brightness are the French horn and the cello played *sul tasto* (a technique of bowing over the fingerboard that gives a soft, velvety kind of sound). Instruments with high brightness include the oboe as well as the trombone played with a mute (which gives it a strident quality). The difference in brightness is illustrated by comparing the instrument spectrograms or frequency–time perspective plots of FH (French horn) and TM (trombone, muted) in Figs 6.4 and 6.5. Note primarily the difference in number of harmonics. The second dimension is related to a combination of the degree of fluctuation in the spectral envelope over the duration of the tone and the synchrony of onset of the different harmonics. This is a spectro-temporal dimension that has been called 'spectral flux' by Krumhansl (1989). Instruments with high synchronicity and low fluctuation include

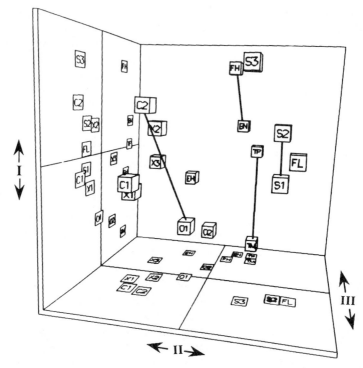

Fig. 6.3 Three-dimensional scaling solution for 16 musical instrument tones equated for pitch, loudness, and perceived duration. Two-dimensional projections of the configuration appear on the wall and floor. Abbreviations for the instruments: 01 and 02, two different oboes; C1 and C2, E♭ and bass clarinets; X1, X2, and X3, saxophones playing softly and moderately loud, and soprano saxophone, respectively; EH, English horn; FH, French horn; S1, S2, and S3, cello playing with three different bowing styles: *sul tasto, normale, sul ponticello*; TP, trumpet; TM, muted trombone; FL, flute; BN, bassoon. Dimension I (top–bottom) represents spectral envelope or brightness (brighter sounds at the bottom). Dimension II (left–right) represents spectral flux (greater flux to the right). Dimension III (front–back) represents degree of presence of attack transients (more transients at the front). Lines connect pairs of timbres that were modified by Grey and Gordon (1978) (see text and Fig. 6.6). (From Fig. 3, Grey and Gordon (1978) p. 1496. © Acoustical Society of America, 1978. Adapted with permission.)

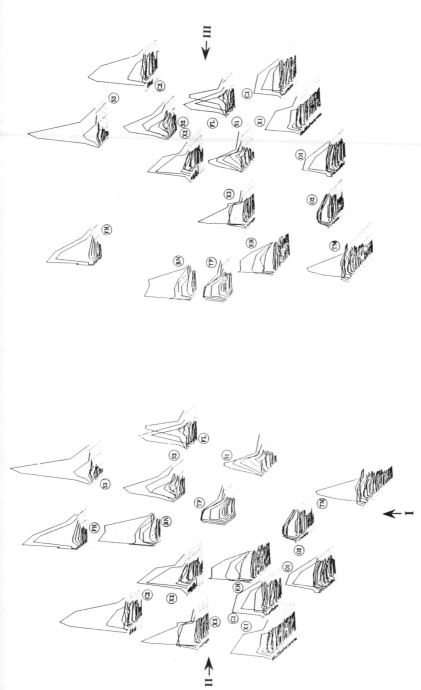

Fig. 6.4 Two-dimensional projections of the three-dimensional solution in Fig. 6.3 on to the dimension-I–dimension-II plane (left) and the dimension-I–dimension-III plane (right). The circle with the abbreviation for the instrument name (see Fig. 6.3 caption) indicates the position in the plane. Next to each label is the time-frequency perspective plot for that instrument tone. (From Fig. 2, Grey (1977) p. 1273. © Acoustical Society of America, 1977. Adapted with permission.)

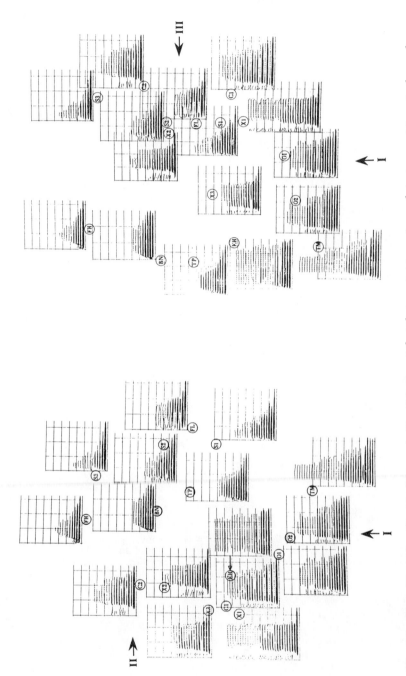

Fig. 6.5 Two-dimensional projections as in Fig. 6.4, except that the spectrogram for each instrument tone is shown here. (From Fig. 3, Grey (1977) p. 1274. © Acoustical Society of America, 1977. Adapted with permission.)

clarinet and saxophone whose harmonics start, stop, and fluctuate together in amplitude. Instruments with low synchronicity and high fluctuation include the flute and cello. The brass (trumpet, trombone, French horn) and double reed (oboe, English horn, bassoon) instruments are somewhere in the middle. The difference in flux is illustrated in Fig. 6.4 by comparing X1 (saxophone) and FL (Flute). Note the relative homogeneity of the envelopes for X1, whereas those for FL are quite varied. The third dimension represents the relative presence of inharmonic transients in the high frequencies just before the onset of the main harmonic portion of the tone. This dimension might be called the 'attack quality' dimension. It is primarily temporal in that the temporal position is crucial, as is the relative lack of periodicity in the transient waveform. Instruments that rate high on this dimension include the strings, flute and single reeds (clarinet, saxophone), whereas the brass, bassoon and English horn have lower ratings. The difference in attack quality is illustrated by comparing EH (English horn) and C1 (E♭ clarinet) in Fig. 6.5 (right). Note the absence of preliminary transients for EH and their abundance in C1. Grey found that there was a strong degree of correspondence among listeners' ratings in this study as well as across two sets of judgements on the same set of stimuli, indicating that the mental representation of the set of timbres is relatively stable and more or less shared by the listeners. He also found a very high correlation between the matrix of similarity judgements and the matrix of confusion errors listeners made when asked to identify the sounds, thus indicating the utility of examining similarity rating studies for developing an understanding of the auditory representations that contribute to recognition processes.

Another study, conducted by Grey and Gordon (1978), hypothesized that since the perceptual dimensions seem closely correlated with acoustic properties, modifying the acoustic properties for a single perceptual dimension in systematic ways ought to cause changes of the position of a given tone along that dimension. To test this hypothesis, they selected four pairs of tones from among the original 16 and exchanged their spectral envelopes, trying to leave the other properties as intact as possible. They then reinserted the modified tones into a multidimensional scaling study with the other eight unmodified tones. The results demonstrate that in all cases the tones exchanged places along the brightness dimension, though in some cases displacements along other dimensions also occurred (compare the connected pairs of instruments in Figs 6.3 and 6.6). These displacements still respected the nature of the perceptual dimensions— envelope changes that also modified the way in which the spectral envelope varied with time for a given tone resulted in appropriate changes along the dimension of spectral flux.

One may question the validity of the assumption that extremely complex sounds like those corresponding to musical instrument tones really differ

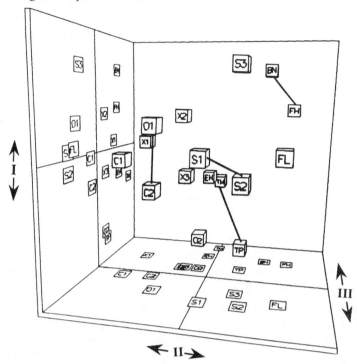

Fig. 6.6   Three-dimensional spatial solution for 16 instrument tones, four pairs of which swapped spectral envelopes. These pairs are connected by lines. Dimensions and abbreviations are described in Fig. 6.3. (From Fig. 2, Grey and Gordon (1978) p. 1496. © Acoustical Society of America, 1978. Adapted with permission.)

in terms of only a few underlying (or common) perceptual dimensions. Each timbre may also have unique characteristics that are not easily coded along continuous dimensions, such as the returning bump of the hopper on a harpsichord, the odd-harmonic structure of the clarinet spectrum, or the 'blatt' of a trombone attack, and so on. This possibility is evidenced by a certain degree of variability in the similarity data from the early scaling studies on timbre which is not accounted for by their scaling solutions. Krumhansl *et al.* (1988) used a set of 'instruments' created by digital sound synthesis (Wessel *et al.* 1987) in which many of the sounds imitated those of musical instruments, while others were intended to simulate hybrids of instruments, e.g. the 'vibrone' is a cross between vibraphone and trombone. A multidimensional scaling analysis technique developed by Winsberg and Carroll (1989*a,b*) was used which, in addition to uncovering the common perceptual dimensions shared by the tones, would allow for specific dimensions or features that applied only to individual timbres. The three-dimensional solution was remarkably similar to those found in previous studies. Within these common dimensions the hybrid instruments were almost always situated somewhere between their two imagined progenitors. Further, the analysis of specificities showed that a significant amount of variability in the similarity judgements, not attributable to the common dimensions, could be accounted for by postulating unique features for some of the instruments, such as harp, harpsichord, clarinet, and vibraphone. Further acoustic and perceptual analyses will be needed to relate these specific features to the acoustic and perceptual properties of the individual instrument tones, but this technique seems promising for tagging sounds that have special perceptual features that may in turn contribute significantly to identification performance. That such is the case is suggested by the studies of Strong and Clark (1967*a*,*b*) who found that the unique spectral envelope of some instruments (such as clarinet and trumpet) contributed more to identification than the amplitude envelope. However, when the amplitude envelope was unique (as in trombone and flute), it had a greater importance. Therefore, listeners appeared to use whatever characteristic was likely to specify the instrument with the least ambiguity and were not constrained to listening for a single cue across all possible sources.

Summary of studies on musical instruments

A number of characteristics of instrument tones presented in isolation seem to be used for their discrimination (Grey and Moorer 1977; Charbonneau 1981). These include, in decreasing order of importance, information present in the attack portion, information concerning the spectral envelope and its evolution through time extracted during the sustain portion, and the presence of small, random variations in the component frequencies. Other characteristics were only weakly discriminable at best, including the degree of coherence in frequency variation on the components, the degree to which the amplitude and frequency variations were simplified (though this was more discriminable for some instruments than for others), and small variations in the temporal pattern of onsets of the frequency components. When similar kinds of tones were placed in musical contexts of various degrees of complexity, temporally based cues seemed to lose importance for discrimination in favour of more spectrally based cues (Grey 1978; Kendall 1986).

Multidimensional scaling studies revealed the importance of spectral envelope distribution, attack character, and spectral evolution in comparisons of the degree of similarity among tones (Grey 1977; Krumhansl 1989), though the perceptual dimensions found to be important are probably quite sensitive to differences in the set of sound events presented to listeners (cf. Miller and Carterette 1975; Plomp 1976). Further analyses have revealed that some tones may possess unique features or dimensions, though the acoustic and perceptual nature of these specificities remain to be determined (Krumhansl 1989; Winsberg and Carroll 1989a,b).

Identification studies have shown a strong inverse correlation with similarity ratings (tones judged as being similar are more often confused in labelling tasks (Grey 1977)). Such studies have also confirmed the importance of the attack portion of the sound event as well as the patterns of change in the sustain portion that signal the nature of the spectral envelope. They showed that the decay portion of the tone contributes relatively little to an instrument's identity on the basis of an isolated tone (Saldanha and Corso 1964). Other studies confirm the importance of spectral envelope and temporal patterns of change for identification of modified instrument tones (Strong and Clark 1967a,b).

6.3.3   Natural acoustic events other than speech and musical sounds

A large class of sounds that is only beginning to be studied, primarily because the ability to synthesize and control them has been severely limited by the available techniques, is comprised of the complex acoustic events of our everyday environment. What often distinguishes many of these sounds is the complexity of their spectral and temporal structure on the scale of the microproperties seen in connection with musical instrument tones, as well as the complexity of their temporal structure on a larger time scale. The breaking plates example discussed in the introduction demonstrates how the textural and rhythmic evolution over the entire event specifies both the nature of the sources involved as well as the interactions among them that give rise to the global event. Below I will review four studies on the perception and recognition of such complex events, two concerning brief events and two concerning more complicated event structures.

Freed (1990) studied listeners' abilities to rate on a unidimensional scale the relative hardness of a mallet striking metal pans of four different sizes. Each pan was struck with six mallets differing in hardness (metal, wood, rubber, cloth-covered wood, felt, felt-covered rubber). He performed acoustic analyses and extracted four abstract 'timbral predictor' parameters that were derived from a simulated peripheral auditory representation of the acoustic signal. These predictors included measures of overall energy, spectral distribution, rate of spectral evolution, and rate of decay of the event. Listeners' ratings increased with mallet hardness and were completely independent of the kind of pan being struck. Since the sounds contain information both about the nature of the pan (the resonator) and the nature of the mallet (the exciter), it appears that listeners are able to abstract the nature of the mallet alone from the combined acoustic information. The timbral predictors selected by Freed were reasonably well correlated with the mallet hardness ratings. However, while the subjective ratings were independent of the pan type, the timbral predictors varied as a function of both the pan and the mallet type, indicating that they did not succeed in extracting psychoacoustic invariants that specified *only* the mallet. A great deal of research remains to be done on the invariant cues that allow listeners to separately characterize and recognize resonators and their sources of excitation.

Repp (1987) studied the sound of two hands clapping. He was primarily interested in what the spectral information in a hand clap contributed to the identification of both the clapper and the configuration of the clapping hands. He recorded 20 people clapping individually and analysed acoustically the spectral structure of each person's average clap. He performed a data reduction analysis on the individual clap spectra and attempted to recover the principal spectral features that describe the ensemble of analysed claps. The main idea was that if these features exhaustively described all of the claps, each clap should be constructable by mixing together the main features with differing weights, e.g. 50 per cent of feature 1 + 20 per cent of feature 2 + 5 per cent of feature 3 + 25 per cent of feature 4. Another person with another hand configuration would have different weights. It is then the task of the analyst to determine the physical origins of each feature. Unfortunately, as is often the case with this kind of analysis, it is not completely clear what physical properties underly each component. Analysis of various hand configurations produced by the author (Fig. 6.7) suggested that about half the variation in spectral features can be specifically associated with hand configuration, e.g. a low-frequency peak seems to be associated with a palm-to-palm resonance and a mid-frequency peak appears to be associated with a palm-to-finger resonance. Others factors such as hand curvature, fleshiness of palms and fingers, and striking force may also contribute to the variation in spectral features across clappers, but were not specifically analysed in this study.

Listeners had all participated as clappers and knew one another. They were asked to identify the clapper from a list of participants, including themselves. Overall identification of specific individuals was quite poor though people recognized their own claps better than those of their colleagues. From these identifications Repp looked to see if there was any consistency among listeners for identifying a clapper as male or female. They were quite consistent at assigning a male or female person to a given clap, but the judgements showed no relation whatever to the actual sex of the clapper. There seem to be certain features that are used by people to evaluate sex. For example, series of claps that were faster, softer, and had higher resonance frequencies were more often judged as being produced by females. Rather than actually representing perception

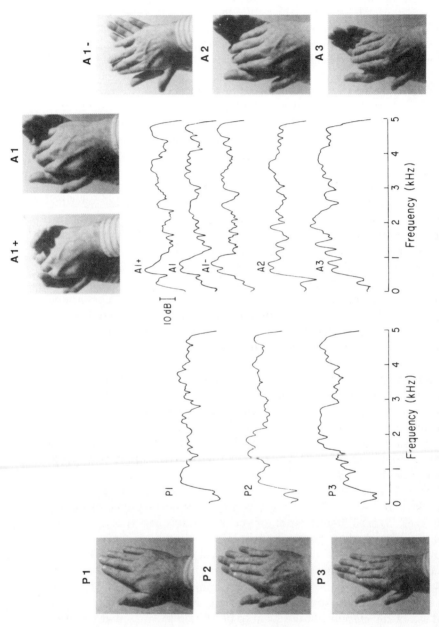

Fig 6.7 Photographs of hand-clapping configurations and their averaged, normalized spectra. (From Figs 3, 4, Repp (1987) pp. 1103–4. © Acoustical Society of America, 1987. Adapted with permission.)

of maleness and femaleness of claps, these results may more reflect certain auditory cultural stereotypes people have about how males and females clap. This result nevertheless suggests that certain classes of acoustic characteristics are associated, in the listener's memory, with gender characteristics. When asked to identify claps in terms of hand configuration, listeners were quite good at the task when all of the claps were performed by the same person. Repp concluded that sound emanating from a source conveys perceptible spectral information about the configuration of that source which the listener can then use to recognize or identify the configuration. However, when the 20 original clappers were intermixed, the configuration was difficult to recover, which weakens this conclusion and indicates that acoustic information specifying hand configuration is not invariant across clappers.

Warren and Verbrugge (1984) conducted an experiment in which listeners were asked to classify sound events as representing either 'bouncing' or 'breaking' glass objects or as events that did not correspond to either class. They were particularly interested in the importance of time-varying properties of sound patterns in specifying mechanical events in the world. In the first experiment, stimuli consisted of recordings of glass jars falling from various heights on to a hard surface. Several features distinguished the bouncing and breaking events: bouncing events are specified by simple sets of resonances which have the same accelerating rhythm pattern, and breaking events are specified by several sets of different resonances with different rhythmic patterns. In the bouncing event, each impact sets the entire bottle or jar into vibration and the different vibration modes are heard as resonances that decay rapidly until they are restimulated by the next impact. This spectral structure stays relatively constant across the several impacts. The rhythm of the impacts is a kind of irregular but accelerating pattern (called damping) where the impacts follow closer and closer together and decrease in amplitude as the object is pulled to rest by gravity. In the breaking event, a noise burst is present at the beginning which corresponds to the initial rupturing of the object. Then a series of overlapping, independent accelerating rhythms are heard which correspond to each piece of the broken object bouncing and coming to rest. The broken pieces do not have as much resilience and so come to rest more quickly which gives a much shorter total duration to the breaking than to the bouncing event. The spectrum for a breaking event also covers a wider range of frequencies. Results for these recorded natural sounds showed a 99 per cent correct classification of the original bouncing and breaking events.

In another experiment, synthetically reconstructed sound events were derived from the recordings. In the artificial events, the rhythm pattern over the course of the event was modified. These artificial sounds were designed to control for effects of duration and width of the frequency spectrum present in the natural sounds. In other words, Warren and Verbrugge (1984) wanted to test for the importance of the global rhythmic pattern in identification, by keeping the spectral and temporal microproperties constant across conditions. Four broken pieces were individually dropped and their bouncing behaviour was recorded. They were then digitally combined such that their successive impacts were either synchronous, following the same rhythmic pattern to simulate bouncing, or completely independent, to simulate breaking. Results for these constructed sequences showed an 89 per cent correct identification of the predicted categories based on the rhythmic behaviour. A single damped sequence with all resonances on each impact was heard as bouncing since there was a spectral invariance across the impacts as well as an appropriate damping behaviour. Overlapping damped sequences at different rates with different resonances on each sequence were heard as a breaking event due to the rhythmic diversity in the overall pattern. In some additional demonstrations, Warren and Verbrugge showed that a single resonance in a natural bounce sequence (i.e. with accelerating rhythm) but without the normal decreasing amplitude pattern was still heard as bouncing since the appropriate rhythmic pattern was combined with an invariant spectral structure. Also, a periodic sequence with all resonances heard on each event, but which did not accelerate, was not heard as bouncing in spite of a decreasing amplitude pattern, since this sequence did not reproduce the appropriate rhythm. These results demonstrate that combined spectral and temporal patterning provides the information necessary to distinguish between the two event categories.

Van Derveer (1979) studied the free identification and classification of a series of complex acoustic events such as shuffling cards, jingling keys, knocking, and sawing. In the free identification task, listeners most often named mechanical events and only reported abstract perceptual qualities when they could not recognize the source. In the classification task, the events were clustered into categories such as repetitive, percussive sounds (hammering, knocking), crackling sounds (crumpling or tearing paper, shuffling cards), or clinking sounds (glasses struck together, a spoon striking porcelain). When these classification judgments were combined with confusion errors in the identification task, they showed grouping by temporal patterns and spectral content. Confusions were made primarily within classes and only rarely occurred across classes, e.g. hammering might be confused with knocking (lower frequency sounds with a regular rhythm), but rarely with jingling (higher frequencies with an irregular rhythm). According to Handel (1989, Ch. 8), it would seem most natural to refer to sounds by the object and mechanical event that produce them, which suggests the possibility that listeners judged the similarity of the actions that produced the sounds (presumably on the basis of transformational invariants). This hypothesis would seem, however, to ignore the fact that the groups could also be partially interpreted with respect to the acoustic properties of the materials involved (i.e. structural invariants), which would certainly entail differences in the constraints on spectral and temporal behaviour, e.g. pounding or grating on wood, shuffling, tearing and crumpling paper, jingling metal, striking glass or ceramic. The question of whether these phenomena truly demonstrate a direct auditory perception of the physical cause of the event, or a more likely post-auditory semantic reconstruction based on recognizable acoustic characteristics of the source materials and knowledge of the ways they are excited, cannot be answered within the experimental framework of this study.

In summary, it seems clear that the way complex sound events are produced gives rise to spectral and spectro-temporal properties (Repp 1987; Freed 1990) as well as more global patterns of change (Van Derveer 1979; Warren and Verbrugge 1984) that are used by the auditory system in the process of acoustic event recognition. What remains to be elucidated are the precise cues used for various sound sources and the way they are used in various sound contexts. It is also important to conduct more systematic research on the way the auditory system is capable of independently extracting cues that specify the resonators or exciters that are involved in mechanical sound-producing events (cf. Huggins 1952). Recent progress in the development of physical models for digital sound synthesis should provide the necessary tools and impetus to carry this important work forward.[2]

6.3.4 Discussion of the experimental evidence

Auditory representations

From the set of studies that we have looked at, we can summarize some of the acoustic properties that appear to be useful for the auditory comparison and recognition of sound sources and events. It should be kept in mind that, according to the information-processing approach adopted here, the discussion of *useful* acoustic properties implies that they are somehow successfully represented in the auditory system, at least to the level of input to the matching process. Two large classes of properties can be distinguished: microproperties and macroproperties, though the boundary between the two remains a bit fuzzy. The two classes are primarily distinguished by the rates at which things occur.

Microproperties would be extracted over relatively short time periods

---

2. For more information on digital sound synthesis using physical models see Adrien (1991), Florens and Cadoz (1991), Cadoz (1992) as well as a forthcoming special issue (in preparation) of the *Computer Music Journal* on 'Physical models of instruments'.

(tens to hundreds of milliseconds) corresponding to a single percussive or continuous excitation of a resonant body. *Spectral microproperties* define the shape of the spectrum at given points in time (or the average shape over a short time period). They include the form of the spectral envelope (related to general resonance properties of the sound source) as well as the frequency content of the spectrum (harmonic, inharmonic, noise: related both to the nature of the exciter and to the relations between the modes of vibration of the object). All of these microproperties have been shown to contribute to sound source comparison and identification in the studies described above. *Temporal microproperties* concern the variation over time of the amplitude or frequency of the sound or of the spectrum as a whole. They include ongoing fine-grained temporal characteristics (related to rapid amplitude and frequency modulations that give rise to perceptions of roughness and jitter or vibrato), the form of the amplitude envelope (related to articulation style and onset rate), and the presence of low-amplitude, inharmonic transients at the beginning of an event which are due to non-linear behaviour of the vibrating object as it is set into motion and before it settles into a stabilized oscillatory behaviour. *Spectro-temporal microproperties* describe the change in shape of the spectrum over time. They include the pattern of onsets of frequency components in a sound event (synchrony of onsets), and fluctuations in the spectral envelope during the course of a sound event. The relative importance of the various cues has been shown to depend on the stimulus context. Much more work is needed to refine our knowledge of the degree to which these different cues are necessary and sufficient for recognition and of *how* the local stimulus context might influence their necessity and sufficiency. For example, the change in relevance of temporal and spectral cues when musical instruments must be discriminated and recognized on the basis of single tones or full melodies suggests that reliable sensory information accumulated over time is based more on spectral than on temporal cues, although this depends on the instrument being studied . It may also be, as suggested by the ecological position, that reliable detection of stimulus invariants requires variation in irrelevant cues so that the listener can detect what does not change.

Macroproperties would be extracted over longer periods of time (hundreds of milliseconds to a few seconds) corresponding to multiple stimulations of the sound sources participating in the event as in bouncing, knocking, jingling, and so forth. *Temporal patterning macroproperties* represent the rhythmic and textural structure of an extended event and are related either to the gesture by which an object (or a group of objects) is set into vibration, or to changes in the state of integrity of an object (such as a breaking plate or glass jar). *Spectral variation macroproperties* have been found to correspond to the nature of the material being stimulated as well as to the transformations of its geometry. They would include the presence of temporally co-ordinated resonances or, conversely, the diverse unco-ordinated resonances that indicate the presence of multiple sources (e.g. a single bouncing jar versus several jar pieces bouncing independently).

The experimental data on identification confusions among musical instrument tones suggest that a continuous dimensional representation is in general more appropriate than a discrete featural representation. Salient common dimensions that have been shown to be used in comparing instrument timbres and which are highly correlated with data on confusions among timbres include brightness, attack quality, and spectral flux. Furthermore, results from experiments that treated tones as consisting of parts (attack, sustain, decay) can most likely be explained in terms of these dimensions. On the other hand, the new techniques of specificity analysis for similarity data (Winsberg and Carroll, 1989a,b) may require us to refine this position since they may allow us to isolate unique properties in order to conduct further experimentation to determine whether they are continuous or featural. For example, the spectral envelope is a continuously varying (multiple) 'dimension', whereas properties like the 'bump' of the hopper on the harpsichord may be featural within the context of musical instrument recognition, since the 'bump' is either present or absent (cf. Garner 1978). Once their featural or dimensional status has been established, the extent to which such features contribute to recognition remains to be determined. For the moment, though, models that are based on continuous representation would seem to be sufficient to explain the majority of the available experimental evidence.

The application of the notion of continuous dimensions to more complex sound events such as bouncing bottles and jingling keys may also be appropriate. These events can be characterized in part by their macrotemporal patterning, i.e. rhythmic and textural patterns. It seems clear that the application of discrete features to such patterns would be quite difficult. What remain to be determined in greater detail are the nature of the dimensions of representation underlying these patterns and the characteristics which allow listeners to distinctly classify them.

Long-term memory representations

The importance of continuous dimensions in auditory representation suggests their prominence in the representation of sound events in long-term memory as well. The strong correlation between perceived similarity and identification errors found by Grey (1977) supports this notion. It seems intuitively obvious that the more similar two sounds are, the more likely it should be for them to be confused with one another. These results would argue in support of models of recognition that explicate the relation between stimulus similarity and identification errors for stimuli represented along continuous dimensions.

Studies of stimulus modifications such as cutting out bits of sound (Saldanha and Corso 1964; Kendall 1986), simplifying amplitude and frequency behavior on harmonic components (Grey and Moorer 1977; Grey 1978), filtering (Pollack *et al.* 1954), or changing aspects of the resonance structure of a sound source (Kuwabara and Ohgushi 1987) have shown that identification performance degrades progressively over a certain range of variation in these parameters. That performance degradation is progressive rather than abrupt could either reflect the fact that categories have large, fuzzy boundaries or indicate that a large number of cues contribute to identity. It also suggests that if an individual characteristic does not match in the comparison between an auditory and a memory representation, a certain degree of identifiability is maintained by other properties, which would support Handel's (1989, Ch. 8) suggestion that recognition is supported by the accumulation and comparison of multiple cues.

The positive effect of frequency modulation (vibrato) on identification performance in the absence of attack transients (Saldanha and Corso 1964; McAdams and Rodet 1988) as well as the predominance of spectral cues in musical contexts provides evidence that dynamic musical instrument tones may give rise to a representation of the resonance structure that is accumulated over time and then represented as an abstract form in memory. Categories derived from spectral envelopes are ubiquitous in speech (see work on vowels by Macmillan *et al.* 1988) and have also been shown to contribute to the identification of hand configuration in clapping (Repp 1987).

Residual acoustic information following removal or simplification of fine-grained variations in different acoustic parameters (Grey and Moorer 1977; Charbonneau 1981) has been shown to have a lesser or greater degree of impact on identification performance depending on the property that was modified. This further supports the idea that event representation in audition involves abstraction since not all of the detail is preserved. Conversely, since many of these variations can be discriminated, indicating that the detail remains present at least to a level of processing that allows comparison (and, for example, judgement of quality of playing style, Grey and Moorer 1977), it may be that abstraction takes place at the moment of retrieval. For complex sound events, such as those produced by bouncing and breaking objects, there seem to be prototypic spectral and temporal properties (or transformational invariants) that characterize a class of sound events, such as the unitary accelerating rhythm and invariant spectral structure that specifies bouncing and the multiple accelerating rhythms, each with different spectral structures, that specify breaking. These spectro-temporal forms would need to be generalized over a large variety of bouncing rates, degrees of irregularity in the rhythm, and spectral characteristics of the fallen object or the newly created pieces if the object breaks. More systematic research is needed to clarify the nature of the transformational invariants that listeners are able to detect and the form in which they are represented in long-term memory.

The matching process

None of the experiments reported above give a clear indication of the nature of the matching process itself. Work on speech and visual form recognition has approached this problem and will be discussed briefly in Section 6.4. A couple of issues specific to non-verbal audition are raised, however.

Experiments on the multidimensional scaling of judged similarities among instrument tones have usually settled on two- or three-dimensional solutions as adequately describing the data. Intuitively this number of dimensions would seem to be quite small compared with the number of ways the tones can differ. One possible reason for this observed limit is that in making comparisons between successively presented tones, listeners are capable of using (or paying attention to) only a limited number of dimensions at a time. In experimental situations where a large number of stimuli are to be compared, certain dimensions or features may acquire a higher psychological weight that subsequently influences the pattern of similarity judgments. This conclusion is supported by the work of Braida (1988) on identification of multidimensional vibrotactile stimuli in which it was shown that when two dimensions must both be identified, sensitivity for a given stimulus dimension is generally reduced. This reduction in sensitivity is partially responsible for the fact that multidimensional stimuli do not tend to transmit as much information as performance for the individual dimensions would suggest. Another possibility is that the limitation in the number of dimensions that can be taken into account by a listener is not in the degree of detail with which the stimuli are encoded but in the extraction of a longer-term representation of distinguishing properties of the entire set of stimuli. One wonders to what extent this latter limitation may also reflect constraints on the process by which auditory representations are matched with memory representations. If the limitation is due to the matching process itself rather than to the auditory analysis process, it would follow that under some conditions not all the features or dimensions encoded in a category's long-term representation can be activated at any given time, i.e. that there are limits in the parallel matching of the multiple auditory cues that specify the sound source or event. However, the fact that listeners' similarity judgements can be better explained by positing specific dimensions or features attached to individual stimulus items in addition to the common dimensions (Krumhansl 1989; Winsberg and Carroll, 1989*a,b*), suggests that these limitations are perhaps at least partially methodological and that the encoding and matching processes are perhaps not the bottleneck. Unfortunately, no recognition or identification data have been collected on stimuli for which the specificities have been analysed in order to determine the role they might play in such tasks.

With this summary of experimental evidence pertaining to auditory recognition in mind, let us now examine a few models of the recognition process.

6.4 SURVEY OF RELEVANT RECOGNITION MODELS

A number of models have been developed by researchers in cognitive psychology which simulate the processes of acoustic dimension or feature analysis, similarity evaluation, categorization, recognition, and identification. They derive from work in intensity perception, speech, visual form perception, and vibrotactile perception. These models embody to varying degrees the stages of processing outlined in Section 6.1 and implement them in different ways. I will briefly describe the main characteristics of these models in terms of the main issues in non-verbal auditory recognition and will attempt to evaluate their relevance for the experimental data presented above.

6.4.1 Perceptual representations

The primary factors that distinguish the way different models simulate the internal perceptual representations prior to matching with memory are

(1) the degree to which the peripheral sensory representation is further analysed into elementary dimensions, properties, or features, and

(2) the degree to which the internal representation of the stimulus is continuous or discrete.

The design issues underlying these factors involve the search for an economical encoding of stimulus information in a form that captures the appropriate invariants.

In Klatt's (1979, 1989) speech recognition model, the only level of auditory representation is the neural spectrogram encoded in the auditory nerve (see Section 6.1.1). This model postulates a representation based on short-term spectra that describe the relative energy present at a given moment distributed across different frequency bands (see Fig. 6.8). Sequences of these templates are considered to adequately represent important phonetic transitions in the fine structure of the stimulus without

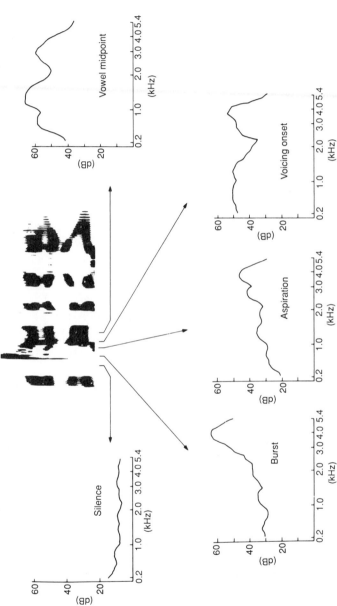

Fig. 6.8 A spectrogram of a speech sample is shown in the upper centre of the figure. A sequence of five static spectra, as represented in the auditory system, approximate the phonetic transition from the middle of the consonant /t/ to the middle of the vowel /a/. At a higher level of the auditory system these spectra would be matched to a series of spectral templates that would recognize the word containing /ta/. (From Fig. 7, Klatt (1989) p. 193. © MIT Press, 1989. Reprinted with permission.)

(a)

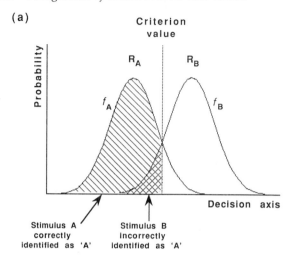

(b)

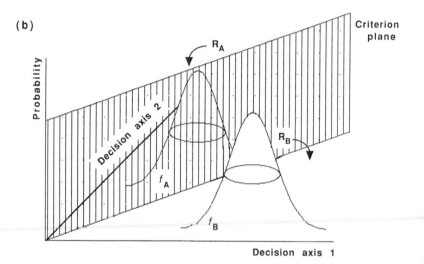

Fig. 6.9 Schematic illustrations of the representations of two categories in a statistical decision model. According to this class of models, stimuli A and B each give rise to a perceptual representation which is a random decision variable. The probability that a stimulus be represented by a given internal value on the decision axis (or axes) is represented by a probability density function, f_A or f_B. The form of this distribution depends on a number of sensory and cognitive factors, depending on the model. The single peak in the function indicates that the perceptual effects of a given stimulus tend to group around a single value. In an identification task, an optimal criterion point is chosen (by the subject) to maximize the likelihood of correctly choosing the appropriate category. This criterion point divides the decision axis into response regions, R_A and R_B. The degree of perceived similarity and confusability is conditioned by the degree of overlap of

imposing a segmentation into discrete features at any stage prior to accessing the lexicon of available words in the listener's memory. The advantage claimed for this representation is that information contained in the fine structure of the stimulus known to be useful in word recognition is not discarded too early in the processing chain. It is unclear, however, what auditory process would have to be postulated to adequately 'sample' the incoming sensory information, since more templates would need to be extracted during consonants (where the spectrum changes rapidly) than during sustained vowels (where the spectrum changes more slowly). If such a model were to be applied to non-verbal stimuli, similar questions would arise. How is the auditory system to be provoked into extracting more templates during attack, transition, and dynamically varying sustain periods than during relatively stable periods?

Some models postulate a continuously valued representation of the stimulus that, if multidimensional, is analysed into separable cues corresponding to the relevant dimensions of stimulus variation (such as angle and size of geometric forms or the frequencies of the first two formants for vowels, etc.). This representation along continuous dimensions can either be deterministic with respect to the stimulus (Nosofsky 1986; Nosofsky *et al.* 1989) or probabilistic (Durlach and Braida 1969; Ashby and Perrin 1988; Braida and Durlach 1988). The probabilistic representation is due in part to the introduction of noise in the sensory transduction process. Instead of a given physical stimulus value being encoded as a single value in the sensory system on all occurrences, it is encoded with a certain degree of variability that is modelled as a random process, e.g. as a Gaussian (bell-shaped) probability density function which describes the probability that a given physical value gets encoded as a given sensory value (see, for example, the function f_A in Fig. 6.9; the representation is unidimensional in (a) and two dimensional in (b)). All perceptual decisions are then performed with respect to this noisy representation. The original model of Durlach and Braida was unidimensional, modelling identification of arbitrarily defined intensity categories that are learned by listeners through feedback concerning correct responses. Subsequent

---

the distributions. (a) Example of two categories for stimuli that vary along a single dimension. The area under the curve f_A to the left of the dotted criterion line represents the probability that stimulus A will result in the response 'A'. The area under curve f_B to the left of the criterion line represents the probability that stimulus B will result in the incorrect response 'A'. (b) Example of two categories for stimuli that vary along two dimensions. The optimal criterion in this case is defined by a planar surface passing between the two peaks. (From Figs 1, 5, Ashby and Perrin (1988) pp. 128, 134. © American Psychological Association, Inc., 1988. Adapted with permission.)

versions have been extended to model the identification of more naturally categorized stimuli with multiple auditory cues, such as vowels and
consonants (Macmillan *et al.* 1988), as well as the identification of consonants from multimodal (auditory, visual lip-reading, vibrotactile)
stimulation (Braida 1991). The visual form recognition models of Nosofsky
et al. (1989) and Ashby and Perrin (1988) are also multidimensional. While
the models treat the dimensions as essentially independent, i.e. they are
represented as being orthogonal in a multidimensional space, it is not
clear to what extent each dimension is initially analysed separately and
then integrated, or whether the stimulus is simply represented as a
multidimensional unit from the start. This question has been explicitly
addressed by Braida (1988) in work on the identification of three-
dimensional vibrotactile stimuli, which has shown that multidimensional
identification performance can be less than the sum of identification
performance as measured for each dimension individually. This implies
limitations of the perceptual representation, memory representation, or
the matching process. His work on multimodal consonant identification
demonstrated that a model that integrates sensory information prior to
assigning a category label better predicts identification performance than
a model that derives a label for each sensory modality and then tries to
integrate the decisions (Braida 1991). It remains to be seen whether such
a model can be successfully applied to the recognition of acoustic sources
and events, though its apparent generality is promising. For example, the
multidimensional version could easily be applied to similarity and recognition data for musical instrument tones.

   Another class of models proposes that the sensory input is analysed
into a number of discrete features that are then integrated prior to matching with memorized categories. In the spoken-word recognition model of
McClelland and Elman (1986), sub-phonetic features, phonemes, and
words are represented as nodes in a pseudo-neural (connectionist) network. Auditory preprocessing results in appropriate nodes being activated according to the presence of given features. The outputs of these
feature nodes converge on phoneme nodes at a higher level of the network, and the phoneme nodes subsequently converge on word nodes.
The activation spreads from lower to higher levels according to the degree of converging activity at each level. So if all the features that signal
the phoneme /b/ are present, they would all be active and this activation would converge on the node for /b/. An additional feature of this
network provides for mutual inhibition of nodes at the same level of
representation, e.g. if a /b/ is stimulated, it inhibits the /d/ and /g/
nodes, phonemes that share similar features. A different kind of feature-
processing architecture is proposed in the (multimodal) speech recognition model of Massaro (1987). In this model, features are assigned a value
according to their relative strength of presence (or according to the

degree to which the sensory information specifies their presence). The resulting 'fuzzy' truth values vary between 0 and 1 in the model rather than simply being labelled as present (1) or absent (0) (hence the label 'fuzzy logical model of perception'). These values are used to calculate the probability that a configuration of features specifies a given syllable in the lexicon (the unit of analysis being the syllable rather than a whole word in this model, for reasons that are supported by experimental research, cf. Massaro 1975; Segui 1989; Segui *et al.* 1990). So for both of these models, primitive features are extracted in some way at relatively early stages and are the unit of auditory representation (either as nodes in a neural network or as strength values in a logical propositional system). In both cases the strength of each feature is also represented (as degree of activation for McClelland and Elman or as a fuzzy truth value for Massaro).

Given the current state of knowledge of non-verbal auditory recognition, the models that have the greatest intuitive appeal are those that maintain some kind of multidimensional continuous representation of the stimulus information until relatively late stages of processing. This is suggested, for example, by the continuous nature of the perceptual dimensions revealed for musical instrument tones as well as the reasonable correspondence between this continuous representation of interstimulus relations and identification errors. However, a mixed model combining continuous common dimensions and discrete unique features for certain stimulus items may turn out to be the most valid simulation of a psychological representation of musical instrument tones, for example (Winsberg and Carroll 1989*a,b*). More systematic research is needed to critically analyse the relative contributions of different characteristics of each of these models to the recognition process as a whole.

6.4.2 Memory representations

The models examined above tend to fall into three basic classes with respect to the way stimulus categories are represented in long-term memory. For the sake of simplicity, these will be referred to as categorized continua, connectionist networks, and propositional descriptions, though any given model may have features that correspond to aspects of more than one of these classes.

Categorized continuum models posit the existence of a continuous auditory representation of the stimulus along one or more dimensions (Nosofsky 1986; Ashby and Perrin 1988; Braida and Durlach 1988). Category boundaries are in some way established along these continuous dimensions dividing the representational space into regions. A stimulus is categorized according to the region within which its auditory representation falls. Categories are defined by the subject according to how the

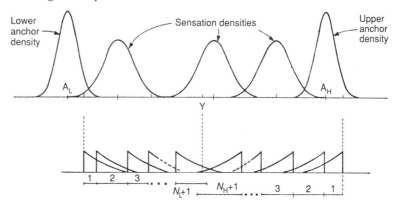

Fig. 6.10 Schematic diagram of the context-coding mechanism of Braida and Durlach (1988). In the upper part of the diagram, the noisy memory representation for the sensations produced by stimuli as well as the perceptual anchors used to categorize them are shown. The sensation Y is encoded by measuring its position relative to the noisy anchors A_L and A_H using a 'ruler' whose step sizes are also noisy. The ruler is illustrated in the lower part of the diagram. The steps are represented as exponentially distributed random variables. The distances of Y from the anchors, A_L and A_H, are measured, and the likely position of Y is estimated by the number of (noisy) steps from each anchor (N_L and N_H). (From Fig. 4, Braida and Durlach (1988) p. 565. © Neurosciences Research Foundation, Inc., 1988. Reprinted with permission.)

stimuli cluster in the space, i.e. subjects try to optimize the placement of category boundaries such that clusters of stimulus representations fall inside the boundaries. Nosofsky (1986) hypothesizes that episodic memory traces of individual experiences of a category can be represented as points in multidimensional space. Multiple exemplars of the same category tend to cluster together in the representational space. The relative weights of the individual dimensions can be varied by selective attending to one or more dimensions in order to maximize correct categorization of the stimuli. In the case of the 'optimal processing' models (Ashby and Perrin 1988; Braida and Durlach 1988), the stimulus representation is probabilistic and the subject must therefore try to optimize category boundaries so as to decrease the likelihood of identification errors given that the representations of stimuli with neighbouring values along one or more dimensions may overlap (see Fig. 6.9). The Braida and Durlach model proposes a context-coding memory mode in which listeners establish perceptual anchors along a given dimension and use these to help define and remember the category boundaries (see Fig. 6.10). In the case of identification of arbitrary categories along the intensity dimension, two anchors are placed just outside the range of intensities presented. For natural categories such as phonemes, different kinds of memory strategies seem to be used, i.e. the anchors are placed at category *boundaries* for vowels and at the *centre* (or prototypical value) of the category for consonants (Macmillan *et al.* 1988). This latter result indicates that different strategies for encoding category boundaries may be used for different classes of stimuli. In the model, a number of factors have been shown to influence the representation of the category boundaries and, consequently, identification performance. Increases in stimulus range result in decreases in identification performance due to increased noise in the encoding of category boundaries that are further away from the perceptual anchors. Variations in the frequency of occurrence of the stimulus categories during an experiment result in shifts in category boundaries to take advantage of higher probabilities of occurrence of members of some categories. The episodic clustering and probability density function representations may not be that different, functionally, since in a formal sense both define bounded regions in a perceptual space.

The connectionist model of McClelland and Elman (1986) represents categories in the network as nodes upon which inputs from the configurations of features that compose them converge. These nodes correspond to phonemes and words. In the model of Klatt (1989), nodes consist of spectral templates organized into sequential networks. A given node is connected backward to nodes for spectra that are expected to precede it and forward to nodes for spectra that are expected to follow it. Specific sequences of such nodes represent words in all their possible acoustic–phonetic variations. As a listener encounters new pronunciations of a word, new elements can be added locally in the sequence decoding network to account for the new variations. As such the network explicitly enumerates all the possible spectral sequences for all possible word combinations of a given language.

Propositional description models represent stimuli as logical propositions concerning the conjunction of features that compose any given category. In the 'fuzzy logical model of perception' (Massaro 1987), the logical terms are the probability of presence (or strength) of a given subphonemic feature (such as voicing—which distinguishes /d/ from /t/— or tongue placement—which distinguishes among /b/, /d/, and /g/, etc.). These are then integrated and the configuration is compared with the proposition for a given syllable, e.g. syllable /ba/ is voiced, has labial rather than dental or velar placement at the beginning of the event, and so on. So syllables are represented as configurations of fuzzy truth values for the individual features that compose them.

Compared with the experimental evidence for auditory recognition of non-verbal sources and events, the models that seem most directly applicable are those proposing categorized continua, primarily because no experimental work has addressed the existence of discrete perceptual features in non-verbal sound events. Even the claim of purely discrete features as the basis for categorical perception of speech phonemes is the object of serious criticism (Macmillan 1987; Massaro 1987). However, the paucity of experimental data from appropriately conceived experiments does not allow us to rule out an eventual role of other types of model at this point.

6.4.3   The matching process

The kinds of matching processes specified or implied by the models discussed above depend strongly on the sensory and memory representations postulated. They may be classed according to whether matching takes place by activation of memory traces or nodes, by the evaluation of the 'goodness-of-fit' between sensory and memory representations, or by a statistical decision process that evaluates the probability of a given sensory representation falling within appropriate category boundaries.

McClelland and Elman's (1986) model is a trace activation model. Klatt's (1989) model can also be formalized in these terms since spectral template nodes activated in an appropriate sequence represent particular words in the lexicon. In a trace activation model, the sensory representation nodes send a wave of activation to configurations of nodes that represent categories in memory. The most highly activated node or sequence of nodes results in recognition of that category (a word in both models). As with lower levels in McClelland and Elman's model, an activated category inhibits other categories according to its degree of activation, i.e. an activated word inhibits its potential competitors for recognition. As such, if sensory information is degraded and several candidates in the lexicon are moderately or weakly activated, ambiguity of recognition results and errors may occur. In the same manner, if several category items are similar in structure, sharing many lower level features, their levels of activation will be similar and errors may also occur.

Massaro (1987) uses a goodness-of-fit measure to compare the auditory representation with a stored prototype description. The fuzzy truth values of all the features composing a syllable are multiplied and normalized to give its goodness-of-fit score. The syllable with the highest score is the one recognized. As in the trace activation models, syllables that share similar feature configurations are more likely to be confused since their goodness-of-fit scores would be comparable. The Klatt (1989) model could also be formalized in terms of goodness-of-fit. According to his conception of the matching process, the input auditory spectra are compared with all available spectral templates using a spectral distance metric. This metric measures how similar the input is to a given template. The spectral template that has the smallest distance score best matches the input spectrum. High scoring templates can subsequently be reduced in number according to whether they satisfy the sequencing constraints that represent allowable phonetic transitions and, ultimately, the best-fitting sequence in the lexicon will give rise to the recognized word.

The 'optimal processing' models (Ashby and Perrin 1988; Braida and Durlach 1988) hypothesize a statistical decision making process that estimates the category within which the sensory information falls. As mentioned in the previous section, an optimal placement of the boundaries would minimize the identification-error rate. For Ashby and Perrin, since the stimulus representation is a multidimensional probability density function, the degree of overlap of the distributions, for stimuli that are adjacent in the space, gives a measure of how similar they are and how probable confusion errors between the two are. So a given analysed sensory representation is compared with the available category boundaries and categorized accordingly. Identification errors result from imprecision in the sensory representation or from biases in the estimation of optimal boundary placement. For Braida and Durlach, the stimulus representation is similar, but the matching process is a bit different. For unidimensional stimuli, category boundaries are remembered with respect to perceptual anchors that are just beyond the end-points of the stimulus continuum. Presuming a stimulus continuum comprised of equally spaced values (such as intensity values every 5 dB across the range from 40 to 90 dB, for example), matching consists of 'measuring' the distance of the sensory representation from the nearest anchor point with a somewhat noisy 'ruler', the units of which are the category boundaries. The further the to-be-identified value is from an anchor point, the noisier its distance measurement is, and thus the greater the probability that it will be incorrectly identified as some neighbouring category (see Fig. 6.10). What this aspect of the model captures is the part of the identification error that is due to the matching process, which is combined in a complete analysis with the error due to stimulus encoding as well as with the error that accumulates in the auditory representation in working memory as the memory trace of the stimulus decays.

6.5   CONCLUSIONS

In reviewing the few studies that have been conducted on the processes of non-verbal auditory recognition and identification, it becomes clear that much remains to be done in the realms of both experimentation and modelling, even just to bring auditory research to the same level of development as research on visual shape recognition. This is particularly true for work concerning memory representations and the matching process involved in non-verbal auditory recognition. The field is certainly wide open and, given the new possibilities of digital signal analysis and synthesis, should see fruitful growth in the years to come.

We have seen that the acoustic micro- and macroproperties to which listeners are sensitive seem to be primarily continuous in nature with the possible exception of a number of unique features that may be represented in discrete fashion. More research on the exact nature of the acoustic cues that are necessary and sufficient for auditory recognition is needed. This work must address the fact that the cues uniquely specifying a given sound source may be quite different from one source to another, as was demonstrated in the work on musical instruments. Further, the utility of these cues can vary a great deal depending on the stimulus context within which recognition takes place. An important experimental question concerns determining how the context modulates the auditory representation that serves as input to the recognition process.

The prominence of continuous auditory representations and the close relation of similarity and identification studies suggest at least some form of fine-grained information encoded in the long-term representation of auditory categories. Furthermore, results that indicate the accumulation of information used for recognition over time and over stimulus variation (dynamic sustained portions of sound events that help define the resonance structure of sound sources, multi-note musical contexts, etc.) suggest the importance of determining the nature of the physical invariants that may also be accumulated in long-term memory over repeated exposure to such sound sources.

Conclusions concerning the matching process can only be speculative at this point given the lack of experimentation directed at this question. Among the more pressing issues might be cited the problem of determining how the matching process constrains the types of recognition error that are made and which cannot be completely accounted for by imprecision in the auditory representation of stimuli or in the long-term memory representation. The analytic approach of Braida and colleagues, who succeed in decomposing the various contributions to identification error (cf. Braida and Durlach 1988), seems the most fully developed at present and presents an interesting framework within which to begin testing hypotheses that are addressed more specifically to the process of auditory recognition of sound sources and events.

ACKNOWLEDGEMENTS

This chapter benefited from the insightful remarks of four *ad hoc* referees, including S. Handel, B. H. Repp, and E. D. Schubert, as well as the students of the fourth (anonymous) reviewer. Comments by E. Bigand, M.-C. Botte, L. D. Braida, A. de Cheveigné, E. F. Clarke, W. M. Hartmann, A. Gorea, J. Grose, J. Segui, and M. Stroppa are also greatly appreciated.

REFERENCES

Adrien, J.-M. (1991). The missing link: modal synthesis. In *Representations of musical signals* (ed. G. De Poli, A. Piccialli, and C. Roads), pp. 269–98. MIT Press, Cambridge, MA.

Anderson, J. R. (1985). *Cognitive psychology and its implications.* Freeman, New York.

Aran, J.-M., Dancer, A., Dolmazon, J.-M., Pujol, R., and Tran Ba Huy, P. (1988). *Physiologie de la cochlée.* INSERM/EMI, Paris.

Ashby, F. G. and Perrin, N. A. (1988). Toward a unified theory of similarity and recognition. *Psychological Review,* **95**, 124–50.

Barrière, J.-B. (ed.) (1991). *Le timbre : métaphores pour la composition.* Christian Bourgois, Paris.

Benade, A. H. (1976). *Fundamentals of musical acoustics.* Oxford University Press.

Braida, L. D. (1988). Development of a model for multidimensional identification experiments. *Journal of the Acoustical Society of America,* **84**, S142(A).

Braida, L. D. (1991). Crossmodal integration in the identification of consonant segments. *Quarterly Journal of Experimental Psychology,* **43A**, 647–77.

Braida, L. D. and Durlach, N. I. (1988). Peripheral and central factors in intensity perception. In *Auditory function: neurobiological bases of hearing* (ed. G. M. Edelman, W. E. Gall, and W. M. Cohen), pp. 559–83. Wiley, New York.

Bregman, A. S. (1990). *Auditory scene analysis: the perceptual organization of sound.* MIT, Cambridge, MA.

Cadoz, C. (ed.) (1992). *Modèles physiques : création musicale et ordinateur.* Collection Recherche, Musique et Danse, Vol. 7, 8, 9. Maison des Sciences de l'Homme, Paris.

Charbonneau, G. R. (1981). Timbre and the perceptual effects of three types of data reduction. *Computer Music Journal,* **5**, 10–19.

Dowling, W. J. and Harwood, D. L. (1986). *Music cognition.* Academic, Orlando, FL.

Durlach, N. I. and Braida, L. D. (1969). Intensity perception. I. Preliminary theory of intensity resolution. *Journal of the Acoustical Society of America,* **46**, 372–83.

Fechner, G. T. (1966). *Elements of psychophysics* (transl. from German, *Elemente der Psychophysik,* Vol. 1, Breitkopf und Härtel, Leipzig, 1860). Holt, Rinehart and Winston, New York.

Florens, J.-L. and Cadoz, C. (1991). The physical model: modeling and simulating the instrumental universe. In *Representations of musical signals* (ed. G. De Poli, A. Piccialli, and C. Roads), pp. 227–68. MIT Press, Cambridge, MA.

Frauenfelder, U. H. (1991). Une introduction aux modèles de reconnaissance des mots parlés. In *La reconnaissance des mots dans les différentes modalités sensorielles: Etudes de psycholinguistique cognitive* (ed. R. Kolinsky, J. Morais, and J. Segui), pp. 7–36. Presses Universitaires de France, Paris.

Frauenfelder, U. H. and Tyler, L. K. (1987). The process of spoken word recognition: an introduction. *Cognition,* **25**, 1–20.

Freed, D. (1990). Auditory correlates of perceived mallet hardness for a set of recorded percussive sound events. *Journal of the Acoustical Society of America,* **87**, 311–22.

Garner, W. R. (1978). Aspects of a stimulus: features, dimensions, and configurations. In *Cognition and categorization* (ed. E. Rosch and B. B. Lloyd), pp. 99–133. Erlbaum, Hillsdale, NJ.

Gibson, J. J. (1966). *The senses considered as perceptual systems.* Houghton-Mifflin, Boston.

Gibson, J. J. (1979). *The ecological approach to visual perception.* Houghton-Mifflin, Boston. (Republished by Erlbaum, Hillsdale, NJ, 1986).

Grey, J. M. (1977). Multidimensional perceptual scaling of musical timbres. *Journal of the Acoustical Society of America,* **61,** 1270–7.

Grey, J. M. (1978). Timbre discrimination in musical patterns. *Journal of the Acoustical Society of America,* **64,** 467–72.

Grey, J. M. and Gordon, J. W. (1978). Perceptual effects of spectral modifications on musical timbres. *Journal of the Acoustical Society of America,* **63,** 1493–500.

Grey, J. M. and Moorer, J. A. (1977). Perceptual evaluations of synthesized musical instrument tones. *Journal of the Acoustical Society of America,* **62,** 454–62.

Handel, S. (1989). *Listening: an introduction to the perception of auditory events.* MIT Press, Cambridge, MA.

Hintzman, D. L. (1986). 'Schema abstraction' in a multiple-trace memory model. *Psychological Review,* **93,** 411–28.

Huggins, W. H. (1952). A phase principal for complex-frequency analysis and its implications in auditory theory. *Journal of the Acoustical Society of America,* **24,** 582–9.

Kendall, R. A. (1986). The role of acoustic signal partitions in listener categorization of musical phrases. *Music Perception,* **4,** 185–214.

Klatt, D. H. (1979). Speech perception: a model of acoustic–phonetic analysis and lexical access. *Journal of Phonetics,* **7,** 279–312.

Klatt, D. H. (1989). Review of selected models of speech perception. In *Lexical representation and process* (ed. W. D. Marslen-Wilson), pp. 169–226. MIT Press, Cambridge, MA.

Krumhansl, C. L. (1989). Why is musical timbre so hard to understand? In *Structure and perception of electroacoustic sound and music* (ed. S. Nielzen and O. Olsson), (Excerpta Medica 846), pp. 43–53. Elsevier, Amsterdam.

Krumhansl, C. L., Wessel, D. L., and Winsberg, S. (1988). Multidimensional scaling with specificity analysis for 21 synthesized tones from a Yamaha TX802 FM Tone Generator. Unpublished data. IRCAM, Paris [reported in Krumhansl (1989)].

Kruskal, J. B. and Wish, M. (1978). *Multidimensional scaling* Sage, Beverly Hills, CA.

Kuwabara, H. and Ohgushi, K. (1987). Contributions of vocal tract resonant frequencies and bandwidths to the personal perception of speech. *Acustica,* **63,** 120–8.

Leipp, E. (1980). *Acoustique et musique,* 3rd edn. Masson, Paris.

Lindsay, P. H. and Norman, D. A. (1977). *Human information processing: an introduction to psychology,* 2nd edn. Academic, New York.

Luce, D. (1963). *Physical correlates of nonpercussive musical instrument tones.* Ph.D. thesis, Massachussetts Institute of Technology. Cambridge, MA.

McAdams, S. and Rodet, X. (1988). The role of FM-induced AM in dynamic spectral profile analysis. In *Basic issues in hearing* (ed. H. Duifhuis, J. W. Horst, and H. P. Wit), pp. 359–69. Academic, London.

McClelland, J. L. and Elman, J. L. (1986). The TRACE model of speech perception. *Cognitive Psychology,* **18,** 1–86.

Macmillan, N. A. (1987). Beyond the categorical/continuous distinction: a psychophysical approach to processing modes. In *Categorical perception* (ed. S. Harnad), pp. 53–87. Cambridge University Press, New York.

Macmillan, N. A., Goldberg, R. F., and Braida, L. D. (1988). Resolution for speech sounds: basic sensitivity and context memory on vowel and consonant continua. *Journal of the Acoustical Society of America*, **84**, 1262–80.

Marr, D. (1982). *Vision*. Freeman, San Francisco.

Massaro, D. W. (1975). Language and information processing. In *Understanding language* (ed. D. W. Massaro), pp. 3–28. Academic, New York.

Massaro, D. W. (1987). *Speech perception by ear and eye: a paradigm for psychological inquiry*. Erlbaum, Hillsdale, NJ.

Michaels, C. F. and Carello, C. (1981). *Direct perception*. Prentice-Hall, Englewood Cliffs, NJ.

Miller, J. D. (1982). Auditory-perceptual approaches to phonetic perception. *Journal of the Acoustical Society of America*, **71**, S112(A).

Miller, J. R. and Carterette, E. C. (1975). Perceptual space for musical structures. *Journal of the Acoustical Society of America*, **58**, 711–20.

Nosofsky, R. M. (1986). Attention, similarity and the identification–categorization relationship. *Journal of Experimental Psychology: General*, **115**, 39–57.

Nosofsky, R. M., Clark, S. E., and Shin, H. J. (1989). Rules and exemplars in categorization, identification, and recognition. *Journal of Experimental Psychology: Learning, Memory and Cognition*, **15**, 282–304.

Pickles, J. O. (1982). *Introduction to the physiology of hearing*. Academic, London.

Plomp, R. (1970). Timbre as a multidimensional attribute of complex tones. In *Frequency analysis and periodicity detection in hearing* (ed. R. Plomp and G. F. Smoorenburg), pp. 397–414. Sijthoff, Leiden.

Plomp, R. (1976). *Aspects of tone sensation*. Academic, London.

Pollack, I., Pickett, J. M., and Sumby, W. H. (1954). On the identification of speakers by voice. *Journal of the Acoustical Society of America*, **26**, 403–6.

Repp, B. H. (1987). The sound of two hands clapping. *Journal of the Acoustical Society of America*, **81**, 1100–9.

Roman, R. (ed.) (1992). *Le système auditif central: anatomie et physiologie*. INSERM/EMI, Paris.

Rosen, S. and Howell, P. (1987). Auditory, articulatory, and learning explanations of categorical perception in speech. In *The psychophysics of speech perception* (ed. M. E. H. Schouten), pp. 113–60. Nijhoff, The Hague.

Saldanha, E. L. and Corso, J. F. (1964). Timbre cues and the identification of musical instruments. *Journal of the Acoustical Society of America*, **36**, 2021–6.

Schiffman, S. S., Reynolds, M. L., and Young, F. W. (1981). *Introduction to multidimensional scaling: theory, methods, and applications*. Academic, Orlando, FL.

Schubert, E. D. (1975). The role of auditory perception in language processing. In *Reading, perception, and language*, pp. 97–130. York, Baltimore.

Segui, J. (1989). La perception du langage parlé. In *Traité de psychologie cognitive*, Vol. 1 (ed. C. Bonnet, R. Ghiglione, and J.-F. Richard), pp. 199–234. Dunod, Paris.

Segui, J., Dupoux, E., and Mehler, J. (1990). The role of the syllable in speech segmentation, phoneme identification, and lexical access. In *Cognitive models of speech processing: psycholinguistic and computational perspectives* (ed. G. T. M. Altmann), pp. 263–80. MIT Press, Cambridge, MA.

Shepard, R. N. (1972). Psychological representation of speech sounds. In *Human communication* (ed. E. E. David and T. B. Denes). McGraw-Hill, New York.

Shepard, R. N. (1981). Psychological relations and psychophysical scales: on the status of 'direct' psychophysical measurement. *Journal of Mathematical Psychology*, **24**, 21–57.

Sloboda, J. A. (1985). *The musical mind: the cognitive psychology of music*. Oxford University Press.

Stevens, S. S. (1956). The direct estimation of sensory magnitudes—loudness. *American Journal of Psychology*, **69**, 1–25.

Stevens, S. S. (1957). On the psychophysical law. *Psychological Review*, **64**, 153–81.

Strong, W. and Clark, M. (1967a). Synthesis of wind-instrument tones. *Journal of the Acoustical Society of America*, **41**, 39–52.

Strong, W. and Clark, M. (1967b). Perturbations of synthetic orchestral wind-instrument tones. *Journal of the Acoustical Society of America*, **41**, 277–85.

Thurstone, L. L. (1927). A law of comparative judgment. *Psychological Review*, **34**, 273–86.

Van Derveer, N. J. (1979). Acoustic information for event perception. Unpublished paper presented at the celebration in honour of Eleanor J. Gibson, Cornell University, Ithaca, New York [cited in Warren and Verbrugge (1984) and in Handel (1989)].

Warren, R. M. (1970). Perceptual restoration of missing speech sounds. *Science*, **167**, 392–3.

Warren, W. H. and Verbrugge, R. R. (1984). Auditory perception of breaking and bouncing events: a case study in ecological acoustics. *Journal of Experimental Psychology: Human Perception and Performance*, **10**, 704–12.

Wedin, L. and Goude, G. (1972). Dimension analysis of the perception of instrument timbres. *Scandinavian Journal of Psychology*, **13**, 228–40.

Wessel, D. L. (1973). Psychoacoustics and music. *Bulletin of the Computer Arts Society*, **30**, 1–2.

Wessel, D. L. (1979). Timbre space as a musical control structure. *Computer Music Journal*, **3**, 45–52.

Wessel, D. L., Bristow, D., and Settel, Z. (1987). Control of phrasing and articulation in synthesis. *Proceedings of the 1987 International Computer Music Conference*, pp. 108–16. Computer Music Association, San Francisco.

Winsberg, S. and Carroll, J. D. (1989a). A quasi-nonmetric method for multidimensional scaling of multiway data via a restricted case of an extended INDSCAL model. In *Multiway data analysis* (ed. R. Coppi and S. Belasco), pp. 405–14. North-Holland/Elsevier, Amsterdam.

Winsberg, S. and Carroll, J. D. (1989b). A quasi-nonmetric method for multidimensional scaling via an extended Euclidean model. *Psychometrika*, **54**, 217–29.

7

Auditory agnosia: a functional analysis

Isabelle Peretz

7.0 INTRODUCTION

Neuropsychology—defined as the study of the relations between cerebral organization and mental functioning—has concerned itself from its earliest days with the recognition of sound events. The first steps were taken in the auditory domain via the observation of selective speech impairments following damage to specific areas of the brain (Broca 1861; Wernicke 1874). These initial observations swiftly prompted the exploration of other essentially auditory functions, such as music (Bouillaud 1865). Indeed, during the latter half of the nineteenth century, the examination of patients suffering from cerebral damage (due to vascular problems, tumours, illness, or war injuries) led to the fascinating realization that cognition was not affected in its entirety, but in particular aspects. The selective nature of these disorders sparked an interest in comparing speech recognition to recognition of other sound events. These early observations are conveyed by the specific labels attached to clinical conditions such as aphasia, amusia, auditory agnosia, and verbal and non-verbal deafness. Although these terms sometimes overlap, they all indicate a concern to describe the specificity of the auditory problems observed. The issue of functional specificity will be the central focus of the present chapter.

Exploration of the selectivity of cognitive disorders is indeed one of the most remarkable contributions of neuropsychology. Although neglected at the beginning of this century, it is the phenomenon of functional selectivity which currently intrigues and stimulates many cognitive scientists. This interest goes back to the 1960s, but more especially to the 1980s, when a large proportion of the work done in neuropsychology started to favour functional explanations of the disorders over neuroanatomical ones. These explanations were couched in terms of transformations sustained by the cognitive system. The search for

Thinking in sound: the cognitive psychology of human audition, ed. S. McAdams and E. Bigand. Oxford University Press, 1993, pp. 199–230.

functional explanations does not, however, imply rejection of explanations formulated in neuroanatomical terms. Rather, this approach represents the awareness that, even if the ultimate goal is to understand the neural bases of cognition, neuropsychological data can only be exploited if theories of normal functioning exist. Without an implicit or explicit model of how a normal system operates, it is difficult to conceptualize how it may be disrupted. Nor may just any type of dysfunction occur, for the disorder is constrained by the organization of the undamaged system, that is to say that of the normal cognitive system.

This approach to neuropsychology is now known as cognitive neuropsychology. It has been pursued with increasing sophistication in many realms of cognition (Ellis and Young 1988; Shallice 1988); the endeavour has proven to be extremely fruitful in the areas of reading (and dyslexia: Patterson *et al.* 1985), of memory (and amnesia: Shimamura 1989) and, more recently, of vision (and visual agnosia: Kosslyn *et al.* 1990). In this chapter, I will discuss how and according to what principles the neuropsychology of non-linguistic auditory functions might be exploited with similar success.

Although my analysis of the auditory disorders will be basically functional, it might be useful here to provide a brief review of the neural background. In theory, knowing how the brain is organized, i.e. studying the 'hardware' of the human cognitive system, might constrain the nature of the functional architecture (or 'software') that is compatible with it. Currently, however, knowledge of the cerebral organization of auditory function emphasizes the importance of the functional analysis, rather than establishing constraints on it. Nevertheless, this brief detour into neuroanatomy will enable me to qualify certain widely held ideas concerning hemispheric specialization which inevitably come to mind.

7.1   CEREBRAL ORGANIZATION

One of the most striking and probably distinctive anatomical correlates of the human species corresponds to the lateralization of linguistic functions to the left hemisphere. A widely held belief attributes the other auditory functions (such as those involving music and environmental sounds) to the right hemisphere. This belief stems from a particularly prolific period of research dating from the 1960s.

The abundance of research conducted on questions of hemispheric specialization is due not only to its obvious intrinsic interest, but also—and especially—to certain methods discovered at that time. One of these methods, though not readily available, played a determining role in spurring researchers' fascination with hemispheric specialization. This method, known as the 'split brain', involves cutting (for therapeutic reasons) the commissures that establish a direct link between the two hemispheres of the brain. Each hemisphere can then be explored independently of the other as long as presentation and response are carefully controlled. Studying such patients has led to the acceptance of the concept of functional autonomy of the two hemispheres. Unfortunately, this technique has never been used, as far as I know, to study the recognition of non-verbal sound events. Another method developed in the 1960s, this time far easier to pursue, is the measure of laterality in normal subjects. The preferred technique in auditory research is the dichotic listening method—this method involves presenting each ear with a different stimulus simultaneously, and observing differences in performance according to ear of presentation. A contralateral relationship between the superior ear and the dominant hemisphere has been demonstrated, thus permitting the inference of hemispheric difference based on lateral difference. This method has been used extensively in auditory research (Hugdahl 1988). Finally, during the same period, the study of brain-damaged patients underwent a paradigmatic shift away from the examination of single cases to the study of groups. This shift has facilitated studies of hemispheric differences since most patients have damage restricted to a single hemisphere. All of these methodological developments taken collectively explain why hemispheric specialization became a dominant theme in neuropsychology during the latter half of this century. These paradigmatic changes also helped to establish the verbal/non-verbal distinction mentioned above, only to challenge it shortly thereafter.

The processing of language and music are two functions that have been considered as representing the verbal and non-verbal domains *par excellence*. Yet it is now generally accepted that this distinction alone does not adequately capture the division of functions between the cerebral hemispheres. While it is relatively clear that speech perception depends critically on the integrity of the left hemisphere, musical perception is far from displaying a comparable lateralization in the right hemisphere (see Zatorre (1984), Lechevalier *et al.* (1985), and Peretz (1985) for recent reviews of research conducted with patients, and Peretz and Morais (1988) for a recent review of research conducted on normal subjects). In fact, the observed bias in favour of the right hemisphere rests on an accumulation of data in a highly specific sector of music perception, namely the organization of pitch presented in isolation, in chords or in melodies. Other aspects of music have received far less attention, such as those depending on the temporal dimension or on access to pre-existing representations, and these would seem to involve rather the left hemisphere (or at least not to be linked to a particular hemisphere).

In fact, the notion of right hemispheric specialization for non-verbal auditory functions stemmed from the idea that the cerebral hemispheres were specialized for dealing with entire functions such as language or music. The possibility that components of these functions, rather than the entire function, might be lateralized was completely overlooked. Today, it is largely accepted that any attempt to explain hemispheric specialization in terms of whole functions or in terms of general-purpose principles, such as the 'analytic–holistic' distinction (Bradshaw and Nettleton 1981), cannot do justice to the complexity of the phenomenon. The current trend is better motivated theoretically, since it is based on the notion that every mental function relies on the involvement of a set of multiple processing components, each of which may be lateralized differently in the brain (Allen 1983). This concept is far more compatible with the observation that both cerebral hemispheres participate in processing music and that auditory agnosia is usually the result of bilateral lesions. Furthermore, this approach stimulates research of a more functionally oriented nature, by the need to define and delineate the processing components at work within each function. The advantage of this orientation of research on hemispheric specialization is that the phenomenon escapes marginalization by becoming an integral part of the cognitive sciences. The drawback is that for certain functions, such as the recognition of non-verbal events, we still lack models describing the nature of the various processing components and the way they are organized to constitute a given function. This directly concerns the level of functional analysis that will be discussed in the following section.

Thus, research carried out on the neural bases of auditory function has acquired a new sophistication by requiring the cognitive components to be well defined in order for their cerebral location to be pinpointed. There are already indications that adopting such an approach to the localization of elementary components is the most appropriate level of analysis. As an example, I will cite work done by Robert Zatorre at the Montreal Neurological Institute on pitch perception of complex tones (Zatorre 1988). Exploiting the phenomenon of the missing fundamental, well known in psychoacoustics and probably due to central rather than peripheral processing (Houtsma and Goldstein 1971), Zatorre suggested that this operation was carried out in a very specific area of the brain, namely at the level of Heschl's gyri in the right hemisphere. Catherine Liègeois-Chauvel is currently pursuing this type of research in Rennes, by attempting to specify the neural mechanisms involved. This type of research conducted on human subjects is far more precise than the efforts summarized in the context of hemispheric specialization, and it furthermore establishes links with animal research. It is probably at this level of elementary functional organization that progress will be the most spectacular, as is now happening with research in vision.[1]

1. The idea that research into cerebral organization can constrain psychological theories at a more elaborate level (notably including speech and music) nevertheless needs to be nuanced. If we take the example of vision, it has to be recognized that the elucidation

In conclusion, research on cerebral organization has not yet yielded clear constraints or indications of the way in which the auditory system is organized functionally. Rather, the following section will show how neuropsychological research can provide further information on this question of functional organization, especially by studying brain-damaged patients, but also by occasionally exploiting hemispheric differences in normal subjects.

7.2 FUNCTIONAL ORGANIZATION

As mentioned at the outset, brain damage may offer unparalleled opportunities to observe clear-cut functional specificity. To illustrate the phenomenon, I will take a well-known example of selectivity between language and music (see Dorgeuille (1966) and Marin (1982) for reviews of published cases). The most famous case is probably that of Shebalin, the Russian composer who, following damage to the left hemisphere, was completely aphasic for the rest of his life; he could neither understand speech nor speak intelligibly. He nevertheless continued to compose, notably completing his fifth symphony, which Shostakovitch considered to be one of his most brilliant and innovative works (Luria *et al.* 1965). Shebalin therefore displayed severe language deficits yet retained his musical skills to a remarkable degree. This dissociation cannot simply be explained by the fact that Shebalin was 'abnormally musical' from the start. Indeed, the inverse dissociation has recently been observed in a person devoid of any special talent, linguistic or musical. This person, C.N., is a young nurse who never received any musical education. As a consequence of successive damage to the two temporal lobes she was unable to recognize the simplest tune. She no longer recognized excerpts from her own record collection, unless the music was accompanied by words. Nor could she sing the children's songs that she used to enjoy singing with her young son. Yet C.N. did not encounter the slightest difficulty in understanding and communicating verbally. This retention of perfect language abilities has enabled her to resume her professional career (Peretz *et al.* 1991).

The straightforward implication of this brief description is that language and music do not share the same processing mechanisms. Rather they

of cerebral organization concerning perception of certain properties such as colour, movement, and depth cannot be easily extended to more elaborate functions such as reading. Indeed, although the various processing elements involved in reading are relatively well delineated and studied, their respective anatomical correlates still largely escape analysis. Consequently, as mentioned previously, if we admit that advances in neuropsychology crucially depend on the study of each function in its most basic elements, whether that be their neural implementation or their functional realization, the integration of these two levels of analysis is no simple matter (Mehler *et al.* 1984).

enjoy functional autonomy. This conclusion may appear trivial to some, but certainly not to everyone. Even today, music is conceived as a sort of epiphenomenon, implying that it relies on processing components used for other functions, such as language (Lerdahl and Jackendoff 1983; but see Jackendoff (1987) for a radically different evolution). For most of us, however, music and language are distinct functions. Accordingly, the interest of cases such as those of Shebalin and C.N. resides mainly in determining the functional locus at which music and language are dissociated. For example, if it were shown that C.N.'s amusia resulted from a perturbation of the mechanisms involved in 'auditory scene analysis' as described by Bregman (1990, Ch. 2 this volume), such an observation would be far from trivial. It would suggest that language and music possess their own scene analysis mechanisms (as argued, in fact, by Liberman and Mattingly (1985) for speech). Consequently, the interest of a given dissociation depends on the theoretical context adopted. Moreover, dealing with two global functions—such as language and music—is not very informative in itself, as was pointed out in the previous section, since the distinction is too broad to be instructive. As will be seen, music is not a monolithic skill that an individual either possesses or not. It is based on numerous components that may be dissociated or isolated, along boundaries as clear cut as those observed between language and music in Shebalin and C.N.

The methodological point to be drawn from the above discussion is the use of *dissociation*. This is the method that derives *par excellence* from the level of functional analysis of neuropsychological data (Teuber 1955; Shallice 1988). The dissociations are of two basic types: selective loss and selective sparing. If a patient can no longer accomplish operation X (selective loss) but is able to perform operation Y (selective sparing) then the dissociation of X from Y suggests that the two operations are performed by different mechanisms. The inference is that much stronger if another patient is found to display the inverse dissociation, that is to say the loss of Y and the sparing of X. These two patients then become an instance of a double dissociation; Shebalin and C.N. fulfil these conditions.

The logic of the argument is quite simple. The validity of inferences on normal functioning are not. First of all, the dissociations concern the performance on tasks and not directly the operations under study. The problem is that any task implies the involvement of multiple operations. Consequently, a dissociation between two tasks is only interesting to the extent that it is not self-evident and enables inferences to be made about a particular component of a mental operation. This methodological problem is not restricted to neuropsychology, but applies to psychology in general (see Dunn and Kirsner 1988). Nevertheless, as will be seen below, the question of the disparity of tasks becomes particularly thorny in neuropsychological practice. Secondly, studying the performance of brain-damaged patients in order to make inferences about normal functioning implies the acceptance of a series of postulates that may turn out to be too rigid (Caramazza 1984). For example, selective loss is assumed to result from elimination of an operation and not from reorganization occurring as an adaptation to brain-damage; these adaptations might relate only indirectly to the way a normal system operates.

In any event, dissociation remains the preferred method for studying brain-damaged patients since it often occurs in an extremely robust and clearly quantitative fashion. Empirical phenomena depending on research involving normal subjects are, in contrast, often fragile, by being small and vulnerable to experimental conditions. Thus, neuropsychological research will continue to be a valuable source of information concerning cognitive functioning, since the problems raised by the study of brain-damaged patients can be offset by seeking points of convergence in normal subjects. This is the approach advocated in the following discussion of auditory agnosia.

7.3 AUDITORY AGNOSIA

Auditory agnosia has been recognized for over a century (Lichtheim 1885). Typical sufferers are persons of about 50 years of age who suddenly complain of hearing all sounds as unintelligible noises (gratings and squeakings). The patients behave like deaf people who can still read, speak, and write; they are not completely deaf, however, since they can usually perceive changes in frequency, intensity, and duration of the sound events presented to them. By way of example, an agnosic patient studied by Klein and Harper (1956, p. 114) made the following remarks: '...I know exactly what I want to say but I don't know whether it is right or wrong.... I know I am speaking but I can't hear the words right, not the actual words, I can hear the voice'. Auditory agnosia therefore involves a problem of recognition and identification that cannot be explained by deafness as such, nor by a difficulty in verbal expression. The disorder is specific to the interpretation of the auditory input: the patient who cannot recognize a sound event can usually do so in another medium, such as by sight or touch. Most descriptions of auditory agnosia are limited to this general description.

Since the 1970s, however, experimentation has become more precise at the functional level. Such research follows two basic lines. One line involves distinguishing between verbal agnosia (involving comprehension of speech) and non-verbal agnosia (involving recognition of sounds other than speech). This distinction has led to changes in terminology; 'auditory agnosia' thereafter refers to a disorder limited to non-verbal events whereas difficulty in recognizing speech is referred to as verbal agnosia or, more often, as verbal deafness. This differentiation of agnosias according to the nature of the sound event involved will be taken up later. The other major line along which agnosia is generally studied concerns the distinction between perception and recognition. This distinction is formulated in neuropsychological terms as apperceptive and associative agnosia, and invokes a very simple recognition model (see also McAdams, Ch. 6 this volume, for a discussion of recognition and identification processes). Since this model guides much research in the non-verbal domain, it will be explained below, followed by a discussion of how neuropsychological data support it.

7.3.1 Auditory recognition: a two-stage process

The term agnosia refers to a problem of recognition. Recognition here means a sense of familiarity stemming from the contact between an external event and the internal representation of previous experiences of that event. This is basically what the two-stage process shown in Fig. 7.1 describes. The first stage involves analysing the sound event in order to abstract its properties; this analysis leads to the perception and discrimination of events. The second stage involves making contact between the percept and mental representations; in other words, the percept activates schemas or previous experience. In so far as this contact or activation is successful, recognition occurs. It should be pointed out that this conceptualization is neither new nor limited to audition; it was proposed in the nineteenth century by Lissauer (1988) to account for visual agnosia.

According to this view, the only way to impair the recognition system, and therefore to induce agnosia, is to disrupt the analysis or to degrade the mental representations. Impairment of the first stage would lead to so-called apperceptive agnosia; impairment of the second stage would lead to associative agnosia. In other words, people suffering from apperceptive agnosia can no longer recognize sound events because their perceptual analysis process is clearly deficient. In contrast, people suffering from associative agnosia can no longer recognize sound objects despite adequate analysis of the relevant features. It is important to determine the extent to which this two-stage process, which would classify agnosic patients with clear perceptual problems separately from those without such problems, is an empirically valid distinction. Indeed, although this recognition model seems intuitively correct (though probably too broad), it is currently being challenged by a new type of modelling that conceives of perception as being an intrinsic part of the process of recognition.

According to these new models—known as connectionist networks or parallel distributed processing—the representations cannot be altered

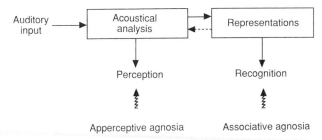

Fig. 7.1 Representation of the two-stage recognition process and classification of the resulting agnosias.

without also altering the perceptual processes (see McClelland and Elman (1986) for the elaboration of such a model for speech recognition). Recognition results from the stabilization of a network, in a state that is maximally consistent with the activation from the stimulus and the knowledge of previous experience encoded in the strength of connections among units in the network. According to this type of conception, the network arrives at a complete or correct interpretation of the stimulus by combining information from the sound event and from the stored perceptual experience. If injured, such a system would not distinguish between apperceptive agnosia and associative agnosia since all forms of agnosia would necessarily entail perceptual disorders.

Most agnosics do, in fact, fulfil this prediction; they exhibit severe perceptual problems leading to the inability to recognize sounds. A common interpretation of these disorders is to attribute them to an impairment in acuity or in temporal resolution (e.g. Albert and Bear 1974; Auerbach *et al.* 1982; Butchel and Stewart 1989).When the agnosia primarily concerns speech sounds, deficiencies in phonemic discrimination are often invoked (Chocholle *et al.* 1975; Denes and Semenza 1975; Saffran *et al.* 1976). In all these cases, and whatever the exact interpretation given to the perceptual difficulties, the perceptual deficit is held to be responsible for the inability to recognize sounds. These observations are compatible with both types of model, that is to say the two-stage process and the connectionist model. The only type of observation that would differentiate them involves cases of associative agnosia. Such patients should, for instance, be able to describe or reproduce the mewing of a cat but be unable to recognize it or to decide whether they have ever heard such a sound. Once shown the cat in question, the patients should be able to identify it immediately.

Such descriptions exist in the case of speech recognition (Kohn and Friedman 1986) whereas nothing similar, to my knowledge, has been reported in the non-verbal domain. Nevertheless, several reports match this 'perception without recognition' phenomenon and have been labelled 'associative agnosia'. These observations arise from three experiments dealing with different types of sound: environmental sounds (ranging from noises made by household objects to animal cries), human voices, and tunes.

The first study to have suggested the existence of associative agnosia in auditory perception was conducted by Vignolo (1982). The experiment entailed two tests. In one, the patient had to decide whether two mixed noises (taken from sound tracks of radio programmes) were identical or not. In the second test, the patient had to recognize a familiar sound event (for example, a braying donkey) by selecting one of four images of the potential source (donkey, cow, elephant, and ambulance). Some patients (with lesions in the left hemisphere) exhibited normal performance in the discrimination test but performed well below normal on the recognition test. The second study followed basically the same design and produced similar results pertaining to the recognition of human voices (Van Lancker and Kreiman 1987; Van Lancker *et al.* 1988). Some patients could distinguish normally the voices of unknown individuals pronouncing the same sentence, yet were unable to recognize famous people from their voices. The same conclusions apparently apply to the recognition of well-known tunes (Eustache *et al.* 1990).

In general, then, the fact that cases of associative agnosia have been observed tends to invalidate the connectionist type of model and to corroborate the two-stage model since it would seem that recognition can be dissociated from perception. Such dissociation, although suggestive, should be treated cautiously. First of all, the absence of perceptual disorders was inferred from the results on a single test. It is highly possible that potentially instructive disorders escaped this limited assessment. This is one of the reasons why a growing number of researchers feel that the detailed examination of single cases, employing multiple tasks, is the only way to achieve tangible progress in this area. Secondly, the tests used to assess perception and recognition were quite different in nature. This disparity might trigger the use of distinct mechanisms that differ not only in perceptual demands but also in decision-making operations. In the cases just cited, those of 'perception without recognition', this disparity in tasks would not seem to be crucial, however, since observations run counter to intuitive expectations. Indeed, the perceptual tasks appear more difficult to perform than the recognition tasks, although it is the former that are spared and the latter, less vulnerable ones that are most affected.

On the other hand, this disparity in tasks may easily account for the inverse dissociations described in these same experiments, with the exception of the one conducted by Eustache *et al.* (1990), to which I will return below. Vignolo (1982) and Van Lancker (Van Lancker and Kreiman 1987; Van Lancker *et al.* 1988) both report cases of 'recognition *without* perception'. This no longer involves apperceptive or associative agnosia for it concerns patients who display the paradoxical phenomenon of being able to *recognize* a noise or a familiar voice while being unable to *discriminate* between unfamiliar noises or voices. The phenomenon loses its strangeness when one considers the difficulty involved in discriminating between events for which we have no previous experience, compared with the processing of familiar events. It is probable that in audition more than in any other area, only part of the stimulus is necessary to activate its representation; this representation can therefore subsequently contribute to its perceptual analysis. This type of interaction is favoured by the intrinsically sequential nature of the information. It is thus conceivable that in hearing—to a greater extent than vision, for example—access to intact representations can compensate for a deteriorated percept and thus lead to recognition. In the absence of the assistance supplied by such representations, as is the case with the stimuli used by Vignolo and Van Lancker in perceptual tasks, the deterioration of perceptual processes is more noticeable than those of recognition.

This explanation in terms of task disparity nevertheless fails to account for the more carefully controlled study of Eustache and his colleagues (Eustache *et al.* 1990, case 2). These authors presented their patient with pairs of familiar tunes. In one situation, the patient had to give the title of both songs after having listened to the pair. In the other situation, the patient had to indicate whether the two songs were identical or different. The patient succeeded in identifying the pairs normally, yet was completely unable to discriminate between them. This condition of spared recognition with severely impaired discrimination cannot be reduced to a methodological issue since the task parameters were identical in the two situations. These surprising results thus raise numerous questions. Notably, if a patient can identify a pair of melodies, say 'Frère Jacques' and 'Au clair de la lune', why doesn't he use these codes to determine that the two melodies are different and thus overcome the difficulties in perceiving? Finally, and more generally, this case of 'recognition without perception' suggests that the two-stage model is probably too simple when it posits a single route of access to representations via the perceptual analysis of a sound event. It is quite likely that more than two stages are required and that various parallel entries are possible, as is already acknowledged for speech (Ellis and Young 1988) and as will be suggested below for music.

To sum up, it is obvious that many questions remain open at this point, since the data are relatively recent and scarce. It would therefore be premature to draw any firm conclusions. Current data nevertheless strongly support the idea that at least two processing components are dissociable in the recognition of non-verbal sound events such as environmental sounds (Vignolo 1982), human voices (Van Lancker *et al.* 1988), and tunes (Eustache *et al.* 1990). These involve the processes that effect perceptual analysis and the mechanisms that allow access to the representations of prior experience, respectively. The two-stage model (Fig. 7.1) would therefore seem to have some psychological reality, although its precise structure has yet to be defined. The question that arises at this point is knowing how many systems of this kind are involved in auditory recognition. In other words, the suggestion that these two stages are of an undifferentiated or general-purpose nature may now be examined on the basis of the various types of agnosia known to exist.

7.3.2   Specific recognition systems

As illustrated previously, speech and music can dissociate after brain damage. This description fits with the widely acknowledged verbal/non-verbal dichotomy mentioned previously. Although this distinction was shown to have limited value when applied to the division of functions between the cerebral hemispheres, it enjoys a respectable reputation outside the field of neuropsychology. This is mainly due to the theoretical and empirical support provided by researchers affiliated with the Haskins Laboratories in the United States. They (see, in particular, Mann and Liberman (1983)) argue that there are essentially two modes of auditory perception. One is dedicated to speech—the phonetic or speech mode—and the other is a general-purpose system handling all the non-speech sounds—the auditory mode. There would thus be essentially two types or two series of dissociable systems depending on whether the information to be processed is speech or not. Consequently, only two broad types of agnosia should be encountered. On the one hand, there would be all those forms of agnosia involving speech without necessarily affecting the recognition of other types of sound. On the other hand, and inversely, there would be non-verbal agnosias that would spare speech recognition but affect any other type of sound, without further distinction. It will be shown that this division into two domains is insufficient to account for the various forms of auditory agnosia.

Usually, auditory agnosia is general or global, in the sense that it applies to all types of auditory event. Numerous cases of dissociation have nevertheless been noted.[2] These seem to confirm the speech versus auditory mode dichotomy. Indeed, there are several reports of agnosia for speech, sparing either music or environmental sounds (Albert and Bear 1974; Metz-Lutz and Dahl 1984; Yaqub *et al.* 1988). In contrast, though less frequently, there have been cases of impaired processing of music

---

2. This article will not present an exhaustive survey of the literature, but will simply examine a few indicative studies. In so far as possible, only research that has quantified the various aspects will be cited.

and environmental sounds, with no impairment of speech (see, in particular, Spreen *et al.* (1965)). This set of studies therefore constitutes evidence of a double dissociation between the recognition of speech and non-speech sounds.

Apparently, however, a single system does not govern all non-speech sounds. My colleagues and I (Peretz *et al.* 1991) have documented two cases of patients with music agnosia who display no difficulty in recognizing environmental sounds or in understanding speech (as mentioned above in the description of C.N.). This selective impairment then completes the double dissociation suggested by a previous study in which recognition of speech and environmental sounds was impossible while recognition of melodies remained unimpaired (Laignel-Lavastine and Alajouanine 1921). Cases of selective impairment involving only environmental sounds (i.e. in sparing speech and music) have never been documented, to my knowledge, except during recovery (see below). The fact that this domain can be selectively spared (Tanaka *et al.* 1987; Eustache *et al.* 1990) suggests, however, that environmental sounds constitute a category distinct from music and speech.

Taken together, the data strongly suggest that at least three distinct systems of recognition exist. This suggestion has direct implications for the functional architecture of auditory perception. It is therefore crucial to seriously entertain the possibility that dissociation by domain corresponds to differences in kind rather than a difference in degree. Indeed, it is plausible that the three domains under consideration could be placed along a continuum of difficulty (if, for instance, perceptual analysis is considered) or automaticity (if access to representations is at issue). Along a continuum, differences in the severity of brain damage could lead to dissociations within a single system of auditory recognition. If brain damage is slight, then the patient would experience difficulty with the most complex, or least automatically recognizable, stimuli. Since speech can be regarded as the most complex stimulus, it would be the most vulnerable domain if the continuum is based on complexity. If, on the other hand, the continuum involves differences in automaticity, speech would be the least vulnerable. Thus, whichever principle is adopted, speech would be located at one of the extremes. As far as music and environmental sounds are concerned, it is difficult to offer an hypothesis at this time, for no normative data are currently available.

Although parsimonious, the notion of a differential gradient of difficulty (or of automaticity) for the various auditory domains encounters serious objections. First of all, stages of recovery are not identical from one patient to another. If a single gradient were involved, recovery of auditory functions should proceed in a consistent order. Yet, two case studies present diametrically opposed sequences of recovery. In the first (Mendez and Gechan 1988), environmental sounds were recovered first, followed by music and finally speech; in the second (Motomura *et al*. 1986), the order was reversed. Although the first case might represent a gradient in complexity (from simplest to most complex) and the second case might represent a gradient in automaticity (from most to least automatic), the fact that both concerned cases of apperceptive agnosia makes this hypothesis unlikely. The strongest argument against the notion of a gradient remains the observation of double dissociation between domains—between speech and non-speech sounds on the one hand, and between music and environmental sounds on the other. If there were only one system of recognition, it should be possible to observe dissociations in one direction only, and not in the other. Consequently, neuropsychological data strongly suggest that several recognition systems exist that are specialized according to the nature of the sound event. From what has just been discussed, at least three such systems would exist: one for speech, another for music, and a third for other, so-called environmental, sounds.

This hypothesis nevertheless raises several questions. The first question concerns the number and nature of domains worthy of examination. Does any newly observed dissociation imply the existence of yet another system? This is a potentially dangerous attitude. Other criteria must be taken into consideration, notably criteria of evolution and specificity, as described by Fodor (1983). A second question follows from this initial one, namely estimating how and to what extent a specific system could process an event outside its own domain. Finally, and above all, it is necessary to determine the level of processing that constitutes the specificity of a given domain. As far as speech is concerned, several hypotheses exist. Specificity is often attributed to phonological encoding, in requiring knowledge of units and combinatory rules that are language specific. Nothing similar yet exists for the other auditory domains (although see Peretz and Morais (1989) for an attempt in this direction in the domain of music). It is therefore important at this stage to formulate hypotheses about the processing components involved in each domain and to measure how and to what extent neurological damage of each of these components can lead to agnosic disorders. This is the approach that will now be taken with music.

7.3.3   The case of music

Music reaches the listener in the form of an extremely rich and complex sound wave conveying an eminently sequential structure. Without seeing the sound source, listeners can infer a vast amount of information from that structure, such as the instruments generating the sound and the musical genre; they can often also appreciate the musical intention. Indeed, music fulfils numerous roles, from the evocation of a certain

emotional ambience (as used notably in films and advertising), to incite-
ment to collective dance and song, to pure aesthetic pleasure (i.e. food
for thought). In the latter case, for instance, the listener[3] must have swift
access to the appropriate tune. It is this particular, and therefore restrictive,
instance of tune recognition that will be discussed here.

Even in the simple case of a tune being distinctly sung or produced by
a computer with no accompaniment or background noise, its recognition
will suppose the intervention of multiple processing components. Their
output should enable the listener to compare it with all the tunes that he
or she knows, in order to determine the closest correspondence and thus
to discover its identity. It is therefore suggested here that musical recognition, like speech recognition, involves the existence of a sort of lexicon
of abstract representations of all the tunes that a listener knows. These
representations would be structural and specific, in the sense that they
would contain no associated extra-musical information (for example,
genre, social context, etc). Such associations are of a more general nature,
and are probably not specific to music but are accessible through other
means and probably vary from one individual to another (but see Halpern
(1984) for a relatively systematic organization of such associations).

Little research has been done on how such a lexicon might be organized.
The ensuing question concerns the nature of the cues that will be effective in activating the appropriate lexical entry. Indeed, knowledge of such
factors would constrain the nature of the prior processing that must
be postulated. If, for example, Serafine and her colleagues (Serafine *et al.*
1984, see Section 3.3.3, and Crowder, Ch. 5 this volume) were right in
postulating that recognition of songs occurs in an integral way in so
far as one cannot access the tune without accessing its text and
vice versa, the existence of a system or processing component for integrating melody and text prior to accessing the lexicon would be required.
It will be seen below how neuropsychology can provide clues as to
what ways of recognizing familiar tunes are more plausible than others.

To make the following argument clearer, I have schematically illustrated (and probably over simplified) in Fig. 7.2, the functional implications of our studies conducted mostly with brain-damaged patients, but
also with normal subjects. These observations tend to indicate that a tune
is the object of parallel structural analyses of its pitch variations, called
melodic organization, and of its temporal features, called temporal organization. Each of these systems of analysis entails a distinct series of

---

3. 'Listener' refers here to both musicians and non-musicians. The argument which follows
is purportedly valid for both types of subject. Indeed, there is no reason to think that,
in terms of relatively basic musical activities, musicians behave differently from non-
musicians (see also Bigand, Ch. 2 this volume). Moreover, there is currently no evidence,
at the level of functional analysis considered here, suggesting that musical education
exerts an influence on cerebral organization.

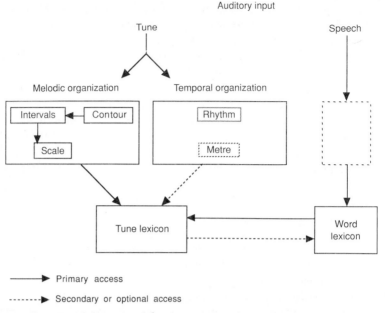

Fig. 7.2   Functional diagram of the recognition of tunes as suggested by research conducted on brain-damaged patients.

components; for the moment, it has been possible to dissociate only certain components participating in the elaboration of a distinct melodic representation. The output representation of this series of melodic operations would be determinant in the activation of a particular tune stored in the lexicon. In other words, and as far as the Western system is concerned, recognition of familiar tunes would be primarily melodic rather than rhythmic. Moreover, this recognition would be independent of the words that go with the music.

The diagram thus recognizes three routes of access to a familiar tune of which one, the melodic route, is given priority status. It is appropriate here to mention that the data on which this schema is based stem from my own recent research. This must therefore be considered a provisional diagram. By making it explicit, however, the model is open to potential falsification and above all has some heuristic value for classifying and discussing disorders related to music recognition. I will therefore follow the diagram, first dealing with the distinction between the melodic and the temporal routes that musical information follows. Then I will discuss the various melodic transformations that such information appears to undergo, and will finally deal with the activation of lexical representations.

Two distinct systems: melodic structure and temporal structure

There are two fundamental dimensions to the recognition of a familiar tune—the melodic dimension (defined by sequential variations in pitch) and the temporal dimension (defined by variations in duration). Variations in intensity (dynamics), in spectral composition (timbre), and in speed (tempo) probably facilitate recognition in so far as they respect the structure of the original tune, or of its most frequent version, but apparently are not determining factors, at least not when highly familiar tunes from the Western musical system are involved. People do recognize their national anthem easily regardless of whether it is sung, played on an instrument lacking dynamics (such as the harpsichord), or played fast or slow. A melodic or rhythmic error, on the other hand, is readily detected and, depending on how serious it is, may lead to ambiguity or failure to recognize the target tune.

These two essential dimensions of music perception, melody and rhythm,[4] have been treated independently, both in theory and practice (see, for example, Deutsch and Feroe (1981) for a model of melody perception, and Povel (1984) for a temporal model). Recently, this tradition has been challenged by Jones and her colleagues (Jones *et al.* 1982; Boltz and Jones 1986; Jones 1987; Jones *et al.* 1987), who have shown on numerous occasions that melody and rhythm are not independent but are processed as a single unit in perception and memory.

Neuropsychological data do not support their hypothesis, however. In behavioural spheres other than listening, several cases have already been described in which melody and rhythm were affected differently by brain damage. In terms of singing skills, rhythm may be spared when melody is lost (Mann (1898) and Josmann (1926) reported in Dorgeuille 1966), and vice versa (Brust 1980; Mavlov 1980). The same double dissociation has been reported in reading music (see Dorgeuille (1966) and Brust (1980) for a selective loss of rhythm; Dorgeuille (1966) and Assal (1973) for a selective loss of melody). Thus, there is evidence that melody and rhythm are dissociable, although the indications are indirect since they address issues somewhat removed from auditory perception and are often reported in an anecdotal (non-quantified) fashion. More recently, I have found evidence for extending this double dissociation to perception (Peretz 1990) and have reproduced the phenomenon under different experimental conditions (Peretz and Kolinsky 1993).

---

4. For the sake of argument, the term rhythm will be used here in a generic, if inaccurate, fashion to refer to the set of mechanisms involved in the temporal organization of a sequence. The term is approximate in that it often refers to a particular level of temporal organization that is distinct, for instance, from metrical organization.

The task involved in these two studies was of the classic 'same–different' classification type. Subjects listened to two short passages and had to judge whether they were identical or different. Unfamiliar musical material was used, and was altered only along one dimension—melody or rhythm—in a way relevant for discrimination. Sometimes the irrelevant dimension was 'neutralized' in the sense that it never varied (for instance, a single duration was used for creating melodic variations), sometimes it was present but of no discriminatory relevance (for example, rhythmic variations might be present in a pair of stimuli that differed in terms of melody, but such variations would remain unchanged across both members of the pair). Finally, sequences that varied in both melody and rhythm were used, following the procedure of Jones *et al.* (1987); instructions to subjects changed since they were now asked to pay selective attention to rhythm in spite of any potential changes in melody. Under all these conditions, we observed a dissociation between the ability to process one of these two dimensions and the inability to process the other dimension. This double dissociation, encountered in a clear fashion in six patients tested under the same experimental conditions, is represented in Fig. 7.3.

Comparison of the results of these patients with those of neurologically healthy subjects (matched in terms of age and education) reveals dissociations that appear robust (expressing a classic dissociation according to the criteria described by Shallice 1988). When performing identical tasks, patients scored well below the normal range (established by control subjects) in the deficient dimension but within the normal range in the unaffected dimension. Normal variations theoretically indicate the level of performance attained by patients prior to brain damage. Consequently, the results given in Fig. 7.3 show that brain damage can produce a selective loss for one of the two dimensions assessed. Since such impairment can affect either melody alone or rhythm alone, the evidence strongly suggests that these two dimensions involve the operation of perceptual systems that are at least partially separable.

That this functional autonomy is easier to observe in brain-damaged subjects than in normal subjects is probably due to the fact that integration is inevitable in a normal brain. Indeed, rhythm and melody are physically integrated elements of music and their joint representation in a percept is probably desirable in order to retain the most faithful, or veridical, copy possible. In brain-damaged subjects, the impairment can affect mainly one system while leaving the other one relatively intact. In these cases, integration of melody and rhythm would take place only partially or not at all. This suggests that their integration does not take place in the early stages of processing of a musical passage, but rather at some later stage. The question that obviously arises is how and at what

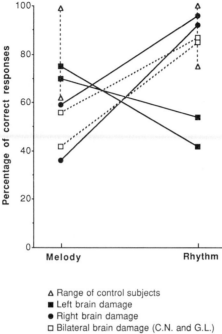

Fig. 7.3   Graph of results showing the double dissociation in discrimination of melody and rhythm by brain-damaged patients displaying a deficit for one or the other dimension.

stage this integration occurs—a question that remains open for the moment. In the issue at hand, it is also important to ask whether such integration is required for the activation of a lexical unit. This point will be taken up later (p. 223).

Whatever the exact nature of the representation required for lexical access, and thus for recognition, neuropsychological data suggest the existence of at least two dissociable routes in the processing of musical information: the melodic route (to be discussed more fully in the next section) and the rhythmic route (about which far less is known). In terms of this latter route, I have suggested that it may involve the operation of two different mechanisms, namely rhythmic organization and metric interpretation (Peretz 1990). Although preliminary results suggest that these two types of mechanism are dissociable in brain-damaged subjects, the conclusions cannot yet be considered definitive, in so far as the different tasks involved did not allow direct comparison.

Components of the melodic system

Recognizing a familiar tune calls on three basic features of the melody: contour, intervals,[5] and tonal function. The exact register is of little importance—a familiar tune will be easily recognized whether sung by a man or a woman. Contour, however, defined as the overall trajectory in pitch, helps to delimit the possibilities; for instance, contour can enable us to guess the song being sung by a young child even when the intervals are unrecognizable. The critical information nevertheless resides in the exact interval size; this is what enables us to distinguish, for instance, the first four notes of Beethoven's *Fifth symphony* (G–G–G–E♭; a falling major third interval) from those of '*Il était un petit navire*' (B–B–B–D; a falling major sixth). Their respective identification is probably also aided by the fact that the *Fifth symphony* implies a key of C minor whereas the song is in G major. Certainly, the fact that these notes obey the tonal constraints of the Western musical system makes recognition more likely than if they violated such rules and evoked an alien melody having no lexical representation. The respective contributions of each one of these three features to melody discrimination have been documented in normal subjects (see, for instance, Dowling and Harwood (1986) for a recent survey).

Recent research in neuropsychology has also focused on these features with respect to melody recognition. The initial impetus, in fact, was given by the influential study of Bever and Chiarello (1974). These authors suggested that musicians used intervals to recognize melodies, thereby depending more heavily on their left hemisphere for melody recognition, whereas non-musicians relied primarily on melodic contour, depending more on the right hemisphere. In addition to the fact that this observation shed new light on hemispheric specialization, the work of Bever and Chiarello raised the possibility that examination of the differences between the cerebral hemispheres could lead to functional dissociations within the melodic perceptual system itself (see also Gates and Bradshaw 1977).

On several occasions, my colleagues and I have verified the notion that melodic contour can be imputed to the right hemisphere whereas extraction of intervals is imputed to the left hemisphere. These experiments have been conducted largely on normal subjects, both non-musicians (Peretz and Morais 1980; Peretz 1987; Peretz *et al.* 1987) and musicians (Peretz and Babaï 1992). More recently, employing the same type of tasks as performed by normal subjects, the relevance of this distinction has

---

5. The difference in pitch between two adjacent sounds can be defined either by a (logarithmic) frequency continuum, for which the term 'interval' will be used here, or by a musical scale. This latter interpretation of pitch will be identified here by the general term of 'tonal function' (see Bigand, Ch. 2 this volume).

been extended to research conducted on brain-damaged subjects (Peretz 1990). This latter research has led me to hypothesize that the extraction of contour was a preliminary and indispensable step to the precise encoding of intervals (see the direction of the arrows in Fig. 7.2).

These experiments entailed running a series of tests on patients who had sustained a unilateral cerebrovascular accident. Four of the tests were designed to measure the use of contour as opposed to intervals in the discrimination and recognition of unfamiliar melodies. It is the convergence of the results obtained across all four tests that are most persuasive concerning the status of processing. By way of illustration, however, the results of just two of the tests will be discussed here. The same melodies were employed and the same tasks were performed in both tests: these involved judging whether two melodies played successively were the same or different. When the second melody differed, it always varied by just a single tone whose serial position changed from one trial to the next. In the 'contour-violated' test, the modified tone altered the contour (and thus also altered the intervals). In the other, the 'contour-preserved' test, the modified tone altered the precise size of the intervals but not the contour (see examples in Fig. 7.4). The use of contour as a discriminating cue should facilitate comparison in the contour-violated condition by comparison with the contour-preserved condition; in this latter condition, exact interval discrimination was necessary to successfully accomplish the task.

The control group performed better in the contour-violated situation than in the contour-preserved situation. This robust effect (already observed under the same conditions by Peretz and Morais (1987) and Zatorre (1985)) indicates that subjects normally used contour in discriminating melodies. This tendency was also present in subjects with a left-hemisphere lesion but not in those with a right-hemisphere lesion. Figure 7.4 gives the results for eight patients (from among 20) with a deficit in one or the other condition. A deficit was considered as such when performance fell below the normal range. The interesting aspect of such an analysis at the individual level is that all the patients who displayed a deficit in using contour (the five patients with a lesion in the right hemisphere, Fig. 7.4) also displayed a deficit in the use of intervals, as shown by their poor performance in the contour-preserved condition. This systematic association between the deficits for processing intervals and processing contour observed in the right-brain-damaged patients stands in sharp distinction to the relatively clear dissociation between these same melodic features exhibited by the left-brain-damaged patients. Thus, the results suggest that it is still possible to use contour when interval processing is deficient, but not vice versa. When contour is affected, intervals are also affected.

Taken in isolation, such results should be interpreted with caution, for

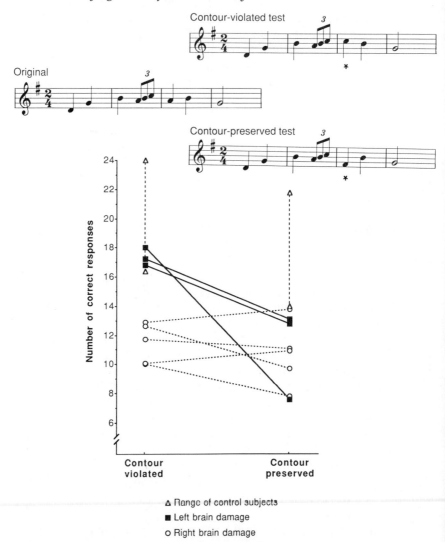

Fig. 7.4   Examples of stimuli and graph of results obtained in the discrimination of these stimuli by brain-damaged patients displaying a deficit in the 'contour-violated' condition or the 'contour-preserved' condition.

a number of reasons. The major one is that, in the case of lesions to the right hemisphere, an association between two disorders was observed. This association does not necessarily indicate a link between the two tasks, since it may stem from the fact that a lesion has damaged two components, and not just one. For two components to be damaged by a lesion, however, they must occupy anatomically adjacent regions; but there is sufficiently strong evidence to suggest, to the contrary, that the two components in question involve neural substrates that are far apart, i.e. in different cerebral hemispheres. This leads to the assumption that the observed association means that extraction of contour is necessary for and occurs prior to the processing of intervals. This hypothesis confirms the two-component theory proposed by Dowling (1978) since it supports a functional distinction between interval processing and contour processing. In addition, the neuropsychological data suggest that this model does not involve parallel processing but rather a serial two-stage process (analogous to the structure of the model shown in Fig. 7.1).

These data illustrate how neuropsychology supports and can shed light on the distinction between the processing of contour and the processing of intervals in melodies. There remains, however, an essential aspect of the melodic organization of these intervals that has not yet been addressed—namely, the tonal interpretation of such intervals. A growing number of experiments conducted with normal subjects shows that the processing of pitch (or interval) reflects the listener's tonal knowledge. This knowledge refers to the schemas or representations specifying the set of pitches and the combination rules that are acceptable in a melody belonging to the Western, or tonal, musical system (see Krumhansl (1990) and Bigand (Ch. 2 this volume) for further details). Moreover, there are empirical and theoretical reasons for supposing that the tonal interpretation of pitch is based on a processing component highly specific to music and relatively autonomous in relation to the two other melodic components involved (Peretz and Morais 1989).

Neuropsychological data support this idea. Francès *et al.* (1973) and myself (Peretz 1993) have found that the tonal interpretation of pitch can be disrupted as a result of brain damage. The selective nature of this disruption nevertheless remains difficult to establish, since patients who display a loss at this level also have serious short-term memory deficits. In both studies, patients were found to have difficulty in remembering melodies of more than six notes. In my own work, I therefore used very short sequences and, once again, employed multiple tasks. One of them was drawn directly from experimental research in normal subjects, and will be given here as an illustration of the loss of tonal sense observed in the patient G.L.

The task in question was one successfully used by Cuddy and Badertscher (1987, the major triad condition) with six-year-old children (see also Trehub and Trainor (Ch. 9 this volume) for even more precocious evidence of this predisposition). In this test, listeners heard a context sequence followed by a tone that could take any chromatic value in the octave (see the example given in Fig. 7.5). Their task was to assess the extent to which this final tone constituted an acceptable conclusion to the melody. Judgements given by children and by adults with no musical

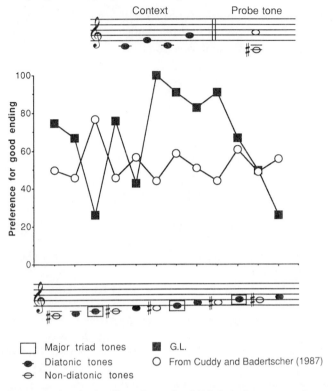

Fig. 7.5   An example of stimuli and graph of G.L.'s judgements of appropriateness of final tone as a function of the pitch of the last tone of the context sequence. The results obtained under the same conditions by six-year-old children tested by Cuddy and Badertscher (1987) are included for comparison.

training preserved tonal constraints—they systematically preferred scale tones (filled notes on the musical staff in Fig. 7.5), and most notably those making up the major triad (boxed notes on the same staff). G.L., however, proceeded otherwise. As he himself explained, his judgements were based on his impression that singers normally conclude on a note that is close but lower in pitch. In other words, he relied on interval size and contour. This is effectively what emerges from an analysis of his responses, as shown in Fig. 7.5. Apart from the most distant tones (A# and B, which in fact had an ambiguous pitch), G.L. felt that the last tone was appropriate when it descended (all those which preceded G) and more particularly so when it was close in pitch, and rejected those that ascended (G#, A). His judgements were thus made irrespective of the tonal status of the pitches.

Once again, this illustration is merely suggestive and does not alone constitute a demonstration of G.L.'s loss of tonal sense. It is only the convergence of the results of this patient on six other tests (in matched individual comparisons with the results obtained by each normal control subject) that allows me to argue that G.L.'s behaviour, described here in the context of Cuddy and Badertscher's task, is representative of his perceptual disorder. In general, G.L. employed contour and intervals to fulfil the requirements of the task, but remained perfectly insensitive to tonal structure. What is involved is therefore not a generalized melodic deficiency, but one basically affecting the tonal component. It is interesting to point out in passing that the inverse dissociation may occur. There has been a recent report of a patient suffering from agnosia and displaying a marked deterioration in the perception of intervals yet retaining traces of tonal interpretation (Tramo *et al.* 1990).

To sum up, neuropsychological data suggest the existence of a tonal component relatively distinct from the other components involved in the melodic organization of a musical sequence. Moreover, the fact that patients with such impaired access to tonal knowledge also display major impairment of short-term memory, as mentioned above, may be taken as further evidence for the important role that tonal interpretation has in melodic organization. In other words, the results are quite compatible with one of the major roles attributed to tonal encoding of pitch, namely that of restricting the number of interval categories so that these can be assimilated by the limited capacity of the human perceptual system (Dowling 1978).

The lexicon

Up to this point, it has been argued that there are probably two basic routes to recognizing a familiar tune based on its perceptual organization: the melodic route (which involves a series of distinct stages) and the rhythmic route (for which an internal trajectory remains to be established; see Fig. 7.2). In theory, a cerebral lesion interrupting one route or the other should yield difficulty in recognizing a familiar tune. The data examined in the section on agnosia did not provide information on this issue since the existence of perceptual disorders was usually inferred on the basis of a single test and, in addition, offered little information on the nature of discrimination cues.

The two cases of music agnosia that I have studied personally—patients C.N. and G.L.—both exhibited amelodia but no arhythmia, that is to say their abnormal difficulty in melodic organization was not accompanied by problems in rhythmic organization (see Fig. 7.3). They also both displayed a total inability to recognize tunes that had once been thoroughly familiar to them. The co-existence of amelodia with the inability to recognize a tune is intriguing. It suggests that access to the lexicon is more strongly determined by melody than by rhythm. Indeed, if rhythm offered such access, C.N. and G.L.—whose rhythmic route seemed intact—should have displayed traces of recognition. Recognizing a tune from its rhythmic pattern alone nevertheless appears possible, according to the available literature, although this possibility remains highly limited (White 1960). In White's experiment, subjects were presented with a modified familiar tune and then had to chose from among ten possible titles for it. When the modification neutralized rhythmic variations (by making all durations equal) yet preserved melodic structure, 88 per cent of the tunes were correctly identified compared with only 33 per cent when the opposite modification was performed and in which only the rhythm would allow identification. Thus, this difference in results supports the idea that melody is more determinant than rhythm. In addition, the low rate of correct responses concerning rhythm could be the result of inferential rather than perceptual processes. The fact that subjects were offered multiple choices highly restricted the possibilities and encouraged reliance on auditory mental imagery.

The idea that the melodic route is crucial for accessing the lexicon, and therefore for recognizing a musical passage, stems from an association observed in two patients and therefore remains an hypothesis requiring verification, notably in normal subjects. This hypothesis does not exclude the possibility that the unit of access results from the combination of melody and rhythm. Nevertheless, within this combination and in the context of Western musical culture in which melodic organization is more sophisticated (and thus more informative) than rhythmic organization, the hypothesis is that melodic structure expressed in terms of tonal intervals is the most determining factor.

The internal organization of this musical lexicon remains largely undefined. The only light that neuropsychology sheds on the nature of the lexicon is that it is probably 'purely' musical and not mixed, as Serafine and her colleagues suggest (Serafine *et al.* 1984). As mentioned above, this team of researchers has shown that given judicious manipulation of the text and tune of newly learned songs, listeners behaved as though they could not access the tune without having access to the words, and vice versa. This phenomenon would seem to imply that we have only a single lexicon, in which words and music are represented as a single unit for a given song. Quite apart from personal experience of this phenomenon that renders such a hypothesis implausible (we have all found ourselves compulsively humming a tune yet unable to recall the words that go with it, though perhaps not the converse—see the directions of the arrows in the diagram in Fig. 7.2), neuropsychological data are incompatible with this idea of a single, mixed lexicon. A patient unable to discern the words can nevertheless recognize the tune (Laignel-Lavastine and Alajouanine 1921; Yaqub *et al.* 1988), and vice versa. C.N. displays this latter condition, since she can unhesitatingly recognize the words to familiar songs yet is unable to recognize the corresponding music.

From a collection of 58 songs known to C.N. prior to her cerebral accident, subsequently played to her without the words, she could recall the words that went with them in only five cases, and with a great deal of hesitation. In a 'lexical decision' task requiring her to judge whether these tunes were familiar or not, 66.6 per cent of her answers were correct—only slightly better than chance. In contrast, when she was asked to make the same type of decision based on the lyrics (whether sung or spoken), she invariably had scores of 90 per cent or more correct responses. This high rate of recognition was independent of whether or not the lyrics were taken from the beginning of the song (and therefore often corresponding to the title, e.g. 'Au clair de la lune') or were mixed in with the titles of films or familiar expressions. C.N. therefore exhibits a clear dissociation between access to lyrics, which she retained, and access to tunes, which was impaired. If the tune were in fact represented together with lyrics in an integral fashion, brain damage at this level should lead to a joint and similar deterioration of words and music. This is not the case. Furthermore, when C.N's responses are analysed song by song, no link between recall of words and that of music emerges; for example, of those songs whose words she recognized as familiar, the music was judged unfamiliar as often as it was judged familiar. Finally, and above all, when music and words were combined, C.N. could recognize the words of the songs irrespective of the tune to which they were sung. Her responses were 91.6 per cent correct, whether these words were sung to the right tune or to a totally unknown tune. Recognition was therefore not any better when words were sung to the usual tune than when they accompanied a totally arbitrary tune.

A possible explanation—not a parsimonious one, but compatible with the neuropsychological data as well as with Serafine's results—is that there are not one or two lexicons, but three. One would be purely musical and a second purely verbal, as argued here (Fig. 7.2), whereas the third would be mixed. This is suggested by the results obtained by Samson and Zatorre (1991), who asked lobectomized patients to perform Serafine's task. The differential involvement of these three lexicons might be conceived in terms of a reliance on the mixed lexicon when a unique relation exists between words and music or when the excerpt was heard just one time. This is the case with songs learned in the laboratory, but not with songs known since childhood. For these latter, two distinct lexicons would be compiled.

In this final section, dealing with the access to and the nature of the musical lexicon, we have seen that neuropsychological data raise many questions. Research in this specific area, more than anywhere else, is particularly in need of development in both cognitive psychology and neuropsychology.

7.4   COMMENTS AND OUTLOOK

This chapter has shown how research in a specific auditory domain, namely music, can lead to the development of functional models far more elaborate than initial reports of auditory agnosia had suggested. It is my conviction that each domain should be explored in similar fashion if we want to understand how sound events are recognized, and what principles of cerebral organization are involved. This should lead to a better appreciation of the question of functional specificity, by distinguishing general-purpose mechanisms from specialized mechanisms, thereby identifying the levels at which cognitive domains divide. For example, it is reasonable to assume that the processing of melodic contour is not specific to music but also participates in the perception of intonation contours in speech. If this is the case, any impairment at this level should necessarily disrupt both melody perception and sensitivity to intonation.

It should be stressed, in this respect, that the marked activity in the musical domain compared with other non-verbal domains is probably due to the fact that cognitive psychology has devoted exceptional attention to this field over the past 20 years. It is therefore likely, though not necessarily certain, that progress in the neuropsychological study of voice recognition and that of other sound events will depend on the interest shown by cognitive psychologists for these topics.

Indeed, it must be acknowledged that neuropsychological research follows, clarifies, and perhaps even inspires, but rarely guides, research on normal functioning. However, even if this situation turns out to be permanent, neuropsychology—like developmental research (see Trehub and Trainor, Ch. 9 this volume)—can shed light on the way in which a system is constructed. Moreover, it would be helpful if the various fields of research referred to the same conceptual and empirical frameworks, namely those based on the cognitive study of young college adults, in order to facilitate the integration of data originating from different perspectives.

ACKNOWLEDGEMENTS

This chapter was prepared with support from the Natural Sciences and Engineering Research Council of Canada.

REFERENCES

Albert, M. and Bear, D. (1974). Time to understand: a case study of word deafness with reference to the role of time in auditory comprehension. *Brain*, **97**, 373–84.

Allen, M. (1983). Models of hemispheric specialization. *Psychological Bulletin*, **93**, 73–104.

Assal, G. (1973). Aphasie de Wernicke sans amusie chez un pianiste. *Revue Neurologique*, **129**, 251–5.

Auerbach, S., Allard, T., Naeser, M., Alexander, M., and Albert, M. (1982). Pure word deafness: analysis of a case with bilateral lesion and a defect at the prephonemic level. *Brain*, **105**, 271–300.

Bever, T. and Chiarello, R. (1974). Cerebral dominance in musicians and non musicians. *Science*, **185**, 537–9.

Boltz, M. and Jones, M. R. (1986). Does rule recursion make melodies easier to reproduce? If not, what does? *Cognitive Psychology*, **18**, 389–431.

Bouillaud, J. (1865). Sur la faculté du langage articulé. *Bulletin de l'Académie de Médecine*, **30**, 752–68.

Bradshaw, J. and Nettleton, N. (1981). The nature of hemispheric specialization in man. *The Behavioral and Brain Sciences*, **4**, 51–91.

Bregman, A. S. (1990) *Auditory scene analysis: the perceptual organization of sound.* MIT, Cambridge, MA.

Broca, P. (1861). Remarques sur le siège de la faculté du langage articulé, suivies d'une observation d'aphémie. *Bulletin et Mémoires de la Société Anatomique de Paris*, **2**, 330–57.

Brust, J. (1980). Music and language: musical alexia and agraphia. *Brain*, **103**, 367–92.

Butchel, H. and Stewart, J. (1989). Auditory agnosia: apperceptive or associative disorder? *Brain and Language*, **37**, 12–25.

Caramazza, A. (1984). The logic of neuropsychological research of patient classification in aphasia. *Brain and Language*, **21**, 9–20.

Chocholle, R., Chedru, F., Botte, M.-C., Chain, F., and Lhermitte, F. (1975). Etude psychoacoustique d'un cas de 'surdité corticale'. *Neuropsychologia*, **13**, 163–72.

Cuddy, L. and Badertscher, B. (1987). Recovery of the tonal hierarchy: some comparisons across age and levels of musical experience. *Perception and Psychophysics*, **41**, 609–20.

Denes, G. and Semenza, C. (1975). Auditory modality-specific anomia: evidence from a case of pure word deafness. *Cortex*, **11**, 401–11.

Deutsch, D. and Feroe, J. (1981). The internal representation of pitch sequences in tonal music. *Psychological Review*, **88**, 503–22.

Dorgeuille, C. (1966). Introduction à l'étude des amusies. Ph.D. thesis, Université de la Sorbonne, Paris.

Dowling, W. (1978). Scale and contour: two components of a theory of memory for melodies. *Psychological Review*, **85**, 341–54.

Dowling, W. and Harwood, D. (1986). *Music cognition.* Academic, New York.

Dunn, J. C. and Kirsner, K. (1988). Discovering functionally independent mental processes: the principle of reversed association. *Psychological Review*, **95**, 91–101.

Ellis, A. and Young, A. (1988). *Human cognitive neuropsychology.* Erlbaum, London.

Eustache, F., Lechevalier, B., Viader, F., and Lambert, J. (1990). Identification and discrimination disorders in auditory perception: a report on two cases. *Neuropsychologia*, **28**, 257–70.

Fodor, J. (1983). *The modularity of mind.* MIT Press, Cambridge, MA.

Francès, R., Lhermitte, F., and Verdy, M. (1973). Le déficit musical des aphasiques. *Revue Internationale de Psychologie Appliquée*, **22**, 117–35.

Gates, A. and Bradshaw, J. (1977). Music perception and cerebral asymmetries. *Cortex*, **13**, 390–401.

Halpern, A. (1984). Organization in memory for familiar songs. *Journal of Experimental Psychology: Learning, Memory and Cognition*, **10**, 496–512.

Houtsma, A. and Goldstein, J. (1971). The central origin of the pitch of complex tones: evidence from musical interval recognition. *Journal of the Acoustical Society of America*, **2**, 520–9.

Hugdahl, K. (1988). *Handbook of dichotic listening: theory, methods and research*. Wiley, New York.

Jackendoff, R. (1987). *Consciousness and the computational mind*. MIT Press, Cambridge, MA.

Jones, M.R. (1987). Dynamic pattern structure in music: recent theory and research. *Perception and Psychophysics*, **41**, 621–34.

Jones, M. R. , Boltz, M., and Kidd, G. (1982). Controlled attending as a function of melodic and temporal context. *Perception and Psychophysics*, **32**, 211–18.

Jones, M. R, Summerell, L., and Marshburn, E. (1987). Recognizing melodies: a dynamic interpretation. *Quarterly Journal of Experimental Psychology*, **39A**, 89–121.

Klein, R. and Harper, J. (1956). The problem of agnosia in the light of a case of pure word deafness. *Journal of Mental Science*, **102**, 112–20.

Kohn, S. and Friedman, R. (1986). Word-meaning-deafness: a phonological–semantic dissociation. *Cognitive Neuropsychology*, **3**, 291–308.

Kosslyn, S., Flynn, R., Amsterdam, J., and Wang, G. (1990). Components of high-level vision: a cognitive neuroscience analysis and accounts of neurological syndromes. *Cognition*, **34**, 203–77.

Krumhansl, C. L. (1990). *Cognitive foundations of musical pitch*. Oxford University Press.

Laignel-Lavastine, M. and Alajouanine, T. (1921). Un cas d'agnosie auditive. *Revue Neurologique*, **37**, 194–8.

Lechevalier, B., Eustache, F., and Rossa, Y. (1985). *Les troubles de la perception de la musique d'origine neurologique*. Masson, Paris.

Lerdahl, F. and Jackendoff, R. (1983). *A generative theory of tonal music*. MIT Press, Cambridge, MA.

Lichtheim, L. (1885). On aphasia. *Brain*, **7**, 433–84.

Liberman, A. and Mattingly, I. (1985). The motor theory of speech perception revised. *Cognition*, **21**, 1–36.

Lissauer, M. (1988). A case of visual agnosia with a contribution to theory. *Cognitive Neuropsychology*, **5**, 157–92 (transl. from the German by M. Jackson; orig. publ. in *Archiv für Psychiatrie und Nervenkrankheiten*, **21**, 222–70, 1889).

Luria, A., Tsvetkova, L., and Futer, J. (1965). Aphasia in a composer. *Journal of Neurological Science*, **2**, 288–92.

McClelland, J. and Elman, J. (1986). The TRACE model of speech perception. *Cognitive Psychology*, **18**, 1–86.

Mann, V. and Liberman, P. (1983). Some differences between phonetic and auditory modes of perception. *Cognition*, **14**, 211–35.

Marin, O. (1982). Neurological aspects of music perception and performance. In *The psychology of music* (ed. D.Deutsch), pp. 453–78. Academic, New York.

Mavlov, L. (1980). Amusia due to rhythm agnosia in a musician with left hemisphere damage: a non auditory supramodal defect. *Cortex*, **16**, 321–38.

Mehler, J., Morton, J., and Jusczyk, P. (1984). On reducing language to biology. *Cognitive Neuropsychology*, **1**, 83–116.

Mendez, M. and Gechan, G. (1988). Cortical auditory disorders: clinical and psychoacoustic features. *Journal of Neurology, Neurosurgery, and Psychiatry*, **51**, 1–9.

Metz-Lutz, M. N. and Dahl, E. (1984). Analysis of word comprehension in a case of pure word deafness. *Brain and Language*, **23**, 13–25.

Motomura, N., Yamadori, A., Mori, E., and Tamaru, F. (1986). Auditory agnosia: analysis of a case with bilateral subcortical lesions. *Brain*, **109**, 379–91.

Patterson, K. Marshall, J., and Coltheart, M. (1985). *Surface dyslexia: neuropsychological and cognitive analyses of phonological reading*. Erlbaum, London.

Peretz, I. (1985). Asymétrie hémisphérique dans les amusies. *Revue Neurologique*, **141**, 169–83.

Peretz, I. (1987). Shifting ear-asymmetry in melody comparison through transposition. *Cortex*, **23**, 317–23.

Peretz, I. (1990). Processing of local and global musical information in unilateral brain-damaged patients. *Brain*, **113**, 1185–205.

Peretz, I. (1993). A case of auditory atonalia. *Cognitive Neuropsychology*. (In press.)

Peretz, I. and Babaï, M. (1992). The role of contour and intervals in the recognition of melody parts: evidence from cerebral asymetries in musicians. *Neuropsychologia*, **30**, 277–92.

Peretz, I. and Kolinsky, R. (1993) Boundaries of separability between melody and rhythm in music discrimination: a neuropsychological perspective. *Quarterly Journal of Experimental Psychology*. (In press.)

Peretz, I. and Morais, J. (1980). Modes of processing melodies and ear-asymmetry in nonmusicians. *Neuropsychologia*, **20**, 477–89.

Peretz, I. and Morais, J. (1987). Analytic processing in the classification of melodies as same or different. *Neuropsychologia*, **25**, 645–52.

Peretz, I. and Morais, J. (1988). Determinants of laterality for music: towards an information processing account. In *Handbook of dichotic listening: theory, methods, and research* (ed. K. Hugdahl), pp. 323–58. Wiley, New York.

Peretz, I. and Morais, J. (1989). Music and modularity. *Contemporary Music Review*, **4**, 277–91.

Peretz, I., Morais, J., and Bertelson, P. (1987). Shifting ear differences in melody recognition through strategy inducement. *Brain and Cognition*, **6**, 202–15.

Peretz, I., Kolinsky, R., Hublet, C., Labrecque, R., Demeurisse, G., and Belleville, S. (1991) Auditory agnosia can be domain specific: functional analysis of two cases of music agnosia following bilateral cortical damage [unpublished data].

Povel, D. (1984). A theoretical framework for rhythm perception. *Psychological Research*, **45**, 315–37.

Saffran, E., Marin, O., and Yeni-Komshian, G. (1976). An analysis of speech perception in word deafness. *Brain and Language*, **3**, 209–28.

Samson, S. and Zatorre, R. (1991). Recognition memory for text and melody of songs after unilateral temporal lobe lesion: evidence for dual encoding. *Journal of Experimental Psychology: Learning, Memory and Cognition*, **17**, 793–804.

Serafine, M. L., Crowder, R. G., and Repp, B. (1984). Integration of melody and text in memory for song. *Cognition,* **16,** 285–303.

Shallice, T. (1988). *From neuropsychology to mental structure.* Cambridge University Press, Cambridge.

Shimamura, A. (1989). Disorders of memory: the cognitive science perspective. In *Handbook of neuropsychology,* Vol. 3 (ed. F.Boller and J. Crafman), pp. 35–73. Elsevier, Amsterdam.

Spreen, O., Benton, A., and Fincham, R. (1965). Auditory agnosia without aphasia. *Archives of Neurology,* **13,** 84–92.

Tanaka, Y., Yamadori, A. and Mori, E. (1987). Pure word deafness following bilateral lesions: a psychophysical analysis. *Brain,* **110,** 381–403.

Teuber, H. (1955). Physiological psychology. *Annual Review of Psychology,* **9,** 267–96.

Tramo, M., Bharucha, J., and Musiek, F. (1990). Music perception and cognition following bilateral lesions of auditory cortex. *Journal of Cognitive Neuroscience,* **2,** 195–212.

Van Lancker, D. and Kreiman, J. (1987). Voice discrimination and recognition are separate abilities. *Neuropsychologia,* **25,** 829–34.

Van Lancker, D. Cummings, J., Kreiman, J., and Dobkin, B. (1988). Phonagnosia: a dissociation between familiar and unfamiliar voices. *Cortex,* **24,** 195–209.

Vignolo, L. (1982). Auditory agnosia. *Philosophical Transactions of the Royal Society of London,* **298,** 49–57.

Wernicke, C. (1874). The symptom complex of aphasia. A psychological study on an anatomical basis. *Boston Studies in the Philosophy of Science,* **4,** 34–97.

White, B. (1960). Recognition of distorted melodies. *American Journal of Psychology,* **73,** 100–7.

Yaqub, B., Gascon, G., Alnosha, M., and Whitaker, H. (1988). Pure word deafness (acquired verbal auditory agnosia) in an Arabic speaking patient. *Brain,* **111,** 457–66.

Zatorre, R. (1984). Musical perception and cerebral function: a critical review. *Music Perception,* **2,** 196–221.

Zatorre, R. (1985). Discrimination and recognition of tonal melodies after unilateral cerebral excisions. *Neuropsychologia,* **23,** 31–41.

Zatorre, R. (1988). Pitch perception of complex tones and human cerebral lobe function. *Journal of the Acoustical Society of America,* **84,** 566–72.

8

Contributions of music to research on human auditory cognition

Emmanuel Bigand

(Translated from the French by Deke Dusinberre)

8.0 INTRODUCTION

A look at the body of work devoted to music perception reveals two major ways of conceiving of music as a phenomenon that can contribute to research on auditory cognition.

The first essentially stresses the highly complex acoustical and temporal nature of musical stimuli. For listeners, music is initially just an agglomeration of atmospheric vibrations that strike the eardrums. The question, then, is how listeners manage to transform these vibrations into a set of sound signals having specific auditory qualities and coherence. Numerous experiments have attempted to answer this question by studying the perception of basic attributes such as pitch, timbre, duration, and loudness (Rasch and Plomp 1982; Risset and Wessel 1982; Sundberg 1982; Dowling and Harwood 1986, Chs 1–3).

The second approach deals with music as a complex sequential organization. The question here is how listeners manage to perceive relations between sound events separated in time. As Francès observed (1988, p. 202), 'listeners experience a strictly irreversible succession; they are required to perform the original perceptual task of discovering a structure as the evolving sound unfolds'. Music is a temporal art; comprehending it therefore requires 'not only an act of memorization, but also a constant effort to link past to present in a relationship that is ultimately of an intellectual rather than perceptual order' (Imberty 1969, p. 115). Substantial research has already shed light on the nature of the processes involved at this level; although most experiments used short musical passages of several notes, the current trend is to work with much longer musical passages (Imberty 1979, 1981a; Sloboda and Parker 1985; Deliège 1990; Clarke and Krumhansl 1990).

Given this double complexity, music constitutes rich matter for studying the elaborate perceptual and cognitive processes that human beings

Thinking in sound: the cognitive psychology of human audition, ed. S. McAdams and E. Bigand. Oxford University Press, 1993, pp. 231–77.

employ when confronted with non-verbal auditory stimuli. The way in which a listener perceives and memorizes music therefore offers a unique opportunity to understand the human mind (Peretz and Morais 1989).

It might seem too restrictive, however, to view the contribution of music to the cognitive sciences solely from the perspective of stimulus complexity. Thus Sloboda (1985), right from the outset of his book, reminds readers that the prime feature of music is its ability to evoke a rich and varied range of feelings and emotions. 'Somehow the human mind endows these sounds with significance. They become symbols for something other than pure sound' (Sloboda 1985, p. 10). The acoustic complexity of music is ultimately only a medium for expressing a meaning that should not be confused with the sounds themselves, just as the object with which a child plays is only a medium offering access to another plane of reality—a stick of wood becomes a horse, an aeroplane, a sword, an individual, a boat. The stick possesses symbolic value that distances it from concrete reality (Piaget 1959), and music fulfils a similar symbolic function; for Imberty it

induces meaning in the name of one of humankind's universal ambitions, namely to grasp and represent the world according to fancy, to the sphere of desire and dream, by replacing the immediate perception of nature with a culture dictating new subjective relations that establish a world of values distinct from the universe of objects' (Imberty 1979, p. 12).

Music demonstrates in exemplary fashion that language is not the only type of sound that carries meaning. Understanding this symbolic dimension would lead to a better understanding of certain aspects of human auditory cognition. Three theoretical issues stem from this approach. The first concerns the nature of the meaning actually conveyed by a piece of music, as explored by the fields of musical semiology (Nattiez 1987) and experimental psychology (see Ch. 8 in Dowling and Harwood (1986) for a review). The second issue entails determining the nature of the sound structures that carry meaning in music (Hevner 1935, 1936; Francès 1988; Imberty 1979, 1981a). The last issue, finally, opens on to a considerably vaster theoretical field. As symbolic form, music would appear to be a potential medium for non-verbal communication. Indeed, in all societies it is a social activity basically arising from the desire to communicate or establish a meaningful exchange with others. In the West in particular, 'every musical work communicates a way of feeling, seeing, and interpreting that the artist offers to other people in the hope that they will perceive at least part of his intentions' (Imberty 1979, p. 12). Music could thus be considered a form of non-verbal auditory communication, one that entertains an ambiguous relationship to language. Research might then address the theoretical issue of whether these two forms of expression entail a shared competence for communicating via sound signals (Lerdahl and Jackendoff 1983; Sloboda 1985; Clarke 1989) and whether they are based on similar systems for processing symbolic information. These questions are examined in the chapters by Peretz (Ch. 7) and Trehub and Trainor (Ch. 9) in this volume.

These two conceptions of music—one stressing the complexity of musical stimuli and the other stressing its symbolic dimension—are obviously not incompatible. The first examines the way in which information is processed by listeners to enable them to organize the acoustic field and perceive musical forms, whereas the second examines the symbolic interpretation of those forms. The processes revealed in the first approach produce the mental representations that would seem to constitute the input for the processes studied by the second approach. It is also worth stressing the extent to which these processes must be intrinsically linked since minor changes in the initial acoustic structures sometimes provoke major changes in the musical expressivity perceived by listeners, as demonstrated by work on musical performance (cf. Clarke 1985).

It would be useful, therefore, to reconcile the initial complexity of the stimulus with the wealth of meanings that it is accorded once analysed. In other words, what mechanisms of information processing are used by listeners to attribute a particularly rich and expressive symbolic value to what was originally just a series of acoustic signals?

The goal of this chapter is to provide a functional synthesis of the basic elements of the current response of experimental psychology to this question.

These basic elements will be presented in three parts. The first part concerns the listener's 'abstract musical knowledge structures' (McAdams 1989). As in all other realms of perception, knowledge plays a major role in the perception of music. Numerous experiments have recently demonstrated what this entails (mainly in Western listeners) and how such knowledge is structured. The second part concerns the way in which the knowledge is used and combined with various processes of perceptual organization during 'event structure processing' (McAdams 1989), that is to say during the real-time processing of musical information. The final part concerns the symbolizing processes involved once the event structure has been analysed.

8.1 ABSTRACT MUSICAL KNOWLEDGE STRUCTURES

Abstract musical knowledge takes two distinct forms:

a system of relations among musical categories (such as pitch categories, scale structures, and tonal and metric hierarchies), and a lexicon of abstract patterns that are frequently encountered (such as the gallop rhythm, gap-fill melody, sonata or *rāg* form) (McAdams 1989, p. 183).

In most musics throughout the world, sound dimensions such as pitch, duration, loudness, and timbre are divided into categories that are organized into ordered relationships. Listeners possess a knowledge of these categories and systems of relations that are needed to analyse pieces of music produced by the culture to which they belong. In many cases, this knowledge is implicit and is the product of acculturation (Francès 1988). Listeners who are non-musicians are unable to name the different categories of musical dimensions, yet they are perfectly capable of perceiving them. By way of comparison, it might be said that music is understood by non-musician listeners in the same way young children understand their native language—they obviously know the rules of syntax because they are able to apply them, though they are unable to name these rules. Such knowledge becomes explicit only after specific study, as is the case with trained musicians.

The (implicit/explicit) knowledge of the system of relations between categories has been particularly well explored for pitch in Western tonal music. In such music, whether the specific form is baroque, classical, Romantic, jazz, popular (tango, rock, pop, film scores, advertising music, military marches, etc.) or traditional folk music, pitch is the main form-bearing element. That is why pitch has been the focus of a good deal of research in cognitive psychology.

8.1.1   Knowledge of tonal hierarchies

In order to appreciate these studies, some music theory is required. Figure 8.1 presents a diagram of the system of tonal relations used in Western music.

Western music is based on an alphabet of twelve notes, known as the chromatic scale. The system then constitutes subsets of seven notes from this alphabet, each subset being called a scale or key. The key of C major (C, D, E, F, G, A, B) is an example of one such subset. Since there are twelve notes in the alphabet, twelve keys can be elaborated. And since each key can be in the major mode or minor mode, a total of twenty-four basic keys is possible.

It has been established that Western (or Westernized) listeners, even non-musicians, posses an implicit knowledge of these various keys (Francès 1988). This has been confirmed by experiments employing paradigms of melodic completion (Teplov 1966), memorization (Krumhansl 1979, experiments 2, 3), and detection of a changed note (Dewar *et al.* 1977). Dewar *et al.*, for example, noted that a changed note within a tonal melody is easier to perceive when the note is from a different key than when it belongs to the original key. Listeners therefore possess knowledge of the

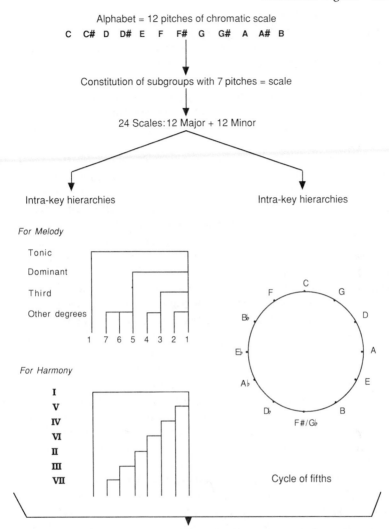

Fig. 8.1 Schematic diagram of the tonal system. Based on an alphabet of 12 notes organized in scales (major and minor), the system establishes two types of hierarchy—hierarchies internal to each key (left) that emerge from the melody and from sequences of chords, and hierarchies that exist between keys (right), represented here by the 'cycle of fifths.'

different keys. This knowledge enables them to detect the moments at which music modulates, that is to say changes key.

Music theory distinguishes hierarchies within these keys. The note by which the key is called (the tonic) is the most important hierarchically, followed by the fifth note in the scale, called 'the dominant' because it dominates the others. Several experiments have shown that listeners posses knowledge of these hierarchies (Krumhansl 1979; Krumhansl and Kessler 1982) even if they are not musicians (Francès 1988, experiment 4). One of the most famous experimental paradigms on this issue—even if it has been the object of methodological debate (Butler 1989, 1990a; Krumhansl 1990a,b)—was developed by Krumhansl and her colleagues. Krumhansl and Shepard (1979) played all seven notes of the C major scale, followed by one of the twelve notes of the chromatic scale. Subjects had to rate, on a scale of one to seven, the extent to which the single note completed the passage. The results indicated that, for all listeners, the notes judged to give the least adequate completion of the passage were those notes not belonging to the key of C major, which confirms the implicit knowledge of various keys. Above all, however, the authors noted a hierarchy within the notes comprising the key of C. All listeners felt that the tonic note best completed the passage played. Among those subjects with the most musical training, the fifth, followed by the third, obtained systematically higher ratings than the other notes of the scale. In another experiment, the authors managed to reveal such hierarchies by using pure tones. These results are important because they indicate that subjects' responses cannot be explained by interference between the harmonics of the notes comprising the original passage and those of the single note. Similar results have been obtained by Bharucha (1987). It would thus seem that these hierarchies are cognitive in origin and not sensory.

Such knowledge indicates that listeners are potentially able to attribute a specific weight to each note within a tonal melody. In the C major passage shown in Fig. 8.2, notes not belonging to the key (C#, D#) are assigned the least weight in the tonal hierarchy. Somewhat more weight is given to notes located on the weak degrees of the key (D, F, A), followed by the third (E) and the fifth (G), all of these being subordinated to the tonic (C).

These different hierarchical weights create differences in musical function—hierarchically important notes are notes on which the musical passage may end, whereas less important notes (from a hierarchic standpoint) are only passing tones. On the psychological level, these differences in function generate patterns of musical tension and relaxation; notes low on the tonal hierarchy produce strong tensions that will be resolved by the arrival of more stable notes.

Numerous experiments have demonstrated this. Francès (1988, experiment 2) mistuned certain notes on a piano. In some instances, lowering

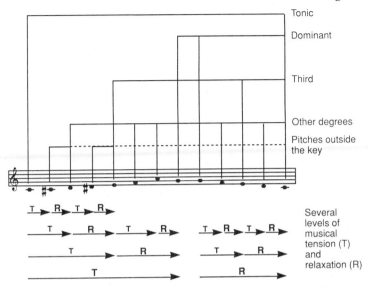

Fig. 8.2 Each note in a melody in C major is assigned a tonal weight (above); the corresponding levels of musical tension (T) and relaxation (R) are noted underneath.

the pitch of the note increased the musical tension created by that note, while in other instances, it moved toward relaxation. For example, in the key of C major, the sequence B–C creates a local pattern of tension/relaxation. Increasing the absolute pitch of B means moving toward resolution, lowering it means moving in the opposite direction. Subjects were then asked to indicate which notes of the piano were out of tune. Francès observed that the ear's tolerance concerning approximations of tuning accuracy was greater when such approximations moved toward increased musical tension.

The existence of musical tension and relaxation was confirmed, moreover, by the phenomena of asymmetry noted by Krumhansl (1979) and Bharucha (1984). Following a procedure similar to that used by Krumhansl and Shepard (1979), Krumhansl (1979) observed that a C followed a D less well when played after a sequence in C major than did the same two notes played in reverse order (D and then C). In the first instance, the D (second interval) is a note hierarchically less important than C (the tonic). The only interpretation for this asymmetry is that the C/D pair contained greater musical tension than the D/C pair, leading listeners to assign greater dissimilarity to the elements comprising it.

Since a hierarchy of structural importance exists, it might be thought that these patterns of tension and relaxation are also perceived in hierarchic fashion. This is one of the central hypotheses of the model proposed by Lerdahl and Jackendoff (1983), to which we will return in Section

8.2.3. In Fig. 8.2, for example, the C# creates strong tension that is immediately resolved by the appearance of D, a hierarchically more important note. But D, itself a note low on the hierarchy of the C major scale, creates musical tension that will be resolved by the appearance of a hierarchically more important note—E. This engenders two levels of musical tension/relaxation patterns: local patterns at the first level (C–C#–D; D–D#–E) are included in a larger tension/relaxation pattern produced by C–D–E. The same type of analysis can be applied iteratively to the rest of the melody. The note E, which is hierarchically less important than G, establishes a third level in the tension/relaxation pattern, namely C–E–G. This pattern is itself part of a more fundamental musical progression going from C to G and resolving to the final C.

Only hierarchies within a melodic line have been discussed so far (Fig. 8.1). Musical theory also assigns a group of seven chords, or degrees, to each key. These chords are represented by the Roman numerals I, II, III, IV, V, VI, and VII.[1] From the standpoint of theory, a hierarchy exists between these chords. The first degree chord is the most important, followed by the fifth and the fourth degrees. In various experiments, Bharucha and Krumhansl (1983) and Krumhansl and Kessler (1982) observed implicit knowledge of these hierarchies, even among listeners who had never studied music theory—the seventh degree appeared less structurally important than the third degree, itself less important than the second degree, which was less important than the sixth degree, and so on.

This knowledge allows for the perceptual organization of any series of chords according to a strict hierarchy of structural importance, as illustrated in Fig. 8.3. All chords are subordinated to I. The other degrees are subordinated to V, either directly (like IV in this instance) or indirectly (like II and VI).

As before, these harmonic hierarchies induce musical tension and relaxation. A hierarchically weak chord generates strong musical tension that will be resolved by a hierarchically more important chord. Thus, in Fig. 8.3, II creates tension that is locally resolved by VI, which establishes a second level of musical tension resolved by IV, itself establishing a higher level of tension partially resolved by V. This entire set of musical tensions is ultimately resolved by a return to I. The psychological reality of such musical tension and relaxation as generated by harmonic hierarchies is confirmed by the phenomenon of asymmetry noted by Bharucha and Krumhansl (1983), and it might be assumed, following Lerdahl and

1. The first chord (marked I) is composed of the tonic plus two higher notes at intervals of a third. In C major, this gives C–E–G. The second chord (marked II) is derived from the same principle, starting on the second note of the scale. So in C major, chord II would include the notes D–F–A. In similar fashion, the fourth chord (IV) is composed of the notes F–A–C, whereas the fifth chord (V) is composed of G–B–D.

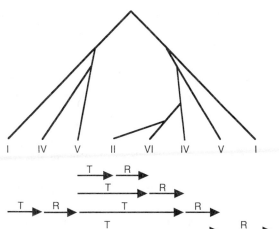

Fig. 8.3 Tonal hierarchy of chords. The roman numerals indicate the degree of each chord, and the tree diagram shows the relative hierarchic importance between these degrees. The arrows under the staff show how this hierarchy will be interpreted at several levels of tension (T) and relaxation (R) by listeners.

Jackendoff (1983), that listeners organize levels of musical tension and relaxation in hierarchic fashion.

Such intra-key hierarchies constitute an initial aspect of the organization of the tonal system. As is shown in the right half of Fig. 8.1, this system also comprises 24 different keys. A second aspect of its organization concerns the relation between these keys.

The distance between these keys has been represented by a circle called the cycle of fifths. This circle shows that the distances between the keys of C and F# is greater than the distance between C and A, which itself is greater than the distance between C and G. These distances lead to inter-key hierarchies.[2] Modulation into a distant key creates a rupture in the musical flow that is much stronger than a modulation into a nearby key. These breaks create tensions having a specific musical character that can be resolved by returning to the initial, or primary, key.

Several experiments have demonstrated that listeners possess implicit knowledge of the distance between keys (Dowling 1978; Cuddy *et al.* 1979; Krumhansl *et al.* 1982*a,b*; Bharucha and Krumhansl 1983; Trehub and Trainor, Ch. 9 this volume). Krumhansl, Bharucha, and Kessler (Krumhansl *et al.* 1982*b*) asked subjects to rate (on a scale of one to seven) the degree of concord between two chords. They observed that judgements expressed on pairs constructed with chords from the key of C major varied according to the distance between C major and the key of the musical

2. For a more elaborate representation of the distances between keys, see Lerdahl (1988, 1992).

context that preceded the playing of the pairs—nearby, moderately distant, or very distant (G major, A major, and F# major, respectively).

Thanks to this knowledge of hierarchies between keys, listeners were able to detect the moments when the musical passage modulated, and could attribute varying importance to such modulations. This knowledge of the distance between keys plays an important role in the mental representation of long musical fragments. Thus in a recent experiment I asked 40 musicians and 40 non-musicians to indicate the boundaries of the salient groupings within a long passage of chords (Bigand 1991b). The harmonic structure of this passage is indicated by the tree diagram in Fig. 8.4. The first 14 chords constitute a harmonic progression in C major, passing through V on chord 7 (half cadence), with a return to I on chord 14 (perfect cadence). Chord 15 starts a modulation to the nearby key of F major, in which the passage remains until chord 30. Chord 22 represents the passage to degree V within this key (half cadence). Chord 31 introduces a modulation toward the distant key of B major, which remains the dominant key up to the end of the sequence, chord 38 being degree V within that key.

Since there was no rhythmic, dynamic, or melodic dimension to this sequence, subjects' responses could be based only on their implicit knowledge of tonal hierarchies. For all subjects, the most salient segmentations were observed when the music modulated into a distant key (first level of the tree diagram), followed by modulation into a nearby key (second level of the tree diagram), and then as a function of the hierarchies existing within each key (perfect cadences on chords 14 and 30, half cadences on chords 7, 22, and 38). These results show that listeners can temporally structure long musical passages on the basis of tonal hierarchies alone; musical training does not have a strong impact on this performance.

Superimposing inter-key and intra-key hierarchies generates a multidimensional space (Lerdahl 1988). Each piece of tonal music allows listeners to travel within this space (Lerdahl 1992), which may be limited to short trips within the main key (as in children's songs or music-hall tunes) or may offer longer trips to nearby keys (baroque and classical music by composers such as Vivaldi, Bach, Mozart, and Haydn, as well as most 'standard' jazz themes and pop music), or may even encourage a constant coming and going between distant keys (music from the Romantic period, notably Wagner).

On a musicological level, combining the intra-key and inter-key hierarchies yields the basic framework around which the tonal system is articulated. This means that any piece of tonal music can be conceived as a highly hierarchized structure in which each note is part of a tight network of relations (Schenker 1979; Meyer 1973; Forte and Gilbert 1982; Lerdahl and Jackendoff 1983; Deliège 1984). In psychological terms,

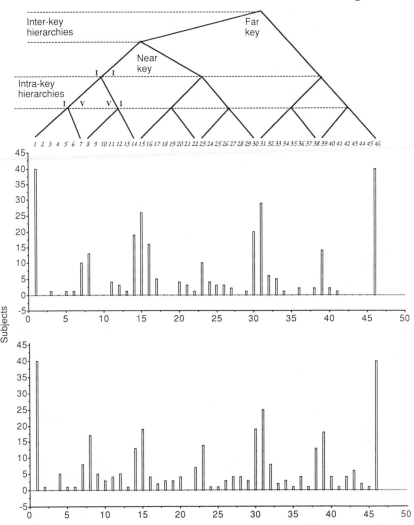

Fig. 8.4 Correspondence between the hierarchic organization of a sequence of 46 chords (top) and segmentation performed by musicians (middle) and non-musicians (bottom). Inter-key hierarchy is manifested by modulations into a distant or nearby key, whereas intra-key hierarchy is expressed as the passage to a fifth degree and a first degree chord.

Section 8.2.2 of this chapter will deal with the way in which this knowledge can be used by listeners to structure an entire set of musical events.

8.1.2 Lexicon of schemas

Knowledge of pitch hierarchies is not the only form of abstract musical knowledge. In every musical culture, rhythmic, melodic and rhythmic–melodic configurations recur frequently enough for listeners to store them in long-term memory in the form of a lexicon of schemas and proto-typical forms. Some experimental research has revealed the existence of a lexicon in Western musical culture.

The early experiments were run in the context of the theory initially proposed by Meyer (1973) and developed by Narmour (1983, 1989). Meyer (1973, Ch. 7) defines a set of melodic patterns that underlie a great number of tonal melodies and are present at various levels of hierarchic organization. The most well known are the 'gap-fill melody' and the 'changing-note process'. The former 'consists of two elements: a disjunct interval—the gap—and conjunct intervals which fill the gap.' The gap never exceeds the interval of an octave (Meyer 1973, p. 145). Figure 8.5(a) illustrates this melodic process. The E–E gap is followed by a series of conjunct notes that fill the gap (D#–C#–B–A–G–F#–E). A comparable pattern can be seen in Fig. 8.5(b). It should nevertheless be noted here that the gap occurs in two stages (E–C, A–F) and that another gap (A–F) is imbedded in the conjunct movement going from high F to low E. This is frequently the case in the examples analysed by Meyer, which underscores the fact that this melodic process can take on highly complex forms.

The 'changing-note' pattern turns around the tonic, beginning on that note and descending to the seventh degree (leading tone), then rising to the second degree and returning to the tonic. In the key of C major, this produces the series of notes C–B–D–C. The order of the B and the D may be inverted, however, and this same pattern may sometimes begin on the third degree (resulting in E–F–D–E, in the key of C major). Figure 8.6(a) provides an illustration of this melodic process in the key of G minor, and the same pattern in F major can be seen in Fig. 8.6(b).

Two studies conducted by Rosner and Meyer (1982, 1986) confirm that listeners manage to recognize these melodic processes when they hear different fragments of music. In the second study, for example, the authors asked subjects ('with no formal musical training') to rate, on a scale of one to nine, the degree of similarity between pairs of melodies containing one or the other of these melodic patterns. The results show that subjects systematically find greater similarity between melodies having the same melodic pattern.

Other experimental research (Francès 1988, experiment 9; Imberty 1979,

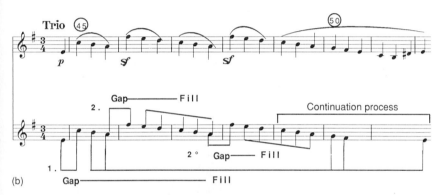

Fig. 8.5 Two examples of a 'gap-fill melody' pattern. ((a) from Ex. 75, Meyer (1973) p. 146, (b) from Fig. 7, Rosner and Meyer (1986) p. 19. © Regents of the University of California, 1973, 1986. Adapted with permission.)

1981*a*) has demonstrated, moreover, that Western listeners possess a knowledge (implicit or explicit) of the various typical formal schemas comprising the temporal macrostructures of pieces of tonal music such as sonata form (exposition, development, recapitulation) and rondo form (couplets, refrain). Imberty (1981*a*, experiments 10, 10*bis*) asked a first group of listeners (musicians and non-musicians) to segment two pieces of music—Brahms' *E♭ Intermezzo*, opus 118 (which clearly presents the ABA form) and Debussy's *La puerta del vino* (where the ABA structure is far less clear). A second group of subjects was asked to indicate, after having listened to them, how many major sections these pieces contained. It appears that all subjects easily managed to identify the typical ABA form in the Brahms piece; the segments they marked and the formal structure they recalled coincided with that form. The Debussy piece produced different results. The knowledge of a stereotyped formal structure only appears when the results of non-musicians in both

(a)

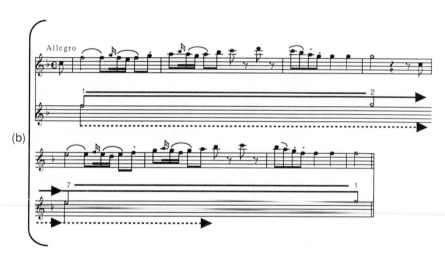

(b)

Fig. 8.6 Two examples of a 'changing-note melody' pattern. (a) from Fig. 1, Rosner and Meyer (1986) p. 3. © Regents of the University of California, 1986 (b) from Fig. 2, Rosner and Meyer (1982) p. 321. © Academic Press, 1982. Adapted with permission.)

experimental situations are compared. In the segmentation experiment, non-musicians no longer recognized the ABA stereotypes; they 'got lost in thousands of details and subtleties', and marked a substantially greater number of segments than did musicians. But the results were inverted in the second experimental situation. Although they could hear no precise form in the Debussy piece, non-musicians in the second group all declared that the piece was structured according to the ABA pattern. In other words, 'it appeared as though [non-musicians] sought the ABA stereotype at all costs because they were unable to represent the piece of music otherwise' (Imberty 1981a, p. 117). In this second experimental situation, non-musicians project their knowledge of typical forms of Western music on to the Debussy piece, an attitude found only to a lesser degree among musician subjects.

These stereotyped macrostructures may provide abstract frames of reference for the temporal organization of musical events. Such stereotypes would be composed of empty slots (A–A–B–A) to be filled during listening by elements specific to the piece heard (Imberty 1981a). They would then represent veritable 'normative structures' that strongly orient the processing of musical information (Lerdahl and Jackendoff 1983).

Knowledge of frequently occurring tonal hierarchies and musical schemas constitute the best-known forms of abstract musical knowledge in the context of Western tonal music (for other musical cultures, see Dowling and Harwood (1986) Ch. 9). But it is probable that other forms can be added to the list, that listeners possess additional musical knowledge of other aspects of musical structure. For example, Arom (1985, 1988) reported that an African listener's perception of a rhythmic passage differs considerably from that of a Western listener, which suggests that culture-specific systems for organizing temporal relations exist. It is likely that experimental research will soon discover new areas of abstract musical knowledge.

Even so, simply revealing the existence of such knowledge does not suffice to explain how listeners perceive and analyse music. How this knowledge is deployed in real listening situations remains unexplained. Returning to the musical fragment illustrated in Fig. 8.6(b), the experiment by Rosner and Meyer cited above (1982) indicates that listeners possess an implicit knowledge of the 'changing-note process'. They therefore possess the competence to understand that this melody is an example of the 'changing-note pattern'. Yet the question remains as to how listeners activate that knowledge during listening, how they actually identify the F–G–E–F pattern rather than some other pattern.

In fact, this competence supposes the execution of complex operations in processing musical information. In order to identify a 'changing-note process,' the perceptual system will have to decide that certain notes in the melody Fig. 8.6(b) are more important than others. Thus the listener

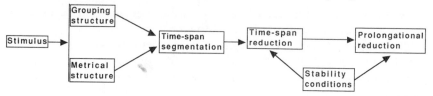

Fig. 8.7 Schematic diagram of the generative theory of tonal music. (From Fig. 5, (1989) Lerdahl p. 72. © Harwood Academic 1989. Adapted with permission.)

must consider the F in measure one to be more important than the initial C in the melody (on an up-beat), than the G in measure one (appoggiatura), than the E (a grace note to the F), than the G (passing tone). Otherwise, the F would not appear to be the first element of the melodic process. The same analysis could be made of the other notes within the pattern (see Meyer 1973).

The goal of research into event structure processing is precisely to explain what these various processes are and how they function.

8.2   EVENT STRUCTURE PROCESSING

The processing of musical information occurs in several stages. The theory proposed by Lerdahl and Jackendoff (1983), although originally designed to describe the final stage of musical understanding, not the real-time event structure processing, encourages specific hypotheses concerning the main stages of this processing. Indeed, it establishes a very strict chronology of the various moments of analysis, as shown in Fig. 8.7. The sound stimulus enters on the left of the diagram. It is then simultaneously analysed by processes of grouping and metrical organization. 'The grouping and metrical structures determine the time-span segmentation, over which time-span reduction takes place'. Prolongational reduction[3] 'derives from the time-span analysis' (Lerdahl 1989, p. 71). The stability conditions represent the abstract musical knowledge of tonal hierarchies discussed above. This theory is therefore based on a strictly ordered sequence of operations. Prolongational reduction is possible only if the musical information has been organized in hierarchic fashion. Yet this organization itself is only possible once the musical information has been segmented into groups (see Lerdahl and Jackendoff 1983, pp. 119, 123).

According to Sloboda (1986), this theory represents the coming of age of music psychology. I feel that it offers the only conceptual framework that currently enables the various stages in musical information processing to be conceived in a global, coherent fashion. McAdams (1987) has

---

3. The term 'prolongational reduction' will be defined later in this chapter.

nevertheless provided an important detail by adding two preliminary processing steps to the three stages described above. This would suggest that there are five major stages in the processing of the event structure.

The first, called 'reading the acoustic surface,' includes all the transduction processes performed by the peripheral auditory system to transform atmospheric vibrations into nerve impulses. The second involves the processing operations that organize acoustic information into coherent auditory images. 'The auditory image is defined as a psychological representation of a sound entity that exhibits an internal consistency (or coherence) it its acoustic behavior' (McAdams 1987, p. 8). Two types of grouping process play an important role at this level (see Bregman, Ch. 2 this volume). The grouping of simultaneous sound elements engenders the perceptual fusion of acoustic elements originating from the same source (for example, fusing the various frequencies of a complex musical sound). Sequential grouping processes group sequences of events originating from the same sound source (auditory stream segregation).

At the conclusion of this second stage of processing, musical information is represented in the perceptual system as a set of notes possessing precise qualities of pitch, timbre, loudness, and duration, constituting a coherent auditory image. The concept of 'musical surface' describes this level of representation of musical information. 'Truly musical organization only begins to occur at subsequent levels of processing' (McAdams 1987, p. 45).

8.2.1 Time-span segmentation

When listening to a musical passage, listeners do not usually feel that they are hearing a simple succession of notes. As Fraisse pointed out (1974, p. 75), this poses a problem in so far as 'physically, there is nothing but succession'. Consequently, it has been admitted that the perception of sequences of temporal events entails 'a psychological present in which successive elements are organized into a series of forms' (Fraisse 1974, p. 75). This psychological present (also called the 'perceptual present') corresponds to a period of time during which auditory stimuli are held present for perception. It certainly indicates the limits of human short-term memory since it rarely exceeds four to five seconds (Fraisse 1974) and can contain only a limited number of elements (seven, plus or minus two, according to Miller (1956)). This number can be significantly increased, however, if elements are organized into subgroups (or 'chunks') as has been demonstrated by Fraisse (1967) and Dowling (1973).

The perceived present is 'the basic feature of the perception of succession' (Fraisse 1974, p. 75). It means that the musical surface is apprehended through a series of 'perceptual centrations' within a window sliding along a string of sound events (Fig. 8.8(a)).

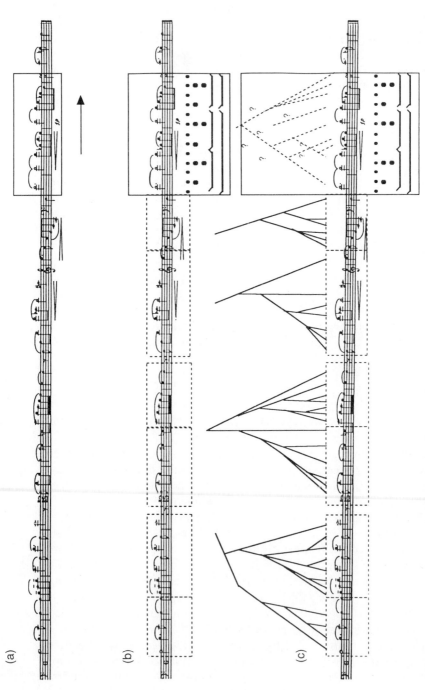

Fig. 8.8 Illustration of the different aspects involved in musical information processing. The listener discovers musical events by focusing on successive zones, symbolized by a sliding window (a). Within each of these zones,, the listener extracts the metric structure of events (represented by black dots) and one or several levels of grouping (represented by parentheses) (b). The musical information contained in each zone is then organized and represented hierarchically (c).

Everything happens as though the subject successively perceived several successive groups of elements in a manner similar to the way we read the letters of a text, that is to say by discontinuous movements that halt from place to place, during which perception occurs (Fraisse 1967, p. 93).

The processes of segmenting the musical surface are processes that help define the position and size of this sliding window. Various experiments have demonstrated that they operate in a fashion conforming to the grouping principles established by Gestalt theories on form. Every group boundary therefore constitutes a segmentation point on the musical surface. Research on this question is sufficiently well known to permit me to discuss just one example in the musical field (for a basic introduction to the question, see Deutsch (1982), Lerdahl and Jackendoff (1983, Chs 2, 3), Sloboda (1985, Ch. 5), Dowling and Harwood (1986, Ch. 6)).

Deliège (1987) conducted a series of experiments on musicians and non-musicians confirming the relevance of grouping principles based on 'proximity', 'similarity' and, to a certain extent, on 'continuity' (experiment 2) and 'symmetry'. Figure 8.9 illustrates the grouping principles tested in her experiment.

According to the grouping principle of temporal 'proximity', the notes E–F–G in the first example should be heard as belonging to the same group, and the notes A–B as belonging to a different group. The arrow between G and A indicates a segmentation point. This segmentation can be explained here by the fact that the time elapsed between the end of the G and the attack of the A is greater than the temporal intervals separating the other notes in the passage (see Lerdahl and Jackendoff 1983, p. 45). A similar analysis can be made for the two following passages.

The other examples illustrate the principle of grouping by 'similarity' ('change rules'). The F–B interval thus creates a group boundary in so far as the principle of 'similarity' of pitch register means that listeners will perceive the notes E–F (in the same register) as being in a different group from the notes B–C–D (in a lower register). The principle of grouping according to 'continuity', on the other hand, is illustrated by a change in melodic contour (Lerdahl and Jackendoff 1983, experiment 2, p. 348)—the boundary between groups is marked here by the change in contour between the notes B–A.

In an initial experiment, Deliège tested these grouping rules using musical excerpts from the baroque, classical, and Romantic repertoires. In a second experiment, she used experimental stimuli of nine notes. In the latter case, the stimuli contained two segmentation cues, creating conflict among the various rules. The last example in Fig. 8.9 shows a case of conflict between segmentation rule 4 (which would call for segmentation between the E and the F) and rule 7 (which would call for

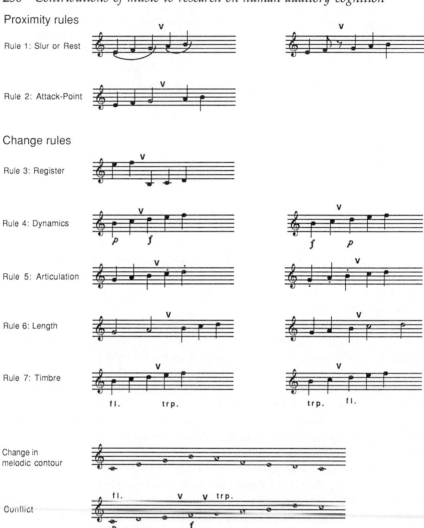

Fig. 8.9   Various segmentation rules. (From Figs 1, 22, 23, Deliège (1987) pp. 328, 347, 348. © Regents of the University of California, 1987. Adapted with permission.)

segmentation between F and G). The subjects' main task was to segment these sequences.

In general, the segments marked by subjects conformed to the ones predicted by the grouping rules. Those marked by musicians conform better than those by non-musicians, this difference being clear only in the first experiment. Listeners seem to prefer the proximity rules based on attack and timbre over other rules. Only the segmentation rule based on continuity, tested in the second experiment, generated mixed results—a change in melodic contour would seem to contribute to the formation of groups without, however, being sufficient change in itself. Finally, in analysing the segmentations that did not conform to the grouping rules tested, Deliège (1987, p. 343) observed that some of them were executed along the lines of the 'symmetry' grouping principle.

Segmenting the musical surface into groups is a crucial stage in the processing of musical information because these groups form veritable processing units that will strongly influence the subsequent perceptual analysis of a given piece of music. The formation of groups is not necessarily a clear-cut phenomenon, however—several grouping processes may enter into conflict (as frequently occurs in contemporary music) and it is not known exactly how these conflicts are resolved by listeners. In other instances, principles may reinforce one another, and the convergence of several grouping principles at the same point on the musical surface may then lead to a grouping of groups (Deliège 1989, 1990) that creates a hierarchy of groups as suggested by Lerdahl and Jackendoff (1983).

Alongside this segmenting into groups, another type of process will lead listeners to detect a regular beat underlying the succession of sound events. Initially, the perceptual system detects a level of regular beats, separated by a uniform time interval. Some of these beats are then interpreted as being more important than others.[4] These beats are strong, metrically speaking, whereas all the other beats are metrically weak. These two levels of regular pulse define the metrical structure of a fragment as perceived by listeners (Povel 1981; Jones 1987). In a waltz rhythm, for example, listeners immediately detect a first level of regular beat at the quarter-note[5] level, then interpret one out of every three beats as being more important. Other levels of regularity (composed of more distant or much closer beats) may be abstracted by listeners; these various levels of regularity then constitute a highly hierarchized metric structure within the piece of music (Jones 1976; Lerdahl and Jackendoff 1983) that is manifested by listeners' ability to 'regularly keep time with the foot' at various speeds.

Processing metric organization nevertheless encounters a certain contradiction: if the physical characteristics of a piece of music are examined closely, it is absolutely impossible to detect a rhythmic level with strictly equal intervals between each beat (see Jones and Yee, Ch. 4 this volume). An analysis of a waltz by Johann Strauss conducted in pure Viennese style provides a revealing demonstration because the last quarter-note of

---

4. These beats are usually represented visually by a series of small dots, as in Fig. 8.8(b).
5. *Editors' note*: all rhythmic values are expressed in the American nomenclature. Their relation to British nomenclature is as follows: half-note = minim; quarter-note = crotchet; eighth-note = quaver.

each measure is systematically delayed. Obviously this pattern, though not strictly metrical from a physical standpoint, possesses a structure sufficiently metric on the psychological level to be clearly perceived by all dancers.

Metric organization is therefore an abstraction, an idealization, implying the existence of complex cognitive processes leading listeners to interpret a succession of sound events as being regular even though they are not strictly regular on an objective level (unless played by a computer). This aspect of processing musical information currently raises numerous issues. Several theoretical models have been proposed to account for the process of metrical abstraction (Steedman 1977; Longuet-Higgins and Lee 1982; Lerdahl and Jackendoff 1983, Ch. 4). Experimental data to confirm such hypotheses, however, are scarce (nevertheless see Collard *et al.* 1981; Gérard and Drake 1990; Palmer and Krumhansl 1990; Drake *et al.* 1991). From this perspective, it appears certain that 'any periodic return of an acoustic difference will tend to be interpreted as a strong beat in the metrical structure' (Fraisse 1974). Other surface markers may be used (see Drake 1990), but the total range of metric markers remains unknown, as does the way they interact in case of conflict (Sloboda 1985, pp. 77–8). Another problem involves the level to which metric hierarchy can be extended—in other words, is there a maximum time lapse beyond which the feeling of a periodic return of accent irrevocably vanishes? Such a limitation is accepted by Lerdahl and Jackendoff (1983, p. 21), and experiments conducted by Fraisse (1974) would seem to suggest that this period cannot exceed four to five seconds (which, as Fraisse points out, corresponds to the duration of the slowest adagio measure). Such results indicate, then, that metric organization is restricted to a local level within the organization of the musical surface.

These metric structures have important repercussions on other aspects of musical information processing. First of all, they constitute a veritable cognitive framework that facilitates the coding of numerous facets of the organization of the musical passage, such as duration (Povel 1981; Essens and Povel 1985). In addition, they create perceptual expectations that lead listeners to focus attention on metrically strong beats within the event sequence (Jones 1976; Jones *et al.* 1981; Jones and Yee, Ch. 4 this volume). Finally, these expectations may underlie the expressive schemas of musical tension and relaxation, as typified by syncopation, off-beats, and changes in metre. Syncopation, for instance, is a rhythmic figure in which a sound event begins on a metrically weak beat and extends into a strong beat. It creates rhythmic tension in so far as no musical event appears on the strong beat, temporarily upsetting the listener's perceptual expectations.

The conjunction of these processes of grouping and metric abstraction leads to a segmentation of the musical surface into different time spans.

Although there is currently no experimental data explaining how the information stemming from these two processes is combined in the perceptual system, Lerdahl and Jackendoff (1983) may be right when they argue that the lower levels of segmentation are defined by metric structures whereas the higher levels are defined by grouping structures. Following this third stage of processing, musical information is probably represented in the form of groups of notes possessing a certain internal structure yet not exceeding the temporal limits of the psychological present (Fig. 8.8(b)).[6]

It is obvious that if information processing stopped at this stage, music would be perceived as a juxtaposition of unrelated groups of notes. For that matter, this would seem to be the case with children up to the age of ten. In a series of experiments, Imberty (1969, 1981*b*) noted that

a child's musical perception proceeds by successive centrations, and each centration provokes an over-emphasis on the zone of focus whereas the preceding zone is definitively banished from the psychological present of the perceptual act (Imberty 1969, p. 114).

Among adults, however, music is perceived in a different manner. It is therefore necessary to consider a fourth stage of information processing, the cognitive function of which is to retain some of the information contained in each of these groups. Relations between the groups of notes will be built up from this local information.

8.2.2 Establishing an event hierarchy

At this level, music raises a general cognitive problem encountered in the structuring of any series of temporal events. Since the successive sound

---

6. This assertion is nevertheless in sharp distinction to Lerdahl and Jackendoff's (1983) theory. These authors feel that segmentation of the temporal framework is exhaustive, that is to say that it extends to groups that last much longer than the psychological present. On a theoretical level this position is understandable because the model contains grouping rules that account for the global features of the organization of the piece, namely grouping preferences rules GPR 4 to GPR 7. Moreover, it is coherent because the theory originally sought to describe only the final stage in musical information processing. It ceases to be coherent, however, for a psychological theory that attempts to account for real-time processing of the event structure, since listeners cannot segment the musical surface as a function of the overall organization of a piece they have not yet heard in its entirety. More specifically, GPR 7, which integrates information from time-span and prolongational reductions, cannot be be invoked at this stage of processing precisely because this information implies the execution of processes that cannot chronologically take place until a later stage of processing. For this reason, only the local segmentation rules proposed by the model could be available at this stage of processing; these rules produce only groups of a temporal scope comparable to that of the psychological present. This observation should lead to a distinction between two forms of segmentation based on radically different perceptual and cognitive processes—that of the narrow level which is one of the first stages in musical information processing, and that of the broader level which produces a deeper level processing of musical structure in its entirety.

events are perceived through the frame of a window sliding along the sequence, 'the immediate availability of information is lost the moment segmentation occurs and a new segment begins' (Michon 1977, p. 275). Of course, this information is not permanently lost. 'As soon as the information in a segment has passed by, it is available only on a conceptual, symbolic level' (Michon 1977, p. 275). Psychology must then try to understand how the information contained in musical segments isolated by the preceding processes is recoded into a more abstract form.

The need for a hierarchization of information

Numerous experiments conducted with series of numbers, lights, letters, and words have shown that a subject's ability to represent a long sequence of events with a hierarchy of operators constitutes an economical way to code information contained in that sequence (Restle 1970; Restle and Brown 1970). Similar representation processes have also been shown to exist in the realm of music (Jones *et al.* 1978; Deutsch and Feroe 1981).

Deutsch (1980), for example, asked musicians to listen to four types of sequence, each of which was to be recalled and notated (Fig. 8.10). Melodies 1 and 3 exhibit hierarchic organization, for they stem from the combination of a chromatic movement (G–F#–G, represented by the algorithm B = (*,p,n)Cr) and a G major arpeggio movement (G–D–B–G, represented by the algorithm A = (*,3p)Gtr) (see caption to Fig. 8.10). There is therefore an algorithm for economically encoding this melodic passage: S = A[pr]B, G5. Melody 2 contains the same notes as the other two but in random order, thereby breaking the hierarchical organization. In this case, no algorithm exists to represent the melody. In melody 3, segmentation into groups of three notes reinforces the organization, whereas in melody 4 segmentation into groups of four notes undermines it. There is therefore no algorithm accounting for the intervals contained in each of those three groups nor in the relations between them.

The author argues that the observed rates of recall (93.5 per cent, 52 per cent, 99 per cent, and 69.2 per cent, respectively) show that listeners perceive and use hierarchies to memorize musical sequences. The comparison of rates of recall obtained for melodies 1, 3, and 4 indicate that memorization is easier when segmentation of the musical surface coincides with the hierarchic structure of the melody. It is much more difficult in the opposite instance. These results underscore the importance of segmentation of the musical surface in this fourth stage of processing.

Musical information can therefore be represented in algorithmic fashion by a hierarchy of operators. However, the main problem is that these results were obtained with melodies so short and stereotypical that it is hard to see how they can be generalized to all pieces of music from the repertoire (for other criticisms, see Jones (1981)). In other words, what

Fig. 8.10 Examples of experimental melodies (top) used by Deutsch (1980). Formal representation of a melody according to a hierarchy of operators. The asterisk stands for the reference note in the algorithm, p stands for a descending movement of one degree within a pattern, n stands for an ascending movement of one degree within a pattern. Gtr stands for the arpeggio pattern of a G major triad, Cr stands for the chromatic scale pattern, and pr expresses the application of one algorithm on another. (From Fig. 1A, Deutsch (1980) p. 38. © Psychonomics Society, Inc., 1980. Adapted with permission.)

types of operators are at work in the case of real pieces of tonal music?

This is the level at which the (implicit/explicit) knowledge of pitch hierarchies (discussed in Section 8.1.1) probably plays a highly important cognitive role. For these hierarchies present themselves as good candidates for defining real operators.

Take, for example, the melody shown in Fig. 8.11, which is closer to common melodies from the tonal repertoire (experiment 2 in Bigand 1990*a*). It contains four groups (A, B, C, D). The relations existing within and between these groups can be specified via rules of the tonal system. These relations are schematically represented in the tree diagram above

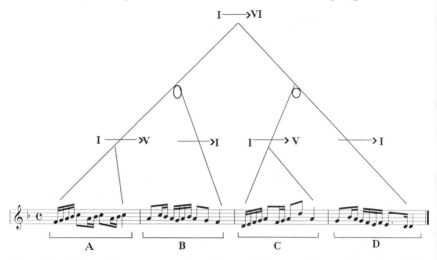

Fig. 8.11 Hierarchic representation of a melody according to the rules of the tonal system. Group A is represented by the progression I–V, group B by a progression returning to I. Groups C and D constitute a transposition of groups A and B into the key of the sixth degree (D minor) of the main key of F major.

the musical staff. The first group constitutes a half cadence (I–V), whereas the second entails a perfect cadence (return to I) providing musical stability for the first part of the phrase. These relations are found again in the second part, which appears as a transposition in the minor key of the first part (the transposition I–VI noted at the top of the tree). The psychological relevance of this type of coding was tested in the following fashion: an initial group of musicians listened to the passage and were asked to transcribe the melody afterwards, while a second group listened to a melody composed of the same groups but played in the order C–B–D–A. From the point of view of their musical surfaces, the second melody is comparable to the first, but from the point of view of tonal syntax the ordering is incoherent in so far as it does not follow the usual hierarchical relations. It ends, for example, on a V chord (group A) which is an inappropriate ending for a tonal melody. The permutation of the groups thus breaks the network of relations that had initially existed between groups, so that a hierarchic coding of the melody becomes impossible. Results of the test showed that the number of notes correctly recalled was significantly higher for the first melody, and that the difference increased as the number of times the passage was played was increased from one to three.

It would therefore appear that harmonic hierarchies established by the tonal system constitute a good way of summarizing musical information contained in relatively long melodies. This hypothesis is partly confirmed

Fig. 8.12 Illustration of the reduction principle. The melody in (a) represents the notes perceived as most important in melody (b). (From Fig. 5.1, Lerdahl and Jackendoff (1983) p. 105. © MIT Press, 1983. Adapted with permission.)

by an experiment conducted by Sloboda and Parker (1985). They had musicians (or music lovers) listen to melodies that were too long to be correctly reproduced after a single hearing. An analysis of errors committed then revealed the musical structures that were encoded and that subsequently guided subjects in the task of recall. Sloboda and Parker report that musicians recall metric structure best (88 per cent correct recall rate), followed by the harmonic structure of the melody (81 per cent).

These various experimental results therefore suggest that when listeners manage to reconstruct the relationships between different segments of a musical surface, it is because the musical information contained in those segments can be represented in a hierarchic way. Thus, as noted by Meyer (1973, p. 80):

hierarchic structures are of signal importance because they enable the composer to invent and the listener to comprehend complex interreactive musical relationships. If stimuli . . . did not form brief but partially completed events (motives, phrases, etc.) and if these did not in turn combine with one another to form more extended, higher-order patterns, all relationships would be local and transient—in the note to note foreground.

The coding of musical information in the form of an event hierarchy currently constitutes one of the main working hypotheses of the cognitive sciences of music. This does not exclude the existence of other possible forms of representation—of an associative nature, for instance—that remain poorly understood today (McAdams 1989).

The Lerdahl and Jackendoff model (1983, p. 106) offers a systematic formulation of this working hypothesis:

The listener attempts to organize all the pitch-events of a piece into a single coherent structure, such that they are heard in a hierarchy of relative importance' [and that] 'structurally less important events are not heard simply as insertions, but in a specified relationship to surrounding more important events. ('strong reduction hypothesis'.)

Consider, for example, the melody shown in Fig. 8.12. The hypothesis of time-span reduction supposes that listeners hear certain notes within each six-note group as being more important than the others. The A would thus be perceived as the dominant element in the first group. The F and the A would be the dominant elements in the second group, the other notes in this group being heard as subordinate ornamentation (passing tones, in this instance). Thus the musical surface of staff (b) could be represented in reduced fashion (hence efficiently by the cognitive system) by the sequence of structurally important notes represented in staff (a).

The process of information reduction can be summarized in the following way: the musical surface is first organized into groups or segments (see above), and then 'within these [groups], the listener compares events for their relative stability' (Lerdahl 1989, p. 71) in order to establish a hierarchic network of relationships providing an abstract representation of the musical structure of those groups. Figure 8.13 offers an example of this type of network. The most ornamental notes are found lowest on the tree (A, D, F), whereas the highest branch of the tree indicates the dominant element within the group (the quarter-note, E).

The question remains as to what extent a listener (and what type of listener?) is able to abstract the reduced structure underlying the musical surface. Serafine *et al.* (1989) directly confronted this issue by playing musical fragments several measures long (the 'model' in Fig. 8.14) to musically trained listeners. Each fragment was followed by four reduced structures. 'Foreground reductions' are only partially reduced compared to 'middleground reductions' that contain far fewer notes (see Schenker 1979; Forte and Gilbert 1982; Deliège 1984). Two of these four reductions contained only structurally significant notes, whereas the two others were traps or 'foils' containing structurally insignificant notes. Subjects were asked to indicate which reductions best fit the model.

Three experiments were conducted along these lines. The results show that 'listeners were able to identify the correct structural reductions at better-than-chance levels, although their success rate was quite variable across items and overall somewhat low' (Serafine *et al.* 1989, p. 403). The percentage of errors was lower for the least-reduced structure (foreground reduction) than for the most-reduced structure (64 per cent versus 59 per cent in the first experiment). In both cases, the results were different from chance, which testifies to the listeners' ability to abstract the two levels of reduced structure.

In three other experiments, Serafine *et al.* (1989) asked subjects to rate the degree of similarity between two melodies. Certain melodies were similar in terms of surface elements (rhythm, melodic contour) and underlying structures. Others were similar in terms of surface elements but different in terms of underlying structure. In general, it appears that 'similarity judgments were based on underlying hierarchic structure' (Serafine *et al.* 1989, p. 397).

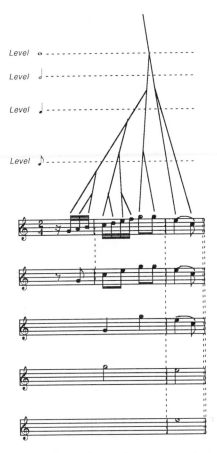

Fig. 8.13 Hierarchic network of relationships encapsulating the musical information contained in a group of notes. The lower staves contain the elements that are most important hierarchically, and the tree diagram (top) displays these hierarchies. (From Fig. 7.9, Lerdahl and Jackendoff (1983) p. 151 © MIT Press, 1983. Reprinted with permission.)

These results therefore lend support to the hypothesis of a hierarchic coding of musical information, even among non-musicians. The question then arises as to the exact cognitive processes involved in the coding operation.

Cognitive processes in the elaboration of an event hierarchy

According to the Lerdahl and Jackendoff model, the structural importance of an event depends not only on its importance within the tonal hierarchy but also on its rhythmic and melodic features as well as the musical context in which it appears. The model supposes, for instance,

Fig. 8.14 Illustration of the melodies used by Serafine *et al*. (1989). (See text for explanation.) (From Fig. 1, Serafine *et al*. (1989) p. 400 © Regents of the University of California. Reprinted with permission.)

that the dominant (the most important note after the tonic in the tonal hierarchy) will have a much greater structural importance for listeners if it occurs on a metrically strong beat with a relatively long duration (a half-note, for example) within a group of notes that has no tonic (a configuration constituting a half cadence), as opposed to occurring on a metrically weak beat for a short period (eighth-note) within a group containing a tonic (yielding a perfect cadence).

Grouping and metric processes apparently play a key role in establishing a hierarchy of events. Not only do they segment music into groups constituting veritable units of musical information processing, but they also 'provide rhythmic criteria to supplement pitch criteria in the determination of the structural importance of events' (Lerdahl and Jackendoff 1983, p. 119).

To fully understand this stage of processing, it is necessary to distinguish tonal hierarchy from event hierarchy (Bharucha 1984; Deutsch 1984; Dowling 1984; Lerdahl 1988). The former refers to an atemporal mental schema representing a system of culturally determined pitch relationships, whereas the latter refers to a structure that listeners must infer from the ongoing temporal sequence of musical events. In Fig. 8.7, the box labelled 'stability conditions' represents the tonal hierarchy, and the box labelled 'time-span reduction' represents the event hierarchy (Lerdahl 1988, 1989). Two questions then spring to a psychologist's mind: what processes activate knowledge of pitch hierarchy? And how can this information be combined with the other sound parameters to define the event hierarchy?

Several experiments have been conducted in an effort to answer the first question. The primary objective is to learn how listeners manage to identify the key in which a passage is played. This identification is absolutely essential in determining the tonal weights of the events. An early model proposed by Longuet-Higgins (1976) suggested that notes were represented in long-term memory in a three-dimensional psychological space. Within this space, the key is defined as a subspace, pictured as a window. When the listener hears a series of notes (C–E–G–A–B), the window is shifted to contain those pitches. The two possible positions correspond to the major keys of C and G—all other keys (major, at least) are excluded. The listener then decides, by taking other criteria into account, which key best corresponds to this passage.

Yet this model does not consider the temporal order in which the notes appear (Deutsch 1984; Brown 1988). The rising sequence D#–E–F#–G–B–C would normally be interpreted as being in C major whereas the same notes in descending order (C–B–G–F#–E–D#) would be interpreted as being in E minor. Although the tonal hierarchies are the same in both cases, the event hierarchies are totally different since in the first instance the structurally important notes are C, G, E, B, F#, D# (in decreasing order of importance) whereas in the second the hierarchy is E, B, G, C, F#, D#. Another approach to the problem of identifying key was proposed by Butler and Brown (1984), Brown (1988), and Butler (1990b). According to this theory, a key is determined by the appearance of intervals specific to that key. For example, the sequence F–B (tritone) is possible only in the key of C major (taking only major keys into account here). Identifying a key would therefore involve recognizing such intervals. However, it is highly probable that these processes also integrate information related to parameters other than pitch alone. Francès (1988, p. 97), for instance, stresses that 'the relative duration of notes and accent . . . can undoubtedly have an effect.' Sloboda (1985) mentions that

(a)

(b)

(c)

Fig. 8.15   Melodies used by Palmer and Krumhansl (1987*a*, experiment 1). (From Fig. 2, Palmer and Krumhansl (1987*a*) p. 119. © American Psychological Association, Inc, 1987. Reprinted with permission.)

the same chromatic passage (E–D#–D–C#–C–B–Bb–A–G#–G–F#–F–E–D#–D) can be interpreted as being in two different keys depending on where the metric accents fall. The impact of duration on the attribution of key was experimentally confirmed by Butler (1990*b*).

Once the key of a musical passage has been determined, it remains to be established how the tonal weight of each event is combined with other sound parameters to determine its importance in the event hierarchy. Research carried out by Palmer and Krumhansl (1987*a*,*b*) directly deals with this issue, though it is limited to the parameters of pitch and rhythm. Musically trained subjects listened to the passages shown in Fig. 8.15 (Palmer and Krumhansl 1987*a*, experiment 1). Melody (c) is the original version of a fugue theme by J. S. Bach. The two other melodies, (a) and (b), are derived from that theme; melody (a) retains only the rhythmic information, whereas (b) retains only the pitch information.

The experiment was designed to measure the structural importance that listeners assigned to each of the events within these three musical passages, on a scale of one to seven. The experimental hypothesis could be summed up as follows. If the structural importance assigned to the notes of a real musical passage (c) is essentially determined by the dimension of pitch, then the responses obtained in (c) should strongly correlate with those obtained in (b) but not with those obtained in (a). The inverse situation should occur if rhythm is the dimension that governs the attribution of structural importance to events within the passage. If the two dimensions contribute equally to the rating of this importance, only a linear combination of responses obtained in (a) and (b) would enable those of (c) to be recovered. A statistical analysis should reveal whether the effects of the rhythmic and pitch dimensions are combined linearly to predict (c) or whether they interact. The results yield a significant correlation between responses obtained in (c) and (a), and between (c) and (b). The correlation between (a) and (b) is not significant. Regression analysis shows that the results obtained in (c) are adequately explained by a linear regression of (a) and (b) on (c).

These results tend to confirm Lerdahl and Jackendoff's hypothesis (1983, p. 119) and suggest that the rhythmic dimension contributes criteria to pitch hierarchies in determining the structural importance of events. It is probable that other sound dimensions, such as loudness and timbre play, a similar role to rhythm at this level, although to my knowledge no experiment has yet demonstrated this.

Following this fourth stage of processing, then, musical information would be represented as a network of hierarchic relations. Figure 8.8(c), partly inspired by the work of Clarke (1988), illustrates this stage of processing. The window marked with a solid line represents the part of the musical passage that the listener apprehends at a given moment; within this group of notes, the listener attempts to organize perceptually present events according to a hierarchy of structural importance, simultaneously taking into account their tonal weights and their rhythmic and metric values. The windows to the left, in broken lines, designate prior zones of perceptual centration. The tree diagrams above (c) represent the hierarchic network of relations as well as the dominant musical event that encapsulates the information contained in those groups. It is by way of such tree-diagram representations that local musical information would be related to higher levels of organization.

8.2.3 Perception of patterns of musical tension and relaxation

The fifth stage of information processing accounts for an aspect of music perception that every listener has certainly experienced. When listening to a piece of tonal music (whatever the style), there is often the very distinct impression that the music is progressing from one point to another—it evolves toward a specific goal that it always ends up reaching, even after a great many detours. The common metaphor of 'musical discourse' clearly conveys this impression that the temporal organization of (tonal) musical is similar to the telling of a tale, with a dynamic temporal development oriented toward a denouement. As Lerdahl and Jackendoff point out (1983, p. 198), 'a tonal phrase or piece almost always begins in relative repose, builds toward tension, and relaxes into a resolving cadence.' Imberty (1981*a*, p. 89) suggests that

this structure, sustained by three centuries of tonal music and imposed by tonal syntax itself, is perhaps related to narrative structure, itself organized according to a relatively similar pattern (tension-problem, crisis, denouement).

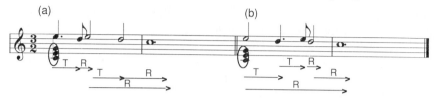

Fig. 8.16   The influence of rhythm on tension/relaxation patterns. A change in rhythm alters such patterns. (From Fig. 8.3, Lerdahl and Jackendoff (1983) p. 180. © MIT Press, 1983. Reprinted with permission.)

As Imberty points out, tonal syntax is partly responsible for this impression of the dynamic progression of musical flow. This dynamic progression, as noted in Section 8.1.1, is based on the alternation of musical tension and relaxation—tension is created when an element that is insignificant from the standpoint of syntax (and therefore of the tonal hierarchy) is inserted between two important events, and vice versa.

Lerdahl and Jackendoff's 'prolongational reduction' hypothesis (1983) makes important distinctions here. The musical relaxation established by an event (or its 'prolongational importance', in the authors' words) does not depend solely on its place in the tonal hierarchy, it also depends on the group in which it appears, its rhythmic value, and its metric position. The prolongational importance of a sound event is therefore defined by its importance within the event hierarchy. As indicated in Fig. 8.7, there is a direct relationship between this hierarchy and the perception of patterns of musical tension and relaxation.

[T]he perceived patterns of tension and relaxation in pitch structure depend crucially on the hierarchy of structurally important events within time-spans as defined by meter and grouping (Lerdahl and Jackendoff 1983, p. 188).

In fact, everything happens as though, during this fifth stage of processing, event hierarchies were interpreted in terms of tension and relaxation so that

each region represents an overall tensing or relaxing in the progression from the beginning to its end, [and] 'tensings and relaxings internal to each region represent subordinate and nonoverlapping stages in the overall progression (Lerdahl and Jackendoff 1983, prolongational hypothesis 1, p. 211).

Taking the two passages in C major illustrated in Fig. 8.16, it emerges that in both of them the most important notes in terms of tonal hierarchy are (in descending order) C, E, and D. The two Ds and the two Es have exactly the same tonal weight. Yet this is no longer the case when event hierarchies are taken into account. Obviously the tonic C, with its long duration and strong metric position, remains the dominant element in both (a) and (b). But there is a shift in the hierarchic relationship between the second and third notes of the first measure (D and E). In (a), the first D (eighth-note) is the least significant element from a structural standpoint, followed by the second D (half-note) and the two Es. In (b), the second E is structurally the least significant element since it is an eighth-note, followed by the first D (dotted quarter-note), the second D (half-note), and the first E. These event hierarchies will then be interpreted by listeners in terms of tension and relaxation. Since the hierarchies differ from (a) to (b), the patterns of tension and relaxation will be perceived differently. As Lerdahl and Jackendoff (1983) note, in (a) the first level of tension/relaxation occurs with the appearance of the D (eighth-note). A second level of tension occurs with the appearance of the half-note D, which is resolved by the C. This second tensing/relaxing pattern is itself part of a progression resolving the tension established by the half-note E to the C. In passage (b), the E (eighth-note) establishes a tension that is resolved locally by the D (half-note). This tension/relaxation pattern is part of a larger tension/relaxation pattern going from the E (half-note) to the D (half-note) and resolving on the tonic C. Furthermore, this second level of tension/relaxation is itself part of a progression going from the E (half-note) to the C. It is the superimposition of these three levels of tension and relaxation that constitute the differences of dynamic progression in the two passages. Readers are strongly encouraged to the play or sing these passages to fully appreciate this phenomenon.

Although very short, this example shows how listeners manage to extract several levels of underlying tension and relaxation from a longer musical passage. These various levels are graphically represented by the prolongational reduction tree diagrams used in Lerdahl and Jackendoff's model. In the passage in D major shown in Fig. 8.17, the first branch of the tree (marked a,b) indicates that listeners perceive the entire piece as progressing toward a final point where all tensions are resolved. This progression occurs in two major stages, represented here by the second level of branchings (marked c). In the first stage, the passage attains weak musical stability on the tonic chord of the relative key of B minor (eighth measure). In the second stage, the passage progressively approaches greater stability by returning to the main key of D major. Within these periods, the musical progression establishes other patterns of tension/relaxation as indicated by the third level of branches (marked d). Finally, the lower levels of the diagram represent local patterns of tension and relaxation.

Several of my own experiments have explored the psychological reality of these various levels of musical tension and relaxation (Bigand 1990*b*, 1991*a*, 1993). In the first experiment, two families of four melodies in A minor were used (Fig. 8.18). The melodies in the first family (a1–b1–c1–d1) had different musical surfaces (intervals, rhythms, contours) and different metric structures, but displayed highly similar musical

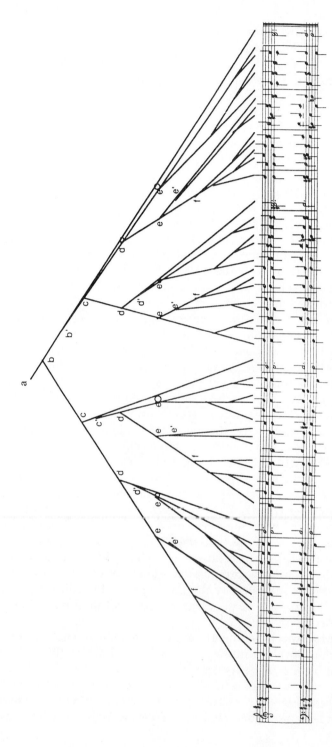

Fig. 8.17 Illustration of the various levels of hierarchic organization of a long musical sequence. (From Fig. 6.25, Lerdahl and Jackendoff (1983) p. 144. © MIT Press, 1983. Adapted with permission.)

Fig. 8.18 Two families of melodies used by Bigand (1990*b*) , with their corresponding prolongational structures shown by tree diagrams as analysed by Lerdahl. The different branchings illustrate differences in the tension/relaxation patterns generated by each family of melody. T1 represents the main key (A minor), T3 is the key a third degree higher (C major), and T5 is the key of the dominant (E major).

progressions, as represented by the prolongational reduction diagram at bottom left. This diagram reveals that, within this family, the primary tension always occurs in the fourth measure and is then regularly resolved by progression toward the final tonic. The melodies in the second family mimicked the first in terms of superficial structure (giving the pairs a1–a2, b1–b2, c1–c2, d1–d2) but displayed a different musical progression, as shown by the prolongational reduction diagram at bottom right. In each of these latter melodies, the primary tension occurs in the third measure and is temporarily resolved in the fourth measure on a major tonic chord in the dominant key of E. This creates a moment of relative musical stability right at the point where there is strong tension in the first family. Thus the two families exhibit radically different tension/relaxation patterns, which should render them distinguishable despite superficial similarities. The experimental procedure confirmed that all listeners managed to perceive these differences in tension/relaxation patterns, which enabled them to correctly identify the family to which each melody belonged.

Two subsequent experiments, employing a single pair of similar melodies (a1 and a2) refined this interpretation. The goal was to measure, on a scale of one to seven, the degree of musical tension perceived by listeners for each of the notes comprising these melodies. If the initial interpretation were correct, the tension profiles of melody a1 should differ significantly from those of a2. Moreover, the prolongational reduction diagram provided predictions of certain aspects of these profiles. The experiment was run twice, on a total of 45 professional musicians and 45 non-musicians. In all instances, the musicians' profiles for a1 and a2 were significantly different (a1r1 versus a2r1 and a1r2 versus a2r2). Among non-musicians, however, this difference only reached a high degree of significance when the experiment was conducted using a between-subjects factorial design (Bigand 1993). In this instance, the profile of non-musicians correlated significantly with that of musicians (Fig. 8.19).

Another goal of these experiments was to verify the importance of rhythmic structure (duration and metre) in the perception of tension/relaxation patterns. As shown in Fig. 8.19, a change in the rhythmic structure of a melody produces highly significant changes in the tension profiles shown by all listeners (r1 vs. r2).

To sum up, these experimental results suggest that following this final stage of processing, musical information is represented as a hierarchic network of tension and relaxation, illustrated by the tree diagrams in Figs 8.17 and 8.18. It is probable that this type of coding partly explains how listeners structure and represent temporal organization in tonal music. Such results, however, will have to be experimentally tested using musical fragments longer than the simple passages discussed above.

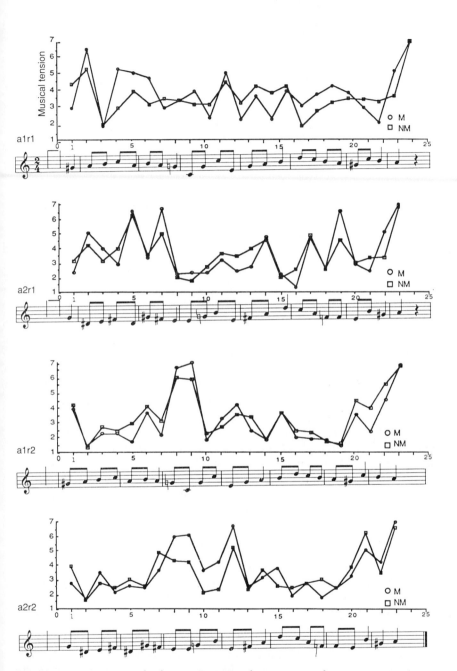

Fig. 8.19 Influence of rhythm and implicit harmony on the perception of tension/relaxation patterns by musician (M) and non-musician (NM) listeners, on a scale of one to seven. The rhythm only changes from r1 (top pair) to r2 (bottom pair). The main change between a1 and a2 involves the implicit harmony of the melodies. Variations in the profiles generated by these four conditions reveal the influence of these two factors on the perception of musical tension.

8.3   SYMBOLIZATION PROCESSES

The question now arises as to what extent the hierarchies of tension and relaxation established in the final phase of information processing constitute input for symbolization processes.

Experiments conducted by Francès (1988) and Imberty (1975, 1979, 1981a) on musical expressivity and semantics led them to develop a theory of symbolic representational activity

based on the phenomenon of assimilation of musical forms to three groups of schemes, whose coordination determines the set of representations that play a role in the association of words to music, via the major types of structures governing the variety and the multiplicity of works and styles (Imberty 1981a, p. 4).

Francès (1988, experiments 14, 15) noted music's capacity for evoking tension/relaxation schemes 'that crystallize the subject's motor and affective experience' (Francès *et al.* 1979, p. 175). These schemes 'assimilate musical dynamism (that is to say, the combined effects of sound intensity, harmonic complexity, and speed) to the subject's physical posture and tonicity' (Imberty 1981a, p. 12). Music that provokes strong tension within listeners will be described using terms such as strong, spasmodic, passionate, tormented, excitable, shattering, flashing, violent, aggressive, sharp, and diabolical. Music provoking only weak tension, on the other hand, is described as languid, lonely, nostalgic, despairing, profound, quiet, gentle, tender, and dreamy. The research discussed above explains the information processing systems involved in establishing the pitch and rhythmic aspects of tension/relaxation patterns. Other aspects of musical stimuli (such as loudness and tempo) certainly play an equally important role in defining musical dynamism—future experimental research should indicate how these parameters interact with the two others.

Imberty (1975, 1979, 1981a) discusses a second type of scheme involving emotional resonance. Such schemes

assimilate degrees of formal complexity (assessed partly in terms of temporal structure . . . and partly in terms of the homogeneity or heterogeneity of component elements) to poles of a subject's affective experience (aggressivity, anxiety—melancholia, asthenia—feelings of self-confidence and strength) (1981a, p. 4).

Imberty effectively observed that as musical complexity increases, the listener's assessment of expressivity is increasingly directed toward negative emotional resonances. The experiment involving pieces by Brahms and Debussy discussed in Section 8.1.2 offers a good illustration of how musical form is associated with this second scheme, according to the degree of complexity with which it is perceived. Imberty first shows how the Brahms piece is organized by listeners into a strong hierarchy 'wherein each "sound event" is closely tied to its context, in which the development strongly embeds units within one another.' The Debussy piece, in contrast, is weakly hierarchized during listening—'the events appear to be unpredictable and unconnected to their context' (Francès *et al.* 1979, p. 188). In a second stage of the experiment, Imberty examined the way in which these differences in perceived musical form (hierarchic/non-hierarchic) affect semantic representations. Subjects were asked to supply semantic descriptions for each of the two pieces of music. An analysis of the correspondence between their responses and the pieces shows that expressions such as 'dislocation, chaos, imbalance, madness, violence, anxiety, aggressiveness, terror,' were basically applied to the Debussy piece, whereas terms such as 'gentle, carefree, gay, vivacious, serene, lively, exalted, transcendent,' were applied to Brahms. The various stages of processing musical information discussed above explain how listeners construct more or less highly hierarchized mental representations of the (tonal) piece to which they are listening. These representations would seem to constitute an input to the emotional resonance schemes. Indeed, Imberty's results show that listeners' representations of these emotional resonance schemes imbue the formal and temporal structure of a work with a symbolic value relating to the integration or disintegration of the inner, affective life of the subject.

Finally, the third type of scheme observed by Imberty involves schemes of spatiality.

Variations (increase or decrease) in sound volume, the superimposition or sequencing of sound strata from bass to treble, as well as melodic 'gesture' are all assimilated to figurative iconic representations (that is, complex visual mental images evoked by the music) (Imberty 1981*a*, p. 5).

These schemes account for the often figurative and visual nature of semantic descriptions given by subjects, such as 'shimmering, crystalline, cascading.'

The co-ordination of these three major schemes would define a rich and complex three-dimensional semantic space pertaining to any musical work (Fig. 8.20). If the musical tensions are strong and the perceived formal structure is weakly hierarchic, then the semantic descriptions associated with it will tend to be located in the upper right section of this space. If the tensions are weak and the formal structure difficult to unify, the semantic associations will be located in the upper left. A similar analysis can be performed for all other sections of this semantic space.

8.4   CONCLUSION

Taken collectively, the experimental results described above provide a glimpse of the types of information processing used by listeners to

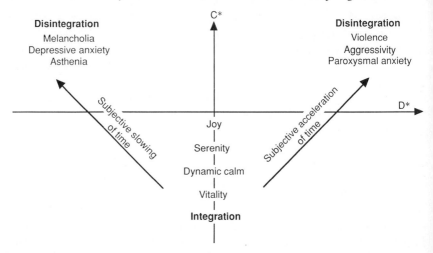

Fig. 8.20   Semantic space of musical forms: the horizontal axis represents the musical dynamism associated with patterns of tension and relaxation, the vertical axis represents the degree of formal complexity associated with schemes of emotional resonance, and the third axis, corresponding to the spatiality scheme, should be seen as emerging from the figure, perpendicular to the page. (From Fig. 1, Imberty (1981*a*) p. 7. © Dunod, 1981. Adapted with permission.)

organize acoustic structures as they are heard, and to interpret this organization in an expressive fashion. As noted, pitch hierarchies established by the tonal system play a determining role in the perception of Western music—on the one hand because they enable various sound events to be woven together, and on the other hand because the more or less strongly hierarchized temporal structure that emerges would seemed to constitute one of the main meaning-bearing elements for listeners. This observation in fact raises two questions for cognitive psychology.

Is the importance of pitch hierarchies a culturally determined phenomenon specific to Western music, with no particular implication for auditory cognition in general? Or, to the contrary, should the perceptual importance of these hierarchies be understood as a general cognitive constraint influencing the processing of long sequences of sound events (including speech) and perhaps even influencing the way in which symbolic information is processed? Here it is worth mentioning the crucial role played by hierarchic representations in the processes of language comprehension on syntactic as well as semantic levels.

If such is truly the case, the pitch hierarchies established by the tonal system would ultimately be merely a response to this constraint. The fact that these hierarchies are primarily defined by the dimension of pitch would be a phenomenon specific to this musical system; other systems (from another historical period or geographical region) could define their hierarchies according to other sound parameters. It would seem, for example, that in contemporary avant-garde music hierarchized musical forms could be built up from timbre hierarchies (Lerdahl 1987). It might also be supposed that with such music, listeners develop hierarchized representations of the work by employing perceptual salience hierarchies, rather than relying on the dimension of pitch (Lerdahl 1989).

Research in music psychology has not yet provided an answer to this question. What is certain is that if the importance played by hierarchic structures were to be confirmed in other musical systems, this would tend to indicate that all sequential processing of auditory information is based on a hierarchization of information, which would have significant implications for the entire body of research into auditory cognition.

ACKNOWLEDGEMENTS

I would like to thank the three *ad hoc* referees and other colleagues for their helpful comments on an earlier version of this chapter: Marie-Claire Botte, Eric Clarke, Jay Dowling, Marie-Dominique Gineste, Anne Grange, Stephen McAdams, and Jose Morais.

REFERENCES

Arom, S. (1985). De l'écoute à l'analyse des musiques centrafricaines, *Analyse Musicale*, **1**, 35–9.

Arom, S. (1988). Du pied à la main: Les fondements métriques des musiques traditionnelles d'Afrique Centrale. *Analyse Musicale*, **10**, 16–23.

Bharucha, J. J. (1984). Event hierarchies, tonal hierarchies, and assimilation: a reply to Deutsch and Dowling. *Journal of Experimental Psychology: General*, **113**, 421–5.

Bharucha, J. J. (1987). Music cognition and perceptual facilitation: a connectionist framework. *Music Perception*, **5**, 1–30.

Bharucha, J. J. and Krumhansl, C. L. (1983). The representation of harmonic structure in music: Hierarchies of stability as a function of context. *Cognition*, **13**, 63–102.

Bigand, E. (1990a). *Perception et compréhension des phrases musicales*. Ph.D. thesis, Université de Nanterre (Paris X), Nanterre [Universal microfiche ISSN: 0294-1767 No. 42, 09882/90, Lille, France].

Bigand, E. (1990b). Abstraction of two forms of underlying structure in a tonal melody. *Psychology of Music*, **18**, 45–60.

Bigand, E. (1991a). La perception de schémas de tensions et détentes musicales dans une phrase musicale. *Analyse Musicale* (special issue), 144–6.

Bigand, E. (1991b). La perception de relations entre les événements sonores dans une pièce musicale. In *Genèse et perception des sons* (ed. J.-C. Risset and G.

Canévet), pp. 159–76. Publications du Laboratoire de Mécanique et d'Acoustique, No. 128, Marseille.

Bigand, E. (1993). The influence of implicit harmony, rhythm, and musical training on the abstraction of 'tension–relaxation schemas' in tonal musical phrases. *Contemporary Music Review*. (In press.)

Brown, H. (1988). The interplay of set content and temporal context in a functional theory of tonality perception. *Music Perception*, **5**, 219–50.

Butler, D. (1989). Describing the perception of tonality in music: a critique of the tonal hierarchy theory and a proposal for a theory of intervallic rivalry. *Music Perception*, **6**, 219–42.

Butler, D. (1990*a*). Response to Carol Krumhansl, *Music Perception*, **7**, 315–38.

Butler, D. (1990*b*). A study of event hierarchies in tonal and post-tonal music, *Psychology of Music*, **18**, 4–17.

Butler, D. and Brown, H. (1984). Tonal structure versus function: studies of the recognition of harmonic motion. *Music Perception*, **2**, 6–24.

Clarke, E. F. (1985). Structure and expression in rhythmic performance. In *Musical structure and cognition* (ed. P. Howell, I. Cross, and R. West), pp. 209–36. Academic, London.

Clarke, E. F. (1988). Generative principles in music performance. In *Generative processes in music: the psychology of performance, improvisation, and composition* (ed. J. A. Sloboda), pp. 1–26. Oxford University Press.

Clarke, E. F. (1989). Issues in language and music. *Contemporary Music Review*, **4**, 9–22.

Clarke, E. F. and Krumhansl, C. L. (1990). Perceiving musical time. *Music Perception*, **7**, 213–52.

Collard, R., Vos, P., and Leeuwenberg, E. (1981). What melody tells us about meter in music. *Zeitschrift für Psychologie*, **1**, 25–33.

Cuddy, L., Cohen, A., and Miller, J. (1979). Melody recognition: the experimental application of musical rules. *Canadian Journal of Psychology*, **33**, 148–57.

Deliège, C. (1984). *Les fondements de la musique tonale*. Lattès, Paris.

Deliège, I. (1987). Grouping conditions in listening to music: an approach to Lerdahl and Jackendoff's grouping preference rules. *Music Perception*, **4**, 325–60.

Deliège, I. (1989). A perceptual approach to contemporary musical forms. *Contemporary Music Review*, **4**, 213–30.

Deliège, I, (1990). Mechanisms of cue extraction in musical grouping: a study of *Sequenza VI* for Viola Solo by L. Berio. *Psychology of Music*, **18**, 18–45.

Deutsch, D. (1980). The processing of structured and unstructured tonal sequences. *Perception and Psychophysics*, **28**, 381–9.

Deutsch, D. (1982). Grouping mechanism in music. In *The psychology of music* (ed. D. Deutsch), pp. 99–130. Academic, New York.

Deutsch, D. (1984). Two issues concerning tonal hierarchies: comment on Castellano, Bharucha, and Krumhansl. *Journal of Experimental Psychology*, **113**, 413–6.

Deutsch, D. and Feroe, J. (1981). The internal representation of pitch sequences in tonal music. *Psychological Review*, **88**, 503–22.

Dewar, K., Cuddy, L., and Mewhort, J. (1977). Recognition memory for single tones with and without context. *Journal of Experimental Psychology: Human Learning and Memory*, **3**, 60–7.

Dowling, W. J. (1973). Rhythmic groups and subjective chunks in memory for melodies. *Perception and Psychophysics*, **14**, 37–40.

Dowling, W. J. (1978). Scale and contour: two components of a theory for melodies. *Psychological Review*, **85**, 341–54.

Dowling, W. J. (1984). Assimilation and tonal structure: comment on Castellano, Bharucha, and Krumhansl. *Journal of Experimental Psychology: General*, **113**, 417–20.

Dowling, W. J. and Harwood, D. L. (1986). *Music cognition*. Academic, New York.

Drake, C. (1990). *Processus cognitifs impliqués dans l'organisation du rythme musical*. Ph.D. thesis, Université René Descartes (Paris V), Paris.

Drake, C., Dowling, W. J., and Palmer, C. (1991). Accent structure in the reproduction of simple tunes by children and adult pianists. *Music Perception*, **8**, 315–34.

Essens, P. and Povel, D. (1985). Metrical and nonmetrical representations of temporal patterns. *Perception and Psychophysics*, **37**, 1–7.

Forte, A. and Gilbert, S. (1982). *Introduction to Schenkerian Analysis*. Norton, New York.

Fraisse, P. (1967). *Psychologie du temps*, 2nd edn. Presses Universitaires de France, Paris. [English transl. of 1st French edn. (1957): *The psychology of time*. Harper, New York (1963).]

Fraisse, P. (1974). *La psychologie du rythme*. Presses Universitaires de France, Paris.

Francès, R. (1988). *The perception of music*. (transl. from the 1st French edn, 1958, by W. J. Dowling). Erlbaum, Hillsdale, NJ.

Francès, R., Imberty, M., and Zenatti, A. (1979). Le domaine musical. In *Psychologie de l'art et de l'esthétique* (ed. R. Francès), pp. 139–93. Presses Universitaires de France, Paris.

Gérard, C. and Drake, C. (1990). The inability of young children to reproduce intensity differences in musical rhythms. *Perception and Psychophysics*, **48**, 91–101.

Hevner, K. (1935). Expression in music: a discussion of experimental studies and theories. *Psychological Review*, **42**, 248–58.

Hevner, K. (1936). Experimental studies of the elements of expression in music. *American Journal of Psychology*, **48**, 248–68.

Imberty, M. (1969). *L'acquisition des structures tonales chez l'enfant*. Klincksieck, Paris.

Imberty, M. (1975). Perspective nouvelle de la sémantique musicale expérimentale. *Musique en jeu*, **17**, 87–109.

Imberty, M. (1979). *Entendre la musique: sémantique psychologique de la musique*, Vol. 1. Dunod, Paris.

Imberty, M. (1981a). *Les écritures du temps: sémantique psychologique de la musique*, Vol. 2. Dunod, Paris.

Imberty, M. (1981b). Acculturation tonale et structuration musicale. Peut-on parler de compétence musicale à propos de la structuration du temps musical chez l'enfant? *Basic musical functions and musical ability*, pp. 81–155. Publication No. 32. Royal Swedish Academy of Music, Stockholm, Sweden.

Jones, M. (1976). Time, our lost dimension: toward a new theory of perception, attention, and memory. *Psychological Review*, **83**, 323–55.

Jones, M. (1981). A tutorial on some issues and methods in serial pattern research. *Perception and Psychophysics*, **30**, 492–504.

Jones, M. (1987). Perspective on musical time. In *Action and perception in rhythm and music* (ed. A. Gabrielsson), pp. 153–75. Publication No. 55. Royal Swedish Academy of Music, Stockholm, Sweden.

Jones, M., Maser, D., and Kidd, G. (1978). Rate and structure in memory for auditory patterns. *Memory and Cognition*, **6**, 246–58.

Jones, M., Kidd, G., and Wetzel, R. (1981). Evidence for rhythmic attention. *Journal of Experimental Psychology: Human Perception and Performance*, **7**, 1059–73.

Krumhansl, C. L. (1979). The psychological representation of musical pitch in a tonal context. *Cognitive Psychology*, **11**, 346–74.

Krumhansl, C. L. (1990a). *Cognitive foundations of musical pitch*. Oxford University Press.

Krumhansl, C. L. (1990b). Tonal hierarchies and rare intervals in music cognition. *Music Perception*, **7**, 309–24.

Krumhansl, C. L. and Kessler, E. (1982). Tracing the dynamic changes in perceived tonal organization in a spatial representation of musical keys. *Psychological Review*, **89**, 334–68.

Krumhansl, C. L. and Shepard, R. N. (1979). Quantification of the hierarchy of tonal functions within a diatonic context. *Journal of Experimental Psychology: Human Perception and Performance*, **5**, 579–94.

Krumhansl, C. L., Bharucha, J. J., and Castellano, M. (1982a). Key distance effects on perceived harmonic structure in music. *Perception and Psychophysics*, **32**, 96–108.

Krumhansl, C. L., Bharucha, J. J., and Kessler, E. J. (1982b). Perceived harmonic structure of chords in three related keys. *Journal of Experimental Psychology: Human Perception and Performance*, **8**, 24–36.

Lerdahl, F. (1987). Timbral hierarchies. *Contemporary Music Review*, **2**, 135–60.

Lerdahl, F. (1988). Tonal pitch space. *Music Perception*, **5**, 315–50.

Lerdahl, F. (1989). Atonal prolongational structure. *Contemporary Music Review*, **4**, 65–88.

Lerdahl, F. (1992). Pitch-space journeys in two Chopin Preludes. In *Cognitive bases of musical communication* (ed. M. R. Jones and S. Holleran), pp. 171–91. American Psychological Association, Washington, DC.

Lerdahl, F. and Jackendoff, R. (1983). *A generative theory of tonal music*. MIT, Cambridge, MA.

Longuet-Higgins, H. (1976). Perception of melodies. *Nature*, **263**, 646–53.

Longuet-Higgins, H. and Lee, C. S. (1982). The perception of musical rhythms. *Perception*, **11**, 115–28.

McAdams, S. (1987). Music: a science of the mind? *Contemporary Music Review*, **2**, 1–61.

McAdams, S. (1989). Psychological constraints on form-bearing dimensions in music. *Contemporary Music Review*, **4**, 181–98.

Meyer, L. (1973). *Explaining music: essays and explorations*. University of California Press, Berkeley, CA.

Michon, J. (1977). Le traitement de l'information temporelle. In *Du temps biologique au temps psychologique*. Symposium de l'association de psychologie scientifique de langue française, pp. 255–87.

Miller, G. A. (1956). The magical number seven, plus or minor two: some limits on our capacity for processing information. *Psychological Review*, **63**, 81–97.

Narmour, E. (1983). Some major theoretical problems concerning the concept of hierarchy in the analysis of tonal music. *Music Perception*, **1**, 129–99.

Narmour, E. (1989). The 'genetic code' of melody: cognitive structures generated by the implication–realization model. *Contemporary Music Review*, 4, 45–64.

Nattiez, J.-J. (1987). *Musicologie générale et sémiologie*. Christian Bourgois, Paris.

Palmer, C. and Krumhansl, C. L. (1987a). Independent temporal and pitch structures in determination of musical phrases. *Journal of Experimental Psychology: Human Perception and Performance*, 13, 116–26.

Palmer, C. and Krumhansl, C. L. (1987b). Pitch and temporal contributions to musical phrase perception: effects of harmony, performance timing, and familiarity. *Perception and Psychophysics*, 41, 505–18.

Palmer, C. and Krumhansl, C. L. (1990). Mental representation for musical meter. *Journal of Experimental Psychology: Human Perception and Performance*, 16, 728–41.

Peretz, I. and Morais, J. (1989). Music and modularity. *Contemporary Music Review*, 4, 279–94.

Piaget, J. (1959). *La formation du symbole chez l'enfant*, 2nd edn. Delachaux et Niestlé, Paris.

Povel, J. (1981). The internal representation of simple temporal patterns. *Journal of Experimental Psychology: Human Perception and Performance*, 7, 3–18.

Rasch, R. and Plomp, R. (1982). The listener and the acoustic environment. In *The psychology of music* (ed. D. Deutsch), pp. 135–46. Academic, New York.

Restle, F. (1970). Theories of serial pattern learning: structural trees. *Psychological Review*, 77, 481–95.

Restle, F. and Brown, E. (1970). Serial pattern learning. *Journal of Experimental Psychology*, 83, 120–5.

Risset, J.-C. and Wessel, D. (1982). Exploration of timbre by analysis and synthesis. In *The psychology of music* (ed. D. Deutsch), pp. 26–54. Academic, New York.

Rosner, B. and Meyer, L. (1982). Melodic process and the perception of music. In *The psychology of music* (ed. D. Deutsch), pp. 317–42. Academic, New York.

Rosner, B. and Meyer, L. (1986). The perceptual roles of melodic process, contour, and form. *Music Perception*, 4, 1–40.

Schenker, H. (1979). *Free Composition* (transl. from German (1935) by E. Oster). Longman, New York.

Serafine, M. L., Glassman, N., and Overbeeke, C. (1989). The cognitive reality of hierarchic structure in music. *Music Perception*, 6, 397–430.

Sloboda, J. A. (1985). *The musical mind: the cognitive psychology of music*. Oxford University Press.

Sloboda, J. A. (1986). Cognition and real music: the psychology of music comes of age. *Psychologica Belgica*, 26, 199–219.

Sloboda, J. A. and Parker, D. (1985). Immediate recall of melodies. In *Musical structure and cognition* (ed. P. Howell, I. Cross, and R. West), pp. 143–68. Academic, London.

Steedman, M. J. (1977). The perception of musical rhythm and metre. *Perception*, 6, 555–70.

Sundberg, J. (1982). Perception of singing. In *The psychology of music* (ed. D. Deutsch), pp. 59–95. Academic, New York.

Teplov, B. M. (1966). *Psychologie des aptitudes musicales* (transl. from the Russian into French by J. Deprun). Presses Universitaires de France, Paris.

9

Listening strategies in infancy: the roots of music and language development

Sandra E. Trehub and *Laurel J. Trainor*

9.0   INTRODUCTION

There has been growing interest in the perception of complex auditory (non-speech) patterns but surprisingly little concern for the origins of such abilities. Nevertheless, contemporary perspectives in this domain often embody implicit, if not explicit, claims about such origins. For some (e.g. Leek 1987; Watson 1987), pattern perception processes are not stable and 'hardwired' but rather have considerable plasticity, being dependent on the experience, training, and expectations of the listener. Indeed, the perceptual organization of particular patterns is thought to depend on extensive formal or informal training with similar materials, with attention, listening strategy, and task demands playing a prominent role (Espinoza-Varas and Watson 1989). The assumption, moreover, is that the amount and kind of information that listeners can extract from a sound pattern is determined primarily by the relative difficulty of the task and secondarily by features of the pattern itself. Accordingly, a difficult task would lead to a synthetic or global mode of listening (i.e. poor sensitivity for pattern components) in contrast to an easy task, which would engage analytic listening skills (i.e. enhanced resolution of individual components) and make alternative representations available to the listener. What is clear, however, is that prolonged practice is deemed essential for *'fully developed* perceptual representations of patterns' (Espinoza-Varas and Watson 1989, p. 90).

This position implies that auditory pattern perception is almost entirely learned. Conceivably, however, pattern perception could be given in its entirety by nature, in which case the perception of auditory events would be uniform across individuals, with learning involved only in such things as the memory for specific patterns (e.g. individual voices, tunes) as well

Thinking in sound: the cognitive psychology of human audition, ed. S. McAdams and E. Bigand. Oxford University Press, 1993, pp. 278–327.

as arbitrary associations between auditory and non-auditory events (e.g. words and meanings). The views of most researchers tend to fall somewhere between these extremes. For example, Handel (1989), Krumhansl (1992), and Jones (1990) consider innate perceptual processes such as grouping to set the stage for perceiving complex patterns such as speech and musical sequences. Beyond these grouping processes, however, there is much to be learned.

According to Krumhansl (1990), adults' perception of pitch relations in music derives from incidental extraction of the regularities in heard music. For Jones (1981, 1982), as well, exposure to music promotes the internalization of prototypes or conventions of a musical culture, with such prototypes generating expectancies that guide the listener's attention. Handel (1989) suggests that innate factors might play a somewhat larger role. For him, heredity supplies the potential perceptual structures that experience 'fine tunes' to the conventions of a particular language or musical system. Just as children acquire their language early, easily, and without formal training, so might they become sensitive to the musical conventions of their culture (Handel 1989, p. 381).

Despite the presumed role of knowledge and experience, few have evaluated these presumptions with novice listeners, notably infants. Such naïve listeners offer unique opportunities for exploring the presence and nature of human pattern processing predispositions as well as the relevance of such predispositions for adult pattern perception. A decade or so of systematic research on the localization of sound patterns in infancy has yielded much valuable information (for reviews, see Clifton (1992), Muir *et al.* (1989)). Unfortunately, there has been considerably less research on other aspects of auditory pattern processing in early life.

To counter this deficiency, we have been pursuing answers to a variety of general questions such as the following. What properties of auditory patterns dominate perception in the early months of life? Do these properties remain influential for more mature listeners? Are the grouping processes that characterize auditory pattern perception (see Bigand, Ch. 8 this volume; Bregman 1990, Ch. 2 this volume) operative in infancy, when instructions to listen synthetically or analytically are necessarily precluded? Although relational processing is the norm for adults' perception of auditory sequences, absolute pitch processing is characteristic of various non-human species such as songbirds and monkeys (D'Amato 1988; Hulse *et al.* 1990). One might ask, then, whether infants are more like human adults in this respect or more like non-human listeners.

Research with adults has revealed that *good* auditory patterns, defined in information-theoretic terms (Garner 1970, 1974) or in terms of conformance to cultural conventions (e.g. Cuddy *et al.* 1981) are perceived and remembered more accurately than poorly structured or *bad* patterns. Is it possible, instead, to define *good* auditory patterns with reference to their relative ease of processing by infant listeners? If so, this would remove the experiential and ethnocentric biases inherent in the notion of a *good* pattern. (Note that aesthetic questions would be irrelevant to this designation of patterns as *good* or *bad*.) Obviously, infants of any age have had the benefit of some listening experience. Nevertheless, patterns that are processed readily in early life could be considered to have special status (i.e. as *good* patterns) and to involve innate attentional predispositions or learning preferences (Locke 1990; Marler 1990). If any such *good* patterns can be identified, one can then ask whether their features are in accord with linguistic (e.g. Kuhl 1986; Liberman *et al.* 1967), psychoacoustic (e.g. Terhardt 1974), music-theoretic (e.g. Butler 1989; Schenker 1954), or mathematical (e.g. Balzano 1982) predictions. One can inquire, as well, whether the perceptual processing strategies that are evident in early life are equally applicable to musical and speech patterns. If so, are there implications of common processing strategies for the acquisition of knowledge about music and language?

9.0.1   Selecting the naïve listener

In principle, the ideal naïve listener is the newborn, who is free from the attentional biases associated with experience, training, and expectations. In practice, however, the newborn is a relatively unco-operative listener by virtue of characteristic drowsiness, a disposition to fuss or cry when awake, and an impoverished response repertoire. For reasons of convenience rather than conviction, we study infants from 6 or 7 months to 10 or 11 months of age. The lower age bound is determined by the onset of a highly reliable and unambiguous response (i.e. turning head and eyes toward a sound source) to salient changes in a sound pattern (Eilers *et al.* 1977; Kuhl 1985; Trehub *et al.* 1984). The upper age bound is determined by the onset of walking, which is generally accompanied by a reluctance to remain seated for the duration of a test session (10–20 minutes).

It would not be surprising for the pattern processing abilities of infants in this age range to have undergone some modification as a result of early exposure to particular patterns. Nevertheless, it is reasonable to consider these abilities as reflecting pattern processing predispositions. In other words, whether infants are predisposed to perceive patterns in particular ways or are predisposed to learn to perceive them in such ways is immaterial.

9.0.2   Selecting the stimuli

In our research on auditory pattern perception, we use musical or music-like patterns for a number of reasons. Music, 'a peculiarly human adaptation to life' (Slobin and Titon 1984, p. 9), is found in every culture. Although few individuals in Western society perform in public contexts, many sing or hum in the shower or elsewhere, and all listen to music, by choice (e.g. concerts, stereo, radio) or otherwise (e.g. commercial background music). What is not generally known, however, is that contemporary Western notions of musical talent, giftedness, and music as art are unusual (Walker 1987, 1990). Historically and cross-culturally, it has been more common for music to be integrated into various facets of work and play, with all community members participating fully (e.g. Bebey 1969). Moreover, there are many widely held beliefs or myths about music including its influence on physical and mental states, its healing powers, and supernatural origins (Walker 1990). The continuing influence of such belief systems can be seen in contemporary uses of music in promoting religious, political, and commercial goals, parental concerns about so-called 'decadent' music, and young children's greater compliance with sung as opposed to spoken requests. The ubiquity of music and its presumed power raise questions about biological significance (Granit 1977; Lerdahl and Jackendoff 1983) for which there are no ready answers. What is clear is that music is prevalent cross-culturally, occupying an important role in daily life.

A further impetus to the use of musical patterns stems from recent progress in the understanding of music perception by musically trained and untrained adults (Deutsch 1982; Dowling and Harwood 1986; Howell *et al.* 1985; Krumhansl 1990; Sloboda 1985). The presumption is that untrained adults, by virtue of informal but extended exposure to the music of their culture, have developed implicit but highly elaborated schemas for music processing. Those with formal training, on the other hand, have more explicit knowledge of musical structure and are capable of more analytic listening. Is it reasonable to assume, however, that the music processing strategies of untrained adults are due entirely to musical exposure, with no carry-over of primitive processing strategies from early life? Terhardt (1987) suggests, instead, that composers, in creating music, intuitively capitalize on universal principles of auditory perception. It would hardly be surprising, then, for some of these principles to be operative in infancy.

Finally, many have drawn attention to numerous parallels between speech and music (e.g. Handel 1989; Lerdahl and Jackendoff 1983; Sloboda 1985), some even suggesting the possibility of innate perceptual principles for organizing speech and musical input (Krumhansl 1992; Lerdahl and Jackendoff 1983). Handel (1989) has applied some of Hockett's (1963) design features of language to music, as well. These include the features of discreteness (i.e. messages in speech or language being constructed from a limited set of units, whether phonemes or scale notes), openness (i.e. an infinite number of possible linguistic utterances or musical

passages), and duality of structure (i.e. meaningless units such as phonemes or notes combined to form meaningful units such as words or
musical phrases).

In short, it is not unreasonable to expect that the study of musical
pattern perception in infancy will yield valuable information about auditory pattern processing in general. In this spirit, we have used sequences
of tones (mostly sine waves) which, despite their harmonic impover-
ishment, are readily recognizable as melodies. This contrasts with the
synthesized speech stimuli in speech perception experiments, some of
which are unrecognizable as speech to adult listeners (e.g. Diehl *et al.* 1981).
In fact, speech synthesis by rule in conjunction with the elimination of all
but a single discriminative cue (the typical procedure for speech perception
experiments) can result in very unnatural-sounding stimuli.

9.0.3   The test procedure

We attempt to overload the information-processing capacities of infants
by presenting them with five- to ten-note sequences or melodies. Assuming that infants are unable to retain the entire melody, then what they do
retain can inform us about their processing strategies. Would they encode
and retain an incomplete but precise description such as the absolute
pitches of the first or last few notes? Such a local-processing strategy
would be uncharacteristic of adults but consistent nevertheless with the
preferred strategy of songbirds (Hulse *et al.* 1990) and monkeys (D'Amato
1988). A global-processing alternative might involve configural information about pitch relations, temporal relations, or both. Some researchers
suggest that local processing has priority over global processing in infant
perception (e.g. Aslin and Smith 1988) whereas others suggest the reverse
(e.g. Morrongiello 1988).

We gather indirect evidence for the use of such strategies by means of
an operant discrimination procedure. The infant sits on the parent's lap
in one corner of a sound-attenuating booth facing an experimenter, who
maintains the infant's attention by manipulating puppets (see Fig. 9.1).
The standard melody or tone sequence is presented repeatedly from a
loudspeaker 45° to the infant's left. The experimenter continually records
(via push buttons) when the infant is looking directly ahead (i.e. ready
for a test trial) and when the infant turns toward the loudspeaker (i.e. a
correct or false-positive response). The parent and the experimenter wear
headphones with masking sounds so that both remain uninformed about
the patterns being presented. Test trials, which are presented only when
the infant is looking directly ahead, are of two types: *change* trials in which
a comparison sequence, which embodies subtle or substantial changes,
replaces the standard sequence for one or two repetitions, and *no-change*
trials in which the comparison sequence is the same as the standard. A

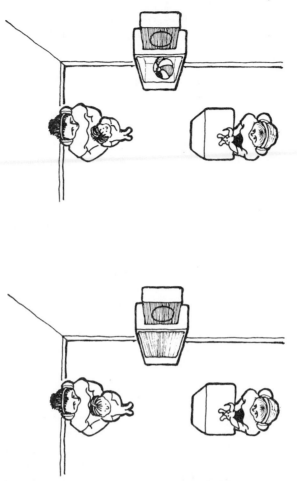

Fig. 9.1 The test situation. The infant sits on the parent's lap facing the experimenter. Sounds are presented repeatedly through the loudspeaker to the infant's left. Turns to the speaker on change trials lead to the presentation of an animated toy near the speaker (From Trehub (1990).)

head turn (45° or more) toward the loudspeaker within 4 s of the sound change results in the illumination and activation of one of four animated toys near the loudspeaker. Turns at other times (i.e. false-positive responses) are unreinforced.

The difficulty of the task can be varied by manipulating the length and complexity of the sequences, the size of the retention interval (i.e. time between standard and comparison sequences), and the degree of deviation from standard to comparison sequences. It is also possible to introduce variations in stimulus parameters across repetitions of the patterns. For example, the repetitions of the standard and comparison patterns could be presented in pitch transposition (i.e. at different pitch levels), precluding the use of absolute pitch cues in the discrimination task. The patterns could also be presented at different tempos or rates, precluding the use of absolute duration cues.

In an initial training phase, infants must meet a training criterion of four consecutive correct responses to a more prominent sound change than that used in the test phase. The subsequent test phase consists of approximately 30 test trials (more or less in some experiments), with a random ordering of 15 change and 15 no-change trials. If infants respond significantly more often on change than on no-change trials, this indicates that they can detect the change.

We make the leap from discrimination data to processing strategy in the following way. If infants are using a particular processing strategy such as encoding the exact beginnings of melodies, then certain changes would evoke a response (e.g. new initial pitches) and others would not (e.g. new final pitches). Likewise, a global-processing strategy would be reflected in infants' failure to respond to certain discriminable changes such as new pitches if the pitch configuration or contour remains the same (e.g. transpositions), or new note durations if the relative note durations (i.e. rhythmic structure) remain the same.

9.1   GROUPING

Perceptual grouping is thought to operate preattentively (Neisser 1967), creating units that optimize cognitive processing (Bregman 1981, 1990). Cues for promoting grouping such as the relative proximity of elements and their similarity were described by the Gestalt psychologists many years ago but their role in auditory contexts has only become clear in recent years (Bigand, Ch. 8 this volume; Bregman 1990, Ch. 2 this volume; Deutsch 1982).

The presumption is that at least some grouping processes are primitive (Bregman 1990) or informationally encapsulated (Fodor 1983), being relatively insensitive to the perceiver's experience. This raises the possibility that these processes would be operative early in life, even in infancy. On the other hand, some grouping phenomena are clearly dependent on experience, that is, they are schema-based (Bregman 1990). For example, the organization of the speech stream into words creates the illusion of pauses between words (Studdert-Kennedy 1975), an illusion that is absent when the sounds belong to a foreign language. In general, however, we tend to group subsets of elements within auditory sequences, even when the elements are totally uniform (Fraisse 1982). Such perceptual grouping has consequences for judgments of duration (Bolton 1894; Woodrow 1909) as well as duration discrimination (Fitzgibbons *et al.* 1974).

If infants grouped auditory sequences in similar ways, we might expect them to have greater difficulty detecting a silent interval or pause *between* groups of sounds compared with an identical pause *within* a group of sounds. In a series of studies (Thorpe and Trehub 1989; Thorpe *et al.* 1988), we assessed the ability of infants 6–9 months of age to detect small temporal changes in patterns of six temporally equidistant tones. The patterns were structured so that the first three tones, which were identical, differed from the last three (also identical to each other) in fundamental frequency (pitch), spectral structure (i.e. waveform: sawtooth vs. sine waves), or intensity. The schematic structure can be represented as XXXOOO. The comparison sequences incorporated increments to the silent interval between the third and fourth tone (XXX OOO), a between-group change, or between the fourth and fifth tone (XXXO OO), a within-group change. Infants detected the temporal alterations when they occurred within a group but not between groups, implying that they had grouped the original pattern of temporally equidistant tones. As a result, the change that altered or disrupted the structure of the standard pattern (from a 3–3 to a 4–2 grouping) was noticeable but not the change that conserved the structure (3–3 in both cases).

Adults tested with the identical sequences but with smaller increment values and a more conventional psychophysical task (two-alternative, forced-choice task) showed a similar pattern of performance (Thorpe 1985). We call this phenomenon the *duration illusion* (Thorpe and Trehub 1989), referring to the inaccuracy of perceiving the duration of silent intervals *between* groups compared to identical silent intervals *within* a group of sounds. This illusion of pauses between sound groups is analogous to the illusion of pauses between words. Discontinuities in pitch, timbre, or loudness typically signal important aspects of pattern structure, triggering the duration illusion, which guides primitive processes of segmentation or parsing. Greater discontinuity or change in any of these parameters leads to greater inaccuracy in detecting the between-group intervals. In effect, listeners override the available temporal information (e.g. temporally equidistant tones), imposing a temporal structure that corresponds to configural aspects (e.g. pattern of pitches) of the pattern.

Another segmentation process that has received considerably more experimental attention with adults is *auditory stream segregation* (Bregman 1978, 1981) or *auditory scene analysis* (Bregman 1990, Ch. 2 this volume). Rapidly repeating sequences of discrete sounds are grouped or segregated on the basis of similarities in frequency, spectral envelope, or other salient properties, leading to the perception of two or more parallel sequences or streams. One consequence of stream segregation is that listeners are unable to track the order of elements across streams but can readily do so within a single stream (e.g. Bregman and Campbell 1971). Bregman (1990) envisions the operation of unlearned as well as learned constraints on auditory scene analysis, with the former reflecting universal regularities in the environment.

Demany (1982) investigated the phenomenon with infants, comparing 7- to 15-week-old infants' discrimination of the temporal order of two sequences of tones. For adult listeners, one of the sequences would remain within a single auditory stream whereas the other would segregate into different streams. Infants showed a pattern of performance similar to that of adults, detecting a change in the temporal order of tones within the hypothesized stream but failing to detect this change across streams. The implication, then, is that stream segregation, like the duration illusion, reflects primitive rather than schema-based parsing.

Our findings and those of Demany (1982) indicate that infants extract the conventional temporal organization of simple auditory sequences. Moreover, infants can also differentiate patterns with contrasting rhythmic structure (Demany *et al.* 1977; Chang and Trehub 1977*a*; Morrongiello 1984). Adults go beyond this, however, generalizing the temporal or rhythmic structure of sequences across variations in tempo or rate. Would infants do likewise? We evaluated their ability to differentiate three-tone sequences with 1–2 (X XX) or 2–1 (XX X) structure and four-tone sequences with 2–2 (XX XX) or 3–1 (XXX X) structure in the context of tempo variations (Trehub and Thorpe 1989). In the training phase, infants were presented with a three- or four-tone pattern at a uniform tempo but at five different pitch levels (changing randomly from one repetition to the next) and were rewarded for responding to the contrasting three- or four-tone pattern with contrasting structure presented at the same tempo (and variable pitch level). In the test phase, we added five (discriminable) tempo variations to the five pitch variations and rewarded infants only for responding to changes in temporal structure. Infants discriminated between patterns with contrasting temporal structure in the context of variations in tempo and frequency (see Fig. 9.2), indicating that they perceived the similarities in rhythmic structure across these variations. Nevertheless, infants found the task difficult, as reflected in their low level of performance and high false-alarm rate. Such a high false-alarm rate has also characterized infants' performance on other difficult tasks with the same procedure (Thorpe and Trehub 1989). In any case, their performance provided evidence of relational processing in the temporal domain.

This does not appear to be a uniquely human feat. Relational temporal processing has been observed in starlings, which are capable of transposing a rhythmic discrimination across changes in tempo (Hulse *et al.* 1984) and in pigeons, which can respond to the longer of two temporal intervals (Fetterman 1987). Nevertheless, such temporal processing is central to

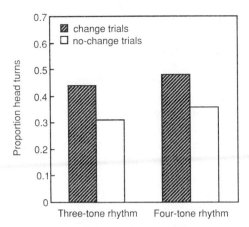

Fig. 9.2 Mean proportion of head turns on change and no-change trials for the three-tone and four-tone rhythms. (Data from Trehub and Thorpe (1989).)

the perception of speech. A verbal message maintains its integrity over changes in rate just as a tune does. There is evidence, moreover, that infants (Eimas and Miller 1980), like adults (Miller and Liberman 1979; Summerfield 1981), make appropriate perceptual compensations for speaking rate.

In a novel approach to the study of grouping in musical patterns, Krumhansl and Jusczyk (1990) explored 4- and 6-month-old infants' sensitivity to phrase structure in music. They presented infants with two distorted versions of Mozart minuets and attempted to establish infants' preference for one over the other. In one version, they added a one-second pause to the end of each phrase, distorting the overall temporal patterning but maintaining the temporal integrity of each musical phrase. In the other, they added the same number of pauses but these were inserted within phrases. This manipulation altered the phrase structure as well as the overall temporal structure of the musical passages. For each infant, the minuets with between-phrase pauses were presented from a loudspeaker on one side and those with within-phrase pauses were presented from the other side. The time spent looking at each loudspeaker during sound presentation was calculated over a series of trials. Infants looked significantly longer at the loudspeaker with intact phrases than at the one with distorted phrases, indicating their 'preference' for the former.

Krumhansl and Jusczyk's (1990) analysis of musical features of the minuets indicated that drops in pitch height and increased duration of the last melody note characterized phrase endings. They suggest that these features signal phrase structure or perceptual units for infant listeners and may account for their preference for intact phrases.

This preference procedure has also been used to explore infants' temporal processing of speech sequences. In these studies (Hirsh-Pasek *et al.* 1987; Kemler Nelson *et al.* 1989), infants heard extended samples of speech in which pauses had been added either between clauses or within clauses. As was the case with music, infants looked longer in the direction of speech with intact clauses (i.e. between-clause pauses) than in the direction of speech with temporally distorted clauses. The implication is that, like musical phrases, spoken clauses are perceptual units, even for prelinguistic infants. Interestingly, this 'preference' for intact clauses was limited to speech directed to infants, being absent in speech directed to adults.

9.2   MELODY PERCEPTION: PITCH CONTOUR

A cursory outline of the melody perception skills of untrained adult listeners can provide a useful backdrop to the consideration of infant skills. It is well known that adults' recognition of melodies is independent of specific pitch levels, being dependent instead on the relations among component pitches. With familiar melodies, the pattern of *intervals* is relevant (Attneave and Olson 1971; Dowling and Fujitani 1971), intervals referring to the precise pitch relations between adjacent notes. Thus transpositions, which have different component notes but an identical pattern of intervals, are perceived as equivalent to one another (Attneave and Olson 1971). With unfamiliar melodies, configural information about pitch is prominent, notably the *melodic contour* or global pattern of changes in pitch direction (up/down/same) (Bartlett and Dowling 1980; Dowling 1978). In addition, unfamiliar melodies that conform to familiar musical principles are encoded in greater detail, remembered more readily, and are also preferred compared with those that deviate from such principles (Cuddy *et al.* 1981; Francès 1988; Krumhansl and Keil 1982; Krumhansl *et al.* 1982; Watkins 1985; Zenatti 1969).

Studies of melodic processing in non-human species have revealed qualitative differences. To the extent that melody discrimination has been demonstrated in monkeys (D'Amato and Salmon 1984), starlings (Hulse and Cynx 1986), and budgerigars (Dooling *et al.* 1987), local (absolute) pitch cues rather than global pattern cues (e.g. contour) have been implicated. By contrast, the perception of single speech sounds by various non-human species, including budgerigars (Dooling *et al.* 1990), chinchillas (Kuhl and Miller 1975), and monkeys (Kuhl and Padden 1982) has revealed remarkable parallels between human and non-human listeners.

Does this imply that the perception of single sounds, including speech sounds, capitalizes on principles common to avian and mammalian species, whereas human adult-like perception of sound sequences depends on experience and the resultant meaningfulness of such patterns? If we adopt a conventional definition of auditory patterns, referring to 'sounds characterized by a perceptual impression that is global . . . elicited by the overall spectral or temporal form' (Espinoza-Varas and Watson 1989, p. 70), then we would have to conclude that the various non-human species that have been studied to date are unable to perceive pitch patterns. What about human infants?

In a series of studies, we focused on three types of melodic information: *contour* (i.e. pitch configuration or up/down/same pattern of pitch change), *interval* (i.e. frequency ratio of successive notes or pitch distance in semitones), and *absolute pitch* (i.e. exact pitch level). Our goal was to determine whether infants' mental representation of melodies was based on absolute pitches, exact intervals, or contour. In one study (Trehub et al. 1984), we tested infants on their discrimination of various changes to a six-tone melody including *transpositions* (i.e. absolute pitch changes, but same intervals and contour), *contour-preserving* changes (i.e. absolute pitch and interval changes, but same contour), and *contour-violating* changes (e.g. interval and contour changes, but same pitches reordered). To preclude the use of obvious cues, the comparison melodies had the same initial and final note as the standard melody except for the transpositions, which necessitated different notes (see Fig. 9.3). For adult listeners, the transposed comparison would seem most similar to the original melody (essentially equivalent to it) and the contour-violating comparison most dissimilar. The contour-preserving changes would be intermediate on the similarity–dissimilarity continuum. In the context of a difficult task such as a single presentation of the standard pattern and a long retention interval, adults might have comparable difficulty detecting contour-preserving changes and transpositions.

Overall, infants' performance was consistent with that expected for adults. Infants performed well on the contour changes but not on the transpositions and contour-preserving (i.e. interval) changes (see Fig. 9.4). In fact, they responded to the latter two types of changed melody as though they were further repetitions of the standard melody. Essentially, their performance was consistent with a global processing strategy, with information about pitch contour dominating at the expense of absolute pitch and interval information. For example, the transpositions had the same contour but contained six new notes and infants seemed to respond on the basis of the unchanged contour. Thus, they treated the transposed melodies as familiar rather than as novel or changed patterns. It is possible, however, that infants responded on the basis of the interval pattern, which was also invariant across transpositions. This seems unlikely

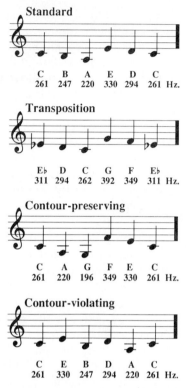

Fig. 9.3 One of the standard melodies and three types of changes to be detected: transposition (same contour, same intervals, different pitches); contour-preserving change (same contour, different intervals, different pitches); contour-violating change (different contour, different intervals, same pitches). (Stimuli from Trehub *et al.* (1984).)

because infants also treated melodies with new intervals but the same contour as though they were familiar patterns. In fact, they responded identically to transpositions and to contour-preserving changes, implying contour-influenced performance in both cases. Moreover, their ease of detecting contour changes was not limited to situations with multiple directional changes in pitch movement. Rather, infants also responded readily to contour-violating comparisons that retained five of the six original notes in their original order but had one note that changed the contour (Trehub *et al.* 1985).

Infants accomplished these contour discriminations with a fixed standard or background melody (i.e. standard and comparison sequences presented at one pitch level) so that absolute pitch cues were available. When we eliminated the potential use of absolute cues (Trehub *et al.* 1987) by presenting a simple standard pattern (up–down contour) repeating

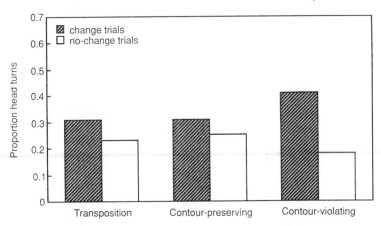

Fig 9.4 Mean proportion of head turns on change and no-change trials for the transposition, contour-preserving, and contour-violating changes. (Data from Trehub *et al.* (1984).)

either in transposition or with changing intervals (but same contour) and a contour-violating comparison (down–up–down contour) with reordered pitches (see Fig. 9.5), infants readily detected the contour changes (see Fig. 9.6). For the most part, they ignored the local pitch changes so long as the contour was retained, responding when the contour changed. Their relational processing strategy was qualitatively similar to adults' characteristic strategy with unfamiliar melodies but distinctly different from the local pitch strategy of non-human species. Note, also, that infants' performance on the contour discrimination tasks was considerably better than their performance on the temporal processing tasks with the same (head-turning) procedure (Thorpe and Trehub 1989; Thorpe *et al.* 1988; Trehub and Thorpe 1989).

These findings suggest that pitch-contour processing may function as an important perceptual organizational device for infants, guiding their parsing or segmentation of complex auditory patterns. Infants have other, perhaps less potent, parsing devices at their disposal including temporal grouping (by pitch, timbre, or loudness) and rhythmic patterning. These organizational processes would be useful not only for processing musical sequences but also for speech sequences, particularly prosodic aspects of speech.

Prosody is thought to be replete with cues to important linguistic units or boundaries (Morgan *et al.* 1987), cues that are enhanced in the unique prosody of speech directed to infants. Indeed, the hallmark of infant-directed speech is its distinctive and perhaps universal pitch contours (Fernald *et al.* 1989; Stern *et al.* 1983). Such speech also embodies higher pitch (by three or four semitones), an increased pitch range, smoother

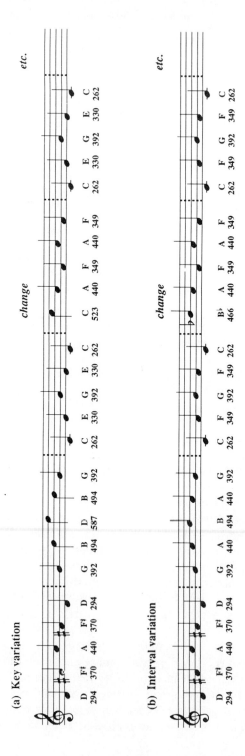

Fig. 9.5 Examples of repeating stimuli for the key-variation (a) and interval-variation (b) conditions. Each example depicts three successive presentations of the standard melody followed by a change and a subsequent return to the standard melody. (Stimuli from Trehub *et al.* (1987).)

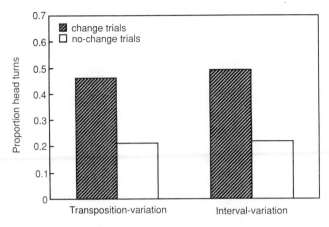

Fig. 9.6 Mean proportion of head turns on change and no-change trials for the transposition-variation and interval-variation conditions. (Data from Trehub *et al.* (1987).)

pitch transitions, simpler pitch contours, slower tempo, more regular rhythms, shorter utterances, and greater repetitiveness compared with adult-directed speech (Fernald and Simon 1984; Fernald *et al.* 1989; Papoušek and Papoušek 1981; Papoušek *et al.* 1985; Stern *et al.* 1983). These various qualities lend unity or coherence to the pitch contours of infant-directed speech, setting them apart from the complex contours of adult-directed speech (Stern *et al.* 1982). In fact, these distinctive prosodic forms are rarely produced by the same individuals in non-maternal contexts (Fernald and Simon 1984).

The characteristic features of infant-directed speech have been designated musical by a number of researchers (e.g. Fernald 1989; Papoušek and Papoušek 1981). The typical pitch contours are unidirectional (rising or falling) but at times bell-shaped (rise–fall, fall–rise) and these are repeated over and over with altered lexical or segmental content and varying tempo. Vowels are usually extended, as in song, and many utterances are contentless from a semantic perspective, consisting of a monosyllable (consonant–vowel or vowel alone) with the vowel stretched out over an expanded pitch contour (Fernald and Simon 1984; Papoušek and Papoušek 1981).

The regular rhythms and slow tempo of infant-directed speech (Beebe *et al.* 1985) also confer a musical quality to such speech. In fact, rhythmic adult-directed speech is atypical, being confined, for the most part, to ritualized or pathological contexts (Jaffe *et al.* 1979). It is also atypical of children's speech, except for ritual chants (Hargreaves 1986; Moorhead and Pond 1978).

There are indications that specific pitch contours are linked universally to particular caretaking contexts (Fernald *et al.* 1989). For example, rising or bell-shaped contours are used to gain and maintain infant attention (Papoušek and Papoušek 1981), falling contours with a narrow pitch range to soothe and hasten sleep (Papoušek and Papoušek 1981), and more variable contours to heighten positive affect (Stern *et al.* 1982). The tempo and rhythm of maternal utterances are also tuned to the infant's presumed needs. Thus slow, rhythmic utterances are provided for attentive infants, increased tempo for inattentive infants, variable rhythms and tempo for fussy infants, and gradually decreasing tempo for infants progressing toward sleep (Papoušek and Papoušek 1981). In sum, maternal vocal stimulation seems to be tuned intuitively to infants' processing abilities in general (Trehub 1989, 1990) and to their fluctuating state in particular.

This care-giving speech register has a dramatic impact on infant listeners. From as young as two days of age, they listen preferentially to infant-directed over adult-directed speech (Cooper and Aslin 1990; Fernald 1985; Werker and McLeod 1989), even to synthesized sine-wave renditions of infant-directed over adult-directed pitch contours (Fernald and Kuhl 1987). Infants also exhibit more positive affect when listening to infant-directed than to adult-directed speech (Werker and McLeod 1989). The universality of a small set of contours tied to specific caretaking contexts and the impact of such contours on infant attention and arousal have prompted some authors to consider their biological basis (Papoušek and Papoušek 1987) and communicative significance (Fernald 1989, 1992).

The pitch contour may well be an important unit of speech processing for prelinguistic listeners, helping to define the boundaries of infant-directed utterances (Trehub 1990). We know that young infants are sensitive to prosodic markers of clauses, phrases, and words in native and non-native languages (Hirsh-Pasek *et al.* 1987; Jusczyk, personal communication; Kemler Nelson *et al.* 1989), perhaps using temporal as well as pitch contour cues to delineate such units. We also know that infants are sensitive to musical phrase structure, with one of the likely cues to phrase boundaries being a falling pitch contour (Krumhansl and Jusczyk 1990).

Although infant-directed speech is music-like in a number of respects, it still differs considerably from the music with which most of us are familiar. If we consider infant-directed song, however, more commonalities might emerge between speech and music. Recently, we unobtrusively recorded mothers of young infants as they informally sang a song of their choice in two contexts, one with their infant present, the other when the mothers were alone (Trehub *et al.* 1993*b*). Most of the chosen materials were play songs, which were appropriate to the presence of awake and lively infants. A tape recording of pairs of identical excerpts from both conditions (infant present, infant absent) was presented to adult listeners, who were required to identify the infant-directed excerpt. Because the musical materials were the same, identification would have to be based on aspects of the singers' performance. Listeners were highly accurate (about 90 per cent correct) in identifying the infant-directed singing of North American mothers. They were also accurate in differentiating *actual* infant-directed singing from *simulated* infant-directed singing in another group of mothers (Trehub *et al.* 1993*a*). They were less accurate (about 60 per cent correct) but still above chance in judging comparable excerpts from a foreign language (Hindi) and musical system (Indian) (Trehub *et al.* 1993*b*). Not surprisingly, listeners of Indian origin were more accurate than native North American listeners with the Hindi songs.

One musical genre, the lullaby, is sung by care-givers throughout the world to soothe infants and induce sleep (Brakeley 1950; Cass-Beggs and Cass-Beggs 1969). There are indications, moreover, that lullabies are structurally and functionally distinct from other songs just as infant-directed speech is structurally and functionally distinct from other speech. For example, lullabies of the Cuna Indians of Panama embody more liberal textual and melodic improvisation than do other songs (McCosker 1974). The text, which includes word reduplication, sequence repetition, and very common words, is incorporated into repetitive rhythmic patterns. Unlike other Cuna songs, Cuna lullabies are indefinitely long, continuing until the infant listener is quieted or asleep. On the melodic front, Cuna lullabies have a narrow pitch range and repeating contours, much like soothing infant-directed speech, which is characterized by low falling contours, a narrow pitch range, and a gentle tone (Fernald and Simon 1984; Papoušek and Papoušek 1981). Vietnamese (Cong-Huyen-Ton-Nu 1979), Afghani Hazara (Sakata 1987), and North American Indian (Sands and Sekaquaptewa 1978) lullabies, among others, also have smooth, re-peating contours, a narrow pitch range, extended vowels, and repetitive rhythms.

In the Hazara culture of central Afghanistan, mothers deliberately alter words to produce mellifluous sounds, with sound effects rather than meaning in mind (Sakata 1987). Indeed, the use of humming and stereotyped syllables such as *loo-loo, lulla, ninna, bo-bo*, and *do-do* is cross-culturally pervasive (Brakeley 1950; Brown 1980). Although lullabies seem to have a distinctive form and style within a culture and some common features across cultures, it is not clear whether any feature or quality of lullabies is universal.

Adults seem to be unaware of the full range of their vocal adjustments in infant-directed speech (Fernald and Simon 1984; Papoušek and Papoušek 1987) but the prosody of such speech is clearly recognizable to adult listeners. In fact, adults easily identify several patterns of maternal prosody including those associated with approval, prohibition, soothing, game-playing, and attempts to capture infant attention (Fernald 1989). Just as universal prosodic features are uncommon in adult-directed speech but are frequent and recognizable in infant-directed speech, so similar universals may emerge in infant-directed music despite their reported absence in other types of music (Harwood 1976).

Recently, we collected a large sample of foreign lullabies and comparison songs (non-lullabies) from diverse cultures and geographic regions (Unyk *et al.* 1992). We prepared a tape in which each of 30 lullabies was paired with a song that was similar in tempo and overall musical style. Adult listeners were required to judge which of the two songs in each pair was a lullaby or song for infants (Trehub *et al.* 1992). They identified the lullabies significantly better than chance (about 63 per cent correct) and performance was unrelated to listeners' level of musical training or their familiarity with any musical culture. When the songs were low-pass filtered (i.e. information below 500 Hz retained) to remove the lullaby lyrics, which had potential cues such as word or syllable repetition, extended vowels, and onomatopoeia, the lullabies were still identifiable. Even the elimination of residual voice quality cues by synthesis of the melody line (with piano timbre) resulted in performance that was highly correlated with performance on the original materials. This suggests that there must be melodic as well as word cues to the identity of lullabies. There are indications, moreover, that simple, descending contours play a role in adults' identification of lullabies (Unyk *et al.* 1992). In short, infant-directed music, whether lullabies or play songs, are identifiable to adult listeners.

9.3   MUSICAL STRUCTURE: DEFINING *GOOD* PATTERNS

Most scholars in the domain of music perception have assumed that specialized schemas for processing the structure of music are developed and progressively refined through exposure (Bharucha 1987; Jones 1982; Krumhansl 1983; Zenatti 1969), although the relevant mechanisms are largely unknown. One possibility is that listeners' mental representations of pitch structure are based on the relative frequency of occurrence of various features in the music of their culture (Krumhansl 1990). If this were the case, then listeners exposed to different musical systems would acquire different musical schemas just as listeners exposed to different languages acquire different speech and language schemas.

Comparisons of various languages have revealed commonalities (but also differences) in the inventory of sound types and in the location of category boundaries for speech (Maddieson 1984). At the same time, sounds that occur frequently across languages (e.g. *ma/pa*) tend to be mastered earlier than those that are relatively infrequent (e.g. *la/ra*) (Jakobson 1968; Locke 1983). This is not the case for the relative frequency of occurrence of sounds within a language. For example, the initial sounds of _this_ and _thing_ occur frequently in English but they are relatively infrequent across languages and are late acquisitions for English-speaking children. One might argue, then, that the selection of phonemes and phonemic boundaries has been guided, to some extent, by their relative ease of processing (Burnham *et al.* 1991; Maddieson 1984; Stevens and Keyser 1989). Indeed, linguists have made considerable progress in defining featural constraints on the selection of candidate speech sounds (e.g. Comrie 1981).

Is it also the case that different musical systems reflect pattern-processing dispositions that go beyond the perceptual organizational principles outlined earlier? One near-universal musical feature is octave-equivalence (Dowling and Harwood 1986), whereby notes an octave apart (having a ratio of 2:1) are considered to be equivalent in some way, even by infants (Demany and Armand 1984). In the music of many cultures, they are even given the same name. Another universal feature is the scaling of musical pitch perception on the basis of log frequency rather than linear frequency. It is likely that these common features reflect processing constraints of the auditory system.

At the level of pattern structure, however, commonalities are more difficult to find. Most musical systems seem to be based on scales, a scale dividing the octave into a small number of discrete pitches (usually 5 to 7). The size of the pitch set likely reflects limits on the chunks of information that can be maintained in working memory (Dowling 1978), thereby facilitating the analysis and coding of relations among pitches. In most musical systems, moreover, the absolute pitch of notes is less important than their relative pitch so that a melody remains essentially the same regardless of pitch level.

Beyond these general features, however, there are few identifiable constraints on pitch relations in scale structures. Indeed, ethnomusicologists are pessimistic about the prospect of finding further universals (Harwood 1976). Nevertheless, the recognition of lullabies across cultures (Trehub *et al.* 1992) is suggestive of possible universal features of musical form beyond those identified to date (Trehub and Unyk, 1992). Such universal features might be evident in musical patterns that have special status for infant listeners (i.e. *good* patterns as defined here). With this long-range goal in mind, we have been attempting to identify the features of *good* musical patterns for infants. As noted, our use of the term *good* does not imply aesthetic or value judgements. Rather, our concern is with auditory patterns that can be processed more readily than others by human listeners with limited exposure to any musical system. Presumably, this would reveal the pattern-processing proclivities of naïve listeners and provide clues to potential musical universals.

In principle, the choice of musical materials could be virtually unlimited with infant listeners. In practice, however, most of the relevant research with adults has been based on Western music. Fortunately, there is a rich music-theoretical tradition in the West on which perceptual hypotheses can be based. Accordingly, we have begun our search for *good* patterns by examining infants' sensitivity to various structural features of conventional Western music. Our reasoning is that features to which infants are sensitive reflect constituent features of inherently *good* musical patterns in the sense that they require relatively limited exposure for their mastery.

It is likely that many *good* musical features and *good* musical patterns are not represented in conventional Western music and, therefore, have been outside the scope of most psychological research to date. A pan-cultural definition of *good* patterns is obviously desirable but this must await research with foreign musical materials which, in turn, depends on foreign informants who can vouch for the appropriateness of the stimuli.

An understanding of potentially *good* musical patterns requires some background information about Western tonal music. The octave in Western music is divided into 12 equally spaced notes (on a logarithmic frequency scale) that form the chromatic scale. This division is repeated in successive octaves. (For a more comprehensive description of the structure of Western tonal music see Bigand, Ch. 8 this volume.) For convenience, we can number the 12 notes of the chromatic scale 0 to 11. It is not this equal-interval scale but rather the major scale, an unequal-interval subset of notes from the chromatic scale, that is most commonly used in Western musical composition (see Fig. 9.7). The successive intervals between notes of the major scale are as follows: tone (i.e. two semitones), tone, semitone, tone, tone, tone, semitone. For example, notes 0, 2, 4, 5, 7, 9, and 11 of the chromatic scale form a major scale, as do notes 4, 6, 8, 9, 11, 1, and 3. In musical composition, moreover, different notes of the scale have different functions (Piston 1969). For example, the first note or *tonic* is considered the most stable, with melodies typically ending on this note. (For a discussion of the relative stability of notes and chords, see Bharucha (1984)). The fifth note or *dominant* is important harmonically, with a chord based on this note generating the expectation of resolution to a chord based on the tonic note. The interval between the tonic and dominant notes is called a *perfect fifth* and consists of seven semitones. Melodically, the notes of the *tonic triad*, that is, the first, third, and fifth notes, are considered most stable in their mental representation (Dowling and Harwood 1986). Musically untrained adults have tacit knowledge of the different functions of various scale notes, as reflected in their ratings of how well each note fits into a major-scale context (Krumhansl 1990).

The tonic triad of a major scale is one instance of a *major triad*. In Western music theory, the major triad (intervals: four semitones, three semitones;

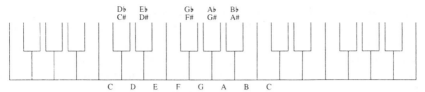

Chromatic scale:

	Db		Eb			Gb		Ab		Bb		
C	C#	D	D#	E	F	F#	G	G#	A	A#	B	C
0	1	2	3	4	5	6	7	8	9	10	11	0

Major scale:

C		D		E	F		G		A		B	C		
0		2		4	5		7		9		11	0		

		Eb			F		G	Ab		Bb		C		D	Eb
		3			5		7	8		10		0		2	3

Major triad:

C		E		G
0		4		7

	Eb		G		Bb
	3		7		10

Augmented triad:

C		E		G#
0		4		8

	Eb		G		B
	3		7		11

Fig. 9.7 Some fundamentals of Western music structure: the chromatic scale, consisting of successive semitones, two major scales, illustrating the interval pattern 2 2 1 2 2 2 1 semitones; two major triads and two augmented trials, illustrating the interval patterns 4 3 and 4 4 semitones, respectively.

e.g. notes 0, 4, 7) is considered to be a consonant, stable, and perhaps prototypical form (Schenker 1954). Raising the third note of a major triad by one semitone (intervals: four semitones, four semitones; e.g. notes 0, 4, 8) results in an *augmented triad*, which is considered to be dissonant and unstable. It is not known, however, whether the major triad is an intrinsically *good* form or whether it achieves this status only after schemas for Western music are developed.

We addressed this question by testing infants on their ability to distinguish between the major and augmented triads (Cohen *et al.* 1987) (see Fig. 9.8). In one condition, a major triad melody was presented as the standard (e.g., notes 0, 4, 7, 4, 0; or C E G E C in the key of C major), that is, it was repeated over and over in transposition, with successive repetitions beginning on different pitches. From time to time, the note highest in pitch was raised by a semitone (G became G#), forming an augmented triad. The infant's task was to respond to this interval (i.e. contour-preserving) change by turning towards the loudspeaker. In another condition, the standard and comparison melodies were reversed so that the augmented triad melody (C E G#E C) now served as standard and the major as comparison. The infant's task in this case was to detect a downward semitone change (G# became G).

If infants engaged their usual contour-processing strategies, as in previous studies (e.g. Chang and Trehub 1977*b*; Trehub *et al.* 1984, 1987), they would necessarily fail on both conditions of this interval discrimination task. In fact, their performance was asymmetrical, being above chance levels when the major triad (a conventional Western pattern) served as the standard but at chance when the augmented triad (an unconventional Western pattern) was the standard (see Fig. 9.9). It is important to note, however, that performance on this interval discrimination task was much poorer than performance on the contour discrimination tasks outlined earlier. It would seem, then, that contour discrimination is relatively easy for infants whereas interval discrimination, although possible in some situations, is considerably more difficult, as it is with adults (Dowling 1978). Nevertheless, one can still consider the major triad to be a *good* pattern for infant listeners because it permits them to go beyond their usual contour-processing strategy to engage a specifically musical or interval-processing strategy. By contrast, the augmented triad is not a *good* pattern in that infants remain limited to their general-purpose strategy of contour processing.

The asymmetric performance on the major-triad/augmented-triad comparison has numerous parallels in adult perception. For example, adults find it easier to detect changes to conventionally structured melodic (Bharucha 1984; Francès 1988), rhythmic (Bharucha and Pryor 1986), and linguistic (Bharucha *et al.* 1985) patterns than to less conventionally structured patterns, even when changes to the latter result in *good*

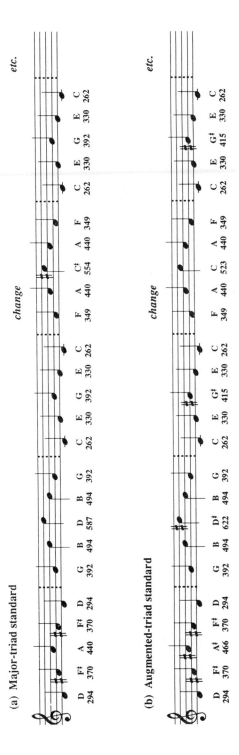

Fig. 9.8 Examples of repeating stimuli with (a) the major-triad melody as standard and the augmented-triad melody as change and (b) the reverse. Each example depicts three successive standard melodies followed by a change and a subsequent return to the standard melody. (Stimuli from Trainor (1991).)

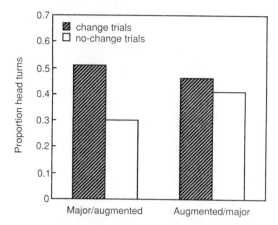

Fig 9.9   Mean proportion of head turns on change and no-change trials with the major-triad and augmented-triad melody serving as standard in one condition and as change in the other. (Data from Trainor (1991).)

patterns. Presumably, the mental representation of a *good* pattern is stable or coherent, thereby facilitating the detection of subtle changes.

There are several possible explanations for the structural significance of the major triad for infant listeners. The major scale is considered to embody special mathematical properties or structural elegance (Balzano 1980, 1982) and the major triad, by virtue of its centrality to major scale structure, would share such properties. According to this perspective, patterns exemplifying major scale structure would be intrinsically easy to process. From a psychoacoustic perspective, intervals approximating simple frequency ratios are considered more consonant than those with more complex ratios (see Burns and Ward 1982; Rakowski 1990). According to this line of reasoning, the notes of the major triad, which approximate simple ratios (4:5:6), would be more consonant than those of the augmented triad, with its complex ratios (16:20:25). In addition, the outer notes of the major triad are related by the perfect fifth interval, which is prominent in the overtone series. This interval is prevalent in naturally occurring sounds, including the simultaneous components of vowel sounds. As a result, ecological considerations may also be implicated in the special status of the major triad.

There is another sense in which the major and augmented triad melodies of these studies were simple, being bilaterally symmetrical and having only three different notes (i.e. the last two notes of these five-note patterns were mirror images of the first two notes). Because of the potential significance of infants' enhanced processing for a conventional Western pattern, it was important to replicate this finding. It was also the case

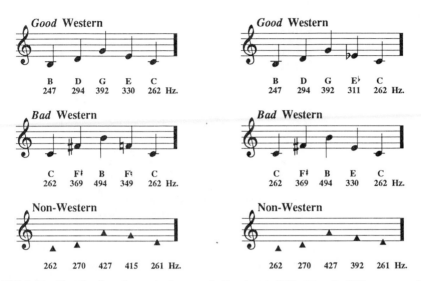

Fig. 9.10 Standard and comparison melodies in *good* Western, *bad* Western, and non-Western conditions. (Note that the non-Western melodies cannot be written in conventional Western notation.) (Stimuli from Trehub *et al.* (1990).)

that the major/augmented comparisons in this study confounded the structure of the standard pattern (major or augmented triad) with upward or downward changes of a semitone. It is possible, then, that enhanced performance with the major triad as standard was attributable to the upward pitch change rather than its structural superiority. To resolve the issue, we evaluated upward and downward changes to major and augmented melodies (Trainor 1991) and still found enhanced processing for major triad melodies by infants as young as six months of age.

We continued to explore the issue of enhanced processing for conventional Western structure by using somewhat more complex, non-symmetrical patterns consisting of five different pitches (Trehub *et al.* 1990). We presented infant listeners with three types of standard pattern (see Fig. 9.10), the comparison patterns all having a downward change of a semitone. One pattern was a conventionally structured Western melody that was based on the major triad but did not begin on the tonic ($B_3 D_4 G_4 E_4 C_4$). Another was less conventionally structured ($C_4 F\#_4 B_4 F_4 C\#_4$), its notes derived from the chromatic division of the octave but not from any major scale. The third melody was essentially non-Western in that some of its intervals were not based on semitones or their multiples. In all three conditions, the task consisted of detecting

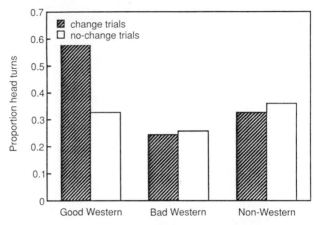

Fig. 9.11   Mean proportion of head turns on change and no-change trials for the *good* Western, *bad* Western, and non-Western melodies. (Data from Trehub *et al.* (1990).)

a change in the fourth note of the melody. We replicated the previous findings of enhanced processing for the major triad in that infants performed above chance levels only on the conventional Western melody (see Fig. 9.11). Naturally, there are differences among the three patterns that go beyond the conventionality of their structure (e.g. interval sizes). Nevertheless, taken together with the previously reported studies of major and augmented patterns, the findings are consistent with the notion that conventional Western melodies confer processing advantages on infants as young as six months of age.

The notion that some objects or patterns serve as cognitive reference points for other exemplars is not new to cognitive psychology (Rosch 1975) although most research of this nature has focused on the visual modality. Such prototypical exemplars are more readily encoded and remembered by adults than are atypical exemplars (Mervis and Rosch 1981; Rosch 1975), as is the case for prototypical musical patterns (e.g. Bharucha 1984; Francès 1988). Even three- and six-month-old infants more readily categorize prototypical visual patterns compared with atypical patterns (Younger and Gottlieb 1988). Moreover, infants respond preferentially to attractive (i.e. as rated by adults) or prototypical faces (Langlois *et al.* 1987; Langlois and Roggman 1990) despite their limited experience with different faces.

In the auditory domain, there are suggestions that some single speech sounds, notably vowels, are rated as better exemplars of their phonetic category than are other instances (Grieser and Kuhl 1989; Kuhl 1991; Miller and Volaitis 1989). Moreover, the rated typicality or *goodness* of a vowel sound exerts substantial effects on perception both for adults and for six-month-old infants (Grieser and Kuhl 1989; Kuhl 1991). Unfortunately, notions of prototypicality have not been evaluated for speech sound combinations or for speech sequences. It is possible, however, that certain intonation patterns or pitch contours, notably those found in infant-directed speech, might be basic forms from which the more complex contours of adult-directed speech are derived.

9.4 *GOOD* CONTEXTS: KEY RELATIONS

Context effects are pervasive in audition as they are in vision. For example, the cues for individual speech sounds vary considerably as a function of the preceding and following sounds (e.g. Dorman and Raphael 1980) or the visible articulatory gestures (e.g. McGurk and MacDonald 1976). Similar context effects are evident in music. For example, the major triad provides a superior melodic context for detecting semitone changes than does the augmented triad or other unconventionally structured melodies (e.g. Cohen *et al.* 1987).

Context effects can operate at different levels of generality. The aforementioned context effects concerned the relations among elements of a pattern, whether the sounds of a word or the notes of a melody. One can consider more global or general contexts for individual sounds or sound units such as the syntactic or semantic relations within and between utterances or the pitch relations between musical patterns or phrases. Having established that infants were sensitive to the context exemplified by relations within a melody, we sought to establish whether they were also sensitive to the more general context exemplified by relations *between* melodies.

One important feature of Western scale structure is that a unique major scale can be formed on each of the 12 notes of the chromatic scale, that is, with each of the 12 chromatic notes serving as tonic. In other words, the particular notes of the major scale with tonic 0 are different from the notes of the major scale starting on any other chromatic note. Each scale is considered to be closely related to two other scales, differing from these by only one note (see Fig. 9.12). These highly related scales have tonic notes that are related by the interval of the perfect fifth, which means that the tonic note of one scale of a highly related pair is the dominant of the other. Musical compositions in the Western tonal idiom often modulate or change from one key to another, although they generally end in the key in which they began. The most common modulation, however, is to the key whose tonic is the dominant of the original key. Western adults have internalized these relations, as exemplified by the so-called *key-distance effect* (Bartlett and Dowling 1980; Cuddy *et al.*

Cycle of fifths

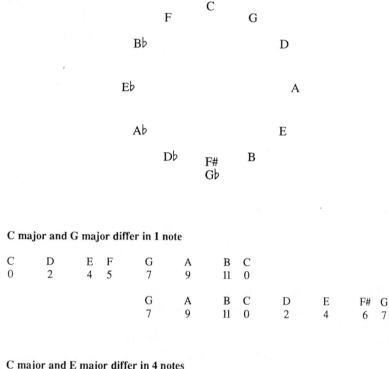

C major and G major differ in 1 note

C	D	E	F	G	A	B	C
0	2	4	5	7	9	11	0

G	A	B	C	D	E	F#	G
7	9	11	0	2	4	6	7

C major and E major differ in 4 notes

C	D	E	F	G	A	B	C
0	2	4	5	7	9	11	0

E	F#	G#	A	B	C#	D#	E
4	6	8	9	11	1	3	4

Fig. 9.12 The cycle of fifths; the distance between any two keys on the cycle of fifths is directly proportional to their relatedness.

1979; Krumhansl *et al.* 1982). For example, Cuddy *et al.* (1979) found that adults' discrimination of melodic changes was most accurate when the keys of standard and comparison melodies were related by a perfect fifth. Does this reflect adults' long-term exposure to Western music or does it arise from primitive processing predispositions? If infants' enhanced processing for the major triad arises from the presence of perfect fifth intervals (i.e. the relation between its outer notes), then keys related by perfect fifths might promote comparable enhancement in melodic processing.

Accordingly, we evaluated infants on their detection of a semitone

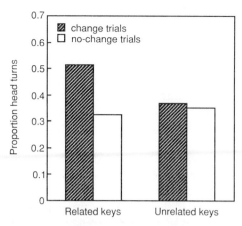

Fig. 9.13 Mean proportion of head turns on change and no-change trials, averaged across major- and augmented-triad melodies, for related and unrelated keys. (Data from Trainor (1991).)

change (upward) in the simple, symmetric major triad melody or augmented triad melody used previously (Trainor and Trehub 1993). In the near-key condition, successive repetitions of the standard and comparison melodies were in closely related keys. The set of keys included B♭, F, C, G, and D, and adjacent melodies were in adjacent keys (in either direction). In the far-key condition, melodies were presented in one of three distantly related keys, C, E, and G# major, again with successive melodies in different keys. Any two of these three keys have only three notes in common (i.e. they differ in four notes). Infants performed better on the major and augmented triad melodies when successive melodies were in related keys (see Fig. 9.13). Thus, interval processing in infancy seems to be enhanced when melodies embody special structures such as the major triad and when musical contexts embody special relations such as those reflected in key relatedness. In short, infants are sensitive not only to the structure of musical patterns but to the macrostructure of pattern repetitions.

It is perhaps significant that the tasks in which infants displayed enhanced processing involved the interval of the perfect fifth. As noted, the outer notes of the major triad form a perfect fifth as do the corresponding notes of melodies transposed to closely related keys. One important but unresolved issue is whether such enhanced processing stems from the simple integer ratio associated with the perfect fifth, that of 3:2. In this regard, it is interesting that individuals from widely different cultures often sing in parallel fifths as well as octaves, thinking that they are singing in unison (Kolinski 1967).

9.5   GOOD SCALES

Recently, there has been increasing interest in the structural characteristics of *good* musical scales, prompted in part by theoretical interest in pattern processing and in part by composers attempting to create new scales suitable for musical composition. Different musical systems seem to use different arrays of intervals, making it possible, in principle, to evaluate the properties of particular scales. In practice, however, most research has been limited to Western scales. Among the findings of such research is that adults have tacit knowledge of major scale structure, as reflected in their ratings of the degree of fit of in-key and out-of-key notes in a major-key context (Krumhansl 1990).

There are claims, as well, that the major scale is special or unique. One approach emphasizes its unique psychoacoustic properties (Burns and Ward 1982; Helmholtz 1954; Krumhansl 1987). With equal-tempered tuning (i.e. all semitones of the chromatic scale equal), the ratios between the fundamental frequency of important scale notes approximate, but do not equal, simple integer ratios, which are considered ideal. For example, notes an octave apart stand in an approximate 2:1 frequency ratio; notes a perfect fifth apart (i.e. seven semitones; e.g. C G) form an approximate 3:2 ratio; notes a perfect fourth apart (five semitones; e.g. C F) an approximate 4:3 ratio; notes a major third apart (i.e. four semitones; e.g. C E) an approximate 5:4 ratio; and so on. Historically, tuning systems embodied these exact ratios but such systems were abandoned because it was only possible for one key to be perfectly in tune at a time, thereby precluding effective key modulation in complex compositions. In line with the notion that small integer ratios are ideal, it is often claimed that singers and players of variable-tuning instruments adjust intervals away from equal temperament toward exact small integer ratios. However, analyses of musical performances are inconsistent with this claim (see Burns and Ward 1982; Rakowski 1990).

Another approach to the uniqueness of the major scale emphasizes mathematical properties of the group of scale notes (Balzano 1980, 1982) independent of psychoacoustic properties. One such property is uniqueness. A scale possesses the uniqueness property if the vector of intervals from each note to every other note in the set is unique. For example, given the set {0 2 4 5 7 9 11}, the vector of intervals formed from the third note (4) is {4–4, 5–4, 7–4, 9–4, 11–4, 12–4, 14–4} or {0 1 3 5 7 8 10}. This pattern of intervals is different from the pattern based on every other note of this scale. On the other hand, all vectors of intervals of the whole-tone scale are the same: {0 2 4 6 8 10}. In this sense, the whole-tone scale is considered to have minimal uniqueness. It is the uniqueness property that allows different notes to take on different functional relations with other notes, facilitating, for example, the tonal hierarchy (Krumhansl 1990).

By contrast, the whole-tone scale has no differentiation of function because all notes are related in the same way. An empirical question, then, is whether these mathematical properties have perceptual consequences, that is, whether melodies based on the major scale are processed more easily than those based on the whole-tone scale.

We are currently evaluating this question by testing infants and adults on their ability to detect a semitone change in a melody based on the major scale (B_3 D_4 G_4 E_4 C_4) or on the whole-tone scale ($B\flat_3$ D_4 $G\#_4$ E_4 C_4). Adults (non-musicians) performed significantly better on the major melody than on the whole-tone melody. Infants showed the same pattern of performance, detecting the change to the major melody but not to the whole-tone melody. This suggests that major scale structure may be more readily encoded than whole-tone scale structure, even by naïve listeners. Despite the failure of cross-cultural studies to uncover universal constraints on intervals in musical scale structure, some scales seem to be intrinsically better than others. Whether this claim is limited to Western infants and adults remains to be determined.

We are conducting further studies with different major and whole-tone melodies and with other scales, both foreign and artificial (Krumhansl 1987; Mathews *et al.* 1987). In particular, the *modal* scales are of interest. For example, the notes 0, 2, 4, 5, 7, 9, 11 form a major scale with tonic 0. These same notes, however, also form a Phrygian modal scale, 4, 5, 7, 9, 11, 0, 2 with tonic 4. Although these scales use the same set of pitches, they are organized around a different tonic so that melodies based on such scales would differ. For example, the melodies would tend to begin and end on different notes and have different statistical properties (i.e. frequency of occurrence of various notes and note combinations). From Balzano's (1982) perspective, the choice of tonic is not involved in the unique properties of the major scale. Consequently, one might expect sensitivity to the choice of tonic to emerge only after considerable musical exposure. Thus adults should find melodies based on the major scale easier than those based on the Phrygian but infants should show no difference.

Our primary focus on Western scale structure stems from convenience rather than its presumed superiority over alternative musical structures. It is reasonable to expect, then, that scales prominent in other cultures would also embody aspects of *good* form. Some recent evidence bears on this question. Lynch *et al.* (1990) investigated Western infants' (six months of age) and adults' ability to detect mistunings (subtle contour-preserving changes) in melodies based on the Western major and Javanese *pélog* scale. Adults with little training but the usual informal exposure performed better with the major than *pélog* melodies whereas infants performed equivalently on both. These findings imply that, in the early months of life, infants' discrimination of such melodic changes is unaffected by culture-specific experience. This raises the possibility of enhanced processing for the *pélog* scale comparable to that observed for the major scale.

9.6   GOOD CHANGES TO GOOD PATTERNS

The aforementioned studies of pattern *goodness* indicate that prototypical patterns in Western music embody features that promote detailed encoding in naïve listeners. Thus infants encode not only global information about melodic contour but also local information about interval size. Even if some analytic skills are present in infancy, it is likely that others are schema-based, emerging only after extended exposure. As a result, infants may not be sensitive to all structural aspects of patterns that conform to the rules of a musical system.

Perhaps *good* and *bad* patterns can be distinguished on the basis of universal principles that are evident in infancy. In the context of a *good* pattern, however, or one readily processed by infants, would there be differential sensitivity to changes that conform to Western musical conventions compared with those that violate such conventions? For adults, a comparison melody in which the changed note goes outside the key of a conventionally structured standard melody is easier to detect than a change that remains within the key (Cuddy *et al.* 1979). In fact, the ease with which adults detect such structural violations (i.e. a non-key note) reveals their knowledge of scale structure.

Would infants be capable of processing comparable aspects of key structure? We presented eight-month-olds and young adults with a ten-note conventionally structured melody (in the key of C major: $C_4 E_4 G_4 F_4 D_4 G_3 C_4 E_4 D_4 C_4$) in transposition (Trainor and Trehub 1992). There were two comparison melodies (see Fig. 9.14). In one, the sixth note (G_3) was raised by a semitone to Ab_3, which was outside the prevailing key and therefore violated Western musical rules. In the second, the same note was raised by four semitones to B_3, which is in the prevailing key. Adults performed as predicted, readily detecting the out-of-key change. In some circumstances, they were at chance levels in detecting the within-key pitch change, even though it was four times as large as the out-of-key change. Infants, on the other hand, performed equivalently and at above chance levels on both pitch changes (see Fig. 9.15). Moreover, they performed significantly better than adults on the within-key change.

Infants' performance is revealing in a number of respects. First, their ability to detect semitone changes in the context of a conventionally structured ten-tone melody increases the generality of our previous findings of enhanced processing (i.e. interval processing) for patterns

Standard melody

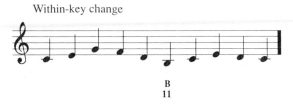

C	E	G	F	D	G	C	E	D	C
0	4	7	5	2	7	0	4	2	0

Within-key change

B
11

Out-of-key change

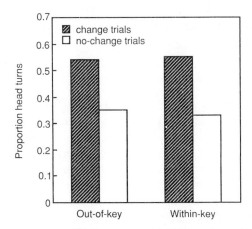

A♭
8

Fig 9.14 The standard ten-note melody (top), the four-semitone within-key change (middle), and the one-semitone out-of-key (bottom) change. (Stimuli from Trainor and Trehub (1992).)

Fig 9.15 Mean proportion of head turns on change and no-change trials for the out-of-key and within-key changes. (Data from Trainor and Trehub (1992).)

based on the major triad. Second, infants' facility in detecting the within-key or structure-conserving change coupled with adults' difficulty on this discrimination implies that infants' performance is culture-independent. Although infants are insensitive to some culturally relevant musical structures, it is difficult to specify their missing knowledge. It is possible, for example, that infants lack tacit knowledge of the notes that belong in a key or scale. As a result, their superior performance for conventional melodies based on the major scale as opposed to unconventional melodies with non-scale notes (Cohen *et al.* 1987; Trainor 1991; Trehub *et al.* 1990) could be due to special properties of the major scale such as the prominence of perfect fifth intervals.

An alternative explanation of this finding is that infants, unlike Western adults, do not process melodies according to their implied harmonic structure. Harmony, the combination of notes sounded simultaneously, or the vertical, as opposed to horizontal (i.e. melodic), structure of music, is a unique feature of Western music (Piston 1969). Thus, one might expect relatively slow emergence of sensitivity to harmonic structure just as rare phonemic distinctions emerge considerably later than those present in many languages (Locke 1983). Even an unaccompanied Western melody is considered to have implied harmonies. For example, the standard melody in Trainor and Trehub (1992), C_4 E_4 G_4 F_4 D_4 G_3 C_4 E_4 D_4 C_4, implies a tonic chord (C_4 E_4 G_4) followed by a dominant chord (F_4 D_4 G_3). Because B_3 (the changed note in one condition) is also part of the dominant chord, this change not only remains within the key of the original melody but also within the implied harmony. A likely possibility, then, is that the performance difference between infants and adults reflects adults' acquired propensity to process the implied harmony of a melody. These findings point to some of the fine tuning or perceptual reorganization that results from extended, informal listening to music. Mapping the timetable of this retuning will be of considerable developmental interest.

9.7   CONCLUSION

At the outset, we posed a number of questions about infants' processing of complex auditory patterns. What answers can we offer on the basis of our findings and those of others? We can say with assurance that perceptual grouping processes such as those described by Bregman (Ch. 2 this volume), Bigand (Ch. 8 this volume), Krumhansl (1992) and others are indeed operative in infancy. Moreover, relational pitch and temporal processing are as characteristic of infants as they are of adults. In particular, relational pitch processing would seem to be a basic and uniquely human disposition, having little to do with acquired knowledge about its utility and more to do with the nature of the human brain. On the other hand, that much vaunted skill, absolute pitch processing, seems to be 'for the birds' (Hulse *et al*. 1990). For reasons that are as yet unclear, extensive childhood exposure to music sometimes results in the addition of 'bird-like' absolute pitch processing to the usual repertoire of human listening strategies (Cohen and Baird 1990).

Pitch contours seem to dominate perception at a time when the infant's world is uncluttered with referential meaning. Thus infants proceed globally, extracting the pitch contours of melodies and spoken utterances and ignoring many of the details within such contours. This is not to say that they are unable to resolve auditory detail. On the contrary, impoverished auditory contexts, such as the typical laboratory experiments with single sounds, reveal impressive phoneme discrimination skills (see Kuhl 1986) and excellent frequency resolution (Olsho 1984) in early infancy.

Our approach to the definition of *good* patterns was empirical rather than theoretical, involving the identification of patterns or pattern elements that are congenial to, or readily processed by, infants. This approach yielded additional perspectives on infants' pattern processing capabilities and provided a means of differentiating universal from culture-specific constraints on musical structure. Specifically, we found that infants could supplement their primary listening strategy of contour processing with a secondary strategy of interval processing, but only in very special circumstances. We know that these circumstances include prototypical melodies from our culture (e.g. melodies based on the major triad) and prototypical contexts (e.g. neighbouring patterns with related keys). What we are likely to learn in the future is that prototypical melodies from foreign musical cultures also promote enhanced processing, engaging both global and analytic strategies. One task that lies ahead is to specify the features associated with such enhanced processing, features that can be considered 'natural' and, therefore, belonging to the set from which musical universals would be drawn.

Our findings cast doubt on some prominent approaches to adult pattern perception. We dispute the view that pattern perception processes have virtually unlimited plasticity, with experience making possible and shaping the perceptual organization of patterns (Espinoza-Varas and Watson 1989). Likewise, we dispute the assumption of a number of twentieth-century composers and music theorists (e.g. Boulez 1971; Forte 1973; Schoenberg 1975) that listeners, given comparable exposure, would perceive or acquire all conceivable types of musical structure as readily as they perceive and acquire conventional musical structure. Not all songs are equivalent as learning stimuli, even for those songbirds that require exposure for song acquisition (Marler 1990). We would argue, instead, that auditory perceptions are initially structured or organized (Trehub 1985; Trehub and Trainor 1990) and that experience leads to alternative organizations including fine tuning to culture-specific circumstances. We would argue, further, that some organizations are more 'natural' or robust than others (Burnham *et al.* 1987; Trehub 1985; Trehub and Unyk 1992) and that the natural organization may prevail throughout life. For example, both infants and adults approach unfamiliar melodies with a pitch contour strategy and, in the case of prototypical melodies, they often add an interval-processing strategy.

Our findings also raise questions about prominent approaches to music perception that involve the internalization of pitch relations or proto-types based on regularities in heard music (e.g. Krumhansl 1990; Jones 1981, 1990). In the absence of data on infant music perception, it may have been reasonable to presume that adults' interval-processing strategy with familiar melodies (Attneave and Olson 1971; Dowling and Fujitani 1971) was attributable to their extensive experience with those melodies and that their superior retention of conventionally structured melodies (e.g. Cuddy *et al.* 1981; Francès 1988) reflected their accumulated know-ledge of musical structure. It turns out, however, that such familiar and unfamiliar but conventional melodies have features that promote analytic or interval processing in infancy. From the infant's perspective, however, these melodies are neither familiar nor conventional but they neverthe-less elicit interval processing. We would argue, then, that it may be unne-cessary for listeners to accumulate information about the frequency of occurrence of structural as opposed to stylistic features of musical pat-terns, constructing internal models based on such statistical information. In fact, comparable approaches have been rejected as viable strategies for the acquisition of linguistic structures (Chomsky 1968). The more likely alternative is that composers intuitively create or select patterns that build on 'natural' and universal principles of pattern perception (Terhardt 1987). The result is that frequency of occurrence and *naturalness* are often confounded. Learning obviously plays a role in perceptual fine tuning or calibration, in the acquisition of some musical conventions, and in mu-sical production. One important goal for the future is to make further progress in differentiating experience-related from natural listening strategies.

Finally, the listening strategies that we have outlined have implica-tions for language as well as musical development. We have suggested that prelinguistic infants parse the speech stream into pitch contours, which may serve as elementary processing units. Adults seem to co-operate in this endeavor by communicating in a special speech register or style that upgrades contour information at the expense of clear articu-lation and informative content. The resulting infant-directed speech is a kind of singsong that captures the infant's attention and promotes posi-tive affect (Fernald 1992; Werker and McLeod 1989). In other words, the simple pitch contours of infant-directed speech seem to have special status or perceptual priority for prelinguistic listeners. Later, infants can use contour information to track phrasal and clausal units and also to distinguish utterance types (questions vs. statements). The transition from global processing to analytic or joint global/analytic processing of speech may depend on important cognitive changes that occur late in the first year. Such changes may promote the perceptual reorganization or fine tuning of some speech sound categories at this time (Werker and Lalonde 1988). Just as culture-specific modes of music processing build on pattern processing predispositions, so mature speech processing seems to build on inherent speech discrimination skills that are evident in infancy (Best *et al.* 1988; Burnham *et al.* 1987; Werker and Lalonde 1988). On the whole, however, pitch-contour processing seems to dominate infants' early perception of connected speech and music. One consequence for production is that native-like intonation contours emerge well before the first words (de Boysson-Bardies *et al.* 1984; Crystal 1973) just as appropriate musical contours predate correct intervals (Davidson *et al.* 1981; Kelley and Sutton-Smith 1987).

It is unclear, however, whether there are speech parallels to the enhanced processing of prototypical musical patterns. In this regard, there is suggestive evidence that *good* or prototypical exemplars of vowels have a more robust representation for infant listeners than do *poor* or less typical exemplars (Grieser and Kuhl 1989; Kuhl 1991). The intonation contours that are prevalent in infant-directed speech across cultures may also function as prototypes for infant listeners and their caretakers but there has been no direct investigation of this question. One perceptual consequence of prototypical status would be enhanced differentiation of such contours from others.

The findings of enhanced processing for major triad melodies and near-key relations raise the possibility that the perfect fifth interval, which approximates a 2:3 frequency ratio, is inherently *good*. Not only does the perfect fifth interval figure prominently in musical sounds, both simultaneous and successive, it also occurs commonly in the simultaneous components (partials or overtones) of complex sounds in the natural environment, including vowel sounds. The special emphasis accorded to vowels in infant-directed speech (i.e. they are greatly extended in duration) may highlight the perfect fifth interval (simultaneously sounded) and contribute to the special status of such speech. Whether the special qualities derive from the perfect fifth interval in particular or intervals that approximate simple ratios in general remains to be determined. Perhaps the relative prominence of the perfect fifth interval affects adults' ratings of the *goodness* of vowel sounds (Grieser and Kuhl 1989; Kuhl 1991) but this has not been evaluated to date. In any case, the cross-cultural prevalence of simple ratios in informal vocal music (Kolinski 1967) is suggestive of their importance.

In the early months of life when the processing of speech and musical sounds is largely (but not entirely) culture-independent, it would not be surprising for both domains to be dominated by common processing tendencies. We have suggested repeatedly that pitch-contour processing is prominent among these processing dispositions, with infants extracting the pitch contours of simple speech and musical passages.

It is also possible that some contours are inherently *good* for infant listeners and that these contours are prominent in speech and song to infants. One example of this is the prevalence of descending contours in soothing infant-directed speech (Fernald and Simon 1984) and music (Unyk *et al.* 1992). Also of interest is the prominence of descending contours in infant vocalization (Fox 1990). Simplicity (e.g. few directional changes in pitch) may be one factor that determines the relative *goodness* of a contour and its resultant ease of encoding. Indeed, simple contours are common in maternal speech (Fernald 1984) as they are in lullabies (Unyk *et al.* 1992) and in infant vocalizations (Delack and Fowlow 1978; Fox 1990). According to one music-theoretic framework (Narmour 1990), adult listeners, regardless of their experience and cultural origins, have certain common expectations about pitch movement within a melody. Preliminary support for this notion has been obtained with American and Chinese listeners (Schellenberg and Krumhansl, personal communication). If such expectations have an innate basis, as Narmour (1990) contends, they might be present in infancy, contributing to the essence of *good* patterns.

The pattern of intervals may also be implicated in the *goodness* of speech and musical patterns. For example, the major triad is asymmetric (a four-semitone interval followed by a three-semitone interval), being derived from a scale with unequal interval structure. The feature of asymmetry in scale systems from which melodic sequences are derived is considered to facilitate the functional differentiation of component notes (Balzano 1982; Butler and Brown 1984; Krumhansl 1987). It is unclear, however, whether comparable asymmetries characterize the intonation patterns of infant-directed speech. Just as there are rules for combining notes into acceptable melodic sequences, so are there rules for combining speech sounds into acceptable utterances. There are suggestions, moreover, that some sequences of speech sounds are more learnable than others (Locke 1990). Perhaps this is also the case for intonation patterns.

Regardless of the ultimate list of common features that will emerge from future studies of speech and musical processing, it is clear that some common features are present. Why might this be the case? In the prelinguistic period, speech directed to infants is not meaningful in the way that it is later on. Rather, the meanings are affective in nature and are conveyed principally through intonation and 'tone of voice' (Fernald 1989; Papoušek and Papoušek 1981). Jusczyk and Bertoncini (1988) have proposed that development in the domain of speech perception is facilitated by innately guided learning such as that described by Gould and Marler (1987) for the acquisition of important species-specific abilities. This process is characterized by considerable selectivity in responsiveness to signals and rapid learning on the basis of limited culture-specific experience. Innately guided learning contrasts with incremental learning, which implicates a flexible and initially unselective system that gradually achieves appropriate organization of the input on the basis of its distributional properties (Mehler and Dupoux, 1990). Early differentiation of the mother's voice from other voices (DeCasper and Fifer 1980; Mehler *et al.* 1978), of the native 'language-to-be' from other languages (Mehler *et al.* 1988), and of infant-directed from adult-directed speech (e.g. Cooper and Aslin 1990; Fernald 1985) are possible examples of such innately guided learning.

The music perception skills that we have uncovered in infants may also reflect innately guided learning, perhaps the same or similar processes that promote the development of speech perception skills (e.g. Werker and Tees 1984) and the appearance of language-specific aspects of babbling (de Boysson-Bardies *et al.* 1989) in prelinguistic infants. It is possible, then, that precocious abilities in both domains stem from common origins. If so, we would expect the processing of speech and music to diverge once infants are ready to assign referential meaning to speech. We know that after the hypothesized separation, the development of speech perception and production skills continues at a rapid pace. It is unclear, however, whether this is also the case for music perception and production. Accordingly, it will be of particular interest to determine whether the precocity of music processing in infancy is dependent on its initial ties to speech. If further progress in music perception and production is considerably slower than in the language domain but comparable to other biologically non-significant domains, this would suggest accidental convergence of speech and music in early infancy. If, on the other hand, music perception continues to exhibit a developmental pace characteristic of innately guided learning, this would revive interest in its biological significance (Granit 1977; Lerdahl and Jackendoff 1983).

ACKNOWLEDGEMENTS

The preparation of this chapter was assisted by grants to the senior author from the Natural Sciences and Engineering Research Council of Canada and the University of Toronto.

REFERENCES

Aslin, R. N. and Smith, L. B. (1988). Perceptual development. *Annual Review of Psychology*, **39**, 435–73.

Attneave, F. and Olson, R. K. (1971). Pitch as a medium: a new approach to psychophysical scaling. *American Journal of Psychology*, **84**, 147–66.

Balzano, G. J. (1980). The group-theoretic description of 12-fold and microtonal pitch systems. *Computer Music Journal*, **4**, 66–84.

Balzano, G. J. (1982). The pitch set as a level of description for studying musical pitch perception. In *Music, mind, and brain: the neuropsychology of music* (ed. M. Clynes), pp. 321–51. Plenum, New York.

Bartlett, J. C. and Dowling, W. J. (1980). Recognition of transposed melodies: a key-distance effect in developmental perspective. *Journal of Experimental Psychology: Human Perception and Performance*, **6**, 501–15.

Bebey, F. (1969). *African music: a people's art*. Lawrence Hill, Westpoint.

Beebe, B., Feldstein, S., Jaffe, J., Mays, K., and Alson, D. (1985). Interpersonal timing: the application of an adult dialogue model to mother-infant vocal and kinesic interactions. In *Social perception in infants* (ed. T. M. Field and N. A. Fox), pp. 217–47. Ablex, Norwood, NJ.

Best, C. T., McRoberts, G. W., and Sithole, N. M. (1988). Examination of perceptual reorganization for nonnative speech contrasts: Zulu click discrimination by English-speaking adults and infants. *Journal of Experimental Psychology: Human Perception and Performance*, **14**, 45–60.

Bharucha, J. J. (1984). Anchoring effects in music: the resolution of dissonance. *Cognitive Psychology*, **16**, 485–518.

Bharucha, J. J. (1987). Music cognition and perceptual facilitation: a connectionist framework. *Music Perception*, **5**, 1–30.

Bharucha, J. J. and Pryor, J. H. (1986). Disrupting the isochrony underlying rhythm: an asymmetry in discrimination. *Perception and Psychophysics*, **40**, 137–41.

Bharucha, J. J., Olney, K. L., and Schnurr, P. P. (1985). Detection of coherence-disrupting and coherence-conferring alterations in text. *Memory and Cognition*, **13**, 573–8.

Bolton, T. L. (1894). Rhythm. *American Journal of Psychology*, **6**, 145–238.

Boulez, P. (1971). *Boulez on music today*. (transl. S. Bradshaw and R. R. Bennett). Faber and Faber, London.

Brakeley, T. C. (1950). Lullaby. In *Standard dictionary of folklore, mythology, and legend*, pp. 653–4. Funk and Wagnalls, New York.

Bregman, A. S. (1978). The formation of auditory streams. In *Attention and performance. Vol. VII* (ed. J. Requin), pp. 63–75. Erlbaum, Hillsdale, NJ

Bregman, A. S. (1981). Asking the 'what for' question in auditory perception. In *Perceptual organization* (ed. M. Kubovy and J. R. Pomerantz), pp. 99–118. Erlbaum, Hillsdale, NJ.

Bregman, A. S. (1990). *Auditory scene analysis: the perceptual organization of sound*. MIT, Cambridge, MA.

Bregman, A. S. and Campbell, J. (1971). Primary auditory stream segregation and the perception of order in rapid sequences of tones. *Journal of Experimental Psychology*, **89**, 244–9.

Brown, M. J. E. (1980). Lullaby. In *The new Grove dictionary of music and musicians*, pp. 313–4. Macmillan, London.

Burnham, D. K., Earnshaw, L. J., and Quinn, M. C. (1987). The development of the categorical identification of speech. In *Perceptual development in early infancy: problems and issues* (ed. B. E. McKenzie and R. J. Day), pp. 237–75. Erlbaum, Hillsdale, NJ.

Burnham, D. K., Earnshaw, L. J., and Clark, J. E. (1991). Development of categorical identification of native and non-native bilabial stops: infants, children, and adults. *Journal of Child Language,* **18,** 231–60.

Burns, E. M. and Ward, W. D. (1982). Intervals, scales, and tuning. In *The psychology of music* (ed. D. Deutsch), pp. 241–69. Academic, Orlando, FL.

Butler, D. (1989). Describing the perception of tonality in music. A critique of the tonal hierarchy theory and proposal for a theory of intervallic rivalry. *Music Perception,* **6,** 219–42.

Butler, D. and Brown, H. (1984). Tonal structure versus function: studies of the recognition of harmonic motion. *Music Perception,* **2,** 6–24.

Cass-Beggs, B. and Cass-Beggs, M. (1969). *Folk lullabies.* Oak Publications, New York.

Chang, H. W. and Trehub, S. E. (1977a). Infants' perception of temporal grouping in auditory patterns. *Child Development,* **48,** 1666–70.

Chang, H. W. and Trehub, S. E. (1977b). Auditory processing of relational information by young infants. *Journal of Experimental Child Psychology,* **24,** 324–31.

Chomsky, N. (1968). *Language and mind.* Harcourt Brace Jovanovich, New York.

Clifton, R. K. (1992). The development of spatial hearing in human infants. In *Developmental psychoacoustics* (ed. L. A. Werner and E. W. Rubel) pp. 135–57. American Psychological Association, Washington, DC.

Cohen, A. J. and Baird, R. (1990). Acquisition of absolute pitch: the question of critical periods. *Psychomusicology,* **9,** 31–7.

Cohen, A. J., Thorpe, L. A., and Trehub, S. E. (1987). Infants' perception of musical relations in short transposed tone sequences. *Canadian Journal of Psychology,* **41,** 33–47.

Comrie, B. (1981). *Language universals and linguistic typology.* Blackwell, Oxford.

Cong-Huyen-Ton-Nu, N.-T. (1979). The functions of folk songs in Vietnam. In *The performing arts: music and dance* (ed. J. Blacking and J. W. Kealiinohomoku), pp. 141–51. Mouton, The Hague.

Cooper, R. B. and Aslin, R. N. (1990). Preference for infant-directed speech in the first month after birth. *Child Development,* **61,** 1584–95.

Crystal, D. (1973). Non-segmental phonology in language acquisition: a review of the issues. *Lingua,* **32,** 1–45.

Cuddy, L. L., Cohen, A. J., and Miller, J. (1979). Melody recognition: the experimental application of musical rules. *Canadian Journal of Psychology,* **33,** 148–56.

Cuddy, L. L., Cohen, A. J., and Mewhort, D. J. K. (1981). Perception of structure in short melodic sequences. *Journal of Experimental Psychology: Human Perception and Performance,* **7,** 869–83.

D'Amato, M. R. (1988). A search for tonal pattern perception in cebus monkeys: why monkeys can't hum a tune. *Music Perception,* **5,** 453–80.

D'Amato, M. R. and Salmon, D. P. (1984). Processing of complex auditory stimuli (tunes) by rats and monkeys (*Cebus apella*). *Animal Learning and Behavior,* **12,** 184–94.

Davidson, L., McKernon, P., and Gardner, H. (1981). The acquisition of song: a developmental approach. In *Documentary report of the Ann Arbor Symposium* (pp. 301–15). Music Educators National Conference, Reston, Virginia.

de Boysson-Bardies, B., Sagart, L., and Durand, C. (1984). Discernible differences in the babbling of infants according to target language. *Journal of Child Language*, **11**, 1–15.

de Boysson-Bardies, B., Hallé, P., Sagart, L., and Durand, C. (1989). A cross-linguistic investigation of vowel formants in babbling. *Journal of Child Language*, **16**, 1–17.

DeCasper, A. J. and Fifer, W. P. (1980). Of human bonding: newborns prefer their mothers' voices. *Science*, **208**, 1174–6.

Delack, J. B. and Fowlow, P. J. (1978). The ontogenesis of differential vocalization: development of prosodic contrastivity during the first year of life. In *The development of communication* (ed. M. Waterson and C. Snow), pp. 93–110. Wiley, Chichester.

Demany, L. (1982). Auditory stream segregation in infancy. *Infant Behavior and Development*, **5**, 261–76.

Demany, L. and Armand, F. (1984). The perceptual reality of tone chroma in early infancy. *Journal of the Acoustical Society of America*, **76**, 57–66.

Demany, L., McKenzie, B., and Vurpillot, E. (1977). Rhythm perception in early infancy. *Nature*, **266**, 718–19.

Deutsch, D. (1982). Grouping mechanisms in music. In *The psychology of music* (ed. D. Deutsch), pp. 99–134. Academic, New York.

Diehl, R. L., Buchwald McCusker, S., and Chapman, L. S. (1981). Perceiving vowels in isolation and in consonantal context. *Journal of the Acoustical Society of America*, **69**, 239–48.

Dooling, R. J., Brown, S. D., Park, T. J., Okanoya, K., and Soli, S. D. (1987). Perceptual organization of acoustic stimuli by budgerigars (*Melopsittacus undulatus*): I. Pure tones. *Journal of Comparative Psychology*, **101**, 139–49.

Dooling, R. J., Brown, S. D., Park, T. J., and Okanoya, K. (1990). Natural perceptual categories for vocal signals in budgerigars (*Melopsittacus undulatus*). In *Comparative perception. Vol. 2: Complex signals* (ed. W. C. Stebbins and M. A. Berkley), pp. 345–74. Wiley, New York.

Dorman, M. F. and Raphael, L. J. (1980). Distribution of acoustic cues for stop consonant place of articulation in VCV syllables. *Journal of the Acoustical Society of America*, **67**, 1333–5.

Dowling, W. J. (1978). Scale and contour: two components of a theory of memory for melodies. *Psychological Review*, **85**, 341–54.

Dowling, W. J. and Fujitani, D. (1971). Contour, interval, and pitch recognition in memory for melodies. *Journal of the Acoustical Society of America*, **49**, 524–31.

Dowling, W. J. and Harwood , D. L. (1986). *Music cognition*. Academic, Orlando, FL.

Eilers, R. E., Wilson, W. R., and Moore, J. M. (1977). Developmental changes in speech discrimination in infants. *Journal of Speech and Hearing Research*, **20**, 766–80.

Eimas, P. D. and Miller, J. L. (1980). Contextual effects in infant speech perception. *Science*, **209**, 1140–1.

Espinoza-Varas, B. and Watson, C. S. (1989). Perception of complex auditory patterns by humans. In *The comparative psychology of audition: perceiving complex sounds* (ed. R. J. Dooling and S. H. Hulse), pp. 67–94. Erlbaum, Hillsdale, NJ.

Fernald, A. (1984). The perceptual and affective salience of mothers' speech to infants. In *The origins and growth of communication* (ed. L. Feagans, C. Garvey, and R. Golinkoff), pp. 5–29. Ablex, Norwood, NJ.

Fernald, A. (1985). Four-month-old infants prefer to listen to Motherese. *Infant Behavior and Development,* **8**, 181–95.

Fernald, A. (1989). Intonation and communicative intent in mothers' speech to infants: is the melody the message? *Child Development,* **60**, 1497–510.

Fernald, A. (1992). Meaningful melodies in mothers' speech to infants. In *Nonverbal vocal communication: comparative and developmental approaches* (ed. H. Papoušek, V. Jurgens, and M. Papoušek), pp. 262–82. Cambridge University Press.

Fernald, A. and Kuhl, P. K. (1987). Acoustic determinants of infant preference for motherese. *Infant Behavior and Development,* **10**, 279–93.

Fernald, A. and Simon, T. (1984). Expanded intonation contours in mothers' speech to newborns. *Developmental Psychology,* **20**, 104–13.

Fernald, A., Taeschner, T., Dunn, J., Papoušek, M., de Boysson-Bardies, B., and Fukui, I. (1989). A cross-language study of prosodic modifications in mothers' and fathers' speech to preverbal infants. *Journal of Child Language,* **16**, 477–501.

Fetterman, J. G. (1987). Same–different comparison of duration. *Animal Learning and Behavior,* **15**, 403–11.

Fitzgibbons, P. J., Pollatsek, A., and Thomas, I. B. (1974). Detection of temporal gaps within and between perceptual tonal groups. *Perception and Psychophysics,* **16**, 522–8.

Fodor, J. A. (1983). *The modularity of mind: an essay on faculty psychology.* MIT, Cambridge, MA.

Forte, A. (1973). *The structure of atonal music.* Yale University Press, New Haven, CT.

Fox, D. B. (1990). An analysis of the pitch characteristics of infant vocalizations. *Psychomusicology,* **9**, 21–30.

Fraisse, P. (1982). Rhythm and tempo. In *The psychology of music* (ed. D. Deutsch), pp. 149–80. Academic, New York.

Francès, R. (1988). *The perception of music.* Erlbaum, Hillsdale, NJ (transl. W. J. Dowling from *La perception de la musique,* 1958; 2nd. edn. 1984. Vrin, Paris.)

Garner, W. R. (1970). Good patterns have few alternatives. *American Scientist,* **58**, 34–42.

Garner, W. R. (1974). *The processing of information and structure.* Erlbaum, Hillsdale, NJ.

Gould, J. L and Marler, P. (1987). Learning by instinct. *Scientific American,* **256**, 74–85.

Granit, R. (1977). *The purposive brain.* MIT Press, Cambridge, MA.

Grieser, D. L. and Kuhl, P. K. (1989). Categorization of speech by infants: support for speech-sound prototypes. *Developmental Psychology,* **25**, 577–88.

Handel, S. (1989). *Listening: an introduction to the perception of auditory events.* MIT, Cambridge, MA.

Hargreaves, D. M. (1986). *The developmental psychology of music.* Cambridge University Press.

Harwood, D. L. (1976). Universals in music: a perspective from cognitive psychology. *Ethnomusicology,* **20**, 521–34.

Helmholtz, H. L. F. (1954). *On the sensations of tone as a physiological basis for the theory of music* (transl. A. J. Ellis from German 4th edn 1877), Dover, New York (reprinted from English 2nd edn, 1885).

Hirsh-Pasek, K., Kemler Nelson, D. G., Jusczyk, P. W., Wright Cassidy, K., Druss, B., and Kennedy, L. (1987). Clauses are perceptual units for young infants. *Cognition*, **26**, 269–86.

Hockett, C. F. (1963). The problem of universals in language. In *Universals in language* (ed. J. H. Greenberg), pp. 1–29. MIT Press, Cambridge, MA.

Howell, P., Cross, I., and West, R. (ed.) (1985). *Musical structure and cognition*. Academic, London.

Hulse, S. H. and Cynx, J. (1986). Interval and contour in serial pitch perception by a passerine bird, the European starling (*Sturnus vulgaris*). *Journal of Comparative Psychology*, **100**, 215–28.

Hulse, S. H., Humpal, J., and Cynx, J. (1984). Discrimination and generalization of rhythmic and arhythmic sound patterns by European starlings (*Sturnus vulgaris*). *Music Perception*, **1**, 442–64.

Hulse, S. H., Page, S. C., and Braaten, R. F. (1990). An integrative approach to auditory perception by songbirds. In *Comparative perception. Vol. 2: Complex signals* (ed. W. C. Stebbins and M. A. Berkley), pp. 3–34. Wiley, New York.

Jaffe, J., Anderson, S., and Stern, D. (1979). Conversational rhythms. In *Psycholinguistic research* (ed. D. Aronson and R. Rieber). Erlbaum, Hillsdale, NJ.

Jakobson, R. (1968). *Child language, aphasia, and phonological universals*. Mouton, The Hague.

Jones, M. R. (1981). Music as a stimulus for psychological motion: Part I. Some determinants of expectancies. *Psychomusicology*, **1**, 14–31.

Jones, M. R. (1982). Music as a stimulus for psychological motion: Part II. An expectancy model. *Psychomusicology*, **2**, 1–13.

Jones, M. R. (1990). Learning and the development of expectancies: an interactionist approach. *Psychomusicology*, **9**, 193–228.

Jusczyk, P. W. and Bertoncini, J. (1988). Viewing the development of speech perception as an innately guided learning process. *Language and Speech*, **31**, 217–38.

Kelley, L. and Sutton-Smith, B. (1987). A study of infant musical productivity. In *Music and child development* (ed. J. C. Peery, I. Weiss Peery, and T. W. Draper), pp. 35–53. Springer, New York.

Kemler Nelson, D. G., Hirsh-Pasek, K., Jusczyk, P. W., and Wright Cassidy, K. (1989). How the prosodic cues in motherese might assist language learning. *Journal of Child Language*, **16**, 66–8.

Kolinski, M. (1967). Recent trends in ethnomusicology. *Ethnomusicology*, **11**, 1–24.

Krumhansl, C. L. (1983). Perceptual structures for tonal music. *Music Perception*, **1**, 28–62.

Krumhansl, C. L. (1987). General properties of musical pitch systems: some psychological considerations. In *Harmony and tonality* (ed. J. Sundberg), Publication No. 54. Royal Swedish Academy of Music, Stockholm, Sweden.

Krumhansl, C. L. (1990). *Cognitive foundations of musical pitch*. Oxford University Press, New York.

Krumhansl, C. L. (1992). Grouping processes in infants' music perception. In *Grouping in music* (ed. J. Sundberg, L. Nord, and R. Carlson). Royal Swedish Academy of Music, Stockholm, Sweden. (In press.)

Krumhansl, C. L. and Jusczyk, P. W. (1990). Infants' perception of phrase structure in music. *Psychological Science*, **1**, 70–3.

Krumhansl, C. L. and Keil, F. C. (1982). Acquisition of the hierarchy of tonal functions in music. *Memory and Cognition*, **10**, 243–51.

Krumhansl, C. L., Bharucha, J. J., and Castellano, M. A. (1982*a*). Key distance effects on perceived harmonic structure in music. *Perception and Psychophysics*, **32**, 579–94.

Krumhansl, C. L., Bharucha, J. J., and Kessler, E. J. (1982*b*). Perceived harmonic structure of chords in three related keys. *Journal of Experimental Psychology: Human Perception and Performance*, **8**, 24–36.

Kuhl, P. K. (1985). Methods in the study of infant speech perception. In *Measurement of audition and vision in the first year of postnatal life: a methodological overview* (ed. G. Gottlieb and N. A. Krasnegor), pp. 223–51. Ablex, Norwood, NJ.

Kuhl, P. K. (1986). The special-mechanisms debate in speech research: categorization tests on animals and infants. In *Categorical perception* (ed. S. Harnad), pp. 355–86. Cambridge University Press.

Kuhl, P. K. (1991). Human adults and human infants show a 'perceptual magnet effect' for the prototypes of speech categories, monkeys do not. *Perception and Psychophysics*, **50**, 93–107.

Kuhl, P. K. and Miller, J. D. (1975). Speech perception by the chinchilla: voiced–voiceless distinction in alveolar plosive consonants. *Science*, **190**, 69–72.

Kuhl, P. K. and Padden, D. M. (1982). Enhanced discriminability at the phonetic boundaries for voicing feature in macaques. *Perception and Psychophysics*, **32**, 542–50.

Langlois, J. H. and Roggman, L. A. (1990). Attractive faces are only average. *Psychological Science*, **1**, 115–21.

Langlois, J. H., Roggman, L. A., Casey, R. J., Ritter, J. M., Rieser-Danner, L. A., and Jenkins, V. Y. (1987). Infant preferences for attractive faces: rudiments of a stereotype? *Developmental Psychology*, **23**, 363–9.

Leek, M. R. (1987). Directed attention in complex sound perception. In *Auditory processing of complex sounds* (ed. W. A. Yost and C. S. Watson), pp. 278–88. Erlbaum, Hillsdale, NJ.

Lerdahl, F. and Jackendoff, R. (1983). *A generative theory of tonal music*. MIT, Cambridge, MA.

Liberman, A. M., Cooper, F. S., Shankweiler, D. P., and Studdert-Kennedy, M. (1967). Perception of the speech code. *Psychological Review*, **74**, 431–61.

Locke, J. L. (1983). *Phonological acquisition and change*. Academic, New York.

Locke, J. L. (1990). Structure and stimulation in the ontogeny of spoken language. *Developmental Psychobiology*, **23**, 621–43.

Lynch, M. P., Eilers, R. E., Oller, D. K., and Urbano, R. C. (1990). Innateness, experience, and music perception. *Psychological Science*, **1**, 272–6.

McCosker, S. S. (1974). *The lullabies of the San Blas Cuna Indians of Panama*. Gothenburg Ethnographical Museum, Gothenburg.

McGurk, H. and MacDonald, J. (1976). Hearing lips and seeing voices. *Nature*, **264**, 746–8.

Maddieson, I. (1984). *Patterns of sounds*. Cambridge University Press.

Marler, P. (1990). Innate learning preferences: signals for communication. *Developmental Psychobiology*, **23**, 557–68.

Mathews, M. V, Pierce, J. R., and Roberts, L. A. (1987). Harmony and new scales. In *Harmony and tonality* (ed. J. Sundberg), Publication No. 54. Royal Swedish Academy of Music, Stockholm, Sweden.

Mehler, J. and Dupoux, E. (1990). *Naître humain*. Odile Jacob, Paris.

Mehler, J., Bertoncini, J., Barrière, M., and Jassik-Gerschenfeld, D. (1978). Infant recognition of mother's voice. *Perception*, **7**, 491–7.

Mehler, J., Jusczyk, P. W., Lambertz, G., Halsted, N., Bertoncini, J., and Amiel-Tison, C. (1988). A precursor of language acquisition in young infants. *Cognition*, **29**, 143–78.

Mervis, C. B. and Rosch, E. (1981). Categorization of natural objects. *Annual Review of Psychology*, **32**, 89–115.

Miller, J. L. and Liberman, A. M. (1979). Some effects of later-occurring information on the perception of stop consonant and semivowel. *Perception and Psychophysics*, **25**, 457–65.

Miller, J. L. and Volaitis, L. E. (1989). Effect of speaking rate on the perceptual structure of a phonetic category. *Perception and Psychophysics*, **46**, 505–12.

Moorhead, G. E. and Pond, D. (1978). *Music of young children*. Pillsbury Foundation, Santa Barbara, CA.

Morgan, J. L., Meier, R. P., and Newport, E. L. (1987). Structural packaging in the input to language learning: Contributions of prosodic and morphological marking of phrases to the acquisition of language. *Cognitive Psychology*, **19**, 498–550.

Morrongiello, B. A. (1984). Auditory temporal pattern perception in 6- and 12-month-old infants. *Developmental Psychology*, **20**, 441–8.

Morrongiello, B. A. (1988). The development of auditory pattern perception skills. In *Advances in infancy research*, Vol. 5 (ed. C. Rovee-Collier), pp. 135–72. Ablex, Norwood, NJ.

Muir, D. W., Clifton, R. K., and Clarkson, M. G. (1989). The development of a human auditory localization response: a U-shaped function. *Canadian Journal of Psychology*, **43**, 199–216.

Narmour, E. (1990). *The analysis and cognition of basic melodic structures: the implication–realization model*. University of Chicago Press.

Neisser, U. (1967). *Cognitive psychology*. Appleton-Century-Crofts, New York.

Olsho, L. W. (1984). Infant frequency discrimination. *Infant Behavior and Development*, **7**, 27–35.

Papoušek, H. and Papoušek, M. (1987). Intuitive parenting: a dialectic counterpart to the infant's integrative competence. In *Handbook of infant development*, 2nd edn (ed. J. Osofsky), pp. 669–720. Wiley, New York.

Papoušek, M. and Papoušek, H. (1981). Musical elements in the infant's vocalization: their significance for communication, cognition, and creativity. In *Advances in infancy research*, Vol. 1 (ed. L. P. Lipsitt), pp. 163–224. Ablex, Norwood, NJ.

Papoušek, M., Papoušek, H., and Bornstein, M. H. (1985). The naturalistic vocal environment of young infants: on the significance of homogeneity and variability in parental speech. In *Social perception in infants* (ed. T. M. Field and N. A. Fox), pp. 269–97. Ablex, Norwood, NJ.

Piston, W. (1969). *Harmony*. Norton, New York.

Rakowski, A. (1990). Intonation variants of musical intervals in isolation and in musical contexts. *Psychology of Music*, **18**, 60–72.

Rosch, E. (1975). Cognitive reference points. *Cognitive Psychology*, **7**, 532–47.

Sakata, H. L. (1987). Hazara women in Afghanistan: innovators and preservers of a musical tradition. In *Women and music in cross-cultural perspective* (ed. E. Koskoff), pp. 85–95. Greenwood, Westport, CT.

Sands, K. M. and Sekaquaptewa, E. (1978). Four Hopi lullabies. A study in method and meaning. *American Indian Quarterly*, **4**, 195–210.

Schenker, H. (1954). *Harmony* (ed. O. Jones), (transl. E. M. Borgese from 1906 German edn). MIT Press, Cambridge, MA.

Schoenberg, A. (1975). *Style and idea* (ed. L. Stein), (transl. L. Black). Faber and Faber, London.

Slobin, M. and Titon, J. T. (1984). The music-culture as a world of music. In *Worlds of music* (ed. J. T. Titon, J. T. Koetting, D. P. McAllester, D. B. Beck, and M. Slobin), pp. 1–11. Schirmer, New York.

Sloboda, J. A. (1985). *The musical mind: the cognitive psychology of music*. Clarendon, Oxford.

Stern, D. N., Spieker, S., and MacKain, K. (1982). Intonation contours as signals in maternal speech to prelinguistic infants. *Developmental Psychology*, **18**, 727–35.

Stern, D. N., Spieker, S., Barnett, R. K., and MacKain, K. (1983). The prosody of maternal speech: infant age and context related changes. *Journal of Child Language*, **10**, 1–15.

Stevens, K. N. and Keyser, S. J. (1989). Primary features and their enhancement in consonants. *Language*, **65**, 81–106.

Studdert-Kennedy, M. (1975). From continuous signal to discrete message: syllable to phoneme. In *The role of speech in language* (eds. J. F. Kavanaugh and J. E. Cutting), pp. 113–25. MIT Press, Cambridge, MA.

Summerfield, A. Q. (1981). Articulatory rate and perceptual constancy in phonetic perception. *Journal of Experimental Psychology: Human Perception and Performance*, **7**, 1074–95.

Terhardt, E. (1974). Pitch, consonance, and harmony. *Journal of the Acoustical Society of America*, **55**, 1061–9.

Terhardt, E. (1987). Gestalt principles and music perception. In *Auditory processing of complex sounds* (ed. W. A. Yost and C. S. Watson), pp. 157–66. Erlbaum, Hillsdale, NJ.

Thorpe, L. A. (1985). *Auditory-temporal organization: developmental perspectives*. Ph.D. thesis, University of Toronto.

Thorpe, L. A. and Trehub, S. E. (1989). Duration illusion and auditory grouping in infancy. *Developmental Psychology*, **25**, 122–7.

Thorpe, L. A., Trehub, S. E., Morrongiello, B. A., and Bull, D. (1988). Perceptual grouping by infants and preschool children. *Developmental Psychology*, **24**, 484–91.

Trainor, L. J. (1991). *The origins of musical pattern perception: a comparison of infants' and adults' processing of melody*. Ph.D. thesis, University of Toronto.

Trainor, L. J. and Trehub, S. E. (1992). A comparison of infants' and adults' sensitivity to Western tonal structure. *Journal of Experimental Psychology: Human Perception and Performance*, **18**, 394–402.

Trainor, L. J. and Trehub, S. E. (1993). Musical context effects in infants and adults: key distance. *Journal of Experimental Psychology: Human Perception and Performance*. (In press.)

Trehub, S. E. (1985). Auditory pattern perception in infancy. In *Auditory development in infancy* (ed. S. E. Trehub and B. A. Schneider), pp. 183–95. Plenum, New York.

Trehub, S. E. (1989). Infants' perception of musical sequences: implications for language acquisition. *Journal of Speech–Language Pathology and Audiology*, **13**, 3–11.

Trehub, S. E. (1990). The perception of musical patterns by human infants: the provision of similar patterns by their parents. In *Comparative perception. Vol. 1: Basic mechanisms* (ed. M. Berkley and W. C. Stebbins), pp. 429–59. Wiley, New York.

Trehub, S. E. and Thorpe, L. A. (1989). Infants' perception of rhythm. Categorization of auditory sequences by temporal structure. *Canadian Journal of Psychology*, **43**, 217–29.

Trehub, S. E. and Trainor, L. J. (1990). Rules for listening in infancy. In *The development of attention: research and theory* (ed. J. Enns), pp. 87–119. Elsevier, Amsterdam.

Trehub, S. E. and Unyk, A. M. (1992). Music prototypes in developmental perspective. *Psychomusicology*, **10**, 31–45.

Trehub, S. E., Bull, D. and Thorpe, L. A. (1984). Infants' perception of melodies: the role of melodic contour. *Child Development*, **55**, 821–30.

Trehub, S. E., Thorpe, L. A. and Morrongiello, B. A. (1985). Infants' perception of melodies: changes in a single tone. *Infant Behavior and Development*, **8**, 213–23.

Trehub, S. E., Thorpe, L. A. and Morrongiello, B. A. (1987). Organizational processes in infants' perception of auditory patterns. *Child Development*, **58**, 741–9.

Trehub, S. E., Thorpe, L. A., and Trainor, L. J. (1990). Infants' perception of *good* and *bad* melodies. *Psychomusicology*, **9**, 5–19.

Trehub, S. E., Unyk, A. M., and Trainor, L. J. (1992). Adults identify infant-directed music across cultures. *Infant Behavior and Development* (In press.)

Trehub, S. E., Trainor, L. J., and Unyk, A. M. (1993*a*). Music and speech processing in the first year of life. *Advances in Child Behavior and Development*, **24**. (In press.)

Trehub, S. E., Unyk, A. M., and Trainor, L. J. (1993*b*). Maternal singing in cross-cultural perspective. *Infant Behavior and Development* (In press.)

Unyk, A. M., Trehub, S. E., Trainor, L. J., and Schellenberg, E. G. (1992). Lullabies and simplicity: a cross-cultural perspective. *Psychology of Music*, **20**, 15–28.

Walker, R. (1987). Musical perspectives on psychological research and music education. *Psychology of Music*, **15**, 167–86.

Walker, R. (1990). *Musical beliefs: psychoacoustic, mythical , and educational perspectives*. Teacher's College Press, New York.

Watkins, A. J. (1985). Scale, key, and contour in the discrimination of tuned and mistuned approximations to melody. *Perception and Psychophysics*, **37**, 275–88.

Watson, C. S. (1987). Uncertainty, informational masking, and the capacity of immediate auditory memory. In *Auditory processing of complex sounds* (ed. W. A. Yost and C. S. Watson), pp. 267–77. Erlbaum, Hillsdale, NJ.

Werker, J. F. and Lalonde, C. E. (1988). Cross-language speech perception: initial capabilities and developmental change. *Developmental Psychology*, **24**, 672–83.

Werker, J. F. and McLeod, P. J. (1989). Infant preference for both male and female infant-directed talk: a developmental study of attentional and affective responsiveness. *Canadian Journal of Psychology*, **43**, 230–46.

Werker, J. F. and Tees, R. C. (1984). Cross-language speech perception: evidence for perceptual reorganization during the first year of life. *Infant Behavior and Development*, **7**, 49–63.

Woodrow, H. (1909). A quantitative study of rhythm. *Archives of Psychology*, **14**, 1–66.

Younger, B. and Gottlieb, S. (1988). Development of categorization skills: changes in the nature or structure of infant form categories. *Developmental Psychology*, **24**, 611–19

Zenatti, A. (1969). *Le développement génétique de la perception musicale* (Monographies Françaises de Psychologie, No. 17). Centre National de la Recherche Scientifique, Paris.

Glossary

A term followed by [*] may be found as an additional entry in the glossary. In certain glossary entries below, rhythmic values are expressed in the American system. Their British equivalents are as follows: whole-note = semibreve, half-note = minim, quarter-note = crotchet, eighth-note = quaver, sixteenth-note = semiquaver. The chapter in which each term appears is given by the chapter number in square brackets, following the entry. NB Terms that are used in a single chapter and defined in that chapter are not included in the glossary.

absolute pitch The exact pitch [*] value of a note (for example, middle C) as opposed to its position relative to other pitches. **Absolute pitch perception** is the ability to name a pitch in isolation from any reference pitch. In **relative pitch perception**, interval relations among pitches are perceived (*see also* pitch). [5,8,9]

accent The perception of an event (tone or syllable) being stronger or more emphasized than neighbouring events. [4,8]

amplitude A parameter of sound related to the extent of oscillation of a vibrating body, of sound pressure, or of an analogue voltage. An **amplitude envelope** is the function describing how the maximum amplitude of a sound waveform evolves over time. The amplitude envelope is often characterized as consisting of three parts: the **attack** portion (or the part during which the amplitude is rapidly increasing) (*see also* transients), the **steady-state** portion (or the part where the amplitude is relatively stable), and the **decay** portion (or the part during which the amplitude is rapidly decreasing). A change in the amplitude according to a periodic or aperiodic function is referred to as **amplitude modulation**. [2,4,6,]

amusia A general term referring to the impairment of musical abilities due to damage to one or both cerebral hemispheres. [7]

analytic listening The ability of a listener to perceptually isolate individual elements of a complex sound [* *see* complex tone] or sequence, such as frequency components [* *see* harmonic] in a complex sound or events in rapid sequences. In **synthetic listening** the tendency is to perceive sound complexes or temporal sequences in a global fashion. [9]

anisochrony (*see* isochrony)

aphasia A general term referring to the impairent of language abilites following damage to the left hemisphere of right-handed people. [7]

appoggiatura From the Italian *appoggiare* which means 'to lean'. A short-duration tone that is a neighbouring note (a semitone [*] or whole tone higher or lower) of the principal note which it precedes. [8]

arpeggio (*see* chord)

atonal (*see* tonal system)

attack (*see* amplitude)

auditory agnosia A general term referring to impairments in recognizing auditory objects, events, and sequences that usually follow damage to both temporal lobes [*]. [7]

auditory beats The periodic sensation of fluctuation that results when two simultaneous components are very close to one another in frequency [*]. [2,3]

auditory Gestalts (*see* Gestalt)

auditory stream A mental description of a (physical or virtual) sound source and its behaviour through time. **Auditory stream segregation** refers to the process of perceptual organization of sound that accomplishes the construction of this description. [2,4,8]

augmented triad (*see* chord)

backward recognition masking (also called **informational masking**) The reduction in the ability to recognize a sound pattern due to the subsequent presentation of another sound pattern with similar information content. This kind of masking is thought to result from a process different from that of normal (sensory) masking [*]. [3,5]

basilar membrane A membrane that runs the length of the **cochlea** which is a fluid-filled spiral in the inner ear. The basilar membrane performs a kind of frequency [*] analysis of the incoming acoustic signal: different locations along the membrane vibrate preferentially in response to different frequencies. The **hair cells** connected to each part of the membrane thus preferentially send neural information about the presence of those frequencies to the brain. [2,6]

beats (*see* auditory beats, metre)

beat period (*see* tempo)

cadence Any chord [*] progression employing dominant (V) [*] and/or tonic (I) [*] chords. Two principal cadences should be distinguished among a number of others. The **perfect cadence**, having a strongly conclusive character, is defined by the succession of V to I. A **half cadence**, less conclusive in nature, is generally formed by a IV (subdominant) to V progression, but other variants are possible. [8]

chord The simultaneous sounding of a group of notes, usually three or more. In Western music, chords of three notes consisting of the first, third, and fifth degrees of a scale [*] are called **triads**. **Major triads** consist of intervals of a major third (four semitones [*]) and perfect fifth (seven semitones) with respect to a reference pitch (the **root**). The third is minor (three semitones) in a **minor triad**. The third is major and the fifth is augmented (eight semitones) in an **augmented triad**. The third is minor and the fifth is diminished (six semitones) in a **diminished triad**. When the notes of a chord are played in ascending or descending succession, the melodic figure is called an **arpeggio**. [7–9]

chromatic scale (*see* scale)

cochlea (*see* basilar membrane)

complex tone A tone composed of two or more pure tones [*] (*see also* spectrum). [2]

connectionist network (*see* neural net)

decay (*see* amplitude)

diminished triad (*see* chord)

discrimination The perception of fine distinctions or differences between stimuli. [3,4,6,7,9]

dissociation Functional dissociation is a term used in neuropsychology. Given that two mental functions, A and B, are present in any normal subject, they are considered to be functionally dissociable if one of them demonstrates a selective deficiency following a neurological disorder (lesion, cerebro-vascular accident) without any deficit being apparent for the other one. [5,7]

dominant In Western tonal music, the fifth degree of the diatonic scale [*] or the triad [* *see* chord] built on it (denoted 'V'). This is an important degree from the standpoint of the tonal hierarchy [*] since, as its name indicates, it dominates the other degrees (excepting the tonic [*]) (*see also* tonal system). [8,9]

echoic memory A hypothetical preperceptual sensory register within which auditory information is temporarily stored without being recoded. The function of this memory would be to preserve sensory information during the time needed for higher-level processing mechanisms to extract useful information. Echoic memory does not last more than a few seconds. It corresponds to iconic memory in the visual modality. [5]

equal-tempered pitch system (*see* scale)

false alarm Judging that a signal is present when it is not or that a change occurred when none did. Also called a **false-positive response**. [9]

fission boundary (*see* temporal coherence boundary)

formants (*see* resonance structure)

frequency A measure of the rate at which something repeats. This term usually refers to the repetition rate of a periodic waveform and is expressed in **Hz** (cycles per second) or **kHz** (thousands of cycles per second). The **period** is the inverse of frequency, or the amount of time a single cycle lasts (*see also* harmonicity). [2–4,6,9]

frequency component (*see* harmonic)

fundamental frequency (*see* harmonic)

Gestalts From the German word for 'form' or 'shape'. The central idea of Gestalt psychology is that the properties of a whole form cannot be derived by simply summing the properties of the individual parts that compose it. The constitution of these forms obeys the perceptual laws (or principles) that were demonstrated for visual perception by the Gestalt psychologists, but which have in general been confirmed for auditory perception as well. These principles include the grouping into forms of elements on the basis of their proximity, similarity, continuity, symmetry, and closure. A configuration of elements that obeys one or more of these principles may be considered to be 'well formed' and as such is a preferred way of experiencing the sensory input (*see also* auditory stream). [2,3,8]

grouping (*see* auditory stream, segmentation)

hair cells (*see* basilar membrane)

harmonic One **component** (or **partial**, or **overtone**) of a complex tone [*] whose component frequencies are all integer multiples of a common **fundamental frequency** [*see* frequency]. The intervals between components of the **harmonic series** are defined by **harmonic ratios** (i.e. ratios of simple integer numbers). The term 'harmonic ratios' can also be applied to very low frequency rates of repetition as are found in rhythms. [2,4,6,8]

harmonicity The state of being harmonic or periodic. **Periodicity** is mathematically synonymous with harmonicity, though the former refers to a regularity in the sound's time description while the latter refers to a regularity in its frequency [*] description. Contrasting terms to this one include **inharmonicity** or **aperiodicity** (usually for complex tones [*]

composed of inharmonically related partials) and randomness (usually employed to refer to noise [*] waveforms). [2,6]

Heschl's gyri (*see* temporal lobe)

hierarchy The organization of a set of elements into subsets according to relations of dominance and subordination. Each element of a subset is subordinate to the subset as a whole which itself is subordinate to the superset of which it is an element, and so on. In a strict hierarchy no element can be a member of more than one subset at a given level of the hierarchy. [4,8]

Hz (*see* frequency)

identification The ability to retrieve from memory a name or concept associated with an object or event. [3,5–7]

immediate memory (*see* short-term memory)

information processing A key concept in cognitive psychology. Drawing on the image of the way computers work, information resulting from stimulation of the sense organs is analysed and transformed by a number of serial or parallel processors [* *see* neural net] each of which takes as input the information output by another processor. [4–6,8]

informational masking (*see* backward recognition masking)

intonation, musical (*see* scale)

isochrony A sequence of events is called isochronous if the time separating each pair of successive events is strictly equal. The absence of isochrony is called **anisochrony**. [4]

key distance Perceptual proximity of the keys of the Western tonal system [*]. Keys sharing more pitches are considered to be more closely related than those with fewer pitches in common. [8,9]

key signature The sign by which the principal key of a piece of tonal music is indicated at the beginning of each musical staff in a score. It contains the flat and sharp signs that specify the key. [5,8]

kHz (*see* frequency)

just noticeable difference, or jnd The smallest change in a stimulus parameter (frequency [*], intensity, duration, etc.) that can be detected by a listener at a predefined level of performance (e.g. 71 per cent of the time) (*see also* Weber's law). [4]

lexicon A term usually used in psycholinguistics to refer to a hypothetical store of words. The process by which incoming sensory information activates a given unit in the lexicon is called **lexical access**. Some researchers in music cognition postulate the existence of an equivalent store of abstract musical forms (familiar melodies, melody prototypes, musical forms) [*see* prototype]. [3,5–8]

long-term memory The experimental paradigm by which permanent storage of experience is measured. Long-term memory (also called **secondary memory** or **permanent memory**) is distinguished from short-term memory [*] in being practically unlimited in its storage capacity. Forgetting seems to be quite progressive (and selective) and can stretch over several decades. [5,6,8]

major scale (*see* scale)

major triad (*see* chord)

masking The process by which one sound (the **masker**) affects the threshold of audibility of another sound (the target or probe) when played at the same time. More intense sounds mask less intense ones. The amount of masking depends on the proximity of the frequency components [* *see* frequency, harmonic] of the two sounds, as well as on the global intensity level of the masker. The greater the level, the greater the extent to which a given masker frequency can mask target components at higher frequencies (*see also* backward recognition masking, comodulation masking release). [2,6,9]

melodic contour The pattern of ascending and descending pitch changes in a melody. [7–9]

memory (*see* echoic memory, short-term memory, long-term memory)

mental representation A hypothetical pattern of mental or brain activity that represents some feature of the world, of the person, or of the interaction between the person and the world. [2,5–9]

mental schema A mental programme or formula that has been proposed by Jean Piaget and other psychologists as a means by which people represent the world and regulate their interactions with it. The concept implies more of an active control mechanism than the concept of mental 'representation' [*] does. [2,4,–9]

metre The group of phenomena related to the musical measure. It consists of the hierarchical ordering of the piece of music into units of equal duration (**beats**; *see also* hierarchy). This ordering is indicated by the **time signature** at the beginning of the score. For example, $\frac{2}{4}$ signifies that the measure (one level of metre) is subdivided into time units equivalent to two quarter-notes (another level of metre). Metrically strong beats are often accented [* *see* accent] and are distributed in a specific way for each kind of measure structure. From a phenomenological point of view, the presence of a metric organization in the heard piece is evidenced by the fact that one can tap one's foot or dance in synchrony with the music. **Non-metric** sequences would be those that do not have a perceptible level of repetition in the rhythmic values. [4,8]

minor scale (*see* scale)

minor triad (*see* chord)

mode, musical (*see* scale)

modularity A process is called modular if it is specific to a well-delimited aspect of a stimulus and is relatively unaffected by other processes. In general, such a process is considered to employ a circumscribed group of neurones. [5,7,9]

neural net A system composed of many simple processing units, formally mimicking the operation of nerve cells, which are connected together in complex patterns of excitation and inhibition and propagate activation to other units by way of these connections. The current state of a given unit and the degree to which it excites other units can be influenced by the success it has had in activating them. Propagated activity among cells can lead the system to stable states in which the activity of the units remains relatively constant. These states constitute the 'response' of the system to a given stimulation by the (external or internal) environment. The main hypothesis concerning this kind of architecture (also called **connectionist** or **parallel distributed processing networks**), is that it is better suited to modelling the microstructure of cognition than more classical data flow or serial processing models: processing, representation, and memory are postulated to be distributed over units in the net rather than being constrained to specific storage locations and processing routines. [6,7]

neural spectrogram (*see* spectrum)

noise A random waveform whose frequency spectrum [*] contains all audible frequencies, called white, broad-band, or wide-band noise. A noise signal that is filtered, removing higher and lower frequencies and just letting through a small band of frequencies, is called narrow-band or band-pass noise. Filtering out the high frequencies starting from a certain cut-off frequency gives low-pass noise, and filtering out low frequencies gives high-pass noise. Taking a noise waveform over a certain time period and then repeating this segment gives what is called frozen noise. [2,3]

non-metric (*see* metre)

non-tonal (*see* tonal system)

octave equivalence (*see* pitch)

overtone (*see* harmonic)

parallel distributed processing (*see* neural net)

partial (*see* harmonic)

passing tone Ornamental notes melodically interleaved between two notes that are part of the triad [**see* chord] of the principal key. [8]

pélog scale (*see* scale)

percept What the perceiver sees or hears as a result of stimulation, as opposed to the physical reality of stimulation. The percept may be considered the 'object' of study in perceptual psychology. This dualist (subjective vs. objective) conception of perception is rejected by the ecological approach to psychology. [2–4,7]

perceptual centration The fixing of one's gaze for sometimes very short periods of time in specific areas as one explores a visual form. These fixation points constitute the zones of perceptual centration. This term was applied to auditory perception by Francès to designate the auditory information upon which listeners focus their attention at a given moment. [8]

perceptual invariance The impression of perceiving the same object, event, or pattern in spite of variations in stimulus structure, due, for instance, to being played louder or softer, faster or slower, higher or lower, or in different acoustic environments. [4,6,9]

period (*see* frequency)

permanent memory (*see* long-term memory)

phonemic restoration A hypothetical active process by which a speech sequence that is interrupted by a noise [*] sound in place of a given phoneme results in the listener's impression of having heard the phoneme. This effect does not occur if a silent gap is left at the place where the phoneme normally occurs. [3,6]

pitch The auditory attribute on the basis of which tones may be ordered on a musical scale [*]. Two aspects of the notion of pitch can be distinguished in music: one related to the frequency (or fundamental frequency [* *see* frequency, harmonic]) of a sound (measured in Hz) which is called **pitch height**, and the other related to its place in a musical scale which is called **pitch chroma**. Pitch height varies directly with frequency over the range of audible frequencies. This 'dimension' of pitch corresponds to the sensation of 'high' and 'low'. Pitch chroma, on the other hand, embodies the perceptual phenomenon of **octave equivalence**, by which two sounds separated by an octave (and thus relatively distant in terms of pitch height) are none the less perceived as being somehow equivalent. This equivalence is demonstrated by the fact that almost all scale systems in the world in which the notes are named give the same names to notes that are roughly separated by an octave, i.e. the labelling system cycles at every octave. Thus pitch chroma is organized in a circular fashion, with octave-equivalent pitches considered to have the same chroma. Chroma perception is limited to the frequency range of musical pitch (50–4000 Hz). [2–9]

primary auditory cortex (*see* temporal lobe)

primary memory (*see* short-term memory)

prototype A notion introduced by Rosch to designate an abstract representation of a whole class of objects, of which the prototype would constitute the central tendency. [6,8,9]

pure tone A tone with a sinusoidal waveform is called a pure tone because it is considered to be the simplest form of tone and sounds pure when played in isolation. [2,5]

recency effect An increase in correct recall rate for the most recently presented items of a list compared with those presented earlier in the list. [5]

recognition The impression that an object, event, or sequence has been experienced before or is familiar. [5–7]

relative pitch (*see* absolute pitch)

resonance structure A resonance structure can be described in terms of the relative level produced at each frequency [*] by a resonating object. Most physical objects (membranes, bars, air columns, strings) have several modes of vibration that resonate at different frequencies, thus constituting a complex resonance structure. In the case of speech, these resonance regions are called **formants**. The placement of the formants is a major clue to the identity of a vowel. The way the resonant frequencies change rapidly over time is a clue to the identity of several classes of consonants. [2,3,6]

rhythm pattern A sequence of events having a specific set of time intervals between the onsets of successive events. Sequences having different onset-to-onset intervals are said to have different **rhythmic structures** or **temporal stuctures**. [2–4, 6–9]

root (*see* chord)

scale, musical A set of pitches (or notes) arranged with certain intervals among them within the span of an octave (*see also* pitch). The scale pattern generally repeats in each octave. Each note constitutes a degree of the scale. Each diatonic scale consists of intervals between adjacent notes that are either minor or major seconds (one or two semitones [*], respectively). The different arrangements of major and minor seconds yield different **modes**. The two most important modes in Western tonal music are the major and minor modes. A **major scale** (such as C major) has the following interval set: whole tone (C–D), whole tone (D–E), semitone (E–F), whole tone (F–G), whole tone (G–A), whole tone (A–B), and semitone (B–C'). There are several versions of the **minor scale** used in Western tonal music, though all have a minor third interval between the tonic [*] and third degree of the scale; for example, the natural minor scale has the interval pattern: whole tone (C–D), semitone (D–E♭), whole tone (E♭–F), whole tone (F–G), semitone (G–A♭), whole tone (A♭–B♭), whole tone (B♭–C'). Other **modal scales** generally also have five whole-tone steps and two half-tone steps. The **chromatic scale** contains all twelve semitone steps within an octave, i.e. C–C#–D–D#–E–F–F#–G–G#–A–A#–B–C'. Another kind of scale which does not fall within the tonal system [*] but which was used extensively in the music of Debussy and Ravel is the **whole-tone scale**, which only has six notes, all separated by whole tones: C–D–E–F#–G#–A#–C'. **Intonation** (or **tuning system**) refers to the exact tuning of the notes of a given scale system. The most widely used tuning system in Western music is the **equal-tempered system** in which all intervals can be expressed as integer multiples of a standardized semitone [*]. This system was brought to Europe from China and adopted during the seventeenth century. The **pélog scale** is a Javanese scale characterized by a pattern of large and small intervals, many of which do not correspond to those found in the equal-tempered Western scale system. [5,7–9]

secondary memory (*see* long-term memory)

segmentation The process by which speech signals are divided into phonemes, syllables or words. It consists of creating boundaries between groups of elements. In music, segmentation refers to the process of dividing an event sequence into distinct groups of sounds. The factors playing a role in segmentation are similar to the principles of grouping addressed by Gestalt [*] psychology. [3,8,9]

semitone The smallest standard musical interval (i.e. step in pitch) in the Western equal-tempered pitch system [*see scale]. All other intervals can be described as containing an integer number of semitones, e.g. the octave contains 12 semitones, the perfect fifth 7 semitones, etc. A tone that is a semitone higher than another is about six per cent higher in frequency [*]. There is a semitone separation between any black key on the piano and its nearest white neighbour or between adjacent white keys that have no black key between them. [2–4,8,9]

shadowing An experimental task in which a listener hears a verbal or musical message and must track the message by, for example, verbally reproducing what has been heard as it is being heard, or by tapping along with a rhythm pattern [*] that is being heard. [4]

short-term memory A memory store (also called **primary memory, immediate memory, working memory**) of relatively short duration (2–10 s according to some accounts) and limited capacity within which incoming sensory information is maintained and processed while being compared with information in long-term store [*], or while being transferred to long-term store. [4–9]

spectral envelope (*see* spectrum)

spectrogram (*see* spectrum)

spectrum A description of the frequency [*] content of a sound waveform, usually presented as a graph with frequency on the abscissa (*x* axis) and amplitude [*] or intensity on the ordinate (*y* axis). A pure tone [*] would have a single vertical line at the appropriate frequency with a height indicating its amplitude. A complex sound [*see* complex tone] would have several such lines, indicating the multiple components. Drawing a curve through the tops of the lines would describe the **spectral envelope**. A **spectrogram** is another representation of a spectrum in which the time component is reintroduced: time is represented on the abscissa, frequency on the ordinate, and amplitude is coded as the darkness of the trace at a given frequency and time. In an auditory **neural spectrogram**, instead of a continuous signal, the probability of occurrence of nerve spikes at a given moment in time is represented. The frequency axis is replaced by a frequency-specific auditory nerve channel [* *see* basilar membrane]. A third type of spectral representation called a time–frequency perspective plot is drawn in three dimensions, with time along the *x* axis, amplitude along the *y* axis, and frequency along the *z* axis. [2,6,9]

steady state (*see* amplitude)

symbolic function Piaget used this term to designate the capacity to evoke, by way of signs or symbols, objects or situations that are not currently being perceived. [8]

synthetic listening (*see* analytic listening)

tempo The speed of occurrence of the beats for a given metric structure [* *see* metre]. In a musical score, the tempo is specified in terms of the number of metric units per minute, for example, quarter-note = 60, in which the time value of each quarter-note is 1 s. The inverse of tempo, the time between beats, is called the **beat period**. [4,7–9]

temporal acuity The degree to which the auditory system can resolve, or separately distinguish, events separated by extremely brief time periods. [3]

temporal coherence boundary Defines the threshold for hearing a repeating two-tone sequence as composed of a single auditory stream [*] across a range of frequency [*] differences between the tones and rates of tone presentation when the listener is trying to hear a single stream. Above the boundary, the sequence is always heard as two streams. Below it, the sequence may be heard as a single stream. This boundary is contrasted with the **fission boundary** which defines the threshold for hearing the same kind of repeating sequences when the listener is trying to hear two separate streams. Above the fission boundary, the sequence may be heard as two streams, but below it the sequence is always heard as a single stream. [4]

temporal lobe A region of the lateral part of cortex (just centre of and slightly behind the ears) concerned with audition and containing **primary auditory cortex** (i.e. the first cortical area to which auditory signals are relayed, also known under the name of **Heschl's gyri**). [7]

temporal structure (*see* rhythm pattern)

tension and relaxation, musical Notions that can firstly be assimilated to the psychoacoustic phenomena of consonance and dissonance, consonant pitch intervals giving rise to relaxation and dissonant ones to tension. However, they may also refer to the syntactic function of notes and chords [*]. The performance of syntactically important chords provokes a sense of musical relaxation in a listener. Cadences [*] generally give rise to varying degrees of relaxation depending on their type. Rhythm, loudness, and duration constitute other sound parameters that interact with syntactic functions in defining the tensions and relaxations perceived by a listener. The terms may also refer to perceptual expectancies. When the music goes against these expectancies, a phenomenon of musical tension is created in the listener due to the effect of surprise. [8]

timbre Also referred to as sound quality or sound colour. The classic negative definition of timbre is: the perceptual attribute of sound that allows a listener to distinguish among sounds that are otherwise equivalent with respect to pitch [*], loudness, and subjective duration. Contemporary research has begun to decompose this attribute into several perceptual dimensions of a temporal, spectral, or spectro-temporal nature. [2–9]

time signature (*see* metre)

time-span This term was used by Lerdahl and Jackendoff to designate the duration between two beats in a metrical structure [* *see* metre]. It takes on a different meaning, however, when the notion of **time-span reduction** is evoked. In this case, it means that the piece is organized during listening into time periods of different durations, smaller ones being nested within larger ones. [8]

tonal system A set of musical rules that characterize Western music since the baroque (seventeenth century), classical, and Romantic styles. This system is still quite prominent in the large majority of traditional and popular musics of the Western world as well as in Latin America. A technical description of this system is proposed by Bigand (Ch. 8, this volume). Other musical systems in use in the West do not conform to these rules, and are consequently called **non-tonal** or **atonal**. [4,5,7–9]

tonic The principal note or chord [*] of a key of the Western tonal system [*]. [8,9]

transients Instabilities present in the oscillation pattern of a physical object that is set into vibration before the object settles into a stable oscillation. Also called **attack transients**. Similar oscillatory instabilities (legato transients) can be observed when the object changes state suddenly as occurs when a musical instrument changes pitch (by changing fingering on a woodwind instrument, pushing on a valve or piston in a brass instrument, pressing down on a string with a finger, or lifting one up on a string instrument). Transients are often characterized by a noisy or inharmonic spectrum [*see* harmonicity, noise, spectrum]. [6]

transposition A change in all the pitches of a melody (or chord [*]) without modifying any of the intervals between the notes. The term 'imitation' is used when the melodic contour [*] is preserved and one or more of the intervals are modified (as often happens when a melody in a major key is subsequently played in a minor key or some other mode [* *see* scale]). [5,8,9]

triad (*see* chord)

tuning system, musical (*see* scale)

universals Musical or cognitive structures that are likely to be observed in all human civilizations. These structures would be the expression of inborn cognitive constraints that would become manifest either in the structure of musical languages (musical universals) or in the processing of musical pieces (cognitive universals). The existence of universals can be demonstrated by studies on newborn infants and babies, as well as by intercultural research. [9]

Weber's law Discovered by Ernest Heinrich Weber in 1834. States that the smallest detectable change (jnd [*]) in intensity is a constant fraction of the level of stimulation, i.e. $\Delta I / I$ = constant, where $\Delta I / I$ is called the *Weber fraction*. Georg Fechner turned Weber's law into a psychophysical scale by expressing the magnitude of sensation (S) as proportional to the logarithm of the magnitude of stimulation (I), or S = k log I. A great deal of psychophysical research has attempted to establish the Weber–Fechner law for sensory dimensions other than intensity, e.g. frequency and duration in audition. While the empirical data conform fairly well to the law over a certain range of values for each dimension, they can differ substantially at extremes of the range of perceptible values. [3]

whole-tone scale (*see* scale)

working memory (*see* short-term memory)

Name Index

Joos, M., 38
Josmann, 215
Jusczyk, P. W., 287–8, 294, 316, 317

Kahneman, D., 70, 73, 75
Kallman, H. J., 119, 120
Kawashima, T., 114
Keil, F. C., 288
Kelley, L., 43, 315
Kelly, W. J., 82, 93
Kemler, D. J., 288, 288, 294
Kendall, R. A., 160, 162, 166, 173, 182
Kennedy, L., 288
Kessler, E., 236, 238–9, 288
Keyser, S. J., 297
Kidd, G. R., 80, 93–4, 102, 215, 252, 254
Kim, J., 19
Kinney, J. A., 38
Kirsner, K., 204, 138
Klatt, D. H., 85, 156, 184, 191–2
Klein, R., 205
Klima, E. S., 118
Kohn, S., 207
Kolers, P. A., 115
Kolinsky, M., 307, 216
Kop, P. F. M., 132
Kosslyn, S., 200
Kristofferson, A. B., 86
Kronman, U., 80
Krumhansl, C., 96, 98, 125, 167, 172,
  173–4, 184, 221, 231, 234, 236–9, 252,
  262, 279, 281, 287, 288, 294, 296, 298,
  306, 308–9, 312, 314, 316
Kruskal, J., 159
Kuhl, P. K., 280, 288, 294, 304–5, 313,
  315
Kuwabara, H., 182

LaBerge, D., 74
Ladefoged, P., 39, 59
Laignel-Lavastine, M., 211, 224
Lalonde, C. E., 315
Lambert, J., 72–3
Lambertz, G., 317
Lane, H., 103
Langlois, J. H., 304
Lapointe, S. G., 103
Larkin, W. D., 92
Lashley, K. S., 86
Lechevalier, B., 201
Lee, M. R., 252
Leek, M. R., 74, 93, 278
Leeuwenberg, E. L., 252
Legge, G. E., 139
Lehiste, I., 101, 102
Lehman, J. R., 93
Leipp, E., 162

Lerdahl, F., 95, 98, 204, 232, 237–8, 240,
  245–6, 249, 251–2, 253, 257–9, 261,
  263, 264–5, 272, 281, 317
Levin, H., 61
Levitan, R., 23, 24, 30
Lewis, J., 72
Lhermitte, F., 221
Liao, C., 23, 24, 30
Liberman, A. M., 204, 280, 287
Liberman, I. Y., 61
Liberman, P., 102, 210
Liègeois-Chauvel, C., 202
Lindsay, P. H., 147
Lissauer, M., 206
Locke, J. L., 280, 296, 312, 316
Lockhart, R. S., 115
Longuet-Higgins, H. C., 252
Luce, D., 162
Lung, K. M., 99
Luria, A., 203
Lynch, M. P., 309

McAdams, S., 5, 7, 30, 114, 123, 135, 163,
  182, 233–4, 246–7, 257
MacCallum, R., 80, 82
McClelland, J. L., 114, 156, 188–9,
  191–192, 207
McCosker, S. S., 295
MacDonald, J., 305
McGurk, H., 305
McHugh, A., 104
MacKain, K., 291, 293
McKenna, T. M., 62–3
McKenzie, B. E., 88, 286
McKernon, P., 315
McLean, J. P., 74
McLeod, P. J., 294, 314
Macmillan, N. A., 92, 159, 182, 188,
  191–192
McRoberts, G. W., 315
Maddieson, I., 296, 297
Majewski, W., 139
Mann, V., 210, 215
Manning, S. K., 119
Marcus, S. M., 119
Marin, O., 203
Marler, P., 280, 313, 317
Marr, D. S., 156
Marshburn, E., 43, 85, 215
Marslen-Wilson, W. D., 280
Martin, J., 90, 104
Maser, D. J., 80, 254
Massaro, D. W., 73, 76, 78, 115, 120, 122,
  127–8, 156, 188–9, 191–2
Mathews, M. V., 309
Mattingly, I., 204
Mavlov, L., 215
Mays, K., 293

Subject Index